ENGLISH GRAMMAR AND COMPOSITION

COMPLETE COURSE

JOHN E. WARRINER
Head of the English Department
Garden City High School
Garden City, New York

CHAPTERS ON SPEAKING AND LISTENING BY

FRANCIS GRIFFITH
Principal, Richmond Hill High School
Richmond Hill, New York

HARCOURT, BRACE AND COMPANY 

New York . Chicago

· THE SERIES ·

▶ English Grammar and Composition: Complete Course

English Grammar and Composition: Grade 11

English Grammar and Composition: Grade 10

English Grammar and Composition: Grade 9

FORTHCOMING: English Grammar and Composition: Grade 8

English Grammar and Composition: Grade 7

TEST BOOKLET FOR EACH TITLE

THE AUTHORS: **JOHN E. WARRINER** has taught English for 27 years, in junior and senior high schools and in college. He is the author of *Handbook of English: I* and *II*, and is also a reader for the College Entrance Examination Board. **FRANCIS GRIFFITH,** who has done graduate work at Columbia University and includes in his experience advanced courses at the National University of Ireland, was for many years Chairman of English and Speech in a Brooklyn, New York, high school.

The photograph on the cover of this book shows part of a type case containing the printing type Perpetua, a face designed in 1932 by the English artist Eric Gill. The chapter headings throughout the book are set in this type. Cover photograph by Lew Merrim from Monkmeyer.

PRINTED IN THE UNITED STATES OF AMERICA

[i · 3 · 59]

CONTINUED ON BACK ENDPAPER

Preface

This book, *English Grammar and Composition, Complete Course,* is the summary volume of a new six-book series. It reviews materials covered in the preceding books of the series and presents advanced subject matter to meet the special needs of students about to enter college or to take their place in the world beyond school.

This book, like the other texts in this series, states the facts about language and the conventions of usage; it gives full explanations of all important skills in writing, speaking, and listening; and it includes enough drills and exercises to meet any teaching demand. The *English Grammar and Composition* series has been planned for teachers who prefer to handle motivation themselves but who need a textbook which presents the subject matter of English arranged for efficient teaching as well as for reference, and functions as a storehouse of carefully prepared exercises.

Part One, a grammar review, helps the student fill gaps in his grammar preparation before undertaking the work on sentence structure to which Parts Two, Three, and Four are devoted. Traditional grammar is employed wherever it will aid teaching and learning. The attitude of the book toward correctness in current usage is explained in the section "What Is Good English?" on page 64. The fourteen chapters on the writing of correct, clear, and smooth sentences represent a major emphasis of the book. Part Five teaches the use of library tools, and includes detailed study of the dictionary and other reference books.

The seven chapters of Part Six, "Writing Compositions," give complete and specific instruction on the planning and writing of exposition, including chapters on clear thinking, the research paper, and letter writing. The chapter on narrative writing is a break in the otherwise purely expository nature of the writing taught in this book.

Part Seven, "Speaking and Listening," presents important skills in these related subjects. Mr. Griffith's concise and lucid treatment of these areas provides a complete description of techniques and an abundance of practical exercises.

Part Eight covers in detail and with a great many exercises the essentials of English mechanics: capital letters, punctuation, manuscript form, and spelling.

The section "College Entrance and Other Examinations," page 644, was written by Peter M. Miller of the California Institute of Technology and formerly of Educational Testing Service. It is planned to acquaint the student with the kinds of tests that he is likely to encounter in advanced work in English.

Although primarily a teaching instrument, this complete course book has been designed for use as a reference tool. The handbook arrangement, now presented with the additional advantage of color, and the exceptionally complete index make the book a handy reference in which the student can easily find the answer to almost any language problem he is likely to encounter. The book is entirely flexible, imposing no chronology. Each chapter is a distinct unit and may be taught at any point in the course.

Teaching Tests, a 64-page booklet containing tests on the material of this book, including exercises that supplement "College Entrance and Other Examinations," is available at a small cost. For the student the booklet provides additional practice, and for the teacher it offers an easy check on student progress.

Author and publishers wish to acknowledge the valuable critical help given by the many teachers who contributed suggestions for this book. Special thanks are due to Miss Margaret B. Dietrich, Westfield Senior High School, Westfield, New Jersey; Mrs. Gladys Kronsagen, Glenbard Township High School, Glen Ellyn, Illinois; and Sister Mary David, O.P., Principal, Junipero Memorial High School, Monterey, California, for their thorough line-by-line critiques.

The author wishes to acknowledge the indispensable assistance given him by his wife in the preparation of this book.

J. W.

Contents

PART ONE

Grammar Review

PART TWO

Writing Correct Sentences

PART THREE

Writing Clear Sentences

PART FOUR

Writing Smooth Sentences

PART SIX

Writing Compositions

PART ONE

GRAMMAR REVIEW

CHAPTER 1

The Parts of Speech

LEARN THE WORK EACH PART OF SPEECH DOES IN A SENTENCE

Adults will tell you that few things you can acquire in school are as important as the ability to speak and write effectively. Success comes to the person who has at his command the words he needs and the necessary knowledge of his language to help him use these words as he wishes. A person's ideas, no matter how good, are of little practical importance unless he can express them clearly. Incorrect and awkward English is a social and business handicap and a frequent cause of failure in school. For these reasons English is a required subject.

Every school subject has its own vocabulary. This vocabulary is composed of the technical terms used in studying the subject; for instance, in mathematics you need to know the meaning of such words as *quotient, equation, polygon, sine;* in science, such words as *molecule, inertia, formula;* in shop, such words as *gauge, mortise, bit.* In your study of language you need to know the terms of grammar. You have probably been learning these terms during your years in junior and senior high school. How well do you remember them? Your future study of English will be much easier and more efficient if you bring to it a clear understanding of grammar terms. Use the following pages for review of these terms and for reference.

In language study a knowledge of the names of words is fundamental. Words are named according to the way they are used in the sentence. Since words may be used in eight different ways, there are eight different word names. These word names are the *parts of speech*. The parts of speech are *noun*, *pronoun*, *adjective*, *verb*, *adverb*, *preposition*, *conjunction*, and *interjection*.

You will find that an understanding of the various parts of speech will be helpful to you in your effort to remove errors from your speech and writing, in your effort to write better sentences, and in your use of language reference books such as the dictionary.

Diagnostic Test on Parts of Speech

To discover whether or not your knowledge of the parts of speech is adequate, take the diagnostic test below. Analyze your results to find out which of the parts of speech you should review.

Copy in a column on your paper the italicized words in the following sentences, numbering them as in the test. Study the use of each word; then write after it what part of speech it is.[1]

a. Only a (1) *handful* (2) *of* students gathered (3) *in* the auditorium to hear (4) *our* (5) *first* (6) *debate*.

b. With the (7) *index* finger and the middle finger of his (8) *left* hand strapped together, Jack (9) *played* the (10) *entire* game (11) *and* was high (12) *scorer*.

c. Just (13) *beyond* the tunnel the road (14) *curves* (15) *very*

[1] The word *our*, which is the possessive form of the pronoun *we*, is called a pronoun throughout this book. Some teachers, however, prefer to think of *our* and other possessive pronouns (*your*, *their*, *her*, etc.) as adjectives because they limit the meaning of nouns: *our* house, *your* friend, etc. Follow your teacher's direction in labeling these words.

(16) *sharply* to the right and (17) *drops* (18) *rapidly* (19) *into* the valley.

d. (20) "*Wow!*" exclaimed Jeff (21) *as* he saw the ball drop (22) *through* the net with a (23) *swish.*

e. (24) *I* did not believe the story (25) *when* I (26) *first* heard (27) *it,* (28) *but* (29) *after* I had talked with George, (30) *who* has a reputation for (31) *honesty,* I (32) *changed* (33) *my* mind.

The Noun

1a. A *noun* is a word used to name a person, place, thing, or idea.

Nouns may be classified in three ways: *proper* or *common; abstract* or *concrete;* and *collective.*

A *proper noun* is the name of a particular person, place, or thing. Proper nouns are capitalized: *Tom, Miami, White House.*

A *common noun* is a noun which does not name a particular person, place, or thing. Common nouns are not capitalized: *man, city, building.*

A *concrete noun* names an object which can be perceived by the senses: *hat, desk, book, box.*

An *abstract noun* names a quality, a characteristic, an idea: *beauty, strength, love, courage.*

A *collective noun* names a group: *crowd, herd, team, class.*

With reference to all three classifications, the noun *team* is a common, concrete, collective noun.

The Pronoun

1b. A *pronoun* is a word used in place of a noun. It may stand for a person, place, thing, or idea.

EXAMPLE During the storm a workman was injured by a falling tree. **He** was pinned beneath **it.** [The pronoun *he* takes the place of the noun *workman*. The pronoun *it* takes the place of the noun *tree*.]

There are several kinds of pronouns: *personal*, *relative*, *interrogative*, *demonstrative*, and *indefinite*.

PERSONAL PRONOUNS

I, me	he, him	it	they, them
you	she, her	we, us	

POSSESSIVE FORMS OF THE PERSONAL PRONOUNS

my, mine	his	its	their, theirs
your, yours	her, hers	our, ours	

Personal pronouns combined with *–self* may be used in two ways:

(1) They may be used *reflexively*.

EXAMPLE George hurt **himself.**

(2) They may be used *intensively* for emphasis.

EXAMPLE George **himself** was not hurt.

REFLEXIVE AND INTENSIVE FORMS

myself	ourselves
yourself	yourselves
himself, herself, itself	themselves

Relative pronouns are used to introduce subordinate clauses (see page 50).

RELATIVE PRONOUNS

who	which	what
whom	that	whose

Interrogative pronouns are used in questions.

INTERROGATIVE PRONOUNS

Who . . .?	Which . . .?	Whose . . .?
Whom . . .?	What . . .?	

DEMONSTRATIVE PRONOUNS

this	these	that	those

MOST COMMONLY USED INDEFINITE PRONOUNS

all	each	many	one
any	either	neither	several
anybody	everybody	nobody	some
anyone	everyone	none	somebody
both	few	no one	someone

● EXERCISE 1. Number in a column on your paper from 1 to 12. Write in order the pronouns in each sentence.

1. Speaking of the newly discovered comet, Mr. Federer said he did not know the direction of its movement.
2. The company announced it will put into operation forty double-decker railroad cars as soon as they are delivered.
3. The Research Corporation was founded in 1912 by Dr. Cottrell, who gave it rights to his inventions.
4. The subject of the President's address had not been made public before he himself announced it.
5. We were able to answer some but not all of the questions they asked.
6. If you had followed the procedure which the teacher suggested, you would not have hurt yourself.
7. Although neither of the stores had the recording that I wanted, both offered to order it.
8. Someone had apparently left the office safe open, but not one of the secretaries would admit she was guilty.
9. If these are not the right size, you may exchange them later.
10. Who would have guessed Gerald himself would be the one for whom the police were looking?
11. I myself thought that none of their arguments was convincing.
12. If each carries out her responsibilities, we will complete the job quickly.

The Adjective

1c. An *adjective* is a word used to modify a noun or a pronoun.

To modify means to describe or to make more definite the meaning of a word. Adjectives may modify nouns or pronouns in any one of three different ways:

1. By telling *what kind:*
   blue eyes, **large** city, **strong** wind
2. By pointing out *which one:*
   this man, **that** suggestion
3. By telling *how many:*
   several reasons, **ten** players

As the preceding examples show, the normal position of an adjective is directly before the word it modifies. Occasionally, for stylistic reasons, a writer may use adjectives after the word they modify.

EXAMPLE The night, **cold** and **foggy,** drove us indoors.

A *predicate adjective* [2] (see page 29) is separated from the word it modifies by a verb.

EXAMPLES Stanley is **capable.**
He looks **tall.**
The food tasted **good.**
His hand felt **cold.**

THE SAME WORD AS ADJECTIVE AND AS PRONOUN

A word may be used as more than one part of speech. This is especially true of the words in the list on the next page, which may be used as either pronoun or adjective.

[2] A predicate adjective is one kind of subject complement. The other kind is the predicate nominative.

all	few	one	this
another	many	other	those
any	more	several	what
both	most	some	which
each	much	that	
either	neither	these	

ADJECTIVE **Which pen do you want?** [*Which* modifies the noun *pen.*]

PRONOUN **Which do you want?** [*Which* takes the place of a noun previously mentioned.]

ADJECTIVE **I like this picture.** [*This* modifies the noun *picture.*]

PRONOUN **I like this.** [*This* takes the place of a noun previously mentioned.]

● EXERCISE 2. Some of the nouns, pronouns, and adjectives in the following sentences are italicized. For each sentence, list these words in order in a column, numbering as in the example. After each word tell what part of speech it is. If a word is an adjective, write after it the word the adjective modifies.

EXAMPLE 1. *These* pictures, which were taken on a *cloudy* day, are better than *those.*

1.	these	adjective	pictures
	cloudy	adjective	day
	those	pronoun	

1. The President's *speech* on the international *situation* silenced *some* of his critics.
2. *This* is the *correct* answer to *this* problem.
3. Although *he* is *blind*, Mr. Hagan is a *skillful* mechanic *who* can repair your *car* better than *anyone* I know.
4. Very *few* of the *seniors* have helped in this year's drive to sell *popular* magazines, but the *sophomores* have sold *many* subscriptions.
5. *Everybody* agreed that extracurricular *activities* are sometimes more *educational* than *regular* classes.
6. Mr. Murphy *himself* told *us* not to pick *any* of *those* apples.

The Verb

1d. A *verb* is a word that expresses action or helps to make a statement.

Action verbs may express either physical or mental action. Examples of verbs expressing physical action: *hit, blow, play, run.* Verbs like *think* and *know* express mental action.

Verbs which do not express action are called *linking verbs.*[3] They help to make a statement by *linking* the subject to a word or idea in the predicate. Commonly used linking verbs are:

appear	feel	remain	sound
be[4]	grow	seem	stay
become	look	smell	taste

EXAMPLES She **is** ill.
You **seem** tired.
The speaker **sounded** angry.

In these sentences the verbs do not express action; they act as a link between the subject and the word following the verb.

Some verbs may be used as either action or linking verbs.

ACTION Sam **looked** everywhere for his wallet.
LINKING Sam **looked** fat.

ACTION In the dark he **felt** his way to the door.
LINKING Everybody in the stadium **felt** cold.

ACTION She **appeared** suddenly at the head of the stairs.
LINKING She **appeared** angry.

[3] Linking verbs are sometimes called *state-of-being* verbs because they help to describe the condition or state of some person or thing.

[4] The following are forms of the verb *to be: am, are, is, was, were, be, being,* and all verb phrases ending in either *been* or *be;* for example, *have been, could have been, can be, should be,* etc.

1d

In general a verb is a linking verb if you can substitute *is* or *was* for it. For instance, in the sentence *Everybody in the stadium felt cold*, you can substitute *was* for *felt* — *Everybody in the stadium* **was** *cold.*

THE HELPING VERB[5] AND THE VERB PHRASE

A *verb phrase* is made up of a main verb and one or more *helping verbs*. Helping verbs are so called because they help the main verb to express action or make a statement. The helping verbs in the following phrases are printed in bold type: **has** *played*, **will be** *coming*, **should have** *paid*, **must have been** *injured*. In other words, a verb phrase is a verb of more than one word.[6]

COMMON HELPING VERBS

do	has	can (may) have
did	had	could (would, should) be
am	can	could (would, should) have
are	may	will (shall) have been
is	will (shall) be	might have
was	will (shall) have	might have been
were	has (had) been	must have
have	can (may) be	must have been

The parts of a verb phrase may be separated from one another by other words; i.e., the helping verb may be separated from the main verb.

Did you **hear** me call?
I **am** not **going** with you.
We **had** at last **completed** our work.

● EXERCISE 3. List in order the verbs and verb phrases in the following sentences, placing before

[5] The helping verb is sometimes called an *auxiliary* verb.

[6] A word ending in *–ing* may be used as part of a verb phrase or as an adjective.

EXAMPLES The boys *were annoying* the girls. [*Annoying* is part of a verb phrase.]
Your interruptions were *annoying*. [*Annoying* is an adjective modifying *interruptions*.]

each the number of the sentence in which it appears. After each verb tell whether it is an action verb or a linking verb. Be sure to list all words in a verb phrase.

1. You will see many natural wonders if you travel through the Southwest.
2. Elliot showed that he was the most consistent ground-gainer on the team.
3. After the mayor has dedicated the new athletic field, the first game of the season will be played.
4. If you are going away during your vacation, leave a forwarding address.
5. As a teacher he is strict and formal, but outside of class he appears good-natured and friendly.
6. Did anyone help you with your homework?
7. The Student Council hopes that a school-wide courtesy drive will improve the manners of all students.
8. Although most students have learned good manners at home, many forget their manners when they come to school.
9. The Radio Club prepares each week a list of outstanding educational radio programs and places this list on the bulletin board in the main corridor.
10. Mr. Horton disliked his classroom on warm days because the children on the playground below the open windows made too much noise, the traffic on State Street drowned out the voices of teacher and students, and trains on the near-by railroad increased the general din.

The Adverb

1e. An *adverb* is a word used to modify a verb, an adjective, or another adverb.

The adverb is used most commonly as the modifier of a verb. It may tell *how*, *when*, *where*, or *to what extent* (how often or how much) the action of the verb is done.

1. **The band played stirringly.** [*Stirringly* tells *how* the band played.]
2. **The band played immediately.** [*Immediately* tells *when* the band played.]
3. **The band played there.** [*There* tells *where* the band played.]
4. **The band played long.** [*Long* tells *to what extent* (how much) the band played.]

An adverb may modify an adjective.

He is extremely capable. [*Extremely* modifies the adjective *capable*, telling how capable he is.]

An adverb may modify another adverb.

We marched very slowly. [*Very* modifies the adverb *slowly*, telling how slowly we marched.]

▶ NOTE: To avoid possible confusion you should know that *not* is classified as an adverb. Because it is so commonly used, you may ignore it in doing the exercises on parts of speech.

● EXERCISE 4. On your paper list in order the adverbs in the following sentences, placing before each the number of the sentence in which it appears. After each adverb write the word or words it modifies and state whether the adverb tells how, when, where, or to what extent.

1. The audience moved rapidly through the exit, and members of the hall squad directed them efficiently.
2. Albert worked hard on his assignment but finally decided he could not finish it.
3. You will soon receive a notice from the office which will explain clearly the new regulations.
4. You should go there now.
5. If you do your daily assignments well, you will pass your examinations easily.
6. Here will stand a monument to two aviators whose heroism deeply impressed the entire world.

7. She told me later that she had changed her mind somewhat.
8. Because very serious accidents have recently occurred at this intersection, the police will soon install traffic lights here.
9. Before we had driven very far, our windshield was completely covered with ice.
10. Mr. Swenson spoke enthusiastically about his new pupil, who, he said, sang beautifully and played the piano exceptionally well.

● EXERCISE 5. Copy in a column on your paper the italicized words in the following sentences, placing before each word the number of the sentence in which it appears. After each word tell what part of speech it is; after each adjective or adverb tell what word or words it modifies.

1. *Each* student in the *class* will read *five* magazine articles on the current topic *which* he chooses for *his* oral report.
2. A *good* speaker *first* attracts the *attention* of his audience and *then* holds *it*.
3. James, *who* talked about experiments in *scientific* weathermaking, *began* his speech with a question.
4. The question he asked *was*, "How would *you* like to be able to make it rain *now*?"
5. Marian's *account* of *life* on the moon was *very entertaining*.
6. In the discussion period after each *speech*, the members of the class *made* comments and asked *questions*.
7. *Sometimes* the class members showed by their comments that *they* knew more about the topic than the *person* who *had given* the speech; furthermore they asked questions which were *embarrassing* to *anyone* who was not *completely* sure of his facts.
8. The boys understood *clearly* Bill's *technical* explanation of *two* different styles of football, but the girls *protested* that the subject was not *clear* to *them*.
9. *Some* speakers *had prepared* good talks but gave them

poorly; others had not prepared very *well,* but *their* presentation was *good.*

10. *We* agreed that this work in oral *English* was more fun than anything else *our* class had done *this* year.
11. *Most* students *prefer* oral work to *written* work because of class periods like *these.*

The Preposition

1f. A *preposition* is a word used to show the relation of a noun or pronoun to some other word in the sentence.

In the following sentences the prepositions are shown in bold type. The words between which the prepositions show relationship are italicized.

1. The *house* **across** the *street* has been sold.
2. Sally *met* me **after** *lunch.*
3. *Everyone* **in** the *car* escaped injury.
4. The *area* **beyond** the white *line* is foul territory.
5. We *flew* **above** the *clouds.*

A preposition always introduces a phrase (see p. 32). The noun or pronoun at the end of a prepositional phrase is the object of the preposition which begins the phrase. In the preceding examples the objects of the prepositions are *street*, *lunch*, *car*, *line*, and *clouds.*

The following words are commonly used as prepositions:

about	at	but (meaning *except*)
above	before	by
across	behind	concerning
after	below	down
against	beneath	during
along	beside	except
amid	besides	for
among	between	from
around	beyond	in

into	since	until
like	through	unto
of	throughout	up
off	to	upon
on	toward	with
over	under	within
past	underneath	without

A group of words may act as a preposition: *on account of, in spite of.*

● EXERCISE 6. Write sentences containing the following prepositions. Draw a line under the phrase which each preposition introduces and draw a circle around the object of each preposition.

above	below	during	into	until
against	by	for	of	up

The Conjunction

1g. A *conjunction* is a word which joins words and groups of words.

In the following sentences the conjunctions are printed in bold type; the words and groups of words which the conjunctions join are printed in italics.

1. *Toys* **and** *games* covered the playroom floor.
2. Your mother *called* **and** *left* a message for you.
3. *The telephone rang* **but** *no one answered it.*
4. Have you met *Mary* **or** *Jean?*
5. *The crowd yelled* **when** *the team came on the field.*
6. *I will go* **if** *you will go.*
7. You must **either** *do the work* **or** *drop the course.*
8. I cannot send **both** *you* **and** your *sister* to preparatory school.

There are three kinds of conjunctions: *co-ordinating* conjunctions; *correlative* conjunctions; and *subordinating* conjunctions.

1f-g

CO-ORDINATING CONJUNCTIONS

and	but	or	nor	for

CORRELATIVE CONJUNCTIONS

either . . . or	not only . . . but (also)
neither . . . nor	whether . . . or
both . . . and	

Correlative conjunctions are always used in pairs:

She didn't know **whether** I was teasing **or** not teasing.

Neither brains **nor** ingenuity will take the place of hard work.

Subordinating conjunctions are used to begin subordinate clauses (see page 47), usually adverb clauses. In the following sentences the subordinating conjunctions are printed in bold type, and the subordinate clauses which the conjunctions begin are printed in italics.

1. Please call at the office **before** *you go home.*
2. I will wait **until** *you have finished your work.*
3. The principal could not see us **because** *he was busy.*
4. We wanted to go **where** *the fishing would be good.*
5. **As** *you turn the corner,* honk your horn.
6. **When** *you have finished the test,* hand it in.

WORDS COMMONLY USED AS SUBORDINATING CONJUNCTIONS[7]

after	inasmuch as	till
although	in order that	unless
as	provided	until
as much as	since	when
because	so that	whenever
before	that	where
how	than	wherever
if	though	while

[7] Some of these words may be used as prepositions: *after, before, since, until;* others may be used as adverbs: *how, when, where. That* is often used as a relative pronoun.

The Interjection

1h. An *interjection* is a word which expresses emotion and has no grammatical relation to other words in the sentence.

EXAMPLES Oh! My goodness! Hurray! Ah! Ouch! Alas! Bravo! Ha!

THE SAME WORD AS DIFFERENT PARTS OF SPEECH

You have already learned that a word may be used as more than one part of speech. For instance, you learned in your study of pronouns and adjectives that a word like *these* may be used as an adjective (*these* books) and as a pronoun (I want *these*). It is the way a word is *used* that determines what part of speech it is.

EXAMPLES I like **school.** [*School* is the name of something, a noun.]
I like **school** dances. [*School* modifies the noun *dances;* hence it is an adjective.]

You **talk** too much. [*Talk* is a verb.]
I enjoyed his **talk.** [*Talk* is a noun.]

● EXERCISE 7. This is an exercise in identifying the same word when used as different parts of speech. Copy on your paper the italicized words in the following sentences. After each word write what part of speech it is. Be prepared to explain your answers.

1. The manager likes to hear the *ring* of the cash registers as the salesgirls *ring* up their sales.
2. According to the *daily* schedule, the boat makes three trips *daily*.
3. She packed an especially large *box* to take to the *box* social.
4. Be sure to turn *right* at the *right* corner; our house is the first one on the *right.*
5. Does *that* answer *that* question *that* you asked?

● REVIEW EXERCISE. Copy in order in a column on your paper the italicized words in the following paragraph, placing before each word the number of the line in which it appears. Consider carefully the use of each word; write after it what part of speech it is.

During the weeks *before* Christmas, Martin worked for the Post Office. *He* received special permission *from* the *school* principal to be absent from *his* last-period study hall so that he could report for *work* at two o'clock. As *luck* would have it, the weather *that* winter was *severe*. A heavy snowfall, zero temperatures, and strong winds, which *drove* the snow into deep drifts, *made* working outdoors unusually strenuous. Martin was sent out as a *substitute* carrier in the north end of town.

Slowly his bare hands *became* accustomed to the cold. He learned to carry his heavy pack so that *its* weight rested *easily* on his back. He enjoyed giving *pleasure* to *little* children *when* he arrived at their homes with *handfuls* of Christmas greetings *and*, at times, with a small present. *But* Martin did not like plowing *through* snowdrifts all afternoon, slipping on icy sidewalks, and balancing himself dangerously on glazed porch steps. When he received cold looks and even reprimands, as though the fault were his for not bringing expected mail, he *felt* unjustly treated and envied the boys *who* had been assigned jobs in the warm sorting room at the Post Office.

When he came home for supper *three* days before Christmas, Martin sniffled and coughed and said he *was* not *hungry*. Dr. Strong, whom his mother called *immediately*, diagnosed the case as grippe and recommended a week in bed. *Although* his Christmas plans were ruined and he had had no opportunity to spend any of his hard-earned money, Martin faced with pleasure the prospect of seven days in bed. "*Whew*," he sighed as he slipped under the covers, "*this* feels good to *me!*"

CHAPTER 2

The Parts of a Sentence

LEARN THE FUNCTION OF SUBJECTS, PREDICATES, AND COMPLEMENTS IN THE SENTENCE

For efficient study of good English, a knowledge of the parts of the sentence is as important as a knowledge of the parts of speech. Your study of the writing of complete, correct, and smooth sentences and of punctuation and usage will be easier if you know the meaning of the terms *subject*, *predicate*, *object*, *predicate nominative*, and *predicate adjective*. This chapter provides a review of these terms, which you will find frequently used in most language textbooks.

Diagnostic Test on Subject, Predicate, and Complements

Give yourself the following two-part diagnostic test. Analyze your results in order to discover which parts of this chapter you should review.

A. First, number on your paper from 1 to 10. After the corresponding number write the simple subject and the verb in each of the test sentences below.

1. The average European knows only the Hollywood *version* of American life.
2. This morning's editorial gives several *reasons* for the President's policy.

3. Behind us lay the most strenuous part of the journey.
4. All of the detectives are *efficient.*
5. Through a radar device the police can determine the *speed* of an approaching car.
6. Last night's television programs were *excellent.*
7. During the crisis the prime minister sent the *king* a full *account* of recent developments.
8. The subjects listed on this sheet are the elective *courses* for seniors.
9. Mr. Smith and Mr. Colburn offered *us* a ride.
10. The outlawing of war is mankind's most pressing *problem.*

B. Now list in order the 10 italicized words in the test sentences above. After each word tell what kind of complement it is: direct object, indirect object, predicate adjective, predicate nominative.

The Sentence

2a. A *sentence* is a group of words expressing a completed thought.

SENTENCE **The latest books are on the counter at the front of the store.** [completed thought]

NOT A SENTENCE **The latest books on the counter at the front of the store . . .** [thought not completed]

SENTENCE **After the fall of France in 1940, the fear of invasion dominated the thoughts and actions of the British.** [completed thought]

NOT A SENTENCE **After the fall of France in 1940, the fear of invasion dominating the thoughts and actions of the British . . .** [thought not completed]

Sentences are classified in two ways. They are classified according to their purpose, and they are classified according to their make-up or structure.[1]

[1] For sentences classified according to structure see p. 58.

2b. Sentences may be classified according to their purpose.

Sentences are used for the following four purposes: (1) to make a statement; (2) to command or request; (3) to ask a question; (4) to exclaim.

(1) A *declarative sentence* is a sentence which makes a statement.

EXAMPLE Israel was admitted to the United Nations in 1949.

(2) An *imperative sentence* is a sentence which gives a command or makes a request.

EXAMPLES Ring the bell at five o'clock.
Please tell Mother that I will be home later.

(3) An *interrogative sentence* is a sentence which asks a question.

EXAMPLE Where have you been?

(4) An *exclamatory sentence* is a sentence which expresses strong feeling. It exclaims.

EXAMPLES What a hot day this has been!
How pretty you look!

Since the same sentence may be spoken with several different purposes, it may be classified in different ways:

We won the game. [declarative]
We won the game! [exclamatory]
We won the game? [interrogative]

Is he crazy? [interrogative]
Is he crazy! [exclamatory]

Subject and Predicate

2c. A sentence consists of two parts: the *subject* and the *predicate*. The *subject* of the sentence

is that part about which something is being said. The *predicate* is that part which says something about the subject.

Subject | Predicate
Thousands of cattle | died in the great storm.

Predicate | Subject
Ahead of the band strutted | the drum majorette.

THE SIMPLE PREDICATE OR VERB

2d. The principal word or group of words in the predicate is called the *simple predicate* or, more commonly, the *verb*.

EXAMPLES Thousands of cattle died in the great storm. [Predicate: *died in the great storm;* simple predicate or verb: *died*]

Ahead of the band strutted the drum majorette. [Predicate: *Ahead of the band strutted;* simple predicate or verb: *strutted*]

THE SIMPLE SUBJECT

2e. The *simple subject* is a word or combination of words naming the person, place, thing, or idea about which something is being said.

EXAMPLES The streamlined appearance of the new models appealed to the public. [Subject: *The streamlined appearance of the new models;* simple subject: *appearance*]

The fuselage of an airplane is shaped like a fish. [Subject: *The fuselage of an airplane;* simple subject: *fuselage*]

Throughout this book the term **subject,** *when used in connection with the sentence, refers to the simple subject; the term* **verb** *refers to the simple predicate.*

COMPOUND SUBJECTS AND VERBS

2f. A *compound subject* is a subject which consists of two or more connected words. The usual connecting words are *and* and *or*.

EXAMPLE Pointed **arches** and vaulted **ceilings** characterize Gothic architecture. [Compound subject: *arches . . . ceilings*]

2g. A *compound verb* is a verb which consists of two or more connected verbs.

EXAMPLE The council **met** at three and **adjourned** at four o'clock. [Compound verb: *met . . . adjourned*]

HOW TO FIND THE SUBJECT OF A SENTENCE

To find the subject of a sentence, first find the verb (the simple predicate); then ask yourself the question "Who or what . . . ?" For instance, in the sentence *Outside the wall walked an armed guard,* the verb is *walked.* Ask the question, "Who or what walked?" You find the answer to be *guard walked. Guard* is the subject of the sentence.

In addition to this simple formula for locating the subject, you should keep in mind the following facts:

1. *In sentences expressing a command or a request, the subject is always* **you,** *even though the word* **you** *may not appear in the sentence.*

EXAMPLES (You) Stamp the envelopes before mailing them.
(You) Please run some errands for me.

2. *The subject of a sentence is never in a prepositional phrase.*

EXAMPLES Neither of the drivers survived the crash. [Verb: *survived.* Who survived? *Neither. Neither* is the subject. *Drivers* is not the subject. It is in the phrase *of the drivers.*]

Thousands of wild geese were making their way south. [Verb: *were making*. Who were making? *Thousands*. *Thousands* is the subject. *Geese* is not the subject. It is in the phrase *of wild geese*.]

3. *To find the subject in a question, invert the question into statement form.*

QUESTION **Into which drawer did you put the box of pencils?**
INVERTED **You did put the box of pencils into which drawer?** [Subject: *you;* verb: *did put*.]

4. *The word* **there** (*or* **here**) *is never the subject of a verb.*

EXAMPLES **There is the book.** [Verb: *is;* subject: *book*. In this sentence the word *there* is an adverb telling where.]

There are arguments on both sides. [Verb: *are;* subject: *arguments*. In this use *there* is called an *expletive*, a word used to get the sentence started. The word *it* may also be used as an expletive: *It* is useless to argue.]

● EXERCISE 1. Number on your paper from 1 to 20. Write after the proper number the subject and the verb in each sentence. Be careful to include all parts of compound forms and all words in a verb phrase.

1. Before the play, we heard an explanation of the plot from Mr. Gaines.
2. Helen's brother and my sister went to the movies with us.
3. Save your hard-earned money and invest it in government bonds.
4. Almost all of our professional basketball players once played college basketball.
5. What were the principal objections to the plan?
6. The setting sun spread a thin layer of gold over the still surface of the pond.
7. Most of the common spelling errors are made with the same 100 words.

8. There will be plenty of time for club meetings after school.
9. In the Soviet Union there are at least six cities of 10,000 population north of the Arctic Circle.
10. During the '50's a new interest in religion swept the country.
11. The opinions of political minorities should be respectfully considered.
12. In what part of Africa is the Congo?
13. Order this book today directly from the publishers or at your local bookstore.
14. One of the manufacturers has produced a trailer with a folding balcony sun deck.
15. The players in the backfield shifted their positions and waited for the snap of the ball.
16. From whom did most of this information come?
17. With the wet weather came hordes of mosquitoes.
18. Give me your telephone number and wait for my call.
19. Into the thickest part of the brawl strode two state troopers.
20. A course in the appreciation of motion pictures and television programs will be included in the curriculum.

Complements

Some sentences express a complete thought by means of a subject and verb only.

EXAMPLES **She works.**
Someone called.

Most sentences, however, contain a third essential part which is called a *complement*. A complement is a completer. It completes the thought of the sentence.

		Complements
EXAMPLES	Marilyn made	the prize-winning **poster**.
	The coach gave	the **team** two new **plays**.
	Harry is	a loyal **friend**.
	This is	**she**.
	The air seemed	**warm**.

OBJECT COMPLEMENTS

Complements which are affected by the action of the verb are object complements. They are of two kinds: the *direct object complement* and the *indirect object complement*, which are commonly called simply *direct object* and *indirect object.*

Only action verbs are completed by object complements.

2h. The direct object (complement) of the verb receives the action of the verb or shows the result of the action. It answers the question "What?" or "Whom?" after an action verb.

EXAMPLES I remember **him** very well. [*I* remember *whom?*]

Fire destroyed the **building**. [*Fire* destroyed *what?*]

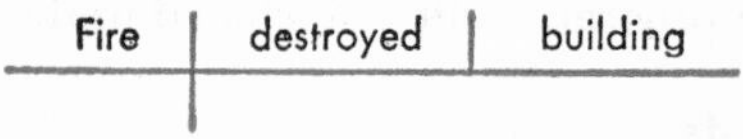

Fire	destroyed	building

▶ NOTE: The diagrams are given to help those students who have already studied diagraming. No attempt is made in this book to teach diagraming or to give practice in diagraming. However, a review explanation may be appropriate. On the main line the subject comes first, then a vertical line crossing the main line, then the verb. Between the verb and the direct object is a vertical line which does not cross the main line. Between the verb and a predicate adjective or a predicate nominative is a similar line slanted to the left. The indirect object occupies a lower line joined to the verb. Single-word modifiers slant downward from the words they modify. The diagraming of other parts of the sentence will be explained as they are encountered in this chapter.

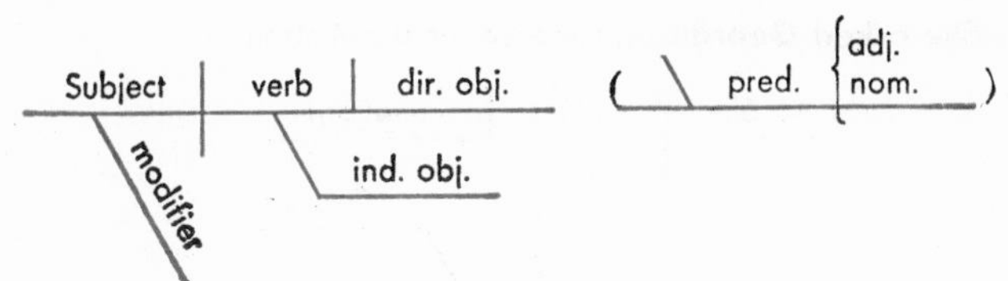

2i. The *indirect object* (complement) of the verb precedes the direct object and usually tells to whom or for whom the action of the verb is done.[2]

EXAMPLES The blizzard brought **us** an unexpected vacation. [brought *to* us]

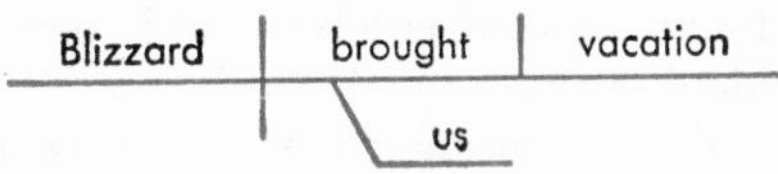

He gave the **house** a coat of paint. [gave *to* the house]

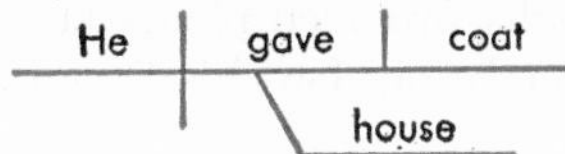

Objects of the verb may be compound:

Have you seen either the **movie** or the **play**?

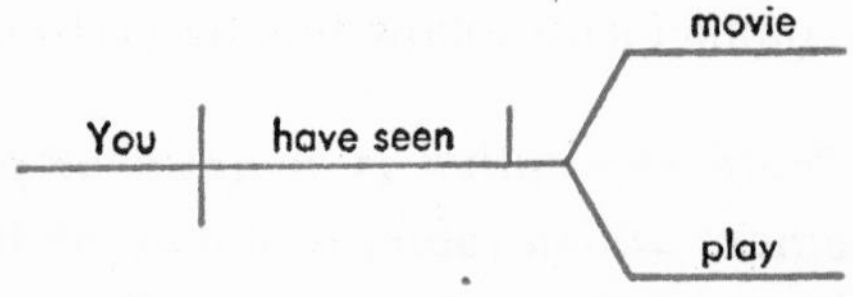

[2] If the word *to* or *for* is used, the noun or pronoun following it is part of a prepositional phrase; it is not an indirect object. Like subjects, objects of verbs are never part of a prepositional phrase.

Father promised *me* the car. [*Me* is an indirect object.]
Father promised the car *to me*. [*Me* is part of the phrase *to me*.]

She asked **George** and **me** several questions.

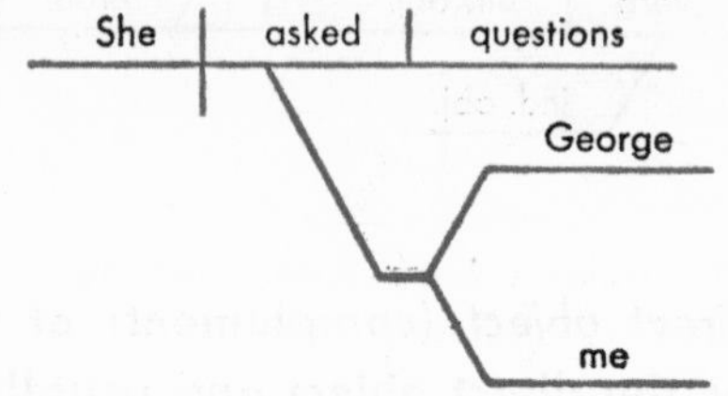

● EXERCISE 2. Number in a column on your paper from 1 to 10. Copy after the proper number the objects of the verb or verbs in each sentence. You need not distinguish between direct and indirect objects.

1. I expected a better mark.
2. Did you lose both your notebook and your textbook?
3. The president of the council told us the facts.
4. Fran gave Jimmy and me the wrong answers.
5. Does anyone else have a key to the building?
6. The committee sent him a special invitation.
7. Finish the job and draw your pay today.
8. Only one of our questions would he answer.
9. The encyclopedia provided plenty of information.
10. That I must see before I will believe it.

SUBJECT COMPLEMENTS

Complements which refer to (describe or explain) the subject are subject complements. They are of two kinds: the *predicate nominative* and the *predicate adjective*.

Subject complements follow linking verbs only.[3]

2j. A *predicate nominative* is a noun or pronoun complement which refers to the same thing as the subject of the sentence. It follows a linking verb.

[3] The common linking verbs are the forms of the verb *to be* (see page 9), and the following: *become, seem, grow, appear, look, feel, smell, taste, remain, sound, stay.*

EXAMPLES **Mr. Smith is the new mayor.** [*Mayor* refers to the same person as *Mr. Smith.*]

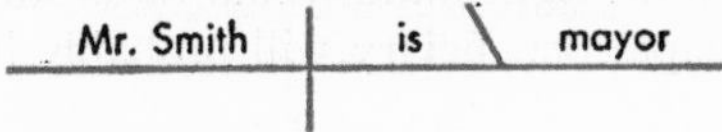

The winners were Allen and he. [compound predicate nominative]

2k. A *predicate adjective* is an adjective complement which modifies the subject of the sentence. It follows a linking verb.

EXAMPLES **The explanation is clear.** [*Clear* modifies *explanation.*]

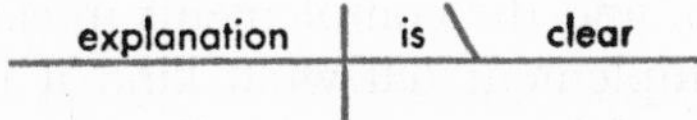

Beside you, he looks tall and thin. [compound predicate adjective modifying *he*]

In the normal order of an English sentence, complements follow the verb. However, a complement may precede the verb.

EXAMPLES **This new car his father gave him as a graduation gift.** [*Car* is the direct object of the verb *gave.*]
Happy and healthy was our life in the open. [*Happy* and *healthy* are predicate adjectives modifying the subject *life.*]

● EXERCISE 3. Number in a column on your paper from 1 to 11. After the proper number write the predicate nominative or predicate adjective in each of the following sentences; identify each with the abbreviation *p.n.* or *p.a.*

1. Many of your sentences seem awkward to me.
2. Phil will be the villain of the play.

2j-k

3. Since his vacation Mr. Willis looks healthier and happier.
4. Nobody in his right mind would be so stubborn.
5. The principal beneficiary will probably be either you or she.
6. Your voice is rather harsh for radio work.
7. After dark the children became frightened.
8. The president of the G.O. must be a senior.
9. Before the game Joe appeared nervous and unsure of himself.
10. Your unknown callers may have been Jean and she.
11. If it is George, tell him I am too tired and sleepy to go out tonight.

● EXERCISE 4. Number in a column on your paper from 1 to 10. Write after the proper number the subject, the verb, and the complements in each sentence. After the complement tell what kind it is, using abbreviations as follows: object (direct and indirect), *obj.;* predicate nominative, *p.n.;* predicate adjective, *p.a.*

1. Every morning the custodian unlocks the doors of all classrooms.
2. Give your father and me a full account of your experiences.
3. Commencement at Dover High is a simple ceremony.
4. None of the seniors offered any objections to the new plans.
5. How did you get my address?
6. Are any of the players ready?
7. Mrs. Stewart lent us a number of new records.
8. Sally's part in the play was short and sweet.
9. The closest and most exciting race of the meet was the relay.
10. Sandy and his brother offered the girls a ride to the beach and a cruise in Sandy's boat.

CHAPTER 3

The Phrase

LEARN THE FUNCTION IN THE SENTENCE OF THE DIFFERENT KINDS OF PHRASES

The most common group of related words in any sentence is the phrase. Phrases (except verb phrases) may be used as modifiers and as subjects, objects, and predicate nominatives. In your study of the sentence, it is important that you understand the various kinds of phrases so that you may learn how to use them in writing correct and clear sentences. You are already familiar with the verb phrase, which is a verb of more than one word (*were going*, *have seen*). This chapter provides a review of the make-up and function in the sentence of other kinds of phrases.

Diagnostic Test on Phrases

To determine which parts of this chapter you need to study in your review of phrases, give yourself the following two-part test.

A. Number on your paper from 1 to 10. Copy in order the 10 prepositional phrases in the following sentences. After each phrase tell whether it is an adjective or an adverb phrase.

1. As we watched from the top of the hill, we saw him walking away alone.
2. The new film at the Mayfair has been praised by the critics.

3. Wishing him well was the only help I could give him at that time.
4. To believe such a story is an indication of childish credulity.
5. Certificates of meritorious service were awarded to three alumni during a special ceremony in Mills Auditorium.

B. Copy on your paper one participial phrase, one gerund phrase, and one infinitive phrase from the test sentences above. Give the number of the sentence for each phrase you select and label the phrases.

3a. A *phrase* is a group of words used as a single part of speech and not containing a verb and its subject.

Four kinds of phrases are explained on the following pages: *prepositional phrases*, *participial phrases*, *gerund phrases*, and *infinitive phrases*.

The Prepositional Phrase

3b. A *prepositional phrase* is a group of words beginning with a preposition and usually ending with a noun or a pronoun.

EXAMPLES **for** John and me | **in** the house
after the game | **to** school

The noun or pronoun which concludes the prepositional phrase is the object of the preposition which begins the phrase.

EXAMPLES at the **door** | from **Helen** and **her**
with my **friends**

Prepositional phrases are used as modifiers. They may be used as adjectives or as adverbs.

THE ADJECTIVE PHRASE

3c. An *adjective phrase* is a prepositional phrase that modifies a noun or a pronoun.

My brother is the boy **in the black coat.**

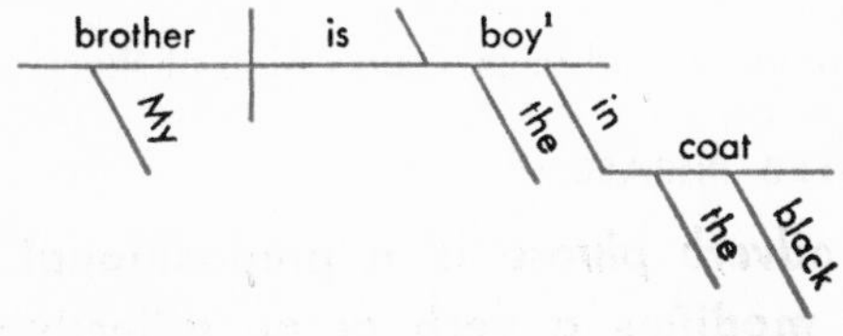

Shelves **of colorful new books** lined the wall **at the back of the room.**

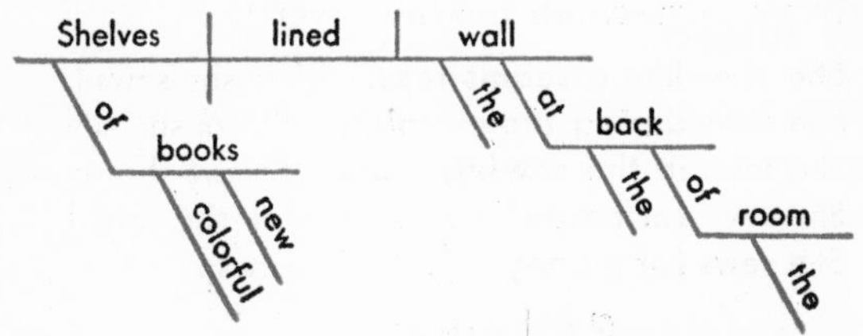

● EXERCISE 1. Number on your paper from 1 to 10. After the proper number copy the adjective phrases in each of the following sentences. After each phrase copy the noun or pronoun the phrase modifies.

1. The letter from Gary brought news of his family.
2. The boys in the minstrel show wanted a book of new jokes.
3. The tunnel under the river is a huge tube of steel.
4. The field beyond the barn is larger than the one between the woods and the barn.

[1] In a diagram the preposition which begins the phrase is placed on a line slanting downward from the word the phrase modifies. The object of the preposition is placed on a horizontal line extending to the right from the line with the preposition. Single-word modifiers are diagramed in the usual way.

5. Bricks for the house across the street were delivered today.
6. The boy behind me has a book by Kenneth Roberts.
7. Have you seen the books on the table by the window?
8. The stones on the ground around second base must be removed.
9. I noticed that the person beside me was a man with a black beard.
10. The road beyond us is a succession of sharp curves.

THE ADVERB PHRASE

3d. An *adverb phrase* is a prepositional phrase that modifies a verb or an adjective or an adverb.

The following sentences show the ways in which an adverb phrase can modify a verb.

1. She sews **like a seamstress.** [*how* she sews]
2. She sews **during the morning.** [*when* she sews]
3. She sews **in the sewing room.** [*where* she sews]
4. She sews **for hours.** [*to what extent* she sews]
5. She sews **for money.** [*why* she sews]

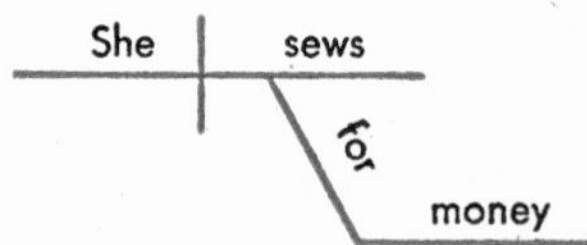

In the sentence below, the adverb phrase modifies an adjective.

Her dress was blue **with a green tinge.**

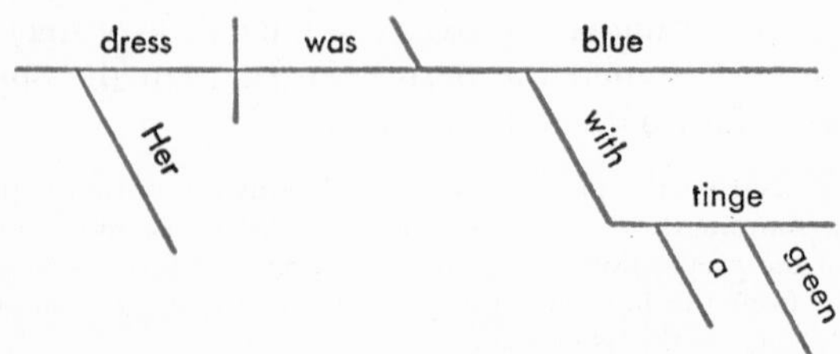

The following sentence illustrates an adverb phrase modifying an adverb.

The bus leaves early **in the morning.**

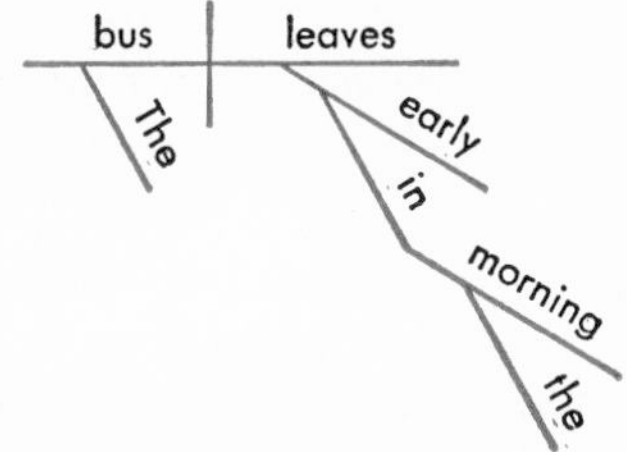

● EXERCISE 2. Number on your paper from 1 to 10. After the proper number copy the adverb phrases in each of the following sentences. After each phrase write the word the phrase modifies.

1. For an hour we waited in the rain.
2. During his childhood he lived on a farm.
3. Teeth should be brushed after meals and before bed.
4. The trip began at dawn and ended in the afternoon.
5. You must stay in school until your eighteenth birthday.
6. He spoke with force but without much sense.
7. Above us roared the jet planes in close formation.
8. Joe swung at a slow ball and missed it; then he hit a fast ball into the bleachers.
9. I stood among the crowd and listened to their comments.
10. A car which was coming toward us veered suddenly into our lane.

Phrases Containing Verbals

Less common than the prepositional phrase but still very useful to a writer are the verbal phrases: the participial phrase, the gerund phrase, and the infinitive phrase. They are called verbal phrases because the most important word in them is a verbal. Verbals are so called because they are formed from verbs. In some respects they act like verbs. For instance, they may express action; they may have modifiers; and they may be followed by complements. In one important respect, however, they are not like verbs. Verbals are not used as verbs in a sentence. They are used as other parts of speech, as nouns, as adjectives, and as adverbs.

Before you can understand verbal phrases, you must understand the verbals on which the phrases are based. On the following pages you will find an explanation of each kind of verbal, followed by a discussion of the verbal as it is most commonly used — in a phrase.

THE PARTICIPIAL PHRASE

3e. A *participle* is a word which acts as both a verb and an adjective.

EXAMPLES The **singing** choir marched onto the stage.
Singing, the choir marched onto the stage.

In these sentences *singing*, like a verb, expresses action; like an adjective, it modifies the noun *choir* — the singing choir.

In the following sentence the participle *dancing*, like a verb, expresses action, and like an adjective, modifies the pronoun *you*.

EXAMPLE I saw you **dancing.**

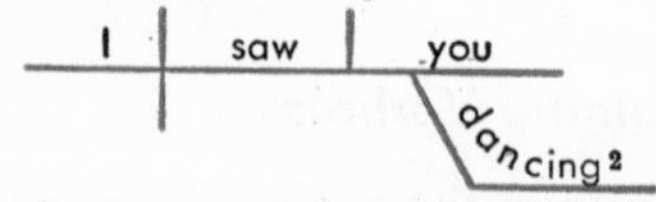

There are two kinds of participles: *present participles* and *past participles*. A present participle, like those in

[2] In a diagram the participle is written on a bent line drawn downward from the word the participle modifies.

the preceding examples, ends in *–ing*. A past participle, which shows action in the past, may end in *–ed*, *–d*, *–t*, *–en*, *–n*: *ask***ed**, *sav***ed**, *deal***t**, *eat***en**, *see***n**.

PRESENT PARTICIPLE He caught two boys **cheating.**
PAST PARTICIPLE The boys, **frightened,** turned around.

Although participles are formed from verbs, they are not used alone as verbs. A participle may, however, be used with a helping verb to form a verb phrase.[3]

PARTICIPLE The boys, **frightened,** . . . [*Frightened* modifies *boys.*]
VERB PHRASE The boys **were frightened.** [The verb phrase *were frightened* consists of the helping verb *were* plus the past participle *frightened.*]

PARTICIPLE The car, **speeding,** . . . [*Speeding* modifies *car.*]
VERB PHRASE The car **had been speeding.** [The verb phrase *had been speeding* consists of the helping verb *had been* plus the present participle *speeding.*]

3f. A *participial phrase* is a group of related words containing a participle.[4]

The participle usually introduces the phrase, and the entire phrase acts as an adjective to modify a noun or pronoun.

EXAMPLES **Expecting trouble,** the guards were fully armed.
The boys, **caught in a sudden downpour,** took refuge in a haystack.

[3] A list of common helping verbs will be found on page 10.
[4] For work on the participial phrase as a sentence fragment, see page 70. For exercises on the dangling participle, see page 212.

3e-f

A participial phrase is made up of a participle and its modifiers and complements. Like verbs, participles may be modified by adverbs and adverb phrases.

EXAMPLE **Leaping gracefully over the wall,** the frightened animal disappeared. [The participle *leaping* is modified by the adverb *gracefully* and the adverb phrase *over the wall.*]

Like verbs, participles may take an object.

EXAMPLE **Turning the knob noiselessly,** I pushed against the door. [The object of the participle *turning* is the word *knob.* (*Turning* what?)]

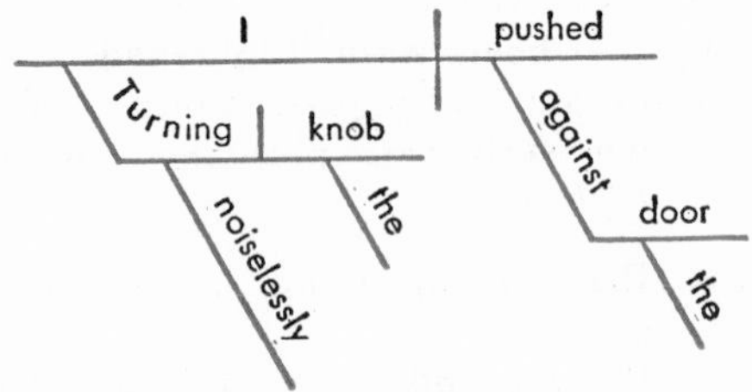

● EXERCISE 3. List on your paper the participial phrases in the following sentences. Before each phrase write the number of the sentence in which it appears. After each phrase write the word the phrase modifies.

1. Disturbed by the news, Father turned off the radio.
2. All girls taking gym today should report to the hockey field.
3. Frightened by the blaze, she rushed from the house, screaming, "Fire!"
4. Walking toward the bus stop, we saw a car lying in the ditch.
5. Left alone, I watched television all evening.
6. Mr. Burt made no comment, leaving us to guess his opinion.
7. Thundering down the home stretch, the horses were neck and neck.
8. Confused by the directions, I entered the wrong door.

9. Jackson's bat, shattered by the mighty blow, lay in pieces at home plate, while Jackson, grinning broadly, jogged around the bases.
10. Still unsatisfied, the employees attending the meeting voted to continue negotiations.

● EXERCISE 4. For each of the following sentences copy in order on your paper the phrases which are italicized. Place each phrase on a separate line and number as shown in the example. After each phrase write the word it modifies and name the phrase: adjective, adverb, participial. Do not list separately prepositional phrases which are included in a participial phrase.

EXAMPLE 1. *Defeated at the polls*, Mr. Sawyer abandoned all hope *of a political career.*

1. Defeated at the polls	Mr. Sawyer	participial
of a political career	hope	adjective

1. *Being obsolete*, trolleys will be replaced *by buses.*
2. *Alarmed by traffic congestion*, the mayor appointed a traffic committee *of four members.*
3. Will the people *standing in the rear* please take the seats *in the front row.*
4. Several reference books *taken from the library without permission* were returned *on Monday morning.*
5. The journey, *estimated at ten days*, actually took only a week.
6. *Standing on the side lines*, we watched Mr. Perkins *drilling the band.*
7. *To his surprise* Bill found his name *in the first-team line-up.*
8. Someone *in the class* was whispering, and Miss Smith, *annoyed by the sound*, kept all *of us* an hour *after school.*
9. *Trapped in a flimsy shack*, the Masked Rider *of the Plains* held off his assailants *for three days.*
10. The sheriff came *to the rescue*, *bringing ample reinforcements.*

11. Money *invested in government bonds* is safely invested.
12. *Received everywhere by enthusiastic crowds*, the candidate became confident, *believing the election already won.*

THE GERUND PHRASE

3g. A *gerund* is a word ending in *–ing* which acts as both a verb and a noun.

EXAMPLE **Plowing** is hard work. [In expressing action, the gerund *plowing* acts as a verb; as the subject of the sentence, it acts as a noun.]

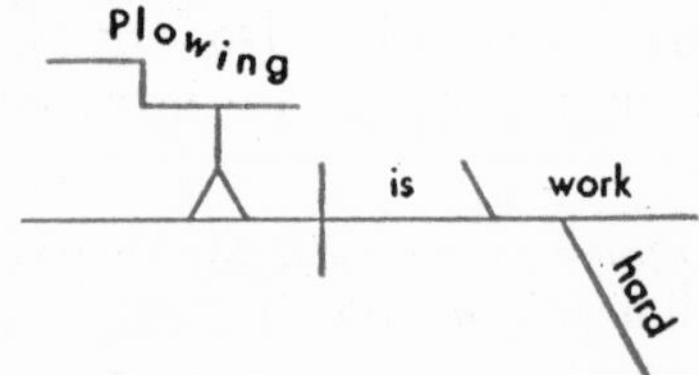

Since a gerund acts as a noun, it may be used as the subject or the object of a verb, as a predicate nominative, and as the object of a preposition.

GERUND AS SUBJECT OF VERB **Talking** is her greatest pleasure.

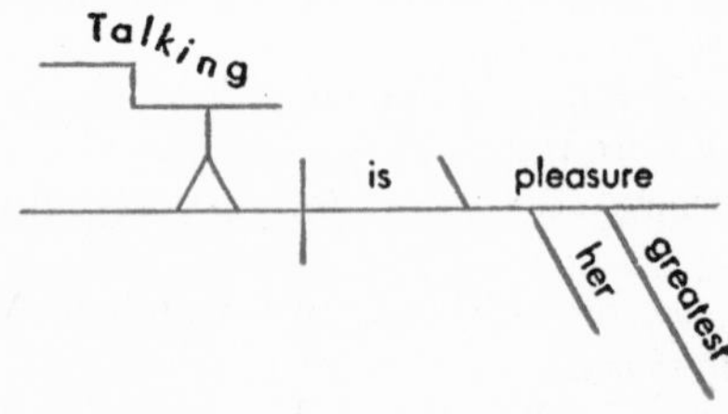

GERUND AS OBJECT OF VERB I enjoyed her **singing.**

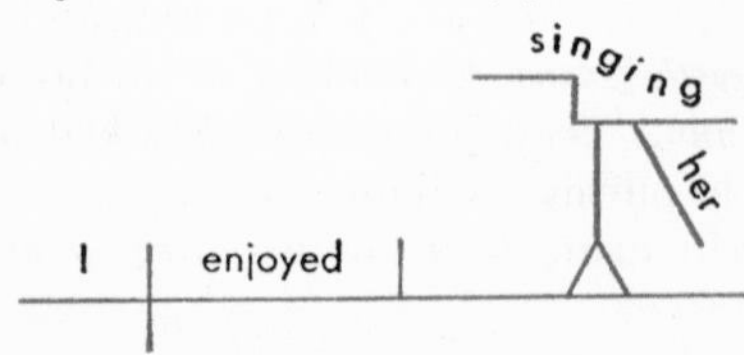

GERUND AS PREDICATE NOMINATIVE **Her greatest pleasure is talking.**

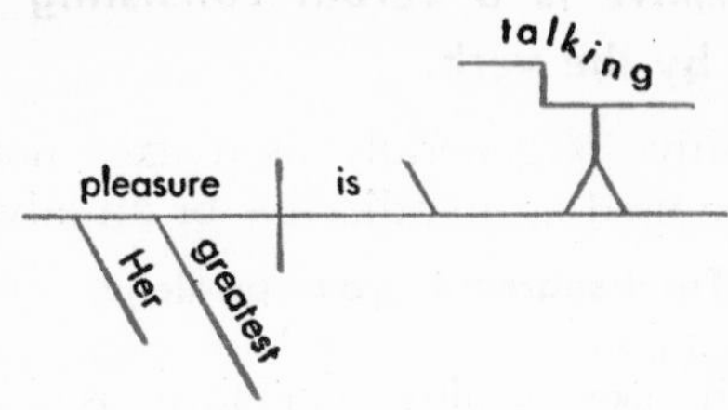

GERUND AS OBJECT OF PREPOSITION By **inquiring,** we found our way.

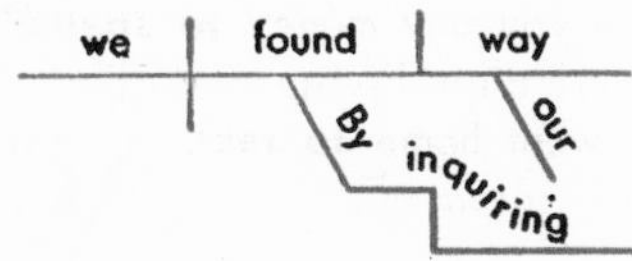

3h. A *gerund phrase* is a phrase containing a gerund.

EXAMPLES **Waiting a long time** was tiresome. [gerund phrase as subject]

He admitted **knowing the murderer.** [gerund phrase as object of verb]

They escaped by **running away.** [gerund phrase as object of preposition]

Making trouble is **courting trouble.** [gerund phrases as subject and as predicate nominative]

A gerund phrase is made up of a gerund and its modifiers and complements.

EXAMPLE **Popping corn on Sunday evenings** was a family custom. [In this sentence the gerund *popping* is modified by the phrase *on Sunday evenings.* The word *corn* is the object of *popping.* (*Popping* what?)]

THE INFINITIVE PHRASE

3i. An *infinitive* is a verbal consisting of *to* followed by the verb.

An infinitive is generally used as a noun, but it may also be used as an adjective or an adverb.

EXAMPLES **To disagree** is your privilege. [infinitive as subject]
He likes **to play.** [infinitive as object of verb *likes* (*likes* what?)]
Our purpose is **to win.** [infinitive as predicate nominative]
Have you any money **to spend?** [infinitive as adjective modifying *money*]
She went home **to rest.** [infinitive as adverb modifying *went*]

▶ NOTE: Do not confuse the infinitive, a verbal of which *to* is a part, with a prepositional phrase beginning with *to*, which consists of *to* + a noun or pronoun.

INFINITIVES	PREPOSITIONAL PHRASES
to fly	to him
to work	to school
to see	to the game

Like a verb, an infinitive may have a subject.

EXAMPLE I wanted **him** *to wait.* [In this sentence the pronoun *him* is the subject of the infinitive *to wait.* The entire group of words *him to wait* is, in turn, the object of the verb *wanted.* (*Wanted* what?)]

3j. An *infinitive phrase* [5] is a phrase containing an infinitive.

EXAMPLES **To get a scholarship** was his ambition.
I don't want **to see anybody.**

[5] For exercises on the use of the infinitive phrase to reduce wordiness, see page 239.

Everyone has some advice to give the coach.
Her job was to operate the switchboard.

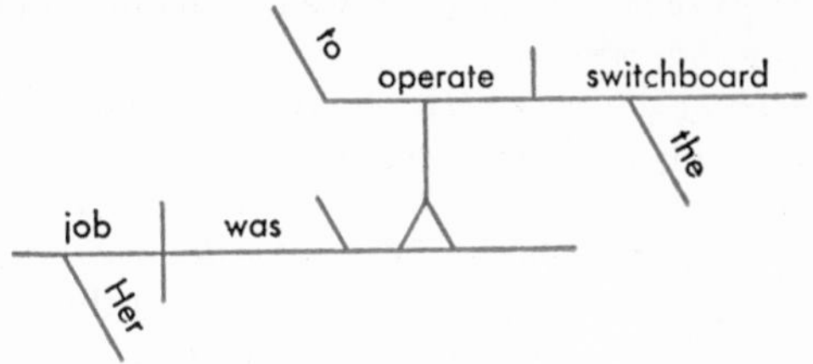

An infinitive phrase is made up of an infinitive and its modifiers and complements.

EXAMPLES We plan **to leave soon.** [*Soon* modifies the infinitive *to leave.*]
He would like **to go with us.** [The phrase *with us* modifies the infinitive *to go.*]
I tried **to sell my car.** [*Car* is the object of the infinitive *to sell.*]

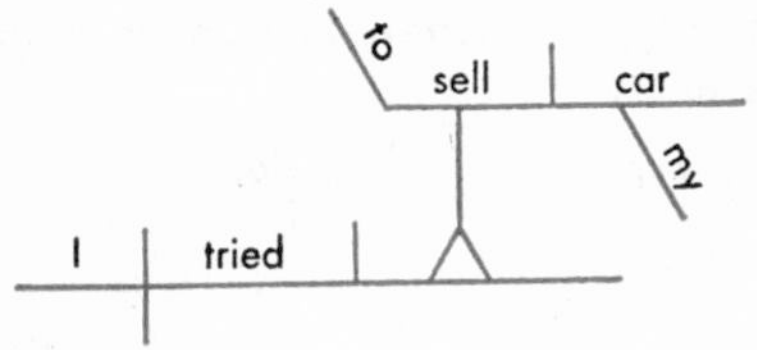

● EXERCISE 5. Number in a column on your paper from 1 to 20. In the following sentences adjective, adverb, participial, gerund, and infinitive phrases are numbered and italicized. Study each phrase and after the corresponding number on your paper, tell what kind of phrase it is.

1. (1) *Driving an obsolete car*, Stan made the trip (2) *to Montville* (3) *in seven hours.*
2. Jones did not wish (4) *to make the decision alone;* (5) *following democratic procedure*, he let the entire class vote (6) *on the proposition.*

3i-j

3. The most interesting part (7) *of our factory visit* was (8) *watching the men* (9) *working on the assembly line.*
4. (10) *Prepared for any emergency,* we began our arduous trek (11) *across the mountain.*
5. (12) *Studying until midnight* leaves you too tired (13) *to work efficiently* (14) *on the following morning.*
6. (15) *Worried about his health,* Mr. McLean went (16) *to Florida* (17) *for a change* (18) *of climate.*
7. (19) *Improving my grades* has been my goal this term, but I do not expect (20) *to make the honor roll.*

The Appositive[6]

3k. An *appositive* is a noun or pronoun — often with modifiers — that follows another noun or pronoun to identify or explain it. An *appositive phrase* is made up of an appositive and its modifiers.

EXAMPLES My opponent **Louis** forfeited the match.
Sandy, **our Airedale pup,** is a dog with personality.

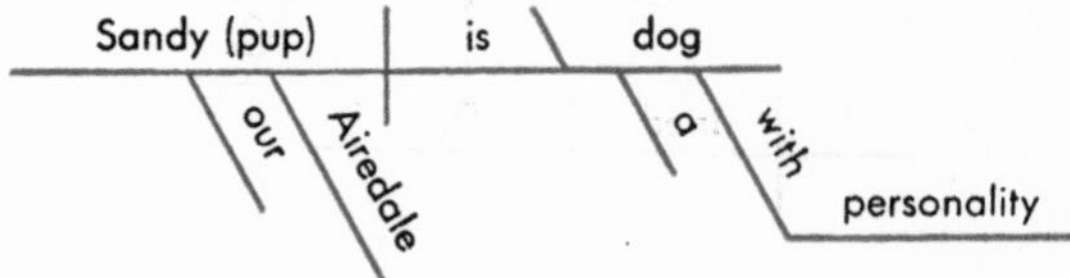

In the following sentences the appositives and appositive phrases are in heavy type.

1. I received the information from Mr. Jackson, **the new mayor.**
2. My sister **Mary** is in the tenth grade.
3. The stranger, **a man of formidable appearance,** stopped the fight.
4. My friend **Bob** had a fine vacation, **a trip to Mexico City.**

[6] For rules on the punctuation of appositives, see page 579. For the use of the appositive in subordination of ideas, see page 196.

● EXERCISE 6. List in the order in which they appear all the phrases in each of the following sentences. Before each list of phrases write the number of the sentence. After each phrase tell what kind it is: adjective, adverb, participial, gerund, infinitive, or appositive. In doing this exercise you will find that a phrase frequently modifies a word in another phrase. For instance, in the sentence *I was impressed by the book with a red cover*, the phrase *with a red cover* modifies *book*, which is in the phrase *by the book*.

1. Living alone appeals to many persons.
2. Left alone, I decided to spend my time in the library.
3. Pedestrians crossing the street against the light will be given a ticket by the traffic officer.
4. At the present time, making money is his only concern.
5. All houses in Cranford, a new real estate development, have been sold.
6. Cars going south were routed through Caldwell.
7. In the last ten yards of the race, Pete tried to outsprint the others.
8. Dismissed early, we decided to practice our diving at Crystal Lake.
9. Promoting higher dues, Adrian Brown, our class president, gave a gloomy picture of our treasury.
10. The girls in the class outvoted the boys on every issue.

CHAPTER 4

The Clause

LEARN THE WORK THAT CLAUSES DO IN THE SENTENCE

As you grow older, your sentences become more mature. One important characteristic of the mature sentence is the subordinate clause, which you are employing more and more frequently in your writing. A knowledge of the subordinate clause — what it is and how it is used — will be helpful to you in learning to write clear, smooth, adult sentences.

Diagnostic Test on Clauses

Give yourself the following diagnostic test. There are 10 subordinate clauses in the following sentences. Copy them in order on your paper. After each clause tell whether it is an adjective, adverb, or noun clause.

1. Professor Wells, who has explored many jungles, will lecture on the new expedition which he is now planning.
2. You will receive a call from me when I have finished the job.
3. No one knew who the stranger was.
4. After you have read the book, tell me what you think of it.
5. I was surprised to learn that the football game had been canceled because the snow was too deep.
6. Since you have been here, we have noticed an improvement in morale, which had been very low.

4a. A *clause* is a group of words containing a subject and predicate and used as part of a sentence.

A *main clause* expresses a completed thought and by itself could be a sentence. A *subordinate clause* does not express a completed thought and must always be attached to a main clause.[1]

MAIN CLAUSES *The dwindling resources of the state are known to the Conservation Department,* **but** *the public does not fully appreciate the need for reforestation.*

In this sentence there are two main clauses joined by the conjunction *but.*

You can see from the following examples that a subordinate clause, although it contains a subject and a verb, differs from a main clause in not expressing a completed thought.

SUBORDINATE CLAUSES which Father bought
when the weather cleared
how I had done the problem

Combined with a main clause, each of these subordinate clauses plays its part in a sentence.

This is the car **which Father bought.**
When the weather cleared, we continued the game.
He asked me **how I had done the problem.**

● EXERCISE 1. Remembering that a group of words is a clause only if it contains a verb and its subject, study the verbs and their subjects in the following sentences to decide whether they are in main clauses (expressing a completed thought) or in subordinate

[1] *Main* clauses are sometimes called *independent* clauses. *Subordinate* clauses are sometimes called *dependent* clauses.

clauses (not expressing a completed thought). Copy on your paper the subordinate clauses.

1. You will receive your pay check after you have completed the job.
2. The governor, who had recently been re-elected, planned several drastic reforms in the government.
3. Although both referees blew their whistles, both teams kept on playing.
4. The skill that he showed in yesterday's match was not apparent this afternoon.
5. When you write to Jane, please give her my regards.
6. I asked for money because the dance tickets were on sale.
7. Do you remember where you put my pen?
8. If you are right, I am wrong.
9. Before you select a college, you should consult your guidance counselor.
10. John will not call you until he has found the necessary information.

● EXERCISE 2. Copy in order on your paper the subordinate clauses in the following sentences. Before each clause write the number of the sentence in which it appears. Some sentences contain more than one subordinate clause. Write *v* above the verb and *s* above the subject of each clause.

1. Frank Martin, who was sent to the office, disappeared on the way.
2. When she was learning to apply lipstick, my sister used to put too much in the wrong places.
3. Come if you can and when you can.
4. You will find wherever you go in this town that people are friendly.
5. Although Bart knows the dance steps, he does not lead his partner, who must guess what he will do next.
6. Since Larry displays talent in art, he should take the major art course which the school will offer next year.
7. When contracts were let for the new courthouse, local

politicians showed the first interest that they had shown in civic affairs for two years.

8. The lowest bidder did not get the contract because he would not share the profits with the politicians.
9. While Carl was cooking lunch, the rest of us took a swim in the river which flowed past our camp site.
10. We could not tell what his purpose was because he kept it to himself.
11. As soon as he arrived, the doctor knew what had happened.

Like a phrase, a subordinate clause acts as a single part of speech — as an adjective or an adverb or a noun.

The Adjective Clause

4b. An *adjective clause* is a subordinate clause which — like an adjective — modifies a noun or a pronoun.

EXAMPLES The look **that she gave him** was discouraging. [The subordinate clause *that she gave him* modifies the noun *look*.]

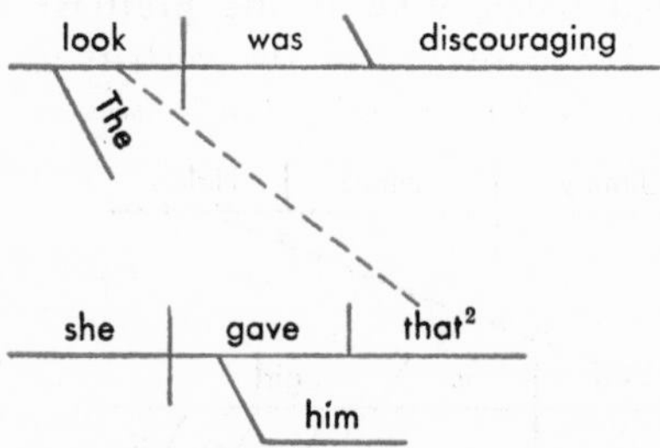

[2] Since a subordinate clause has a verb and a subject and may contain complements and modifiers, it is diagramed very much like a sentence. Adjective and adverb clauses are placed on a horizontal line below the main line. An adjective clause begun by a relative pronoun is joined to the word it modifies by a slanting dotted line drawn from the modified word to the relative pronoun.

I am grateful to the mechanic **who helped me.**

Is it she **whom you mean?**

We showed him the house **where he was born.**

Do you recall the time **when Alec forgot his own party?**

THE RELATIVE PRONOUN

Subordinate clauses often begin with the pronouns *who, whom, whose, which, what, that.*[3] Pronouns used in this way refer to, or are *related to,* some word or idea which has preceded them. Because of this relationship they are called *relative* pronouns.

4c. A *relative pronoun* is a pronoun which begins a subordinate clause and is related to another word or idea.

A relative pronoun may be the subject of the clause it begins.

Jimmy invited Helen, **who is the prettiest girl in the class.** [*Who* is the subject of the verb *is* in the subordinate clause *who is the prettiest girl in the class.*]

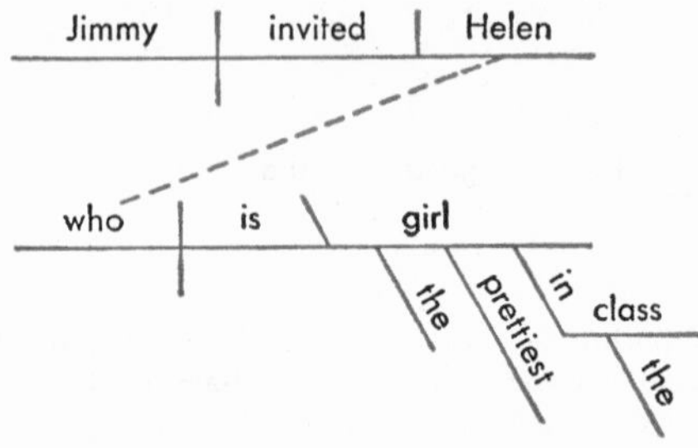

[3] The compound relative pronouns *whoever, whomever, whichever, whatever* may also begin clauses.

A relative pronoun may be the object of the verb in the clause it begins.

Ted Morrison, **whom I recommended,** got the job. [*Whom* is the object of the verb *recommended.*]

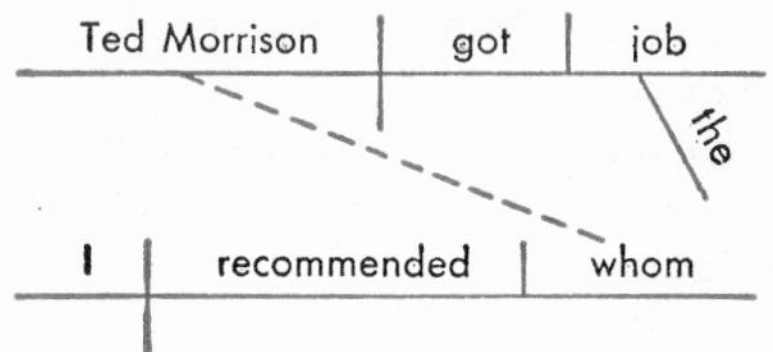

A relative pronoun may be the object of a preposition in the clause it begins.

Are you the man **to whom I gave the order?** [*Whom* is the object of the preposition *to.*] [4]

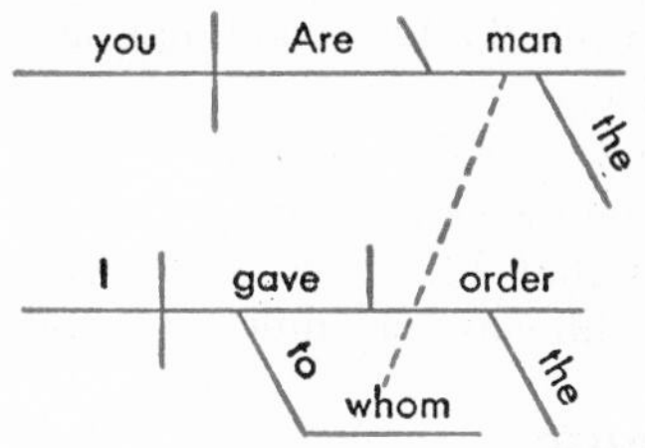

● EXERCISE 3. Copy in order on your paper the adjective clauses in the following sentences. After each clause write the noun or pronoun that the clause modifies. Your teacher may ask you to indicate whether the relative pronoun is used as a subject, an object of a verb, or an object of a preposition.

1. I did not know the girl who spoke to me.
2. Captain Rickenbacker, who is president of the airline, was an ace in World War I.
3. The answer that Joe got was different from mine.

[4] In this sentence two words — *to* and *whom* — begin the clause. Other two-word combinations of a preposition and a relative pronoun to begin a clause are *in which, by whom, for whom.*

4. Beware of shoes that are too small for you.
5. After the game Frank proudly showed us the pictures that he had taken.
6. There is no excuse that I can think of for your bad behavior.
7. The class adviser, whom I consulted, advised me to take more math.
8. Those were experiences which I shall never forget.
9. The bus which carried the team broke down on the way to the game.
10. I could not understand Mr. Perrone, who spoke rather broken English.
11. The team that I backed lost every game in which it tried a passing attack.
12. My uncle who lives in California is a twin of my uncle who lives in Florida.
13. Mr. Macaulay's book, which was published twenty years ago, is still the best book that has been published on this subject.
14. There is no reason that occurs to me for your not getting the money which you inherited.
15. The clothes that I ordered were sent by mistake to my father, who was very much surprised.

The Noun Clause

4d. A *noun clause* is a subordinate clause used as a noun.

EXAMPLE **What the announcer said** was not clear.

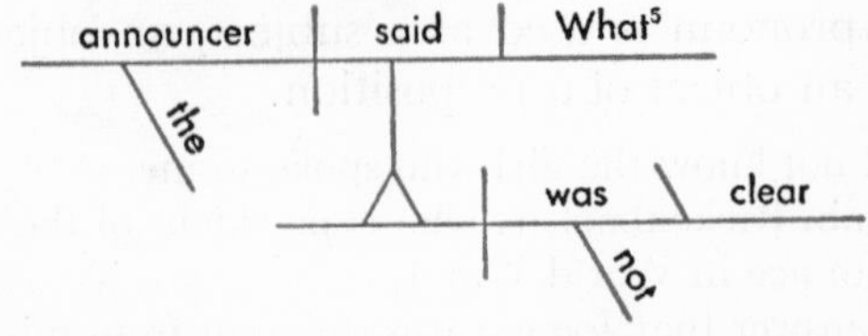

[5] In diagraming, a noun clause is pictured as a unit by being placed at the top of a vertical line, like a pedestal, rising from that part of the diagram (subject, object, predicate nominative) in which the clause belongs.

The entire noun clause *What the announcer said* is the subject of the verb *was.* Study the following pairs of sentences to see how a noun clause may be a predicate nominative, an object of a verb, or an object of a preposition.

1. This is my greatest **need.** [*Need* is a noun used as a predicate nominative.]
   This is **what I need most.** [*What I need most* is a noun clause used as a predicate nominative.]
2. I remember his **comment.** [*Comment* is a noun used as the object of the verb *remember.*]
   I remember **what he said.** [*What he said* is a noun clause used as the object of *remember.*]
3. A prize will be given to the **winner.** [*Winner* is a noun used as the object of the preposition *to.*]
   A prize will be given to **whoever**[6] **wins.** [*Whoever wins* is a noun clause used as the object of the preposition *to.*]

SUBORDINATE CLAUSES NOT BEGUN BY A JOINING WORD

Adjective and noun clauses are frequently used without an introductory relative pronoun or other joining word. Note that the introductory word is omitted in the second sentence in each of the following pairs.

1. Do you believe **that he is guilty?**
   Do you believe **he is guilty?**
2. There is a man **whom everybody admires.**[6]
   There is a man **everybody admires.**

● EXERCISE 4. List in order on your paper the subordinate clauses in the following sentences. Before each clause place the number of the sentence in which it appears. After each clause tell what kind it is — adjective or noun. Be prepared to tell what word each adjective clause modifies and how each noun clause

4d

[6] For work on the use of *who* and *whom* in good usage, see page 106.

is used in the sentence — as a subject, an object of a verb or of a preposition, or a predicate nominative.

1. Whatever you say will be held against you.
2. The criticisms that he made were not constructive.
3. We offered her some water, which she drank eagerly.
4. Do you remember who gave you this information?
5. What he said was not what the audience wanted to hear.
6. The author, who was a brilliant man, explained passages that were puzzling his readers.
7. Whatever you decide will be satisfactory to the students, who have faith in your judgment.
8. The camp will be cleaned up by whoever reaches it first.
9. That you overslept is a poor excuse for tardiness.
10. I told Mr. Long, who is the treasurer, that we needed more money.
11. What you need is a course in dancing like the one that Jim took.
12. We agree with what you said, but we object to the manner in which you said it.
13. Many of my friends whom I had not seen for years came to the reunion that was held last summer.

The Adverb Clause

4e. An *adverb clause* is a subordinate clause which is used like an adverb.

In the following examples the adverb clauses modify the verb *runs*. Each illustrates one of the typical adverbial functions of telling *how*, *when*, *where*, *why*, *to what extent*, *under what conditions*.

1. He runs **as though he had been frightened.** [*how* he runs]
2. He runs **whenever he can.** [*when* he runs]
3. He runs **wherever he goes.** [*where* he runs]
4. He runs **because he likes to run.** [*why* he runs]

5. **He runs as far as he can.** [*to what extent* he runs]
6. **He runs if he feels like it.** [*under what conditions* he runs]

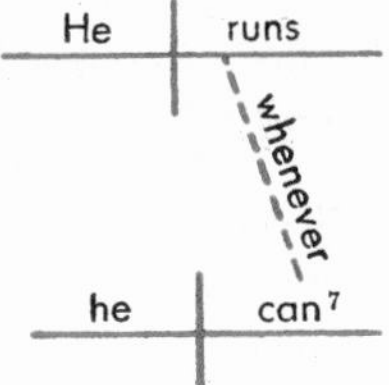

ADVERB CLAUSE MODIFYING AN ADJECTIVE **She is as pretty as a girl can be**. [The adverb clause *as a girl can be* modifies the adjective *pretty*.]

ADVERB CLAUSE MODIFYING AN ADVERB **He ran faster than I did.** [The adverb clause *than I did* modifies the adverb *faster*.]

THE SUBORDINATING CONJUNCTION

4f. A conjunction which begins an adverb clause is called a *subordinating conjunction*. It joins the clause to the rest of the sentence.

The following words are used as subordinating conjunctions.

COMMON SUBORDINATING CONJUNCTIONS [8]

after	before	unless
although	if	until
as	in order that	when
as if	since	whenever
as long as	so that	where
as though	than	wherever
because	though	while

[7] In diagraming, an adverb clause is written on a horizontal line below the main line of the diagram. The subordinating conjunction beginning the clause is written on a slanting dotted line which links the verb of the clause to the word the clause modifies.

[8] Many of these words, as you know, may be used as other parts of speech.

4e-f

THE ELLIPTICAL (INCOMPLETE) CLAUSE

Sometimes in our writing and speaking we do not complete the adverb clauses we use.

EXAMPLES **Is she taller than you (are)?**
While (he was) talking, he waved his arms.

In these adverb clauses, the part of the clause given in parentheses has been omitted. The complete clause, however, is in the writer's and the reader's mind. Such incomplete clauses are said to be "elliptical."[9]

● EXERCISE 5. Copy on your paper the adverb clauses in the following sentences. Before each clause write the number of the sentence in which it appears. Draw a line under the subordinating conjunction which introduces the clause. After each clause write what the clause tells: *how*, *when*, *where*, *why*, *to what extent*, *under what conditions*.

1. When the Secretary of State went to Paris, he conferred with the leaders of the Western powers.
2. If the delegates are willing to compromise, more progress will be made.
3. Private planes have been denied landing privileges at Municipal Airport because the commercial traffic there is already congested.
4. A traveling secretary goes wherever he is needed.
5. Since the air pressure inside the plane is greater, a broken window will break outward.
6. I drove as rapidly as road conditions would permit.
7. You will find the farm more appealing after you have lived in the city for a while.
8. Wherever you go in the West take your camera.
9. Fred put a block of wood under the jack so that it would be steadier.

[9] The dictionary definition of "ellipsis" as applied to grammar is "an omission of one or more words, obviously understood, but necessary to make the expression grammatically complete." For the correct usage of pronouns in elliptical clauses see page 110.

10. Be as quiet as you can until the bell rings.
11. Although there have been major strikes, the stock market has continued to rise.
12. While I was waiting for the train, I watched my fellow travelers.
13. He lived each day as though it were his last.
14. After the ballots had been counted, George asked for a recount.
15. Although the new styles did not suit her, Nan insisted on wearing them.
16. When the doctor measured us, Ted was taller than I was.
17. There will be no school picnic this spring unless the principal changes his mind.
18. If you take my advice, you will read the preface before you read the book.
19. Bill drives more than I do because his family has two cars.
20. Since traffic was heavy, the new highway was opened although it had not been completed.

● EXERCISE 6. Each of the following sentences contains one or more subordinate clauses. Copy the clauses in order on your paper. Before each write the number of the sentence in which it appears. After each write what kind it is — adjective, noun, adverb.

1. Although legislation cannot destroy prejudice, it can destroy unfair discrimination, which may be based on prejudice.
2. After we had seen the film, we read the book, which was even better.
3. Before you can register for this course, you must get the approval of Mr. Thompson, who will be the teacher.
4. If the students object to the plan which the council is proposing, they may vote it down.
5. The president, who addressed new members, told them that they must attend every meeting unless they are ill.
6. When you realize that time is money, you spend it as carefully as you spend money.
7. Mr. Larkin, who was leaving the room in a hurry,

caught his toe and fell forward as he reached the door.

8. Before you decide, let me tell you what I think.
9. Although the actors had not learned their lines, the director decided that the play would be given on the scheduled date.
10. People who read rapidly usually comprehend what they read better than people who read slowly.

Sentences Classified According to Structure

4g. Classified according to their structure, there are four kinds of sentences — *simple, compound, complex,* and *compound-complex.*

(1) A *simple sentence* is a sentence with one main clause and no subordinate clauses.

EXAMPLE The visiting dignitaries from Europe were met at National Airport by the President.

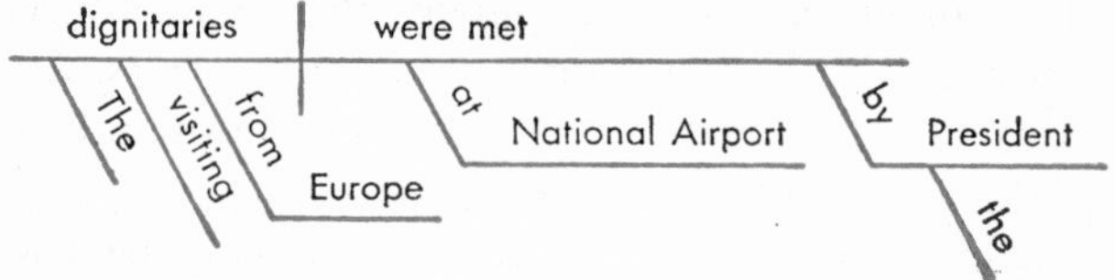

(2) A *compound sentence* is a sentence composed of two or more main clauses but no subordinate clauses.

EXAMPLES The visiting dignitaries landed at National Airport, and they were met by the President.

The visiting dignitaries landed in Washington; consequently, they were met by the President, and they were entertained at the White House.

▶ NOTE: Do not confuse the compound predicate of a simple sentence with the two subjects and two verbs of a compound sentence. Study the two diagrams given on the next page.

SIMPLE SENTENCE WITH COMPOUND PREDICATE The visiting dignitaries **were met** by the President and **entertained** at the White House.

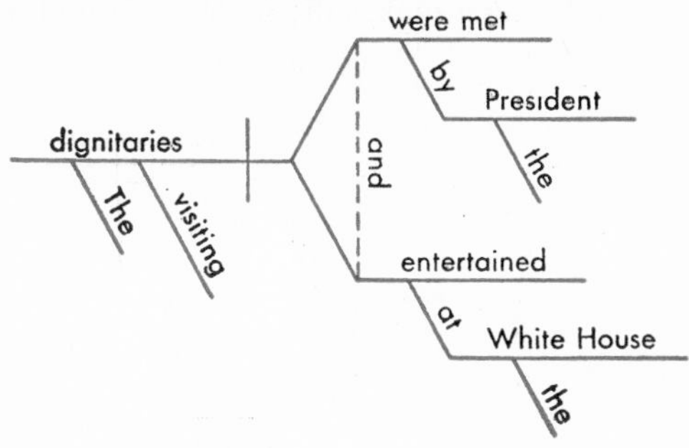

COMPOUND SENTENCE WITH TWO SUBJECTS AND TWO VERBS The visiting **dignitaries were met** by the President, and **they were entertained** at the White House.

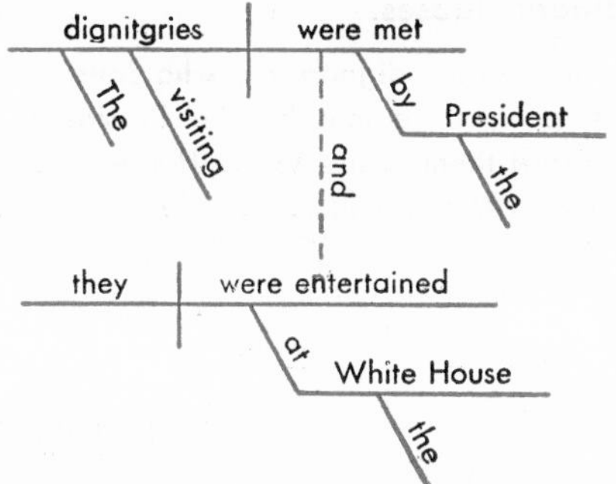

Main clauses may be joined by co-ordinating conjunctions (*and*, *but*, *nor*, *or*, *for*) or by conjunctive adverbs (*accordingly*, *also*, *besides*, *consequently*, *hence*, *however*, *moreover*, *nevertheless*, *otherwise*, *then*, *therefore*, *thus*, *still*).[10]

(3) A *complex sentence* is a sentence which contains one main clause and one or more subordinate clauses.

[10] For rules concerning the punctuation of compound sentences, see pages 587 and 591.

EXAMPLE **The visiting dignitaries arrived at National Airport where they were met by the President.** [The subordinate clause *where they were met by the President* makes the sentence complex.]

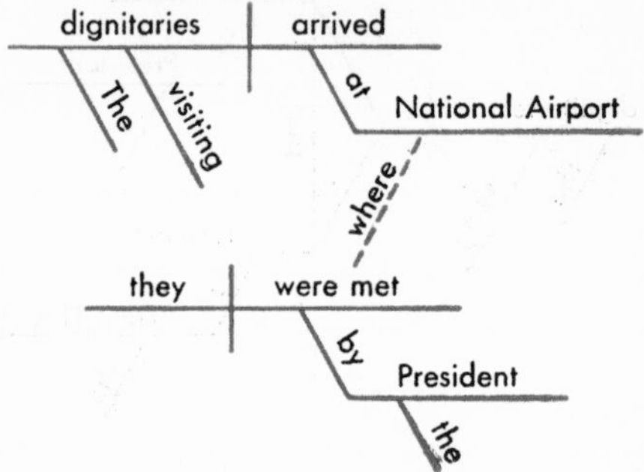

(4) A *compound-complex sentence* is a sentence which contains two or more main clauses and one or more subordinate clauses.

EXAMPLE The visiting dignitaries, who landed at National Airport, were met by the President, and he escorted them to the White House. [Main clauses: *The visiting dignitaries were met by the President; he escorted them to the White House;* subordinate clause: *who landed at National Airport.*]

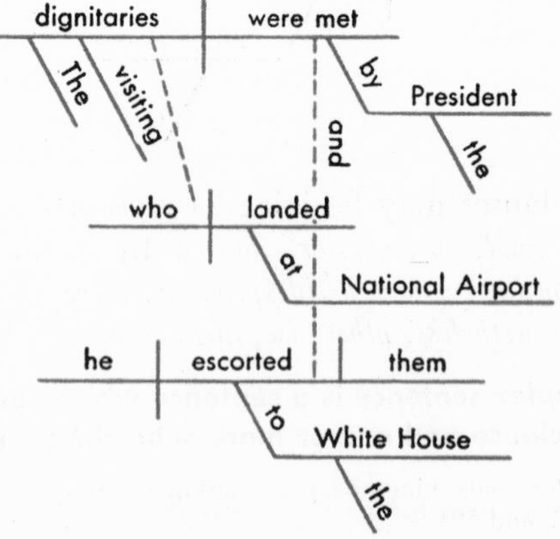

● EXERCISE 7. Number from 1 to 20 on your paper. After the proper number tell what kind of sentence each of the following is: simple, compound, complex, compound-complex. Be prepared to support your answers.

1. A telegram or a telephone call at three in the morning always sends Mother into mild hysteria.
2. If it is the sea voyage that you want, you should take a tramp steamer.
3. Sally learned to knit during the summer, and now she spends most of her time knitting socks for Bill.
4. If employers will not hire inexperienced persons, how is a beginner going to get a job?
5. An attractive display of the new books in the library was a feature of this year's Book Week.
6. To underestimate your opponent is dangerous, but to underestimate yourself is more dangerous.
7. Jack failed English because his grades in composition were too low.
8. When the team has had a little more experience, it will be stronger than last year's championship team.
9. The scene that Mr. Parkhurst saw as he entered the room was enough to break the heart of any teacher, but the scene that followed his entrance was enough to make any student cringe.
10. The conductor sensed that the brass section was confused; therefore he called for greater volume from the basses.
11. Spectators came early so that they would have a chance at the few available unreserved seats.
12. Sales of television sets dropped sharply when authorities announced that there would be no basketball telecasts; however, television dealers believed that the decision would be reversed because of the public demand.
13. Harmful effects of radiation appear in the offspring of irradiated fish.
14. Fish are used for experimentation because they react

to radiation as higher vertebrates, including human beings, react.

15. The search for uranium in northern Ontario was a pleasure to the engineers, who took along their fishing rods as well as their Geiger counters.
16. Although Ontario has long been known as a fisherman's paradise, only in recent years have the northern lakes and rivers become accessible to any but the hardiest adventurers.
17. Mary was offered scholarships at three colleges, and she spent weeks trying to decide which to accept.
18. According to Miss Hilker, the guidance counselor, some basic considerations in choosing a college are your own interests, your personality, your financial resources, and your scholastic record in high school.
19. Although they were almost invariably poor, the early Americans were hard-working people, and they were eager to make a place for themselves in the wilderness.
20. A few telephone calls revealed to Mr. Thayer that his daughters' stories of what other parents allowed their children to do were clever falsifications; furthermore, he learned to his surprise that other children had been holding him up to their parents as a liberal father who made no strict rules for his daughters.

● EXERCISE 8. Write in the following order 2 simple sentences, 2 compound sentences, 4 complex sentences, and 2 compound-complex sentences. In the complex and compound-complex sentences draw a line under each subordinate clause.

PART TWO

WRITING CORRECT SENTENCES

WHAT IS GOOD ENGLISH?

Since the day long ago when you first began to talk, you have been learning to speak English by imitation. That is, you have listened carefully to the words other people used and then have tried to pronounce them and use them in the same way. You have acquired a vocabulary of several thousand words which you pronounce as people around you pronounce them. You have acquired a fair understanding of complicated English constructions without realizing how complicated they are. You have mastered most, perhaps all, of the forms of verbs and pronouns. You have done all this chiefly by imitation and by accepting the helpful corrections made by your parents, friends, and teachers.

"Correction" of your English raises the question: Why is one word or one form correct while another is incorrect? What, in other words, is good English? Good English is the kind of English used by educated people. The fact that educated people use a different kind of English from that used by uneducated people can easily be discovered by listening. The educated person will say, for example, "Jim and I weren't able to see anything in the fog." The uneducated person might say, "Jim and me wasn't able to see nothing in the fog." Although the idea expressed is clear in either form, you, as a high school student, would say it the first way, which, since it is the way an educated person would say it, is the "correct" way.

WRITTEN ENGLISH AND SPOKEN ENGLISH

The distinction between correct and incorrect English is not so simple, so black and white, as the preceding paragraph suggests. There are variations in the way English is used by the well educated. For instance, there is a difference between spoken English and written English. You have discovered in school that you are not permitted to write in the way you speak. Not only must you attend to matters like punctuation and spelling, but you must use whole sentences. You must avoid the dawdling, repetitious, disconnected language of ordinary conversation because such language is confusing when it is written. You *speak* to someone face to face, but you *write* to someone who will not be present at your side when he reads what you have written. For that reason, written language must be more precise and careful than spoken language.

APPROPRIATE ENGLISH

Educated persons also adapt their language to the situation in which they find themselves. You know, for example, that your language in the classroom is different from the language you use on the athletic field, in the locker room, or among your friends. You would not use locker-room English in the classroom because it would promptly gain the disfavor of the teacher and the rest of the class. You would not use very formal English at a party for fear of being thought stilted by the group. Formal English, however, would be appropriate in speaking before a P.T.A. meeting or in addressing the school assembly.

It comes to this: each of us knows and uses several kinds of English. Which kind we use depends upon the situation. We choose language appropriate to an occasion just as we choose appropriate clothes.

THE LEVELS OF ENGLISH USAGE

We can describe three kinds of English, which are known as the three *levels of usage*. They are *standard* English, *colloquial* English, and *illiterate* English. The first two are correct if appropriately used. The third is always considered incorrect among educated people.

Standard English, the top level of usage, is the English used by educated people when they are speaking or writing carefully. Standard English is free of slang. It follows the rules of usage described in the following chapters of this book. It is appropriate in all formal situations: serious articles, "literary" essays, essay-type answers on examinations, research papers, and formal speeches.

Colloquial English is the language used by educated people in conversation and in conversational writing. It is completely acceptable in any informal situation. It uses slang sparingly. It is less formal than standard English in both its vocabulary and its form. Whenever a writer wants to make his writing seem as free and easy as talk, he will write in colloquial English. You will find colloquial writing on the editorial pages of some newspapers, in signed columns, and in stories and essays in most of the popular magazines. It is the natural and appropriate language of friendly letters.

Since standard English is acceptable in most situations, the exercises in this book are designed to help you master standard English. Whenever there is a difference between standard and colloquial English, you will find that difference noted in this book. How far we can depart from standard English in any group depends on the kind of language that group approves.

The *illiterate*, or lowest, level of usage is the language typical of persons who have not had the advantages of much education or who have persisted in the use of poor English in spite of their education. As a high school student you should avoid altogether this level of usage. To be specific, *He don't*, *He seen it*, *You was*, *Them cars*, *ain't* are examples of illiterate English. Similarly, errors in agreement of subject and verb and most errors in the use of pronouns are considered unacceptable in educated circles.

The three levels of English usage may be summarized as follows:

Standard: Always correct although it may sound stilted in some informal situations

Colloquial: Correct in all informal situations

Illiterate: Never correct

THE IMPORTANCE OF GOOD USAGE

Social pressure is a powerful thing. Because of it, you dress in a certain way; you observe certain social customs; you mind your manners. Social pressure affects language customs. In some groups illiterate expressions such as "He come" or "He done it" or "between you and I" may be acceptable. In others they are not acceptable. In these others, if you use such expressions, you are penalized. You may be kept out of a club, or left off invitation lists for parties, or kept out of a better paying job. How can you avoid these penalties? You can avoid them by mastering standard English, the kind taught in this book. Knowing standard English, you can be sure that your English will be acceptable in any situation.

EXCEPTIONS TO GRAMMAR RULES

In some ways, English is a most unsatisfactory language. It is not logically consistent. Its rules are filled with exceptions. Its declensions and conjugations are filled with surprises. For example, we have *ring–rang–rung*, and the unwary person naturally expects *bring–brang–brung*. The explanation for this illogical construction of English lies in its method of growth. Like any living language, English does grow and change as it has grown and changed for centuries. The changes occur slowly. There may be only a half dozen in one person's lifetime. Moreover, the changes arise out of habit and custom, not out of logic. For many generations, there has been a strong psychological urge among English-speaking people to say *It is me*. This expression is at variance with the established pattern of using a nominative after forms of *be*. Yet it has been so persistent and has been so widely used by educated persons speaking and writing carefully, that it has finally become accepted.

The question which naturally arises next is: What about *It is her*, *It is him*, and other such expressions? Logically, if *It is me* is acceptable, these other forms are also acceptable. However, since language does not change logically, these other forms must win approval one by one; they have not yet done so.

The rules of grammar and usage which you find in textbooks are intended as a description of how language is used. Actually the use of a language comes first; then the description of it follows and gets into the textbooks. It is the language that is important; no living language can be confined within arbitrary rules. Rules are guides for people who are learning to speak and write English which will be accepted by any group in which they find themselves.

Since the English language is not a logically developed thing, the rules have exceptions such as that noted above. Since there are not many of these exceptions, they can be learned easily enough.

CHAPTER 5

The Completed Sentence

LEARN HOW TO AVOID FRAGMENTS, RUN-ON SENTENCES, AND THE COMMA FAULT IN YOUR WRITING

There are two kinds of "sentence error." The first kind is the writing of a part of a sentence, a *fragment*, as though it were a whole sentence, able to stand by itself with a capital letter at the beginning and a period at the end. The second kind of error is the *run-on error*, which results from using a comma (or no punctuation at all) at the end of a sentence, instead of a period or other end mark.

If *sentence fragments* and *run-on sentences* still find their way into your compositions, you should study this chapter. The chapter cannot remove the carelessness which is responsible for many sentence errors, but it can increase your understanding of what is and what is not a sentence.[1]

[1] In order to understand this chapter, you should know the following common grammar terms: *participial phrase*, *prepositional phrase*, *subordinate clause*, *appositive*, *infinitive phrase*. If you need to do so, look them up in Chapters 3 and 4.

Sentence Fragments

A group of words is a complete sentence when it has a subject and a verb and expresses a completed thought.

COMPLETED	After the flood the barn roof lay in the front yard.
NOT COMPLETED	After the flood the barn roof in the front yard
NOT COMPLETED	After the flood the barn roof lying in the front yard

Because they lack a verb, the last two examples do not express a completed thought. Words ending in *–ing*, like *lying*, are not verbs when they are used alone. Such words may, of course, be used with a *helping verb* to form a verb phrase (see page 10). Unless a word ending in *–ing* does have a helping verb, it cannot be used as the verb in a sentence.[2]

NO VERB	The barn roof *lying* in the front yard
VERB PHRASE	The barn roof **was lying** in the front yard.
NO VERB	Jane *going* with us
VERB PHRASE	Jane **will be going** with us.

5a. A *sentence fragment* is a group of words which does not express a completed thought. Since it is part of a sentence, it should not be allowed to stand by itself, but should always be kept in the sentence of which it is a part.

THE PHRASE FRAGMENT

A phrase is a group of words acting as a single part of speech and not containing a verb and its subject.

[2] The following helping verbs may be used with words ending in *–ing* to form a verb phrase:

am	were	can (may) be
are	will (shall) be	could (would, should) be
is	has been	will (shall) have been
was	had been	might have been

There are many kinds of phrases (participial, gerund, prepositional, infinitive) but regardless of their kind, they all have one important characteristic — they are parts of a sentence and must never be separated from the sentence in which they belong. When a phrase is incorrectly allowed to stand by itself, unattached to a sentence, it is referred to as a fragment.

Study the way in which the unattached phrase fragments in the following examples are corrected.

FRAGMENT **On the school steps I saw Alice. Waiting for her mother to pick her up.** [This participial phrase fragment modifies the word *Alice*. It should be included in the sentence with the word it modifies.]

FRAGMENT REMOVED **On the school steps I saw Alice, waiting for her mother to pick her up.**

FRAGMENT **The camps were filled with thousands of displaced persons. Deprived of home and country by the fortunes of war.** [This participial phrase fragment modifies the word *persons*. It should be included in the sentence with the word it modifies.]

FRAGMENT REMOVED **The camps were filled with thousands of displaced persons, deprived of home and country by the fortunes of war.**

FRAGMENT **The new cottage is on the north side of the lake. At the edge of a grove of pine trees.** [This prepositional phrase fragment modifies the verb *is*, telling where the cottage is. The phrase belongs in the sentence.]

FRAGMENT REMOVED **The new cottage is on the north side of the lake at the edge of a grove of pine trees.**

FRAGMENT **My parents finally gave me permission. To go with Bill to the game at West Point.** [Here an infinitive phrase fragment has been separated from the word *permission*, which it explains. It should be written in the same sentence with the word it explains.]

FRAGMENT REMOVED **My parents finally gave me permission to go with Bill to the game at West Point.**

THE APPOSITIVE FRAGMENT

A second type of fragment is the appositive fragment. An appositive is a word or group of words which follows a noun or pronoun and means the same thing. It *explains* the noun or pronoun which it follows. In the following example the appositive has been incorrectly separated from the sentence in which it belongs.

FRAGMENT **Uncle Frank came bearing gifts. A wrist watch for Jean and a ring for me.**

FRAGMENT REMOVED **Uncle Frank came bearing gifts, a wrist watch for Jean and a ring for me.**

THE SUBORDINATE CLAUSE FRAGMENT

A third type of fragment is the subordinate clause which is incorrectly separated from the sentence in which it belongs. A clause is a group of words containing a subject and predicate and used as a part of a sentence. A subordinate clause does not express a completed thought and cannot stand alone.

FRAGMENT **I was grateful for his financial assistance. Which enabled me to go to college.**

FRAGMENT REMOVED **I was grateful for his financial assistance, which enabled me to go to college.**

5b. Do not separate a phrase, an appositive, or a subordinate clause from the sentence of which it is a part.

● EXERCISE 1. Some of the items in this exercise consist of one or two completed sentences; others contain fragments of sentences. Number from 1 to 20 on your paper. If all the parts of an item are completed sentences, write *C* after the proper number. If an item contains a fragment, rewrite it to include the fragment in the sentence.

1. After a vote, the minority should abide by the decision. Until, by the same process, the consensus can be changed and the decision reversed or modified.
2. Shortly after the puff of flame came a tremendous explosion.
3. History shows few men as versatile as Franklin. Who was an inventor, scientist, public benefactor, writer, statesman, and philosopher.
4. We left the boys at the rink. Uncertain as to whether or not they should skate for another hour.
5. A student gradually learns the danger of putting off homework until the next morning. Interruptions are always cropping up at the last minute.
6. You could not make a better choice for captain. Jack being the conscientious boy he is.
7. Although the editors resented the criticisms of their paper, they frankly admitted that the criticisms were fair.
8. Katherine met me at the appointed place. Surprising me by being on time, too.
9. Committees composed of teachers and parents met every week during the year. To discuss the school program and plan a new building.
10. The librarian threatened to hide the magazine rack. Because too many students were wasting time just thumbing the pages of the popular periodicals.
11. One automobile insurance company has reached a surprising decision. Not to insure drivers under twenty-five years of age.
12. His training gave him a good background for pursuing important research. First at the university and later at the Rockefeller Institute.
13. Standing on this huge boulder, a relic of the glacial era, one commands a striking view of the entire valley.
14. At the end of the street stands a dilapidated home. Its windows broken and its porches crumbling.

15. Authorities at the trial of war criminals had to face a fundamental question. Whether a soldier can be held responsible for what he does under orders from his superiors.
16. There was no excuse for his refusing to co-operate. Knowing, as he did, that his services were desperately needed.
17. Team play is as important on the stage as on the athletic field. Every actor must work for the total effect, not just to show off himself.
18. From beneath a ledge of rock flowed a clear spring. Undoubtedly the headwaters of a stream.
19. Each student was asked to write down what he considered his worst fault. As far as appearance is concerned.
20. Conflicts at home should be settled in the same way as conflicts among nations. By talking the problem over.

The Run-on Sentence

When a comma (instead of a period, a semicolon, or a conjunction) is used between two completed sentences, the result is referred to as a "run-on sentence." One sentence is permitted to "run on" into the next. In high school writing, this type of sentence error is more common than the fragment error. Usually it is the result of carelessness in punctuation rather than of lack of understanding. Because the error involves the misuse of a comma — to separate sentences — it is sometimes referred to as the "comma fault" or "comma blunder." A worse, but far less common, kind of run-on sentence results from completely omitting punctuation between sentences.

5c. Avoid the run-on sentence. Do not use a comma between sentences. Do not omit punctuation at the end of a sentence.

RUN-ON SENTENCE The choice of a camera is difficult, there are many good kinds on the market.

These two sentences should either be completely separated by a period or joined into one sentence by means of a conjunction or a semicolon. There are four ways of removing the error:

1. The choice of a camera is difficult**.** There are many good kinds on the market.
2. The choice of a camera is difficult**,** **but** there are many good kinds on the market.
3. The choice of a camera is difficult **because** there are many good kinds on the market.
4. The choice of a camera is difficult**;** there are many good kinds on the market.

As you grow older and do more and more writing, you develop a "sentence sense," which is the ability to recognize at once whether a group of words is or is not a completed sentence. Reading your compositions aloud, so that your ears as well as your eyes can detect completeness, will help you find any run-on sentences in your own writing.[3]

● EXERCISE 2. The items in this exercise are run-on sentences. Copy after the proper number on your paper the final word in the first sentence in each item and follow it with the first few words of the second sentence. Indicate how you would eliminate the faulty comma. You may use a semicolon, a comma and conjunction, or a period and a capital letter. Do not be satisfied with using a period and a capital letter in

[3] Do not be surprised, after being warned against sentence fragments and run-on sentences, if you find them being used occasionally by writers in the best newspapers and magazines. Professional writers (who have a strong sentence sense, or they would not be professionals) do at times write fragments and use the comma between sentences, especially when the ideas in the sentences are very closely related. Leave this use of the comma and the use of the fragment to the experienced judgment of the professional.

every case; to make clear the relationship between ideas, some of the items should be corrected in other ways.

EXAMPLE 1. Ford didn't hear about the party until Thursday, he had to get a date in a hurry.

1. **Thursday; therefore he had . . .**

1. In social studies this year we are studying our major national problems, so far we have covered highways, conservation, and education.
2. Each year Marilyn hands in a new book report on *Gone with the Wind*, she rereads the book every year, too.
3. Galileo discovered that most substances expand when heated, but contract when cooled, this was an important step in the scientific study of heat.
4. Every young person should learn one important fact about his social bearing, you do not have to be beautiful to have an attractive personality.
5. Milton took an art elective and discovered he had talent, now he spends his afternoons in the art room.
6. At an advanced age she began to write the story of her colorful life, at least she thought her life had been colorful.
7. The astounding scientific developments of one generation are accepted commonplaces in the next generation, the airplane and the telephone, for instance, are taken for granted by everyone today.
8. A new club is being formed for the study of social behavior, instead of just reading an etiquette book, students will give and attend teas, receptions, and dinner parties.
9. A large suggestion box has been placed in the hall just outside the principal's office, students can, by this means, express their pet peeves about the school. names should not be signed to the suggestions.
10. First try to do the assignment by yourself, if you can't do it, ask your teacher for help.

● EXERCISE 3. The following exercise contains sentence fragments and run-on sentences. Prepare to explain to the class how you would eliminate the sentence errors. Use the blackboard when giving your explanation.

1. I have never known anyone who was a better worker than Paul. Who always did his homework in half the time I took, he usually had it done twice as well, too.
2. Concentration was the secret of his success. Although he undoubtedly had a keen mind.
3. I asked Paul to help me with my math once. When I was particularly desperate, I hadn't been getting good grades for several weeks.
4. He could do the problems easily, but he couldn't explain them to me. So that I could understand them, anyway, I didn't ask him again.
5. Mr. Rehman wants all musicians to continue to study their instruments in high school. Because he knows that as they get busier and busier, many students stop taking lessons, sports and other activities cut in on their practice time.
6. The United Nations must avoid the mistakes made by the League of Nations. If it is to endure. Most nations apparently want the United Nations to succeed. Although some occasionally seem unco-operative.
7. A mammoth crane was brought here to lift into place the steel girders. Huge orange-colored beams that were easily set into place. Almost as though they were matchsticks.
8. The time when a radio station may broadcast is determined by its license, some stations must go off the air at sundown.
9. Everyone was asking me about Fred. Where he was and what he was doing, wild rumors had been circulating.
10. The city's water supply has been threatened. Very little rain or snow having fallen during the past weeks.
11. I learned to like poetry when I read Kipling, his

poems appealed to me. Because of their strong rhythm and their rhyme.

12. I stopped at the bank on my way home and cashed a check, then I hurried on my way. Leaving my brief case and books in the bank.
13. Today's submarine is very difficult to locate and to destroy. It is a far more serious threat than it was years ago. Being larger and more powerful.
14. Some detective and confession magazines are examples of sensational journalism, they have, in the opinion of many people, an unwholesome effect on the younger generation. Millions of copies being sold every month.
15. Women's colleges were established in America in the nineteenth century. During the Victorian period. When girls were considered frail flowers to be kept safe at home.
16. In bad weather we go to the movies on Saturday afternoon, in good weather we prefer to be outdoors. Getting our exercise and fresh air.
17. Audiences appeared to enjoy the play, the reviews in the papers, however, were unfavorable.
18. A back-to-school night for parents convinced the taxpayers of the inadequacy of our building, consequently the bond issue for a new building was passed by a large vote. When it was presented later in the year.

CHAPTER 6

Agreement

LEARN TO MAKE WORDS AGREE ACCORDING TO STANDARD USAGE

Agreement of Subject and Verb

6a. A verb agrees in number with its subject.

Two words are said to agree in number when both of them are singular or both of them are plural. A word is singular when it refers to one *single* thing; a word is plural when it refers to more than one thing.

SINGULAR	PLURAL
book	books
child	children
either	both
this	these

When a singular word is used as a subject, it takes a singular verb; when a plural word is used as a subject, it takes a plural verb.

SINGULAR A small **child was playing** in the street.
PLURAL The small **children were playing** in the street.

SINGULAR The main **road goes** through the center of town.
PLURAL Both main **roads go** through the center of town.

▶ NOTE: *Is*, *was*, *has*, and most verbs ending in a single *s* are singular: he *thinks*, he *works*, he *tries*, etc. *Are*, *were*, *have*, and most verbs not ending in *s* in the present

6a

tense are plural: they *think*, they *work*, they *try*, etc. Exceptions, of course, are verbs used with singular *I* and *you*. (Singular: *I think; you think.*)

Although you may understand clearly what is meant by agreement, you must be careful not to be misled by certain constructions which tend to cause lack of agreement between subject and verb.

(1) The number of the subject is not usually changed by a phrase following the subject.[1]

A phrase following a singular subject may easily mislead you, especially if the phrase contains a plural word. Study the following pairs of sentences.

1. The **performance was** very funny.
   The **performance** of the three clowns **was** very funny. [*performance was*, not *clowns were*]
2. The **decision was** overruled.
   The **decision** of the umpires **was** overruled. [*decision was*, not *umpires were*]

● EXERCISE 1. Number on your paper from 1 to 20. Write after the proper number the subject of each sentence. After the subject write the one of the two verbs in parentheses which agrees in number with the subject. Check your answers before going on to the next exercise.

1. The signs at the top of the building (was, were) barely visible.
2. The boats in the fishing fleet (goes, go) out at eight o'clock.
3. Everything but the eggs (were, was) in the same box.
4. The final performances of the play's run (are, is) to be given on Saturday.
5. His answers to our question (changes, change) everything.

[1] Exceptions to this rule are explained in rule (3) below.

6. Trespassing on these grounds (are, is) prohibited.
7. The leaders of the party (are, is) looking for a strong candidate.
8. Poe's stories of mystery and imagination (appeals, appeal) most to me.
9. Employees of the mill (lives, live) in bunkhouses.
10. The winner of both races (were, was) from Central.
11. The girls in the cast (objects, object) to evening rehearsals.
12. Clearness in writing and speaking (are, is) essential to success.
13. The wing span of these planes (are, is) so small that the planes must be launched from bombers.
14. Her shyness among strangers (is, are) appalling.
15. The time for courage and decision (are, is) here.
16. His objections to our program (seems, seem) trivial.
17. The depth of some of these lakes (has, have) never been measured.
18. His use of discord and strained harmonies (do, does) not appeal to me.
19. Working under these conditions (is, are) exasperating.
20. The demand for teachers (has, have) not been met.

(2) The following words are usually singular: *each, either, neither, one, everyone, everybody, no one, nobody, anyone, someone, somebody.*

When used as subjects, these words are frequently followed by a phrase. Do not let a phrase coming between subject and verb affect the agreement of the verb with the subject.

1. **Each has** a motorcycle.
   Each of the boys **has** (not *have*) a motorcycle.
2. **Everyone wants** more money.
   Every **one** of the workmen **wants** (not *want*) more money.

(3) The pronouns *some, all,* and *most* may be either singular or plural, depending upon whether they

refer to a quantity of something (singular) or to a number of things (plural).

1. **Some** of the money **was stolen.**
   Some of the dimes **were stolen.**
2. **All** of the fruit **looks** ripe.
   All of the cherries **look** ripe.
3. **Most** of the book **was** interesting.
   Most of the books **were** interesting.

In expressions like these a word in the phrase following the subject does change the number of the subject. Hence this rule is an exception to rule (1) above.

(4) The words *none* and *any* may be either singular or plural, depending upon whether the speaker is thinking of one thing or several.

EXAMPLES **None** of the players **was injured.** [*Not one* was injured.]
None of the players **were injured.** [*No players* were injured.]

Any of these authorities **is** reliable. [*Any one* is reliable.]
Any of these authorities **are** reliable. [*All* are reliable.]

(5) The following words are plural: *several, few, both, many*.

EXAMPLES **Several** of the club members **were** absent.
Few of my family **look** like me.

(6) Phrases like *together with, as well as, accompanied by, in addition to, including* . . . do not, as a rule, affect the number of the subject.

EXAMPLES The **captain**, as well as the coaches, **was** disappointed in the team.
Mr. Douglas, together with his two sons, **has gone** fishing.

● EXERCISE 2. Number on your paper from 1 to 25. Write after the proper number on your paper the subject in each sentence. After it write the one of the two verbs in parentheses which agrees in number with the subject.

1. Each of these dresses (have, has) a wide belt.
2. One of my best friends (were, was) playing against me.
3. All of our study periods (are, is) spent in the library.
4. Some of these errors (is, are) preventable.
5. Ford, as well as Chrysler and General Motors, (were, was) willing to compromise.
6. Every one of my summer dresses (are, is) too small.
7. A few of the guard (was, were) left behind.
8. The loss of his sons (was, were) a cruel blow.
9. Everybody living in these states (pay, pays) a state income tax.
10. An amateur in competition with these professionals (hasn't, haven't) a chance.
11. A porpoise, like whales and sharks, (swim, swims) near the surface.
12. Every one of the buildings (were, was) damaged.
13. Tickets for the entire season (is, are) now on sale.
14. Both of these laws (have, has) been broken more than once.
15. One carload of cherries (was, were) shipped to Chicago.
16. Several of our boys (were, was) unfairly treated.
17. One of the sisters (learn, learns) more easily than the other.
18. His struggle to overcome the waves and the tides (was, were) not successful.
19. Every classroom in the new buildings (has, have) been equipped with typewriters.
20. (Has, Have) all the tickets been accounted for?
21. Neither of the jobs (requires, require) much technical knowledge.
22. Everyone in both cars (was, were) injured.
23. Mr. Stark, together with his wife and children, (is, are) leaving for New York.

24. The sky, as well as the wind and water, (look, looks) favorable.
25. As a pinch hitter, Morgan, like the other players, (strike, strikes) out.

● EXERCISE 3. *Oral Drill.* The oral drill exercises are composed of short, conversational-type sentences. The sentences should be read *aloud* many times to fix the habit of using the correct form. Ear training is important in correcting usage. In reading aloud, stress italicized words.

1. *One* of the girls *was* late.
2. The *cause* of both fires *was* the same.
3. *Has either* of them any money?
4. *Each* of the boys *is* dependable.
5. *All* of my friends *have* left.
6. Not *one* of the teachers *approves* our conduct.
7. *Both* of the cars *were* damaged.
8. Every *one* of us *is* hungry.
9. The *result* of his efforts *seems* uncertain.
10. The *number* of A's *was* disappointing.

(7) *Don't* and *doesn't* must agree with their subjects. With the subjects *I* and *you*, use *don't (do not)*. With other subjects use *doesn't* (*does not*) when the subject is singular, and *don't (do not)* when the subject is plural.

EXAMPLES **I don't** remember the score.
You don't look well.
It (he, she, this) doesn't run fast enough.
They don't swim.

By using *doesn't* after *it*, *he*, and *she*, you can eliminate most of the common errors in the use of *don't* and *doesn't*.

● EXERCISE 4. Write in a column on your paper the correct form (*don't* or *doesn't*) for the following sentences. When your answers have been corrected, use the sentences for oral drill.

1. That —— mean a thing.
2. The mayor —— approve.
3. They —— want to come.
4. She —— live here.
5. It —— matter.
6. Frank —— believe me.
7. He —— agree with me.
8. It —— seem fair.
9. She —— understand you.
10. You —— need to hurry.
11. The job really —— have to be done today.
12. That picture —— look like him.
13. She —— read many books.
14. Your arguments —— impress me very much.
15. He —— work very hard.

● EXERCISE 5. Number on your paper from 1 to 25. Read each of the following sentences aloud. If a sentence is correct (verb agrees with subject) put a + after the proper number on your paper; if the sentence is incorrect, put a 0.

1. Each of the students are responsible for one lesson.
2. She don't obey her parents.
3. Neither of the stories were good enough to publish.
4. Every one of the stations was out of gasoline.
5. Some of the crops have been ruined by frost.
6. The height of the office buildings are unusually great.
7. One of the club members has not yet voted.
8. Don't he look like George?
9. The principal, as well as the school board and the faculty, was enthusiastic.
10. All of the mines has been closed.
11. Don't it bother you?
12. Some of the criminal's motives were apparent.
13. The result of so many attempts was disappointing.
14. One of the Army planes are missing.

15. She don't usually arrive until nine o'clock.
16. Each of the salesmen have a definite territory to cover.
17. Fear of open spaces is known as agoraphobia.
18. The ocean, as well as the gulf and the bay, provides good fishing.
19. It don't look far on the map.
20. Neither of his paternal grandparents are living.
21. Several of our best news sources have been cut off.
22. The boys in R.O.T.C. goes to camp in July.
23. Few members of the party approve the chairman's appointments.
24. A sophomore, as well as a freshman, is allowed to take public speaking.
25. The vessel, with its entire crew and cargo, were lost.

(8) Most compound subjects joined by *and* are plural and take a plural verb.

EXAMPLES A **truck and** a **sedan were** in the ditch.
Gerald and he look alike.
The **walls and** the **ceiling are** beautifully decorated.

(9) When a compound subject is considered as a unit, not as two distinct things, it takes a singular verb.

EXAMPLES **Macaroni and cheese is** the cafeteria special on Friday.
The **sum and substance** of the speech **was** anti-American.
Broadway at 48th Street **and** the surrounding **area is** known as Tin Pan Alley.

(10) Singular subjects joined by *or, nor, either . . . or,* and *neither . . . nor* are singular and take a singular verb.

EXAMPLES **Neither** my **mother nor** my **father is** a high school graduate.
Either Lucille or Mildred has a dress like that.
Neither Don nor Russell wants the job.

(11) When two subjects, one of which is singular and the other plural, are joined by *or* or *nor*, the verb agrees with the nearer subject.[2]

ACCEPTABLE *Either* the judge *or* the **lawyers are** wrong.

Whenever possible avoid such constructions.

BETTER Either the judge is wrong or the lawyers are wrong.

(12) When the subject comes after the verb as in sentences beginning with *here is, there is,* and *where is,* be especially careful to determine the subject and make sure that the verb agrees with it.

WRONG There's three routes you can take.
RIGHT There **are** three **routes** you can take.

WRONG Where's your mother and father?
RIGHT Where **are** your **mother and father?**

● EXERCISE 6. Number on your paper from 1 to 25. Read each of the following sentences aloud. If a sentence is correct (verb agrees with subject) put a + after the proper number on your paper; if the sentence is incorrect, put a 0.

1. Where's the maps you were using?
2. One of the islands appear to be inhabited.
3. The extent of his injuries have not been determined.
4. Neither the milk nor the groceries have been delivered.
5. Was there any letters for me?
6. Either Pete or his father is going to pick us up.
7. Both the funds appropriated by the legislature and the income from the sales tax were exhausted.
8. Each of the stowaways have been questioned by immigration officials.
9. One of our best suggestions was spurned by the council.

[2] When the subjects are in different *persons*, the verb agrees in person with the nearer subject. This kind of construction should be avoided.

ACCEPTABLE Neither my brother nor *I am* going to summer camp.
BETTER My brother is not going to summer camp, and neither am I.

10. Not one of these cases have ever been solved.
11. Private ownership and free competition is characteristic of capitalism.
12. Neither of these reference books contains the information I want.
13. There's several important differences between the democratic and the totalitarian forms of government.
14. She just don't want to obey any rules.
15. Not one of her many children has offered to help her financially.
16. There has been very few unhappy moments in her life.
17. Neither Ken nor Sid have enough energy to walk such a distance.
18. Some of his best stories have been sold for the smallest amounts.
19. The teacher, as well as her pupils, was nervous during the superintendent's visit.
20. Speaking and writing involves different skills.
21. The outcome really don't interest me.
22. Where's the magazines you told me about?
23. The ambassador, accompanied by his family and secretaries, is returning to Washington.
24. Every one of the culprits has agreed to plead guilty.
25. The results of yesterday's election has not been made public.

(13) Collective nouns may be either singular or plural.

A collective noun names a group: *crowd*, *committee*, *jury*, *class*. A collective noun takes a plural verb when the speaker is thinking of the individual parts of the group; it takes a singular verb when the speaker is thinking of the group as a unit.

1. The **crowd were fighting** for their lives. [The speaker is thinking of the individuals in the crowd.]
   The **crowd was** a quiet one. [The speaker is thinking of the crowd as a single thing, a unit.]
2. The **team were talking** over some new plays.
   The **team was** the best in the country.

3. The **family have agreed** among themselves to present a solid front.
   The **family is** the basic unit of our society.

COLLECTIVE NOUNS

army	faculty	jury
audience	fleet	squadron
class	flock	swarm
club	group	team
committee	herd	troop
crowd		

(14) Words stating amount (time, money, measurement, weight, volume, fractions) are usually singular.

EXAMPLES **Three years** in a strange land **seems** like a long time.
Ten dollars is not enough.
Three fourths of the money **has** been recovered.

Words stating amount may sometimes be affected in number by a plural word in the phrase which follows them.

EXAMPLE **Three fourths** of his losses **have** been recovered.

MINOR PROBLEMS IN AGREEMENT OF SUBJECT AND VERB

(15) The title of a book, a story, a work of art, even when plural in form, takes a singular verb.

EXAMPLE Johnson's *Lives of the Poets* **was published** in the 18th century.

(16) A few nouns, although plural in form, take a singular verb. The following are examples of such nouns: *mumps, measles, civics, economics, mathematics, physics*.

EXAMPLES The **measles is** a nuisance.
World **economics has** a direct bearing on world peace.

The following similar words are more often plural than singular: *athletics*, *acoustics*, *gymnastics*, *tactics*. The word *politics* may be either singular or plural, and *scissors* and *trousers* are always plural.

For a detailed discussion of the use of words ending in *–ics*, look up *–ics* in your dictionary.

(17) When the subject and the predicate nominative are different in number, the verb agrees with the subject, not with the predicate nominative.

ACCEPTABLE The most appreciated **gift was** the clothes that you sent us.

ACCEPTABLE The **clothes** that you sent us **were** the most appreciated gift.

BETTER Most of all we appreciated the clothes that you sent us.

(18) *Every* or *many a* before a word or series of words is followed by a singular verb.

EXAMPLES **Every** *man, woman, and child* **was** asked to contribute.

Many a college *student* **wishes** to return to the easy days in high school.

Many a *boy* in these circumstances **has** hoped for a lucky break.

● EXERCISE 7. Number on your paper from 1 to 25. After the proper number write the correct one of the two verbs in parentheses in each sentence.

1. The cost of his explorations (was, were) paid by scientific societies.
2. Neither the President nor the FBI (were, was) willing to release any information.
3. Every one of his sons (have, has) been successful.
4. Each of these products (stands, stand) up under hard wear.
5. The question of taxes (don't, doesn't) belong in this discussion.

6. Neither our car nor the cars of the others (was, were) able to plow through the drifts.
7. Fifteen minutes (is, are) enough time for this exercise.
8. There (seem, seems) to be many arguments on both sides.
9. Every planet, including the earth, (revolve, revolves) around the sun.
10. *The Magnificent Ambersons* (is, are) worth reading.
11. Most of the Roosevelt papers (have, has) been made available to the public.
12. The mayor of the city and the governor of the state (have, has) been in conference.
13. It (don't, doesn't) matter to me where you go.
14. Neither his secular music nor his religious compositions (appeal, appeals) to the popular taste.
15. Probably some of the oranges (don't, doesn't) ripen until April.
16. The fruit on the outdoor stands (look, looks) tempting.
17. Neither the doctor nor the nurse (was, were) in the patient's room when the crisis came.
18. College life and high school life (is, are) vastly different.
19. (There are, There's) not many selfish people in the world.
20. Two weeks (are, is) enough for a trip of that length.
21. Every one of my teachers (knows, know) the same jokes.
22. The acoustics in this room (have, has) always been bad.
23. Each of the cheeses (were, was) sampled by the inspector.
24. Few members of the scientific world (is, are) able to explain the theory of relativity.
25. The mumps (is, are) not exclusively a children's disease.

● EXERCISE 8. *Oral Drill.* To fix the "agreement habit" in your speech, read each of the following sentences aloud several times, stressing the italicized words.

1. *Neither Barbara nor Louise was* with me.
2. Every *one* of my brothers *is* tall.
3. *Both Joe and Bob are* smart.
4. *It doesn't* look like him.
5. Where *are* your *books?*
6. *Four dollars is* more than I can afford.
7. *One* of the roads *has* been resurfaced.
8. *Has Ellen or Dorothy* seen you?
9. *Each* of the boys *plays* a different kind of game.
10. There *were seven* of us in the car.

Agreement of Pronoun and Antecedent

6b. A pronoun agrees with its antecedent in number and gender.

All that you have learned about agreement of subject and verb will be useful to you in making pronouns agree with their antecedents. The antecedent of a pronoun is the word to which the pronoun refers. Study the following examples, in which the antecedents and the pronouns referring to them are printed in heavy type. Notice that the pronoun is singular when the antecedent is singular, and plural when the antecedent is plural. Notice, too, that the pronoun is masculine (*he*, *him*, *his*) when the antecedent is masculine; feminine (*she*, *her*, *hers*) when the antecedent is feminine; neuter (*it*, *its*) when the antecedent is neither masculine nor feminine. This kind of agreement is agreement in *gender*.

1. **Mr. Jameson** did **his** best.
2. **One** of the boys injured **his** ankle.
3. **Neither** of the girls achieved **her** purpose.
4. The **women** in the League expressed **their** opinions forcefully.

5. The **city** is proud of **its** parks.
6. I recognized **one** of the boys, but I didn't speak to **him.**

(1) The words *each, either, neither, one, everyone, everybody, no one, nobody, anyone, anybody, someone, somebody* are referred to by a singular pronoun – *he, him, his, she, her, hers, it, its.* The use of a phrase after the antecedent does not change the number of the antecedent.

EXAMPLES **Each** of the men had removed **his** parachute.
Nobody in a position of authority had given **his** approval of the bill.
If **anyone** calls, tell **him** I'll be back later.

▶ NOTE: When the antecedent may be either masculine or feminine, as in the example directly above, use the masculine pronoun in referring to it. Avoid the awkward use of two pronouns: "If *anyone* calls, tell him or her I'll be back later."

Strict adherence to the general rule of agreement between pronoun and antecedent may lead to a construction so absurd that no one would use it.

ABSURD Did *everybody* leave the dance early because *he* wasn't enjoying *himself?*

In instances of this kind, use the plural pronoun.

BETTER Did **everybody** leave the dance early because **they** weren't enjoying **themselves?**

(2) Two or more singular antecedents joined by *or* or *nor* should be referred to by a singular pronoun.

EXAMPLE **Neither Jack nor Dick** had **his** key with **him.**

(3) Two antecedents joined by *and* should be referred to by a plural pronoun.

EXAMPLE **Jack and Dick** came with **their** uniforms on.

6b

(4) The number of a relative pronoun (*who, which, that*) is determined by the number of the word it refers to, its antecedent.

EXAMPLES This is one of the ships **that were** loaned to England. [*That* is plural because its antecedent is *ships*, not *one*.]

She is one of those girls **who are** too shy to be popular.

● EXERCISE 9. This exercise covers errors in agreement of verb and subject and of pronoun and antecedent. Number on your paper from 1 to 25. If a sentence is correct, write a + after the proper number; if it is incorrect, write a 0. One error makes a sentence incorrect. Be prepared to revise all incorrect sentences.

1. One out of every three automobile accidents are caused by a teen-age driver.
2. At this point the law of diminishing returns begins to operate.
3. A correspondent who answers too promptly the letters they receive is a nuisance to their friends.
4. Neither of the proposed bills were accepted in their entirety.
5. Each of the papers read in class were good.
6. Two thirds of the estate was left to the children.
7. Has either of the orders been sent?
8. When an employer is interviewing you, one of the first things they look for is experience.
9. Every political candidate flatters the people they speak to.
10. In his opinion, the classics present many difficulties, the surmounting of which are of little value.
11. Neither the Department of Agriculture nor the farmers were too sure of their position.
12. He was one of the advisers who were with Roosevelt at Yalta.

13. Each of these suggestions must be taken only for what they are worth.
14. Every member of the crew was decorated for his part in the rescue.
15. Where's the letters we received from Ruth?
16. The acting in amateur productions are always the same.
17. Everybody who enters politics knows that he will have to take criticism.
18. The toll of traffic accidents are rising.
19. In the past, close co-operation among nations have brought many improvements to the world.
20. Is there any old magazines in the cellar?
21. Assault and battery is a criminal offense.
22. Are you one of the boys who were tardy?
23. Anyone who does not get their parents' permission will not be permitted to make the trip.
24. Only one of his objections were sensible.
25. After the government had persuaded somebody to take this important position, they refused the appointment.

CHAPTER 7

Correct Use of Pronouns

LEARN TO USE PRONOUNS ACCORDING TO STANDARD USAGE

The function of a pronoun in a sentence is shown by the case form of the pronoun. Different uses demand different forms. For instance, a pronoun which acts as a subject is in the *nominative case;* a pronoun which acts as an object is in the *objective case;* and a pronoun which possesses something is in the *possessive case.*

PRONOUN AS SUBJECT	**I paid the manager.**
PRONOUN AS OBJECT	**The manager paid me.**
POSSESSIVE PRONOUN	**This is my money.**

Observe that the pronoun has a different form (*I*, *me*, *my*) in each case.

CASE FORMS OF PRONOUNS

7a. Learn the case forms of pronouns and when to use each form.

PERSONAL PRONOUNS[1]

Singular

	NOMINATIVE CASE	OBJECTIVE CASE	POSSESSIVE CASE
1ST PERS.	I	me	my, mine
2ND PERS.	you	you	your, yours
3RD PERS.	he, she, it	him, her, it	his, hers, its

Plural

	NOMINATIVE CASE	OBJECTIVE CASE	POSSESSIVE CASE
1ST PERS.	we	us	our, ours
2ND PERS.	you	you	your, yours
3RD PERS.	they	them	their, theirs

INTERROGATIVE AND RELATIVE PRONOUNS[2]

NOMINATIVE CASE	OBJECTIVE CASE	POSSESSIVE CASE
who	whom	whose
whoever	whomever	whosever

At present, concentrate on the personal pronouns. (*Who* and *whom* are discussed on page 106.) Since *you* and *it* do not change their forms, ignore them. Memorize the following lists of nominative and objective forms.

NOMINATIVE CASE	OBJECTIVE CASE
I	me
he	him
she	her
we	us
they	them

[1] Personal pronouns are those pronouns which change form in the different persons. There are three persons, first, second, and third. The meaning of *person* is as follows:

1st person is the person speaking: *I* (*We*) come.
2nd person is the person spoken to: *You* are coming.
3rd person is the person or thing spoken about: *He* (*She*, *It*, *They*) will come.

[2] *Who* and *whom* (*whoever* and *whomever*) are not personal pronouns. They may be relative pronouns (see page 50); when used to ask a question they are interrogative pronouns.

Uses of Nominative Forms

7b. The subject of a verb is in the nominative case.

This rule means that whenever you use a pronoun as a subject, you should use one of the pronouns in the left-hand column above. Ordinarily, you do this without thinking about it. You say, for instance, "*I* am sixteen years old," not "*Me* am sixteen years old," or "*We* are good friends," not "*Us* are good friends." In sentences like these you select the correct pronoun quite naturally. When the subject is compound, however, many persons do make mistakes in their selection of pronouns. Whereas they would never say "*Me* am sixteen years old," they will say "*John and me* are sixteen years old." Since in both sentences the pronoun is used as a subject, it should be in the nominative case in both.

(1) To determine the correct pronoun in a compound subject, try each subject separately with the verb. Your ear will tell you which form is correct.

WRONG *Her and me* are good friends. [*Her* is a good friend? *Me* is a good friend?]

RIGHT **She and I** are good friends. [*She* is a good friend. *I* am a good friend.]

WRONG *Neither Bill nor him* was in school today. [*Him* was in school today?]

RIGHT **Neither Bill nor he** was in school today. [*He* was in school today.]

(2) When the pronoun is used with a noun (*we boys, we seniors, etc.*), determine the correct form by reading the sentence without the noun.

EXAMPLE **We** (not *Us*) **boys** will do the job. [*We* will do the job.]

● EXERCISE 1. *Oral Drill.* Read aloud several times the following sentences, stressing the italicized words. The purpose of this exercise is to train your ear to the correct pronoun forms in the nominative case.

1. Sally and *I* have a date.
2. Mother and *he* will be home later.
3. Our family and *they* were neighbors for years.
4. The boys and *we* girls will take the same bus.
5. Either Jerry or *she* will write to you.
6. He and *I* saw the same movie.
7. Have Joe and *she* written to you?
8. When are you and *he* going?
9. *We* juniors won the contest.
10. Neither Ed nor *they* can come.

7c. A predicate nominative is in the nominative case.

A predicate nominative is a noun or pronoun in the predicate which refers to the same thing as the subject of the sentence. For the present purpose think of a predicate nominative as a pronoun following any form of the verb *to be.*

COMMON FORMS OF "TO BE"		NOMINATIVE PRONOUNS
am	are followed by	I
is, are		he
was, were		she
may be, can be, will be, etc.		we
may have been, etc.		they
want to be, like to be, etc.		who

EXAMPLES **Are you sure it was they?**
It might have been she.
This may be he coming up the walk.

▶ EXCEPTION: Current usage of educated people ignores this rule in the case of *It's me,* which is considered acceptable English although contrary to the rule. Usage varies as to other predicate nominative forms like *It's him, them, us*, etc., which are apparently *becoming* acceptable. While these expressions are certainly no longer regarded as serious errors in colloquial English, they are not so widely accepted as *It's me*. When you find these expressions in the exercises in this book, take the conservative attitude, which is always safe, and abide by the rule.

● EXERCISE 2. Number on your paper from 1 to 20. After the proper numbers write pronouns in the correct case to fill the blanks in the following sentences. Use as many different pronouns as you can. Do not use *you*. Make an oral drill of this exercise by repeating aloud several times your corrected sentences.

1. Allan and —— are going out for basketball.
2. He and —— are brother and sister.
3. —— (*We* or *Us*) students will support the principal.
4. That might have been ——.
5. Did you think Sally and —— were close friends?
6. Can you or —— do these problems?
7. Are —— (*we* or *us*) boys invited too?
8. I wish that I were ——.
9. Neither Sandra nor —— was chosen.
10. Stan and —— won our matches.
11. You and —— are wrong.
12. Either your teacher or —— will advise you.
13. First she thought she had seen them; then she said she wasn't sure it was ——.
14. Mildred and —— borrowed my homework paper.
15. If John or —— is absent, I'll get the assignment.
16. Ruth and —— have gone shopping.
17. —— (*We* or *Us*) seniors are giving a dance.
18. Dorothy and —— are going together.
19. —— and —— will help you.
20. She and —— solved the problem.

Uses of Objective Forms

7d. The object of a verb is in the objective case.

The object of a verb answers the question "What?" or "Whom?" after an action verb.

EXAMPLE **I saw her.** [Saw whom? Answer: *her*, which is the object.

As their name suggests, the objective forms (*me*, *him*, *her*, *us*, *them*) are used as objects.[3]

EXAMPLES **I caught him by the shoulder.**
She greeted me cordially.
Him I remember very well.

Like the nominative forms of pronouns the objective forms are troublesome principally when they are used in compound objects. You would hardly make the mistake of saying, "I caught *he* by the shoulder," but you might say, "I caught *Jim and he* by the shoulder." Trying each object separately with the verb will help you to choose the correct pronoun for compound objects: "I caught *him* by the shoulder."

● EXERCISE 3. Referring to the list of objective forms, supply correct pronouns for the blanks in the following sentences. Use a variety of pronouns.

1. Have you seen the janitor or ——?
2. We invited the Smiths and ——.
3. Calvin and —— I refused to believe.
4. Leave —— (*we* or *us*) girls alone for a while.
5. The paper mentioned both you and ——.
6. I'll take Janet and —— in my car.
7. I reminded both the boss and —— of the meeting.

[3] Since both direct and indirect objects are in the objective case, there is no point in distinguishing between them in applying this rule.

EXAMPLES I saw *him*. [direct object]
I told *him* the story. [indirect object]

7d

8. Please tell your father and —— when you leave.
9. Will you please help Susan and ——?
10. Mr. Heater sent Jack and —— to the office.
11. She left Ray and —— behind.
12. Why are you always teasing —— (*we* or *us*) girls?

● EXERCISE 4. *Oral Drill.* Read each of the following sentences aloud several times, stressing the italicized words. This is ear training.

1. *Ask* Dick and *him.*
2. Letter writing *bothers* Pauline and *me.*
3. *Take* Louis and *her* with you.
4. Have you *met* the Whites and *them?*
5. Couldn't you *hear us* girls?
6. I *admire* Carl and *him.*
7. *Show* Ellen and *me* your essay.
8. I'll *give* you and *her* one more chance.
9. The officer *caught* Tom and *him.*
10. She *called them* and *us.*

● EXERCISE 5. This exercise covers the use of personal pronouns as subjects of verbs, predicate nominatives, and objects of verbs. Number on your paper from 1 to 20. Write after the proper number the correct one of the two forms in parentheses in each sentence.

1. Who told Sam and (she, her)?
2. Have you and (she, her) had an argument?
3. That was probably Steve and (them, they).
4. Mr. Thompson said that (we, us) girls were late.
5. Tell the headmaster and (him, he) what you did.
6. Are you expecting Jean and (she, her)?
7. I don't believe it was (him, he).
8. Did you know that (him, he) and (she, her) are engaged?
9. Please tell (us, we) girls where you were.
10. Do not annoy the driver or (me, I).

11. Certainly you must remember Edna and (me, I).
12. You misunderstood the teacher and (me, I).
13. Who will drive Peggy and (she, her) to the airport?
14. That must be (him, he).
15. I'll send you and (he, him) by different routes.
16. The doctor offered to treat her husband and (she, her) without fee.
17. We didn't want to leave Anne and (her, she) behind.
18. Our callers were probably (them, they).
19. Ray and (I, me) don't need advice.
20. We know it was (he, him).

● EXERCISE 6. Write 3 sentences of your own, each containing a pronoun as part of a compound subject; 3 sentences, each containing a pronoun as part of a compound predicate nominative; 4 sentences, each containing a pronoun as part of a compound object.

7e. The object of a preposition is in the objective case.

Prepositions, as well as verbs, take objects. The final or principal word in a prepositional phrase is the object of the preposition which begins the phrase. In the following prepositional phrases the objects are printed in bold type:

at **home**	in the **morning**	from **him**
to **Chicago**	under the **house**	for **George** and **him**

A list of commonly used prepositions will be found on page 14.

Errors in the use of the pronoun as the object of a preposition, like those made when it is the object of a verb, usually occur when the object is compound. Since you would not say "I had a letter from *she*," you would not say "I had a letter from *Geraldine* and *she*." By omitting the first of the two objects in a compound object, you can usually tell what the correct pronoun is.[4]

WRONG **Give the message to either Belle or she.**
RIGHT **Give the message to either Belle or her.** [to *her*]

WRONG **I begged a ride with Frank and he.**
RIGHT **I begged a ride with Frank and him.** [with *him*]

WRONG **Dad bought the typewriter for my brother and I.**
RIGHT **Dad bought the typewriter for my brother and me.** [for *me*]

● EXERCISE 7. Number on your paper from 1 to 10. Select the preposition from each sentence and write it after the proper number on your paper. After the preposition write the correct one of the two pronouns in parentheses. Remember to choose the objective form. When you have checked your answers, use the sentences for an oral drill.

1. I played against Sam and (him, he).
2. He showed a friendly attitude toward my sister and (me, I).
3. How long did you work with John and (they, them)?
4. I addressed the card to both Carol and (her, she).
5. Bill came in after Joan and (me, I).
6. She put the blame on (us, we) boys.
7. Did you sit beside Jim and (he, him)?
8. A dispute arose between their leader and (they, them).
9. Miss Sprague is looking for you and (her, she).
10. Were they talking about the girls or (we, us)?

● EXERCISE 8. This exercise covers four uses of the personal pronouns:

A. Subject of a verb
B. Predicate nominative (after a form of *to be*)

[4] This formula does not apply in correcting the common error "between you and I" because *between* is never used with just one object. After *between* you will have to remember to use the objective form of the pronoun — "between you and *me*."

C. Object of a verb (direct and indirect)
D. Object of a preposition

Number on your paper from 1 to 25. Select the correct one of the pronouns in parentheses in each sentence and write it after the proper number on your paper. After each pronoun write the letter of its use as listed above.

1. I will ask Carter and (he, him).
2. Have you heard from the Whites or (they, them)?
3. Bruce and (me, I) did our homework in school.
4. Did you think it was (her, she)?
5. Tell Mr. Clark and (he, him) what you want.
6. It might have been (them, they).
7. (Him, He) and (I, me) are on our way to the movies.
8. The book was written by Mr. Hall and (he, him).
9. You can count on (we, us) students.
10. (She, Her) and (I, me) volunteered to help.
11. The next speaker will be (he, him).
12. If (we, us) seniors support the production, others will support it.
13. Have you ever worked for either Miss Berger or (her, she)?
14. Did you leave the baby and (she, her) together?
15. Do I look like my father or (her, she)?
16. Don't go without (we, us) girls.
17. When Gene and (I, me) saw what was coming, we ran.
18. How do you know it was (he, him)?
19. When do you expect your family and (they, them)?
20. Bring Isabel and (she, her) with you.
21. Neither you nor (I, me) was right.
22. The trouble with Bob and (I, me) is that we are lazy.
23. The Browns and (them, they) are coming together.
24. She thought it was (they, them) who owned the house.
25. I talked to Dan and (he, him) for twenty minutes.

Uses of *Who* and *Whom*

WHO AND WHOM AS INTERROGATIVE PRONOUNS

Who and *whom* are interrogative pronouns when they are used to ask a question. The four rules (pages 98–103) governing the case forms of the personal pronouns apply also to *who* and *whom*. *Who* is nominative; *whom* is objective.[5]

EXAMPLES **Who left his books here?** [The nominative form is required because *who* is the subject of the verb *left.*]
Whom did he call? [The objective form is required because *whom* is the object of the verb *did call.*]

When the interrogative pronoun is used immediately after a preposition, *whom* is the only correct form.

EXAMPLE **To whom were you speaking?**

On the colloquial level of usage, however, *whom* is not usually used as an interrogative pronoun. *Who* is used regardless of whether the case is nominative or objective.

COLLOQUIAL **Who do you know in Birmingham?**
Who does the manager want?

On the standard level of usage, the distinction between *who* and *whom* is still recognized.

STANDARD **Whom do you know in Birmingham?** [*Whom* is the object of the verb *do know.*
Whom does the manager want? [*Whom* is the object of the verb *does want.*]

[5] You may find it helpful, at first, to substitute *he–him* for *who–whom* respectively. If *he*, a nominative pronoun, fits the sentence, then *who*, also nominative, will be correct. If *him* fits, then *whom* will be correct.

EXAMPLES (Who, whom) left his books here? *He* left his books here. Hence, *Who* left his books here?
(Who, whom) did Mary call? Mary did call *him.* Hence, Mary did call *whom.*

WHO AND WHOM BEGINNING SUBORDINATE CLAUSES

When *who* and *whom* (*whoever* and *whomever*) are used to begin a subordinate clause, their case is governed by the same rules that govern the case of a personal pronoun. The distinction between *who* and *whom* in subordinate clauses is usually observed in writing. Study the following explanations and refer to them whenever you need help with relative pronouns in your compositions.

7f. The case of the pronoun beginning a subordinate clause is determined by its use in the clause which it begins. The case is not affected by any word outside the clause.

In order to analyze a *who–whom* problem, follow these steps:

1. Pick out the subordinate clause.
2. Determine how the pronoun is used in the clause — subject, predicate nominative, object of verb, object of preposition — and decide its case according to the usual rules.
3. Select the correct form of the pronoun.

PROBLEM The new teacher, (who, whom) has taken Mr. Collins's position, came from the South.

STEP 1 The subordinate clause is (*who*, *whom*) *has taken Mr. Collins's position.*

STEP 2 In this clause the pronoun is used as the subject of the verb *has taken;* as a subject it should be, according to rule, in the nominative case.

STEP 3 The nominative form is *who.*

SOLUTION The new teacher, **who** has taken Mr. Collins's position, came from the South.

PROBLEM The new teacher (who, whom) I met today, came from the South.

STEP 1 The subordinate clause is (*who*, *whom*) *I met today.*

STEP 2 In the clause the subject is *I;* the verb is *met;* and the pronoun is the object of the verb *met* (*I met whom*). As an object it is in the objective case according to rule.

STEP 3 The objective form is *whom.*

SOLUTION **The new teacher, whom I met today, came from the South.**

PROBLEM **Does anyone know (who, whom) the new teacher is?**

STEP 1 The subordinate clause is (*who, whom*) *the new teacher is.*

STEP 2 In the clause *teacher* is the subject; *is* is the verb; the pronoun is a predicate nominative (*the new teacher is who*). As a predicate nominative it is in the nominative case according to rule.

STEP 3 The nominative form is *who.*

SOLUTION **Does anyone know who the new teacher is?**

In writing the preceding sentence, one might tend to use *whom,* thinking it the object of the verb *know,* but *know* is outside the clause and cannot affect a word in the clause. The object of the verb *know* is the entire clause *who the new teacher is.*

PROBLEM **I do not remember (who, whom) I loaned the book to.** [Following the three steps, you will find that the pronoun here is used as the object of the preposition *to;* it should be in the objective case, hence *whom.*]

SOLUTION **I do not remember whom I loaned the book to.**

BETTER **I do not remember to whom I loaned the book.**

▶ NOTE: In determining whether to use *who* or *whom,* do not be misled by a parenthetical expression like *I think, he said,* etc.

EXAMPLES **They are the people who, *I think,* are the foundation of society.** [*who* are the foundation of society]

He is a man who, *Mr. Bryan said,* should be rewarded. [*who* should be rewarded]

● EXERCISE 9. Number on your paper from 1 to 20. Using the three steps for determining the case of a relative pronoun, determine the correct form for each of the following sentences and write it on your paper after the proper number. Take plenty of time. Don't guess.

1. In *Hamlet* the two characters (who, whom) I most admire are Hamlet and Horatio.
2. If I had known (who, whom) he was, I should have been more cordial.
3. Next month's chairman will be (whoever, whomever) the delegates elect.
4. Since I did not know (who, whom) the package was for, I opened it.
5. Everybody (who, whom) received an invitation sent a reply.
6. The club members (who, whom) have paid their dues are qualified to vote.
7. He was one of the men (who, whom) the politicians could not influence.
8. No one has figured out (who, whom) the teacher was referring to.
9. The church is looking for someone (who, whom) it can depend on as a leader of the young people's group.
10. John Wallace is a boy (who, whom), I think, is well qualified for the work.
11. The poets (who, whom) the reading public takes to its heart are not always great poets.
12. Everyone in the courtroom wondered (who, whom) the mysterious witness would be.
13. Many men (who, whom) are on strike would prefer to be working.
14. She is one of the French students (who, whom), I believe, will make the most of an opportunity to study abroad.
15. Two men (who, whom) police arrested for a parking violation were wanted for robbery in three states.
16. He couldn't plan his strategy until he knew (who, whom) his opponents would be.

17. You may tell anyone (who, whom) you think is interested that our fight has just begun.
18. The reporters must rely for information on certain persons (who, whom) they know well and whose trust they have obtained.
19. The coach's reply to the grandstand strategists (who, whom) were criticizing him was an undefeated season.
20. He is a man (who, whom) nobody has any faith in.

Pronouns in Incomplete Constructions

An "incomplete construction" occurs most commonly after the words *than* and *as*. To avoid repetition, we say *The captain played better than he.* (*played* is omitted) *Are you as tall as she?* (*as she is*) The interpretation of the sentence may depend upon the form of the pronoun used.

EXAMPLES **I like Fred better than he.** [than he likes Fred]
I like Fred better than him. [than I like him]

7g. After *than* and *as* introducing an incomplete construction, use the form of the pronoun you would use if the construction were completed.

● EXERCISE 10. Number on your paper from 1 to 10. Write after the proper number the part of each sentence beginning with *than* or *as*, using the correct pronoun and completing the sentence to show that the pronoun is correct. In several sentences either pronoun may be correct depending on how the sentence is completed.

EXAMPLE 1. Philip is more popular than (him, he).
1. **than he is.**

1. Did you stay as long as (them, they)?
2. I don't know Pat so well as (she, her).
3. Sam is much stronger than (me, I).

4. You played harder than (they, them).
5. Mr. Eldred was more helpful than (he, him).
6. Is he older than (I, me)?
7. The race proved that Mason could not stand the pace so well as (he, him).
8. Are you willing to trust Carl more than (I, me)?
9. Are they as fast as (us, we)?
10. I can understand him better than (her, she).

Minor Problems in the Use of Pronouns

7h. In standard English the pronouns ending in *–self, –selves* should be used only to refer to another word in the sentence or to emphasize another word in the sentence.

EXAMPLES I hurt **myself.** [*Myself* refers to *I.*]
He told me the whole story **himself.** [*Himself* emphasizes *he.*]
The **boys themselves** made the suggestion. [*Themselves* emphasizes *boys.*]

In other words, avoid the use of pronouns ending in *–self, –selves* in place of other personal pronouns.

EXAMPLES John and **I** (not *myself*) are sixteen years old.
His letter was intended only for the Nortons and **us** (not *ourselves*).

7i. An appositive is in the same case as the word with which it is in apposition.

WRONG Two freshmen, Abe and him, made the best speeches.
RIGHT Two freshmen, **Abe and he,** made the best speeches.

Abe and he is in apposition with *freshmen,* the subject of the sentence. Since the subject of a verb is nominative, the appositive is also nominative, hence *he* is correct.

RIGHT The truant officer was chasing two boys, **Abe and him.**

In apposition with *boys*, which is the object of *was chasing*, *Abe and him* is also in the objective case, hence *him* is correct.

7j. Use the possessive case of a noun or a pronoun before a gerund — a verbal noun ending in *–ing*.

This use of the possessive case will appear reasonable if you understand that a gerund is a noun form.

EXAMPLES I was surprised by the **child's question.** [*Question* is a noun possessed by *child's.*]

I was surprised by the **child's asking** such a question. [*Asking* is a gerund possessed by *child's.*]

Do you object to **my presence?** [*Presence* is a noun possessed by *my.*]

Do you object to **my being** present? [*Being* is a gerund possessed by *my.*]

Sometimes a participle ending in *–ing* may be confused with a gerund. The following use of the objective case before a participle is correct.

EXAMPLE I watched **him coming** up the street.

The use of the possessive *his* in this sentence would change the meaning to a far less likely idea: *I watched his coming up the street.* Distinguish in meaning between the sentences in the following pairs:

1. I do not approve of **your doing** that.
   I do not approve of **you doing** that.
2. Can you imagine **Helen's singing?**
   Can you imagine **Helen singing?**
3. Do you remember **his speaking** to you at the game?
   Do you remember **him speaking** to you at the game?
4. I hate to think of **their losing** all that money.
   I hate to think of **them losing** all that money.

7k. The subject of an infinitive is in the objective case.

An infinitive is a verb form consisting of *to* followed by a verb: *to go*, *to see*, *to play*, etc.

EXAMPLE I wanted you and him **to help** me.

In this sentence the words *you* and *him* may seem to you to be objects of the verb *wanted;* actually they are subjects of the infinitive *to help*, the whole infinitive phrase being the object of *wanted.*

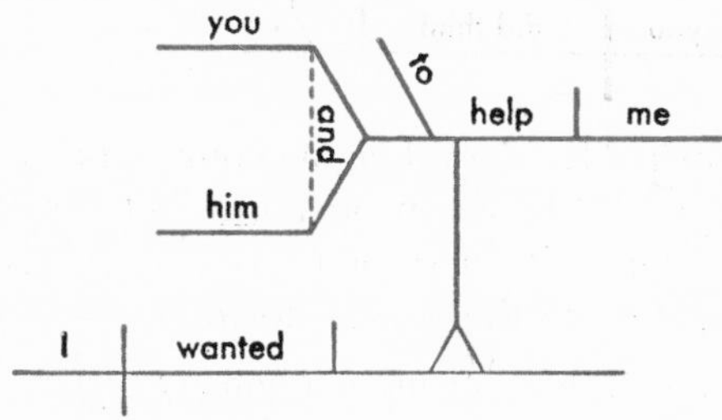

In most sentences like this one, since the subject of the infinitive is in the same case as the object of the verb, you will encounter little difficulty in using the correct pronoun. In one instance, that of the infinitive *to be*, the distinction between the subject of the infinitive and the object of the verb is important. In this rather involved construction, you find a pronoun following the infinitive.

EXAMPLE I believed **it** to be **him.**

The explanation of the use of *him* in this construction is that the same case follows a form of *to be* as precedes it. Since *it*, the subject of the infinitive, is in the objective case, the pronoun following the infinitive *to be* is also in the objective case, hence *him*. In other words, when you wish to determine the case of a pronoun following *to be*, look to see whether a noun or pronoun immediately precedes *to be*. If it does, use the objective case of the pronoun after *to be*.[6]

Most difficult of all such constructions is one involving *who* and *whom*.

EXAMPLE **Whom did you think me to be?** [You did think *me* to be *whom*.]

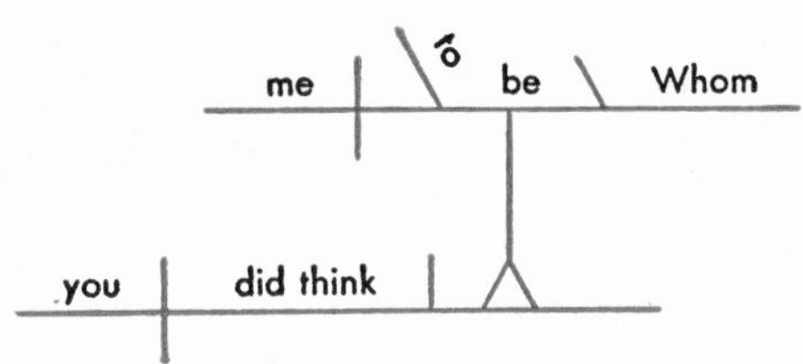

● EXERCISE 11. Number on your paper from 1 to 15. Write a + after the proper number for each correct sentence; write a 0 for each incorrect sentence. After each 0 write the correct form.

1. The school's being open on a holiday surprised us.
2. Jean and myself did not have dates.
3. I do not enjoy his playing.
4. No one could understand Bob failing a math course.
5. The best players, Carl and him, were too ill to play.
6. Did you think me to be he?
7. After him warning us, we decided to study for the test.
8. Somebody, either Harold or he, answered the question.
9. I had not been notified of their coming.
10. I offered the position to his brother and himself.
11. The class's taking the test without preparing for it was a mistake.
12. Who did you want the winner to be?

[6] When the infinitive *to be* does not have a subject, it is followed by the nominative case. See rule **7c**, page 99.

EXAMPLES I wouldn't like to be *he*. [no subject before *to be*]
Who would you like to be?

Strict adherence to this rule, however, is rare except in the most formal English.

COLLOQUIAL How would you like to be *me?*

13. He was especially fond of his grandchildren, Ella and she.
14. He expected it to be us.
15. Pete was worried about Bill driving too fast.

● EXERCISE 12. Number on your paper from 1 to 33. Select the correct one of the two pronouns in parentheses in each sentence and write it after the proper number on your paper. Be prepared to explain your answers.

1. Helen and (me, I) stayed after school.
2. Have you seen Sally and (her, she)?
3. No one could be sure that it was (they, them).
4. Today I had letters from both Nancy and (she, her).
5. The Congressmen (who, whom) I talked with objected to the President's policy.
6. He is a boy (who, whom), I think, has always had his own way.
7. You should have seen Dick and (I, me).
8. I do not know (who, whom) he had in mind.
9. He said that you and (me, I) are his best friends.
10. How can anyone be sure (who, whom) it was?
11. Can you cook as well as (her, she)?
12. These are the students (who, whom), I think, Mr. Langley referred to.
13. The disagreement between John and (he, him) was easily settled.
14. My sister and (me, I) did most of the cooking.
15. I do not know (who, whom) it was.
16. I know that it might have been (she, her).
17. His sister is better looking than (him, he).
18. Please call on either Mr. Nash or (me, I) if you need help.
19. (Him, He) and (I, me) have been in the same homeroom for three years.
20. The flowers came from Harry and (I, me).
21. You go ahead and (we, us) girls will follow later.
22. Why do you dislike Tom and (him, he)?

23. That is the girl (who, whom) I want you to meet.
24. Bob and (he, him) have their driver's license.
25. He refused to let (we, us) boys drive his car.
26. Ask the co-editors, Roy and (she, her), when the book will be published.
27. It was (his, him) whistling which annoyed us.
28. Two teachers, Mr. Bryce and (she, her), are sponsoring the Ski Club.
29. Did you hear about (Howard, Howard's) breaking his leg?
30. Sue and (me, I, myself) did the homework together.
31. I do not approve of (them, their) habitually talking in class.
32. Herb and (me, I) took turns at the wheel.
33. An investigation uncovered the story of the (Senator, Senator's) refusing a bribe.

CHAPTER 8

Correct Form and Use of Verbs

LEARN TO USE VERBS ACCORDING TO STANDARD USAGE

A verb is a word that expresses action or helps to make a statement.

ACTION VERB A trailer truck **had plunged** into the river.

A verb which does not express action is called a *linking verb*. It *links* the subject to a word or idea in the predicate.

LINKING VERB The river **was** deep. [*Was* links *river* to *deep*.]

Every verb has four principal parts. These are the *present*, *past*, *past participle*, and *present participle*.

PRINCIPAL PARTS OF THE VERB "TO CHANGE"

PRESENT	PAST	PAST PARTICIPLE	PRESENT PARTICIPLE
change	changed	(have) changed	(is) changing

The words *have* and *is* are given with the past and present participle forms to remind you that these forms are used with a helping verb: *have*, *has*, *had*, *am*, *is*, *are*, *was*, *were*, *has been*, *will be*, etc.

Regular verbs form their past and past participle forms by adding *–d* or *–ed* to the present form.

PRESENT	PAST	PAST PARTICIPLE
live	live*d*	(have) live*d*
play	play*ed*	(have) play*ed*

Irregular Verbs

Irregular verbs do not form their past and past participle forms by adding *–d* or *–ed* to the present form. They form their past and past participle in various other ways such as: by changing the vowel in the verb; by adding *–en*; or by making no change at all.

PRESENT	PAST	PAST PARTICIPLE
sw*i*m	sw*a*m	(have) sw*u*m
wr*i*te	wr*o*te	(have) wr*itten*
hit	hit	(have) hit

The major problem in the correct use of verbs is the choice of the correct past and past participle forms of irregular verbs. Since irregular verbs make these forms in a variety of ways, you must know the principal parts of each irregular verb.

Three principal parts of common irregular verbs are given in the following alphabetical list. Use this list for reference. For the principal parts of other irregular verbs, consult a dictionary. Drill exercises on irregular verbs frequently misused are given following the list.

PRINCIPAL PARTS OF IRREGULAR VERBS

PRESENT	PAST	PAST PARTICIPLE
bear	bore	(have) borne
beat	beat	(have) beaten
begin	began	(have) begun
bite	bit	(have) bitten

PRESENT	PAST	PAST PARTICIPLE
blow	blew	(have) blown
break	broke	(have) broken
bring	brought	(have) brought
burst	burst	(have) burst
catch	caught	(have) caught
choose	chose	(have) chosen
come	came	(have) come
creep	crept	(have) crept
dive	dived [1]	(have) dived
do	did	(have) done
draw	drew	(have) drawn
drink	drank	(have) drunk
drive	drove	(have) driven
eat	ate	(have) eaten
fall	fell	(have) fallen
flee	fled	(have) fled
fling	flung	(have) flung
fly	flew	(have) flown
freeze	froze	(have) frozen
get	got	(have) got *or* gotten
give	gave	(have) given
go	went	(have) gone
grow	grew	(have) grown
hurt	hurt	(have) hurt
know	knew	(have) known
lay	laid	(have) laid
lead	led	(have) led
lend	lent	(have) lent
lie	lay	(have) lain
lose	lost	(have) lost
ride	rode	(have) ridden
ring	rang *or* rung	(have) rung
rise	rose	(have) risen
run	ran	(have) run
say	said	(have) said
see	saw	(have) seen

[1] Colloquial: *dove.*

PRESENT	PAST	PAST PARTICIPLE
set	set	(have) set
shake	shook	(have) shaken
shine	shone	(have) shone
sing	sang *or* sung	(have) sung
sink	sank *or* sunk	(have) sunk
sit	sat	(have) sat
slay	slew	(have) slain
speak	spoke	(have) spoken
spring	sprang *or* sprung	(have) sprung
steal	stole	(have) stolen
sting	stung	(have) stung
swear	swore	(have) sworn
swim	swam	(have) swum
swing	swung	(have) swung
take	took	(have) taken
tear	tore	(have) torn
throw	threw	(have) thrown
wear	wore	(have) worn
write	wrote	(have) written

8a. Learn the principal parts of common irregular verbs.

To help you learn the correct use of irregular verbs, those which are commonly misused are presented on the following pages in four groups. Memorize the principal parts of the verbs in each group and do the exercises. Make note of any verbs you have not used correctly and review their principal parts, saying them over until the correct forms are fixed in your mind and the incorrect forms "hurt" your ears. In doing the exercises, remember that the past participle is used with auxiliary verbs: *is*, *are*, *was*, *were*, *have*, *has*, *had*, *have been*, etc. As you say the principal parts, place *have* before the past participle: *beat*, *beat*, *have beaten*.

GROUP I

PRESENT	PAST	PAST PARTICIPLE
beat	beat	(have) beaten
begin	began	(have) begun
blow	blew	(have) blown
break	broke	(have) broken
burst	burst	(have) burst
choose	chose	(have) chosen
come	came	(have) come
do	did	(have) done

● EXERCISE 1. Number on your paper from 1 to 20. After the proper number write the form of the verb given at the beginning of each sentence which will fill correctly the blank in the sentence.

1. *begin* I had already —— to work.
2. *blow* The wind has —— hard all day.
3. *come* He —— in last night at 10 o'clock.
4. *choose* Has everyone —— a partner?
5. *beat* We have —— them three times.
6. *do* Jack —— the best he could.
7. *break* Was his arm ——?
8. *burst* As I drove up, three dogs —— from the gate.
9. *do* We —— what was expected of us.
10. *begin* You should have —— earlier.
11. *blow* His boat had been —— out to sea.
12. *beat* This team has never been ——.
13. *burst* They thought the water pipes had ——.
14. *come* We watched as the band —— slowly up the street.
15. *choose* I wished we had —— the other route.
16. *break* He has —— his promise.
17. *come* I —— along right after the accident.
18. *do* The actors —— well in last night's performance.
19. *begin* When the bad news came, I —— to regret my decision.
20. *come* She has —— to get your advice.

GROUP II

PRESENT	PAST	PAST PARTICIPLE
draw	drew	(have) drawn
drink	drank	(have) drunk
drive	drove	(have) driven
fall	fell	(have) fallen
fly	flew	(have) flown
freeze	froze	(have) frozen
give	gave	(have) given
go	went	(have) gone

● EXERCISE 2. Number on your paper from 1 to 20. After the proper number write the form of the verb at the beginning of each sentence which will fill correctly the blank in the sentence.

1. *drink* Have you —— all the milk?
2. *fall* If I hadn't ——, I'd have caught him.
3. *freeze* The water hasn't —— yet.
4. *go* He has —— to Chicago.
5. *give* She —— me a make-up test yesterday.
6. *fly* Have you —— the Atlantic?
7. *drive* George has —— since he was twelve.
8. *draw* Marilyn —— the cartoons for the yearbook.
9. *go* Mac has —— to the library.
10. *give* I —— him the money last week.
11. *freeze* All of us were nearly ——.
12. *fly* You could have —— up here in two hours.
13. *draw* No child could have —— that picture.
14. *drink* He —— more than I did.
15. *drive* We have —— more than 500 miles today.
16. *fall* I thought he had —— from the tree.
17. *give* He —— me only a dollar.
18. *drive* If you had —— a little farther, you would have found us.
19. *go* He has —— home already.
20. *give* He should have —— me more time for the test.

● EXERCISE 3. *Groups* I *and* II. Number on your paper from 1 to 33. After the proper number write a

+ for each sentence in which the italicized verb is correct; write a 0 for each sentence in which the verb is incorrect.

1. Janet *drew* the picture for us.
2. I *begun* to think you had forgotten me.
3. No one *had drank* very much.
4. You *have broke* the window.
5. He's *drove* this road hundreds of times.
6. You *should have chosen* Jimmy.
7. She *had* not *fell* very far.
8. The boys *done* the heavy work.
9. I *had flown* as far as St. Louis.
10. She *come* home an hour ago.
11. The food *must be frozen* immediately.
12. During the heavy rain the ripest cherries *had bursted* open.
13. He *give* me what I wanted.
14. Strong winds *blowed* us off our course.
15. We *could* not *have gone* any farther.
16. You *should have beat* him easily.
17. His plow *was drawed* by a team of mules.
18. *Have* you ever *drunk* papaya juice?
19. He *had chose* her for his partner.
20. You *could have flew* to Newark.
21. As I reached the car, the bag of groceries suddenly *burst* open.
22. You *should have went* earlier.
23. Since then he *has* never *been beaten.*
24. Who *give* you the pearls?
25. Pete *come* in third in the first race.
26. You *might have fallen* on your head.
27. The axle *must be broke.*
28. The game *begun* about two o'clock.
29. He *had drunk* too much.
30. We *had driven* for miles in the fog.
31. Who *done* it?
32. The river *had frozen* solid.
33. Dad *come* after us about noon.

GROUP III

PRESENT	PAST	PAST PARTICIPLE
grow	grew	(have) grown
know	knew	(have) known
ride	rode	(have) ridden
ring	rang *or* rung	(have) rung
run	ran	(have) run
see	saw	(have) seen
sing	sang *or* sung	(have) sung
speak	spoke	(have) spoken

● EXERCISE 4. Number on your paper from 1 to 20. After the proper number write the form of the verb given at the beginning of each sentence which will fill correctly the blank in the sentence.

1. *ring* The bell has ——.
2. *run* When the rain came, everyone —— for shelter.
3. *sing* Had she —— in the choir before?
4. *speak* If I had recognized you, I'd have —— to you.
5. *see* The boys —— some rattlesnakes.
6. *ride* He's —— every horse in the stable.
7. *know* You should have —— better.
8. *grow* He has —— too fast.
9. *see* I —— him at the drugstore.
10. *know* We found that no one —— the correct answer.
11. *ride* Barry had —— over to see us.
12. *grow* In one year the trees had —— a foot.
13. *speak* Have you —— to her yet?
14. *sing* Has anyone here ever —— this song?
15. *run* We —— home as soon as school was out.
16. *ring* Has she —— the bell?
17. *speak* I wish I hadn't —— so severely.
18. *see* Who —— me last night?
19. *ring* The telephone has —— ten times in the past hour.
20. *run* I don't think he —— as fast as he could.

GROUP IV

PRESENT	PAST	PAST PARTICIPLE
spring	sprang *or* sprung	(have) sprung
steal	stole	(have) stolen
swim	swam	(have) swum
swing	swung	(have) swung
take	took	(have) taken
tear	tore	(have) torn
throw	threw	(have) thrown
write	wrote	(have) written

● EXERCISE 5. Number on your paper from 1 to 20. After the proper number write the form of the verb given at the beginning of each sentence which will fill correctly the blank in the sentence.

1. *spring* The lock had been —— by force.
2. *swim* I could not have —— another foot.
3. *tear* Have you —— your coat?
4. *write* Has she —— to you?
5. *throw* Jackie —— him out at first base.
6. *take* She should have —— the children with her.
7. *swing* Last year they —— in the playground swings nearly every day.
8. *steal* They thought their car had been ——.
9. *throw* The first ball Gary —— was a wide curve.
10. *write* My uncle has —— several books.
11. *tear* You have —— my homework paper.
12. *swim* Yesterday she —— alone to the raft.
13. *spring* In a moment he had —— into the saddle and galloped away.
14. *take* I should have —— a course in typing.
15. *swing* All morning the balloon —— back and forth on its cable.
16. *steal* I'm sure no one has —— your wallet.
17. *write* If you had —— to me, I'd have helped you.
18. *swim* Where were you when we —— the channel?
19. *throw* A sudden lurch of the boat —— everyone overboard.
20. *write* When you have —— your essay, show it to me.

● EXERCISE 6. *Groups* III *and* IV. Number on your paper from 1 to 33. After the proper number write a + for each sentence in which the italicized verb is correct; write a 0 for each sentence in which the verb is incorrect.

1. You *have growed* much taller this year.
2. Who *had rang* the bell?
3. He *has ran* his last race.
4. We *have sung* that number in every concert.
5. He *has spoke* at our school several times.
6. They *swam* until they were tired.
7. I *had tore* my shirt.
8. You *have* never *wrote* a better story.
9. *Had* I *known* your number, I'd have called you.
10. I *had* not *rode* horseback for years.
11. He thinks I *seen* him there.
12. Who *throwed* you out?
13. We *should have taken* more money with us.
14. Several pages *have been torn* from this book.
15. The acrobat *swung* himself over the swinging bar.
16. Someone *must have stolen* my watch.
17. On both plays they *threw* us for a loss.
18. Mr. Maxwell *seen* at once what the trouble was.
19. Dad thought we *had ridden* far enough.
20. He *would have knowed* what to do.
21. *Have* you *wrote* your composition yet?
22. The gale *had tore* both sails.
23. No one *could have swum* that far.
24. I *have* not *spoken* to Everett.
25. She *has sung* her way to stardom.
26. When Mr. Stoltz appeared, the boys *run* away.
27. I did not know the bell *had rang*.
28. This town *has grown* rapidly.
29. You *should have knowed* better.
30. Nothing *had been stolen*.
31. She *had tore* her new gloves.
32. You *could have took* Jane to the dance.
33. I *shall have written* my letter by that time.

● EXERCISE 7. *Groups* I–IV. Number on your paper from 1 to 50. After the proper number write the form of the verb at the beginning of each sentence which will fill correctly the blank in the sentence.

1. *burst* In the bus station my suitcase suddenly —— open.
2. *freeze* The doctor said I had —— both feet.
3. *break* Were any bones ——?
4. *fly* We'd be home now if we had ——.
5. *blow* The storm had —— down a telephone pole.
6. *fall* She could not have —— more than six feet.
7. *begin* We —— the job yesterday morning.
8. *know* You should have —— what to do.
9. *beat* Has anyone —— him this season?
10. *ring* Someone had —— the bell.
11. *drive* How far have you —— today?
12. *ride* Father had never —— in the back seat.
13. *drink* During last spring's flood, we —— only bottled water.
14. *run* When I saw him pass the house, I —— after him.
15. *do* She —— her homework before school was out.
16. *swim* When I called for help, Helen —— out to me.
17. *come* He —— in about an hour ago.
18. *steal* Jack thought someone had —— his bicycle.
19. *choose* The council could have —— a better representative.
20. *sing* You should have —— louder.
21. *grow* The school has —— beyond capacity.
22. *speak* How many times have I —— to you about that?
23. *go* Alice had —— to the movies.
24. *see* I'm sure Raymond —— me as I left the room.
25. *give* Who —— you the black eye?
26. *take* I wish he had —— me with him.
27. *tear* The trainer said I had —— a ligament.
28. *throw* We lost the game when Bob —— the ball over Ben's head.

29. *tear* Someone had —— the draperies.
30. *write* Why haven't you —— to your mother?
31. *throw* Who —— away this fountain pen?
32. *go* We could not have —— any earlier.
33. *see* How do you know they —— you last night?
34. *freeze* If he had not been rescued promptly, he would have ——.
35. *run* The truck —— into us when we were parked at the curb.
36. *come* After dinner last night Don —— over to hear some records.
37. *write* You should have —— more.
38. *drink* Who —— the coke I left here?
39. *know* I had —— June when she was a little girl.
40. *break* Two convicts had —— away from the work gang.
41. *begin* A little later I —— to see what he meant.
42. *swim* During last week's cold wave we —— in the pool.
43. *fall* We thought he must have —— through the ice.
44. *beat* The defendant claimed his jailers had —— him.
45. *see* I —— him at the dance last night.
46. *throw* That horse has never —— a rider.
47. *run* Mr. Smith —— for mayor last year.
48. *speak* I wish he had —— about his travels.
49. *come* I couldn't find the family when I —— home.
50. *write* Both men have —— an autobiography.

Six Special Irregular Verbs

Three pairs of irregular verbs have been reserved for special study and drill because they are more difficult to use correctly than any other verbs. These special verbs are *lie*, *lay*, *sit*, *set*, *rise*, and *raise*. Most difficult to use correctly are the verbs *lie* and *lay*.

LIE AND LAY

The verb *lie* means *to recline*, *to rest* or *remain in a lying position*. Its principal parts are *lie*, *lay*, (have) *lain*, (is) *lying*.

The verb *lay* means *to put, to place something.* Its principal parts are *lay*, *laid*, (have) *laid*, (is) *laying.*[2]

Memorize the principal parts of these verbs:

PRESENT	PAST	PAST PARTICIPLE	PRESENT PARTICIPLE
lie (to recline)	lay	(have) lain	(is) lying
lay (to put)	laid	(have) laid	(is) laying

If you do not habitually use these verbs correctly, you must begin your work on them slowly and thoughtfully. Only by taking time to think through each form you use can you eventually establish the habit of using the verbs correctly. When faced with a *lie–lay* problem, ask yourself two questions:

1. What is the meaning I intend? Is it *to be in a lying position*, or is it *to put something down?*

2. What is the time expressed by the verb and which principal part is required to express this time?

PROBLEM **After the alarm had awakened me, I (lay, laid) in bed too long.**

QUESTION 1 Meaning? The meaning here is *to remain in a lying position.* The verb which means *to remain in a lying position* is *lie.*

QUESTION 2 Principal part? The time is past and requires the past form, which is *lay.* [lie, *lay*, lain]

SOLUTION **After the alarm had awakened me, I lay in bed too long.**

PROBLEM **Mac (lay, laid) his coat on the table.**

QUESTION 1 Meaning? The meaning here is *to put.* The verb which means *to put* is *lay.*

QUESTION 2 Principal part? The time is past and there-

[2] If you are familiar with the terms "transitive" and "intransitive," it may help you to know that the verb *lie* is intransitive; it does not take an object. The verb *lay* is transitive; it may take an object.

INTRANSITIVE (no object) For weeks he had to *lie* in a cast.

TRANSITIVE (with an object) *Lay* the *box* down, please.

fore requires the past form, which is *laid.* [lay, *laid*, laid]

SOLUTION **Mac laid his coat on the table.**

PROBLEM **How long had it (lain, laid) there?**

QUESTION 1 Meaning? The meaning here is *to remain in a lying position.* The verb which means *to remain in a lying position* is *lie.*

QUESTION 2 Principal part? The time requires the past participle with *had.* The past participle of *lie* is *lain.* [lie, lay, *lain*]

SOLUTION **How long had it lain there?**

PROBLEM **The dog is (lying, laying) on the doormat.**

QUESTION 1 Meaning? The meaning here is *to remain in a lying position.* The verb which means *to remain in a lying position* is *lie.*

QUESTION 2 Principal part? The time here requires the present participle, which is *lying.*

SOLUTION **The dog is lying on the doormat.**

It will pay you to use this two-question formula each time you are in doubt about a problem in the use of *lie* and *lay.* Although slow at first, the process will speed up after a few trials, and you will be able to select the correct verb quickly. Of course, you must have memorized the principal parts of the verbs before you can use the formula.

Two facts about the use of *lie* and *lay* may be of additional help.

1. Most errors in the use of these verbs are made when the speaker means *to rest, recline, to remain in a lying position.* When this is the meaning you intend, be especially cautious.

2. When you wish to express the idea of *putting* or *placing something* **in the past tense,** always use *laid.*

● EXERCISE 8. Number on your paper from 1 to 10. After the proper number write the correct one of the two words in parentheses. Use the two-question formula.

1. He spent the summer just (lying, laying) around home.
2. Someone (lay, laid) the dictionary on my glasses.
3. He had (laid, lain) a burning cigar on the edge of the table.
4. Jimmy (lay, laid) down on the back seat of the car.
5. I saw your hat (lying, laying) on the hall table.
6. She had just (lain, laid) down when the telephone rang.
7. Have they (laid, lain) the cornerstone yet?
8. We were (lying, laying) on an old army blanket.
9. She (laid, lay) her sewing aside and went to the door.
10. Don't leave any money (lying, laying) in plain sight.

● EXERCISE 9. Number on your paper from 1 to 10. After the proper number write the correct form of *lie* or *lay* to fill the blank in each sentence. Use the two-question formula.

1. Where was he ——?
2. —— on your back and stretch yourself.
3. An hour ago I —— down for a nap.
4. Everyone was —— on the beach.
5. Have they —— the flooring yet?
6. I think he is —— in the hammock.
7. He —— the boxes on the porch yesterday.
8. She had —— there only a short time.
9. We were —— in the shade.
10. She —— the pattern on the cloth.

● EXERCISE 10. Number on your paper from 1 to 20. After the proper number write the correct one of the two verbs in parentheses. Use the two-question formula.

1. The wreck (lay, laid) in twenty feet of water.
2. The cat loves to (lie, lay) on the window sill.
3. The missing book was (lying, laying) on the top shelf.
4. Do you remember where you (laid, lay) my pen?
5. You shouldn't have (laid, lain) there so long.

6. Jack was (laying, lying) on the deck.
7. Here the coal (lays, lies) near the surface.
8. We gathered driftwood while Doug (laid, lay) a fire.
9. I planned to (lie, lay) down for only ten minutes.
10. Gently she (laid, lay) down the injured child.
11. Sandy usually (lies, lays) near the fire.
12. I could not persuade him to (lay, lie) down.
13. Yesterday Dad and I (lay, laid) the new carpet.
14. The cat never (lays, lies) in the bed we made for her.
15. Someone had (laid, lain) a paintbrush on the chair.
16. His clothes were (lying, laying) about the room.
17. Frank had (laid, lain) his camera on the railing.
18. The shells had (laid, lain) there for a million years.
19. Beneath his rough exterior (lies, lays) a kind heart.
20. I keep forgetting where I have (laid, lain) the hammer.

SIT AND SET

Sit usually means *to rest, to be in an upright, sitting position.*[3] The principal parts of *sit* are *sit, sat,* (have) *sat,* (is) *sitting.*

Set usually means *to put, to place something.* The principal parts of *set* are *set, set,* (have) *set,* (is) *setting.*[4]

Since all forms of *set* are made without changing the vowel, the problem of using these two verbs is rather simple. You need only keep in mind the fact that when you mean *to put something down,* you use *set* or *setting.* For all other meanings use *sit* or *sat* or *sitting.*[5]

Memorize the principal parts of these verbs:

PRESENT	PAST	PAST PARTICIPLE	PRESENT PARTICIPLE
sit (to rest)	sat	(have) sat	(is) sitting
set (to put)	set	(have) set	(is) setting

[3] Such expressions as "Sit the baby in his high chair" or "Sit him up" really mean *to put* or *to place*, and the expressions, which are acceptable, are exceptions to the general rule.

[4] Like *lie, sit* is an intransitive verb; it does not take an object. Like *lay, set* is a transitive verb; it may take an object.

[5] The expressions "The sun sets," "the setting hen," and "Wait for the cement to set" are exceptions to the rule.

● EXERCISE 11. Number on your paper from 1 to 10. After the proper number write the correct one of the two verbs in parentheses in each sentence.

1. She has been (sitting, setting) by the telephone all evening.
2. Bill just (set, sat) still and said nothing.
3. In what row were you (setting, sitting)?
4. Extra chairs were (set, sat) in the aisles by the ushers.
5. Had you (sat, set) there a little longer, you would have caught a fish.
6. We decided to (set, sit) quietly and await results.
7. Passengers (setting, sitting) in the rear seats were not injured.
8. If you (sit, set) on the damp ground, you may catch a cold.
9. He plans to (set, sit) the new cabin on the beach.
10. Someone had (set, sat) in the fresh paint.

RISE AND *RAISE*

The verb *rise* means *to go up.* Its principal parts are *rise, rose,* (have) *risen,* (is) *rising.*

The verb *raise* means *to force something to move upward.* Its principal parts are *raise, raised,* (have) *raised,* (is) *raising.*[6]

Memorize the principal parts of these verbs:

PRESENT	PAST	PAST PARTICIPLE	PRESENT PARTICIPLE
rise (to go up)	rose	(have) risen	(is) rising
raise (to force up or be forced up)	raised	(have) raised	(is) raising

● EXERCISE 12. Number on your paper from 1 to 10. After the proper number write the correct one of the two verbs in parentheses in each sentence.

1. The river has been (rising, raising) all night.
2. The effect of the law was to (rise, raise) prices again.

[6] Like *lie* and *sit, rise* is intransitive; it does not take an object. Like *lay* and *set, raise* is transitive; it may take an object.

3. Our hopes (raised, rose) and fell in the same instant.
4. We saw a column of smoke (raising, rising) above the farmhouse.
5. The moon (raises, rises) about nine o'clock.
6. If taxes (raise, rise) any higher, we shall have to move.
7. With its extra load of fuel, the plane would not (rise, raise) from the runway.
8. Workmen (raised, rose) the house six feet.
9. Clouds were (rising, raising) on the horizon.
10. Rents are (raising, rising) rapidly.

● EXERCISE 13. Number on your paper from 1 to 25. After the proper number write the correct one of the two words in parentheses in each sentence. Work slowly. Try for 100 per cent.

1. A film of oil (lay, laid) on the water.
2. Can't you (sit, set) a while longer?
3. If his temperature (rises, raises), call the doctor.
4. The dog had been (laying, lying) in my bed.
5. We hardly (set, sat) down at all during the final quarter of the game.
6. Your letter was (lying, laying) at the bottom of the pile.
7. The waves (rose, raised) to mountainous height.
8. I had (laid, lain) the flashlight on the car seat.
9. From where we were (setting, sitting), the stage was barely visible.
10. She forgot where she had (laid, lain) her gloves.
11. Piles of books and papers were (lying, laying) on the desk.
12. Clouds of black smoke were (rising, raising) from the hills.
13. If we (sit, set) here much longer, we'll be late.
14. (Lie, Lay) down, Butch!
15. Boulders and jagged rocks (lay, laid) across the highway.
16. Since the election, stocks have been (raising, rising) steadily.
17. The dog must have been (laying, lying) under the car.

18. We spent the afternoon just (sitting, setting) and visiting.
19. Where do you want to (set, sit)?
20. The child refused to (lie, lay) under the beach umbrella.
21. Beyond this point the road (rises, raises) sharply.
22. Who (lay, laid) out this tennis court?
23. No one expected the tide to (raise, rise) so high.
24. We were (setting, sitting) before the fireplace.
25. The ties on which the track (lays, lies) must be firm and level.

Tense

Verbs change in form to show the time of their action or of the idea they express. The time expressed by a verb (present, past, future) is its tense. There are six tenses. As the following conjugation of the verb *to go* will show you, the six tenses are made from the principal parts of the verb. Study this conjugation and use it for reference in your work on tense.

8b. Learn the names of the six tenses and how the tenses are formed.

CONJUGATION OF THE VERB *TO GO*

Present infinitive: *to go* Past infinitive: *to have gone*

PRINCIPAL PARTS

PRESENT	PAST	PAST PARTICIPLE	PRESENT PARTICIPLE
go	went	gone	going

PRESENT TENSE

Singular	*Plural*
I go	we go
you go	you go
he, she, it goes	they go

Present progressive: *I am going*, etc.

PAST TENSE

Singular	*Plural*
I went	we went
you went	you went
he, she, it went	they went

Past progressive: *I was going*, etc.

FUTURE TENSE

(*shall* or *will* + the present)

Singular	*Plural*
I shall go	we shall go
you will go	you will go
he, she, it will go	they will go

Future progressive: *I shall be going*, etc.

PRESENT PERFECT TENSE

(*have* or *has* + the past participle)

Singular	*Plural*
I have gone	we have gone
you have gone	you have gone
he, she, it has gone	they have gone

Present perfect progressive: *I have been going*, etc.

PAST PERFECT TENSE

(*had* + the past participle)

Singular	*Plural*
I had gone	we had gone
you had gone	you had gone
he, she, it had gone	they had gone

Past perfect progressive: *I had been going*, etc.

FUTURE PERFECT TENSE

(*shall have* or *will have* + the past participle)

Singular	*Plural*
I shall have gone	we shall have gone
you will have gone	you will have gone
he, she, it will have gone	they will have gone

Future perfect progressive: *I shall have been going*, etc.

8c. Learn the uses of each of the six tenses.

Each of the six tenses has its own particular uses, some of which require explanation. Study the following explanation of these uses; learn rules for the uses of the tenses; do the exercises. Use these pages for reference when you are confronted by a problem in tense in your own writing.

(1) The *present tense* is used to express action (or state of being) occurring now, at the present time.[7]

EXAMPLES **I work here.**
I am working now. [progressive form]

▶ NOTE: In all tenses, as in the preceding example, continuing action may be shown by the use of the progressive form, which ends in *–ing*.

The *present tense* is also used to indicate habitual action.

EXAMPLE **He works every evening.**

The *present tense* is also used to express a general truth, something which is true at all times.

EXAMPLES **He apparently thought that seeing is** (not *was*) **believing.**
I did not know that Salem is (not *was*) **the capital of Oregon.**

The *present tense* is also used occasionally to achieve vividness in writing about past events. This use of the present tense is known as the *historical present.*

EXAMPLE **Napoleon promptly senses the danger to his left flank and dispatches reinforcements.**

(2) The *past tense* is used to express action (or state of being) that occurred in the past but did not continue

[7] *Linking* verbs do not express action; they express state of being.

8c

into the present. The past tense is formed regularly by adding *–ed* to the verb.

EXAMPLES **I worked** there during the holidays.
I was working there during the holidays.

▶ NOTE: Past action may be shown in other ways:

EXAMPLES **I used to work** there.
I did work there. [The verb with *do* or *did* is called the emphatic form of the verb.]

(3) The *future tense* is used to express action (or state of being) at some time in the future. The future tense is formed with *shall* or *will*.

EXAMPLES **I shall work** in the library after school.
I shall be working in the library after school.

▶ NOTE: The future may be indicated in other ways:

EXAMPLES **I am going** to work there.
I am about to work.
I work there tomorrow. [present with another word indicating future time]

(4) The *present perfect tense* is used to express action (or state of being) occurring at no definite time in the past. It is formed with *have* or *has*.

EXAMPLE He **has worked** for us many times.

The *present perfect tense* is also used to express action (or state of being) occurring in the past and continuing into the present.

EXAMPLES **I have worked** here for six weeks. [I am still working here.]
I have been working here for six weeks. [I am still working here.]

(5) The *past perfect tense* is used to express action (or state of being) completed in the past *before some other past action or event*. It is formed with *had*.

EXAMPLES When I **had worked** for a week, I **asked** for my pay. [The working preceded the asking.]
When I **had been working** for a week, I **asked** for my pay.

(6) The *future perfect tense* is used to express action (or state of being) which will be completed in the future *before some other future action or event*. It is formed with *shall have* or *will have*.

EXAMPLES By the time school **opens, I shall have worked** here eight weeks. [The working precedes the opening of school.]
By the time school **opens, I shall have been working** here eight weeks.

● EXERCISE 14. Explain the difference in meaning between the sentences in the following pairs. The sentences are correct. Name the tense used in each sentence.

1. Katherine went to high school for two years.
   Katherine has gone to high school for two years.
2. How long has she been here?
   How long was she here?
3. When she's twenty-one, she will learn some important lessons.
   When she's twenty-one, she will have learned some important lessons.
4. What has been going on here?
   What went on here?
5. Have the ballots been counted?
   Had the ballots been counted?
6. We learned that he had been there for three hours.
   We learned that he has been there for three hours.
7. Mary will have finished college when you return from abroad.
   Mary will finish college when you return from abroad.
8. The coach thought the team was playing well.
   The coach thought the team had been playing well.

9. The doctor said Carl had tuberculosis.
   The doctor said Carl had had tuberculosis.
10. Mr. Edwards was president of the bank for twenty years.
    Mr. Edwards has been president of the bank for twenty years.

Special Problems of Tense Usage

THE PAST PERFECT TENSE

The past perfect tense requires special consideration because young writers frequently fail to employ it in expressing two actions which happened at different times in the past. The function of the past perfect tense is to make clear which of the actions preceded the other.

8d. Use the past perfect tense for the earlier of two past actions.

WRONG **Suddenly I remembered** (past) **that I forgot** (past) **the tickets.** [The same tense has been incorrectly used for two actions which did not happen at the same time. Since the forgetting preceded the remembering, the past perfect form of *forget* should be used.]

RIGHT **Suddenly I remembered** (past) **that I had forgotten** (past perfect) **the tickets.**

WRONG **Everything he told** (past) **me I heard** (past) **before.** [The hearing preceded the telling.]

RIGHT **Everything he told** (past) **me I had heard** (past perfect) **before.**

WRONG **There was** (past) **a beautiful park where the city dump was** (past). [Since the two verbs in this sentence are in the same tense, the sentence suggests that the park and the dump were there together.]

RIGHT **There was** (past) **a beautiful park where the city dump had been** (past perfect). [The past perfect *had been* makes it clear that the dump was there before the park.]

RIGHT There **had been** (past perfect) a **beautiful park** where the city dump was (past). [Making the other verb past perfect reverses the time order; the park preceded the dump.]

8e. Avoid the use of *would have* in "if clauses" expressing the earlier of two past actions. Use the past perfect.

WRONG If he would have worked harder, he'd have made the honor roll.

RIGHT If he **had worked** harder, he'd have made the honor roll.

WRONG If I would have thought of it, I'd have called for you.

RIGHT If I **had thought** of it, I'd have called for you.

● EXERCISE 15. Correct the following sentences, which contain errors in the use of tenses. Refer, if necessary, to the rules on pages 137–41 for the uses of the various tenses.

1. The class officers canceled the party after I made all arrangements for it.
2. Gerald based his decision on the old proverb that honesty was the best policy.
3. By the time I graduate, my brother will be practicing law for five years.
4. Even though his innocence was previously proved, he was not released.
5. If you would have been here earlier, you'd have met Joe.
6. Since the new manager came, there were no serious financial problems.
7. The company hired Mr. Littmann because he lived for many years in Arabia.
8. We thought that Bill went already.

9. The candidate listed effectively the errors his opponent made while in office.
10. When I introduced them, they acted as if they never met before.
11. He already lost confidence in himself before he was fired.
12. By that time we will withdraw all our occupation troops.
13. If she would have asked me, I could have helped her.
14. The police said they thought we imagined the whole incident.
15. If we had matches, we could have built a fire.
16. When I was doing my homework last night, I was sure I took down the assignment correctly in class.
17. I didn't know that Lake Superior was the largest of the Great Lakes.
18. After totaling the scores, we found that we won by twenty points.
19. If we would have stayed at home, we'd have missed a good show.
20. The receptionist thought that Dr. Berg has been out of town until this morning.

HAVING WITH THE PAST PARTICIPLE

8f. In participial phrases, use *having* with the past participle to express action completed before another action.

WRONG Being tardy three days in succession, I was kept after school today. [The present participle *being* is incorrectly used to express an action which had obviously been completed *before* the second action in the sentence.]

RIGHT **Having been** tardy three days in succession, I was kept after school today.

WRONG Making his decision, Martin stuck to it. [The decision had to be made *before* he could stick to it.]

RIGHT **Having made** his decision, Martin stuck to it.

THE PRESENT AND THE PAST INFINITIVE

8g. Use the present infinitive (*to go, to see, etc.*) to express action following another action.

WRONG **The children were disappointed because they had hoped to have gone with us.** [What had the children hoped, *to have gone* or *to go?* The present infinitive *to go* should be used because the action it expresses follows the action of the verb *had hoped.*]

RIGHT **The children were disappointed because they had hoped to go with us.**

WRONG **He intended to have written to all of us.** [Was his intention *to have written* or *to write?*]

RIGHT **He intended to write to all of us.**

8h. Use the past infinitive (*to have gone, to have seen, etc.*) to express action before another action.

EXAMPLE **I am glad to have seen that movie.** [The past infinitive is correct because the action it expresses came before the time of the other verb *am.*]

● EXERCISE 16. The sentences in this exercise contain errors in the use of tense and in the use of the present participle and the infinitive. Correct the sentences according to the rules you have just studied. Discuss your corrections in class before doing Exercise 17.

1. Listening to the committee argue for two hours, we excused ourselves.
2. I should have liked to have seen the races.
3. In the afternoon woodsmen trimmed the trees which they cut in the morning.
4. The date of the opening of school has always varied because Labor Day was a holiday.

5. We did not wish to have become involved in any scandal.
6. By the time you specify, I shall be practicing medicine for many years.
7. Although the morning forecast predicted rain, the afternoon was clear.
8. Every boy has at some time wished to have been a fireman.
9. If I knew your address, I would have written to you.
10. By the time he called me, I finished my homework.

● EXERCISE 17. The following sentences contain errors in the use of tense and in the use of the present participle and the infinitive. Correct the sentences.

1. I had hoped to have been a successful writer.
2. Receiving a four-year, all-expense scholarship, Dick did not work during the summers.
3. Nancy was shocked to have learned that a diamond was merely a form of carbon.
4. If the team won, we would have celebrated.
5. Being ill during the morning, I went home at noon.
6. I learned that the Nile was the longest river in the world.
7. She asked whether the new books arrived yet.
8. We should have liked to have met your sister.
9. If I didn't eat breakfast this morning, I'd have been on time.
10. I tried to explain to him that I already saw the movie twice.

Minor Problems in the Use of Verbs

ACTIVE AND PASSIVE VOICE

A verb is in the *active* voice when it expresses an action performed *by* its subject. A verb is in the *passive* voice when it expresses an action performed *upon* its subject or when the subject is the result of the action.

ACTIVE VOICE Lightning struck the barn. [subject acting]

PASSIVE VOICE The barn was struck by lightning. [subject acted upon]

PASSIVE VOICE This house was built by my grandfather. [The subject is the result of the action.]

Whether you use an active or a passive verb is usually more a matter of personal taste than a matter of correctness. For example, the two sentences below, which express the same meaning, are equally good sentences. The only reason a writer might choose one in preference to the other would be that one sentence fitted more smoothly into his style than the other.

ACTIVE VOICE A foul ball hit the umpire.
PASSIVE VOICE The umpire was hit by a foul ball.

You should understand, however, that, unless sparingly and skillfully used, the passive voice may produce awkwardness in writing and that, in general, a passive verb is weaker in its effect than an active verb.

AWKWARD PASSIVE At the beginning of his senior year, a secondhand typewriter was purchased by Bill, and a course in typing was signed up for by him.

ACTIVE At the beginning of his senior year, Bill purchased a secondhand typewriter and signed up for a course in typing.

WEAK PASSIVE The game was won when a home run was hit by Jerry.

ACTIVE Jerry won the game by hitting a home run.

WEAK PASSIVE An exciting game was expected by everyone, but a victory was predicted by no one.

ACTIVE Everyone expected an exciting game, but no one predicted a victory.

Not only may the passive voice be weak and awkward, but too many passive verbs may easily cause a monotonous style, as in the following paragraph.

We *were invited* by Dr. Rowland to see his famous collection of precious stones. A large table *had been placed* in the center of his study. The green cloth by which the table *was covered was removed* by Dr. Rowland, and a glittering collection of exquisite jewels *was revealed* beneath the glass top of the table. Although we *were delighted* by the display, there were so many precious stones that they *could* not *be* fully *appreciated* by us. It *was concluded* by all of us that we *would be* more *impressed* by one beautiful ruby than by a dozen.

8i. Use the passive voice sparingly. Avoid weak and awkward passives. In the interest of variety, avoid long passages in which all the verbs are passive.

There are, however, some qualifications of this general rule which should be mentioned. The passive voice is particularly useful in two common situations.

(1) Use the passive voice to express an action in which the actor is unknown.

EXAMPLE The door **had been closed** before we arrived.

(2) Use the passive voice to express an action in which it is desirable not to disclose the actor.

EXAMPLE A mistake **has been made** in issuing this order.

In some instances the passive voice is more convenient and just as effective as the active voice. The following sentences containing verbs in the passive voice are entirely acceptable.

1. America **was discovered** in 1492.
2. We **were drenched** by the rain and **frozen** by the icy wind.

3. **Because he played baseball for money, Carl has been barred from interscholastic athletics.**
4. **Miss Green, who is very well liked by the students, has been invited to act as chaperon.**

Remember, however, that, in general, the active voice is stronger than the passive and less likely to get you into stylistic difficulties.

● EXERCISE 18. Revise the following sentences by changing the passive verbs to active verbs wherever you think the change is desirable. In some sentences the change is more important than in others.

1. After the car had been washed by us, it was waxed and polished by the garage man.
2. We were held spellbound by Lieutenant Douglas as a number of his harrowing experiences in the Air Force were related by him.
3. A formal protest against the location of the new school building has been presented by the Student Council, which was urged on by the entire student body.
4. The rules of the school must be understood and followed by every student.
5. Since dinner had been prepared by the girls, the dishes were washed by the boys.
6. Her new, high-heeled shoes were worn by her to the dance.
7. The new surprise play which had been taught to the team on Thursday was completely forgotten by them in the game on Saturday.
8. Mr. James was known by everybody and liked by everybody.
9. Our sport of baseball may be borrowed by foreigners and played by them as played by us, but it will always be regarded by them as the great American game.
10. Because proof of his accusations was unable to be provided by Mr. Brown, the case against the accused man had to be dropped by the FBI.

THE SUBJUNCTIVE MOOD

Verbs may be in one of three moods: *indicative*, *imperative*, or *subjunctive*. Almost all the verbs you use are in the *indicative mood*. The *imperative mood* is used to express a request or a command.

IMPERATIVE **Form** a single line along the left wall.
Please **reply** to this letter as soon as possible.

The only common uses of the *subjunctive mood* in modern English are to express a condition contrary to fact and to express a wish. These usages occur principally in written English and usually apply to only one verb form — *were*. The following partial conjugation of *to be* will show how the subjunctive mood differs from the indicative.

PRESENT INDICATIVE		PRESENT SUBJUNCTIVE[8]	
Singular	*Plural*	*Singular*	*Plural*
I am	we are	I be	we be
you are	you are	you be	you be
he is	they are	he be	they be

PAST INDICATIVE		PAST SUBJUNCTIVE	
Singular	*Plural*	*Singular*	*Plural*
I was	we were	I were	we were
you were	you were	you were	you were
he was	they were	he were	they were

8j. The subjunctive *were* is used in contrary-to-fact statements (after *if* or *as though*) and in statements expressing a wish.

[8] The present subjunctive is used only in certain rather formal situations.

EXAMPLES I suggest that *he be* admitted to membership.
Mr. Black insists that *I be* punished.
I move that *he be* reprimanded.

CONTRARY TO FACT **If I were** (not *was*) **you, I'd save the money.** [I am not you.]

If he were (not *was*) **taller, he'd be a champion** [He is not taller.]

He talked as though he were (not *was*) **my father.** [He is not my father.]

WISH **I wish it were** (not *was*) **true.**

I wish he were (not *was*) **my adviser.**

● REVIEW EXERCISE. Some of the following sentences contain errors in the use of verbs. Others are correct. Number in a column on your paper from 1 to 25. If the verbs in a sentence are correct, place a plus (+) after the corresponding number on your paper. If a verb is incorrect, write the correct form after the proper number.

1. If I was his father, I'd give him a thrashing.
2. We lay logs under the boat and used them as rollers.
3. I had forgotten that February 22 is a holiday.
4. Instead of working, I should have preferred to have gone to the game.
5. If he weren't so lazy, he'd be a good student.
6. When he entered the bank, the custodian discovered that the vault was opened during the night.
7. If you would have told the truth, you would have been forgiven.
8. The pilot of a search plane spotted wreckage laying at the bottom of a ravine.
9. As the warm air rises, the cool air pushes in beneath it.
10. If I was a year older, I could get a driver's license.
11. Survivors swum to the raft and pulled themselves up on it.
12. If you had taken your time, you would not have had an accident.
13. The driver did not see the second of the two children who run into the path of his car.
14. Would you have preferred to go to the movies?

15. When his new orders come through, Captain Martin was on his way overseas.
16. If Jim was in my position at that time, he would have done what I did.
17. Her mother found her lying at the foot of the stairs.
18. If he were a more liberal thinker, I'd vote for him.
19. I am not sure whether she seen us.
20. We soon realized that someone entered the house ahead of us.
21. I had just lain down when I heard the doorbell.
22. Mr. Stern told us that the Mississippi was the largest river in the United States.
23. If the judge would have listened to me, I'm sure he would not have fined me.
24. When we added our income, we found we made more than a hundred dollars.
25. Was it Jean who give you the assignment?

CHAPTER 9

Correct Use of Modifiers

LEARN TO USE ADJECTIVES AND ADVERBS ACCORDING TO STANDARD USAGE

An adjective modifies a noun or a pronoun. An adverb may modify a verb, an adjective, or another adverb. These are familiar statements, but applying them to usage is sometimes difficult. Should you say "left quick" or "left quickly," "tastes strong" or "tastes strongly," "played good" or "played well"? These and other usage problems are answered in this chapter.

Adjective and Adverb Forms

Before reviewing the usage of adjectives and adverbs, you should make sure that you are able to tell which is the adjective form of a word and which is the adverb form. The fact that most adverbs end in *–ly* (*clearly*, *happily*, *eagerly*) will be helpful if you understand that not all adverbs end in *–ly* and that a few common adjectives do end in *–ly*. Some words have the same form whether used as an adjective or as an adverb. The following list, which gives adjectives and adverbs that have the same form, shows that not all adverbs end in *–ly*.

ADJECTIVES	ADVERBS
a *fast* ball	He ran *fast.*
a *slow* trip	Go *slow.*
hard candy	He works *hard.*
a *tight* fit	Hold *tight.*
a *long* job	He worked *long.*
a *loud* noise	He sang *loud.*
a *late* train	He came *late.*
a *low* bridge	Swing *low.*
a *straight* road	Go *straight.*

ADJECTIVES ENDING IN "–LY"

daily practice
friendly people
early bird
kindly gentleman
lively child
homely dog
lovely island

9a. Linking verbs, especially the verbs of sense (*taste, smell, feel,* etc.), are usually followed by an adjective. The most commonly used linking verbs are *be, become, seem, grow, appear, look, feel, smell, taste, remain, stay,* and *sound.*

EXAMPLES **The dinner tasted delicious.** [The adjective *delicious* is correct after the linking verb *tasted.* It modifies the subject *dinner.*]
Everyone felt happy. [The adjective *happy* is correct after the linking verb *felt.* It modifies the subject *everyone.*]

Some verbs may be used as either linking or action verbs. When they are used as action verbs, the modifier which follows modifies the verb rather than the subject and is, therefore, an adverb; for example, *looked* may be used as a linking verb and as an action verb.

EXAMPLES **He looked sleepy.** [After the *linking* verb *looked*, the adjective *sleepy* is correct. It modifies *he.*]

He looked sleepily in my direction. [After the *action* verb *looked*, the adverb *sleepily* is correct. It modifies *looked.*]

When you are in doubt as to whether a verb is a linking verb or not, try substituting for it a form of *to be: am, is, are, was, were,* etc. If the substitution can be made without greatly changing the meaning of the sentence, the verb is a linking verb and should be followed by an adjective.

EXAMPLES He *looked* sleepy. [*He was sleepy* gives about the same meaning; hence *looked* is a linking verb.]

He *looked* sleepily in my direction. [*He was sleepily in my direction* does not make sense; hence *looked* is not a linking verb in this sentence.]

9b. In making a choice between an adjective and an adverb, ask yourself what the word modifies. If it modifies a noun or pronoun, choose the adjective. If it modifies a verb, choose the adverb.

PROBLEM We built the raft (strong, strongly) enough to hold us.

SOLUTION We built the raft **strong** enough to hold us. [The adjective *strong* modifies the noun *raft.*]

PROBLEM Has he been playing golf (regular, regularly)?

SOLUTION Has he been playing golf **regularly**? [The adverb *regularly* modifies the action verb *has been playing.*]

● EXERCISE 1. Number on your paper from 1 to 20. Select the correct one of the two words in parentheses in each sentence and write it after the proper

9a-b

number. If the word modifies the subject, select the adjective; if it modifies the verb, select the adverb. Remember that a linking verb is followed by an adjective.

1. I thought she looked (beautiful, beautifully) today.
2. The plane appeared very (sudden, suddenly).
3. Do your work as (careful, carefully) as you can.
4. I can finish this job (easy, easily) within an hour.
5. I can't forget how (cold, coldly) he looked at me.
6. The fruit tastes (bitter, bitterly).
7. What are you feeling so (sad, sadly) about?
8. Apparently Sam was feeling (angry, angrily) about his bad luck.
9. Judy does her homework (regular, regularly).
10. He slunk very (quiet, quietly) around the corner.
11. The whole orchard smelled (fragrant, fragrantly).
12. The play ended (abrupt, abruptly) and (disappointing, disappointingly).
13. She feels (miserable, miserably).
14. He did not appear so (brave, bravely) as his brother.
15. The first batch of fudge looked (horrible, horribly).
16. If you just speak (sharp, sharply), the dog will behave.
17. I was driving very (careful, carefully).
18. Finish the test as (quick, quickly) as you can.
19. His story sounded (suspicious, suspiciously) to me.
20. The trip cannot be made so (rapid, rapidly) as you think.

Three Special Problems

BAD AND BADLY

The use of *bad* and *badly* requires special mention, because in colloquial usage *badly* is sometimes accepted as an adjective.

COLLOQUIAL **He felt badly about his loss.** [Strictly speaking, *bad*, the usual adjective form, should be used in this sentence; it is an adjective following a linking verb and modifying the subject *he.*]

STANDARD **He felt bad about his loss.**

In standard written English the distinction between the adjective *bad* and the adverb *badly* is carefully observed.

EXAMPLES The team played **badly.** [The adverb *badly* modifies *played.*]
The situation looks **bad.** [The adjective *bad* modifies the subject *situation.*]

WELL AND *GOOD*

Well may be used as either an adjective or an adverb. As an adjective, *well* has three meanings.

1. *To be in good health:*

EXAMPLES He feels **well.** He seems **well.**

2. *To appear well-dressed or well-groomed:*

EXAMPLE She looks **well** in that dress.

3. *To be satisfactory:*

EXAMPLE All is **well.**

As an adverb, *well* means to perform an action capably.

EXAMPLE She sang very **well.**

Good is always an adjective. It should never be used to modify a verb.

WRONG She spoke good.
RIGHT She spoke **well.**

WRONG They work very good together.
RIGHT They work very **well** together.

SLOW AND *SLOWLY*

Slow is used as both an adjective and an adverb. *Slowly* is an adverb. Except for the expressions *Drive slow* and *Go slow*, which have become acceptable because of their wide use on highway signs, you will be on the safe side if you use *slow* only as an adjective.

● EXERCISE 2. Number on your paper from 1 to 20. If the *italicized* modifier in a sentence is correct, write a + after the proper number on your paper. If it is incorrect, write the correct form and after the correct form write the word it modifies.

1. The old car held up fairly *good.*
2. We were surprised to find him looking so *well.*
3. I always do my homework as *quick* as I can.
4. Some of the food tasted *bad.*
5. Work *slow*, and you will make fewer mistakes.
6. Jean appeared quite *happy.*
7. I can do these errands *easy.*
8. Was George feeling very *bad?*
9. His clothes never fit him very *good.*
10. The family felt *bitterly* about Uncle Fred's will.
11. Drive *careful.*
12. Nancy looks *well* in blue.
13. I was afraid you had been hurt *bad.*
14. She went *direct* to the principal.
15. We couldn't hear very *good* because of the storm.
16. Isn't it possible for you to drive *slowly?*
17. He looked *hopefully* in my direction.
18. The prisoners said they had been treated very *cruel.*
19. If the food smells *bad*, throw it away.
20. Each of us wrote the assignment down *separate.*

Comparison of Adjectives and Adverbs

9c. *Comparison* is the name given to the change in the form of adjectives and adverbs when they are used to compare the qualities of the words

they modify. There are three degrees of comparison: *positive, comparative,* and *superlative*.

POSITIVE	COMPARATIVE	SUPERLATIVE
big	bigger	biggest
anxious	more anxious	most anxious
good	better	best
fast	faster	fastest
easily	more easily	most easily

COMPARATIVE AND SUPERLATIVE FORMS

(1) Most adjectives and adverbs of one syllable form their comparative and superlative degrees by adding *–er* and *–est*.

POSITIVE	COMPARATIVE	SUPERLATIVE
long	longer	longest
hard	harder	hardest

(2) Some adjectives of two syllables form their comparative and superlative degrees by adding *–er* or *–est;* other adjectives of two syllables form their comparative and superlative degrees by means of *more* and *most*.

When you are in doubt as to how a word is compared, consult an unabridged dictionary.

POSITIVE	COMPARATIVE	SUPERLATIVE
happy	happier	happiest
eager	more eager	most eager

(3) Adjectives of more than two syllables and adverbs ending in *–ly* form their comparative and superlative degrees by means of *more* and *most*.

POSITIVE	COMPARATIVE	SUPERLATIVE
capable	more capable	most capable
rapidly	more rapidly	most rapidly

(4) Comparison to indicate less or least of a quality is accomplished by using the words *less* and *least* before the adjective or adverb.

POSITIVE	COMPARATIVE	SUPERLATIVE
bright	less bright	least bright
excited	less excited	least excited
willingly	less willingly	least willingly

IRREGULAR COMPARISON

Adjectives and adverbs which do not follow the regular methods of forming their comparative and superlative degrees are said to be compared irregularly.

POSITIVE	COMPARATIVE	SUPERLATIVE
bad	worse	worst
good, well	better	best
many, much	more	most

● EXERCISE 3. Write the comparative and superlative forms of the following words. If you are in doubt about any of them, look them up in an unabridged dictionary.

1. tall
2. beautiful
3. well
4. short
5. graceful
6. satisfactory
7. ill
8. little
9. industrious
10. bravely
11. bad
12. casually
13. reckless
14. clear
15. good
16. humble
17. dear
18. stealthy
19. diligently
20. small

CORRECT USE OF COMPARATIVE AND SUPERLATIVE DEGREES

9d. In standard English usage employ the comparative degree when comparing two things,

and the superlative degree when comparing more than two.

Comparison of two things

EXAMPLES Although both the plaintiff and the defendant presented strong arguments, those of the defendant were **stronger** (not *strongest*).
The doctors tried both penicillin and sulfanilamide; the penicillin proved to be the **more** (not *most*) **effective** drug.

Comparison of more than two things

EXAMPLES I chose this book because it was the **shortest** (not *shorter*) of the **three.**
Of the **three** branches of the armed services, the Air Force has been the **most** (not *more*) **favored** in recent years.

9e. Do not omit the word *other* when comparing one thing with a group of which it is a part.

WRONG At the end of the war, the United States was stronger than any country in the world. [Since the United States is one of the countries in the world, this sentence says illogically that it was stronger than itself.]

RIGHT At the end of the war, the United States was stronger than any **other** country in the world.

WRONG He has better marks than any student in his grade. [He is a member of his grade; he cannot have better marks than himself.]

RIGHT He has better marks than any **other** student in his grade.

9f. Avoid the double comparison.

A double comparison is one in which the degree is formed incorrectly by both adding *–er* or *–est* and using *more* or *most*.

WRONG She is a more prettier girl than I.
RIGHT She is a **prettier** girl than I.

WRONG He is the most happiest child I know.
RIGHT He is the **happiest** child I know.

● EXERCISE 4. Number on your paper from 1 to 25. For each correct sentence write a + after the proper number; revise each incorrect sentence and write the revised form.

1. Speak soft.
2. I played as good as he did.
3. Bill works harder than any boy in his group.
4. Whatever she does, she does well.
5. If negotiations proceed too slowly, the work will not be completed this year.
6. Since there were two recommended procedures, the committee had to decide which procedure would be best.
7. To our palates the highly seasoned food tasted strongly.
8. Try to speak as convincingly as you can.
9. Albert arrived unexpectedly and took charge of the meeting.
10. His greeting was more friendlier than hers.
11. When the tide is in, the water is many feet more deep.
12. Although he writes badly, his books are popular.
13. *Gone With the Wind* sold better than any American novel.
14. The judges were given ten manuscripts and asked to select the best one.
15. Eat moderate, and you will lose weight.
16. The tiger rushed menacing toward me.
17. I found Mr. Trumbull the more co-operative of the two men.
18. Has he been working regular?
19. The entire menu looked good to us.
20. Three jobs faced us, and we did the harder job first.
21. Pine Lake has the most clearest water.
22. I didn't believe he could act so bad as that.
23. She makes up her mind too slow.
24. Jack is a lot more faster than his brother.
25. When he ran out of money, he went unwilling on relief.

CHAPTER 10

Glossary of Usage

The words and expressions in this glossary are listed for study and for reference. You may, if you wish, work straight through the glossary, using the exercises to test your knowledge of the various items. Refer at any time to the glossary for an explanation of usages of which you are not sure.

The usage items here are of two kinds. There are those which require you to choose between two words, one of which is less acceptable than the other, and there are those which simply should not be used in good writing. You will find frequent mention of the distinction between colloquial and standard usage. This distinction is explained in detail on page 66. In order to use the glossary properly, you should note the meaning of the following terms, which are used to describe items in the glossary:

Wrong: Incorrect English, not to be used at all
Colloquial: Used only in informal speaking and writing
Standard: Used in any situation, informal or formal

The exercises for the glossary, like those for other parts of this book, are to be corrected on the basis of standard usage.

Problems of spelling, such as the difference between *already* and *all ready*, are listed in the spelling chapter (page 619).

accept, except. *Accept* is a verb; it means *to receive. Except* as a verb means *to leave out;* as a preposition it means *excluding.*

EXAMPLES We *accept* your invitation with pleasure.
If you *except* his freshman grades, he has a good scholastic average.
My grades are satisfactory in every subject *except* English.

affect, effect. *Affect* is always a verb; it means *to impress* or *to influence* (frequently the mind or feelings). *Effect* as a verb means *to accomplish, to bring about. Effect* as a noun means the result of some action.

EXAMPLES How did the defeat *affect* the team?
A number of improvements were *effected* (brought about) by the new student council.
Effects (results) of the strike were felt everywhere.

ain't. Avoid this word in speaking and writing.

all the farther, all the faster. Poor English when used to mean *as far as, as fast as.*

WRONG I did not know that was all the faster the car would go.
RIGHT I did not know that was *as fast as* the car would go.

allusion, illusion. An *allusion* is a *reference* to something. An *illusion* is a *mistaken idea.*

EXAMPLES His writing is full of classical *allusions.*
In spite of the evidence, he clung to his *illusions.*

alumni, alumnae. *Alumni* (pronounced ȧ·lŭm′nī) is the plural of *alumnus* (male graduate). *Alumnae* (pronounced ȧ·lŭm′nē) is the plural of *alumna* (female graduate). The graduates of a coeducational school are referred to (as a group) as *alumni*.

EXAMPLES It was a stag party; *alumnae* were not invited. I attended a reunion of Princeton *alumni*. Every high school should keep track of its *alumni*.

amount, number. *Amount* refers to *quantity thought of as a unit*. *Number* refers to *quantity thought of as several things*. Use *amount* with a singular word; use *number* with a plural word.

EXAMPLE This *amount of money* (singular) will buy a large *number of tickets* (plural).

and etc. Since *etc.* is an abbreviation of the Latin *et cetera*, which means *and other things*, you are using *and* twice when you write "and etc." The *etc.* is sufficient.

WRONG We carry a complete stock of newspapers, magazines, stationery, school supplies, tobacco, candy, and etc.

RIGHT We carry a complete stock of newspapers, magazines, stationery, school supplies, tobacco, candy, *etc.*

and which, but which. The expressions *and which*, *but which*, (*and who*, *but who*) should be used only when a *which* or *who clause* precedes them in the sentence.

WRONG The public was shocked by the council's revelations and which the commissioner had tried to suppress.

RIGHT The public was shocked by the revelations *which* the council published *and which* the commissioner had tried to suppress.

RIGHT The public was shocked by the council's revelations *which* the commissioner had tried to suppress.

anywheres, everywheres, nowheres. Use these words and others like them without the final *s*.

EXAMPLE We looked *everywhere*, but the children were *nowhere* in sight.

apt, likely, liable. In colloquial use these words are commonly used interchangeably to express probability, but they do have specific meanings which should be observed in standard English.

Apt means *habitually inclined* or *tending toward something.*

EXAMPLE Being the nervous type, Mr. Johnson is *apt* to worry.

Likely means *probable.*

EXAMPLE He is not *likely* to object to our plans. [It is not *probable* that he will object to our plans.]

Liable means *to be subject to a probable misfortune.*

EXAMPLE If you turn in a false fire alarm, you will be *liable* to arrest.
If you don't do your homework, you are *liable* to fail.

at. Don't use *at* after *where.*

WRONG Where were you staying at?
RIGHT *Where* were you staying?

● EXERCISE 1. The sentences in this exercise contain usage problems presented on the preceding pages in the glossary. Number on your paper from 1 to 20. Write after the proper number on your paper the correct one of the two words in parentheses.

1. She graciously (accepted, excepted) our congratulations.
2. What do you think the (affect, effect) of the decision will be?

3. I did not understand his (allusions, illusions) to my brother.
4. The (alumni, alumnae) of a local school for girls are holding a reunion today.
5. We have sold an unusually large (number, amount) of fountain pens this year.
6. On tour we met friends (everywheres, everywhere) we went.
7. Everyone agreed with me (except, accept) you.
8. His expectation of a large fortune proved to be only an (allusion, illusion).
9. The medicine had no (effect, affect) on him.
10. All (alumni, alumnae) of our high school are very loyal.
11. This is (all the farther, as far as) the bus goes.
12. How did her son's departure (affect, effect) Mrs. French?
13. Everyone (accept, except) George and me finished the assignment on time.
14. You should not (accept, except) money for doing a good deed.
15. Do you know any Vassar (alumnae, alumni)?
16. How was the team (effected, affected) by the loss of their captain?
17. After our panel discussion, the audience asked a large (amount, number) of questions.
18. Milton's poetry is full of obscure classical (allusions, illusions).
19. If you can't (accept, except) my invitation, please let me know.
20. I was surprised at the (affect, effect) of his words on the audience.

because. The use of *because* after *reason is* (*The reason is because* . . .) is common in spoken English and in informal writing, but it is generally avoided in formal writing. In a sentence beginning *The reason is* . . ., the clause following the verb is a noun clause used as a predicate nominative. A noun clause may begin with *that* but not with *because*, which usually introduces an adverb clause.

ACCEPTABLE The reason she refused to go was *that* (not *because*) she had no money.

BETTER She refused to go because she had no money.

being as, being that. Poor English when used for *since* or *because*.

WRONG Being as my mother was away, I had to do the housework.

RIGHT *Because* my mother was away, I had to do the housework.

beside, besides. *Beside* means *by the side of* someone or something. *Besides* means *in addition to.*

EXAMPLES Who sits *beside* you in English class?
Besides my homework, I have to write a letter.

between, among. The distinction in meaning between these words is usually observed in standard written English. Use *between* when you are thinking of *two* items, regardless of whether they are part of a series of more than two.

EXAMPLES The ball went *between* Phil and him.
Do you know the difference *between* a Pomeranian, a Pekingese, and a Chihuahua? [*Between* is correct because the speaker is thinking of one dog and another dog — *two* at a time.]

Use *among* when you are thinking of a group rather than of separate individuals.

EXAMPLES She is never at ease *among* strangers.
Petitions were circulated *among* the voters.

bring, take. Use *bring* when the meaning is to convey something *to the person speaking*. Use *take* when the meaning is to convey something away *from the person speaking*. *Bring* is related to *come; take* is related to *go*.

RIGHT When you come back, *bring* your textbooks.
WRONG I'll bring this note to my father when I go home.
RIGHT I'll *take* this note to my father when I go home.

bursted. Sometimes incorrectly used for the past form of *burst*. The principal parts of *burst* are *burst*, *burst*, (*is*) *bursting*, (*has*) *burst*.

WRONG The angry crowd bursted through the police cordon.
RIGHT The angry crowd *burst* through the police cordon.

bust, busted. Use *broke* or *burst* instead.

WRONG He busted his new bat.
RIGHT He *broke* his new bat.

WRONG The overripe fruit busted open.
RIGHT The overripe fruit *burst* open.

can't hardly, can't scarcely. See *Double negative* (page 179).

can't help but. See *Double negative* (page 179).

could of. Sometimes carelessly written for **could have.** Do not write *of* for *have*. Similar expressions frequently written incorrectly are *ought to of*, *might of*, *must of*.

WRONG He could of warned me about the dangerous roads.
RIGHT He *could have* warned me about the dangerous roads.

data. The plural form of the Latin *datum*. In colloquial English *data* is frequently used, like a collective noun, with a singular pronoun and verb.

COLLOQUIAL This data was collected by the investigating committee.

However, since *data* has only recently become acceptable as a singular word, you will be safer if, in your writing, you use the word as a plural. See **phenomena** and **strata.**

STANDARD *These data were* collected by the investigating committee.

done. Not the past form of *do*. *Done* always needs a helping verb: *has done*, *was done*, *will be done*, etc. The past form of *do* is *did*.

WRONG The doctors done all they could.
RIGHT The doctors *did* all they could.
RIGHT The doctors *had done* all they could.

don't. A contraction of *do not*, *don't* should not be used with a singular noun or the third person of singular pronouns (*it*, *he*, *she*). Use *doesn't*. See page 84.

WRONG It don't matter to me.
RIGHT It *doesn't* matter to me.

effect, affect. See **affect, effect.**

emigrate, immigrate. Emigrate means *to go from a country* to settle elsewhere. Immigrate means *to come into a country* to settle there.

EXAMPLES Residents of crowded countries have been advised to *emigrate* from their homelands to less crowded regions.
His parents *immigrated* to this country in 1910.

etc. See **and etc.**

except, accept. See **accept, except.**

farther. See **all the farther.**

fewer, less. *Fewer* is used to refer to a *number of things*. *Less* is used to refer to a *quantity of one thing*. Use *fewer* if the word it modifies is plural; use *less* if the word it modifies is singular.

EXAMPLES There are *fewer* apples (plural) in this basket.
There is *less* fruit (singular) in this basket.

good, well. *Good* is an adjective. Do not use *good* to modify a verb.

WRONG He dances good.
RIGHT He dances *well.*

For a complete discussion of the uses of *well*, see page 155.

● EXERCISE 2. The sentences in this exercise contain usage problems explained on pages 165–69. Double negatives and the listed items explained elsewhere in this text are not covered. Number on your paper from 1 to 20. Write after the proper number the correct one of the two words in parentheses.

1. The rear axle had (busted, broken).
2. (Beside, Besides) the excellent meals, the hotel provides superb recreational facilities.
3. Pine trees have been planted (between, among) the trees in the grove.
4. I'll (take, bring) your letters to the post office when I go downtown.
5. It took courage to (emigrate, immigrate) from an established home and settle in the American wilderness.
6. There are (fewer, less) students enrolled here this year than last year.
7. Do you intend to divide the work (among, between) the four of us?
8. (Being that, Because) Father was tired, I did the driving.
9. There are (fewer, less) students in the third-period class.
10. Harry does (good, well) enough in the subjects in which he is interested.

11. There has never been a serious disagreement (between, among) Betty, Mary, and me.
12. Please (bring, take) this card to the librarian.
13. Has anyone (beside, besides) you been in the room?
14. You have (fewer, less) friends than she.
15. We (done, did) the lessons according to instructions in the textbook.
16. His schoolwork (don't, doesn't) bother him very much.
17. There were eight people in the plane (beside, besides) the crew.
18. She sang as (good, well) as anyone could with a sore throat.
19. The government found it necessary to discourage (immigration, emigration) into this country.
20. Will someone volunteer to (take, bring) these books to the storeroom?

● EXERCISE 3. This exercise covers all usage items explained in the glossary to this point.

Number on your paper from 1 to 25. If a sentence does not contain a usage error, write a + after the proper number on your paper. If it does contain a usage error, write a 0 and write after the 0 the correct form. It will not be necessary to copy whole sentences.

1. He has less friends than his brother.
2. Being as the mayor was going away, he appointed an assistant to handle emergencies.
3. How will the new laws affect the school?
4. Besides my teachers, my family have been making me study.
5. The reason for the failure of our campaign was because we didn't work hard enough.
6. Mr. Standish threatened to sue the newspaper because of its unflattering allusions to his private life.
7. "Wrong-way" Corrigan made a transatlantic flight and which he claimed was made by mistake.
8. Both women are alumni of a famous women's college.

9. Several disputes arose between members of the committee.
10. Is that all the faster you can work?
11. Please take this brief case to your father.
12. Mrs. Corbin hunted everywheres for her lost book.
13. In the confusion no one knew exactly where he was at.
14. Doctors are studying the effects of this new drug.
15. I found the people full of allusions about the real causes of the strike.
16. I am sure I could of done better on my test if I had had more time.
17. Without family or a job, Francis had no other choice than to emigrate.
18. I hope you will take your family when you come East this summer.
19. As you grow older, you will encounter less opportunities to change jobs.
20. If you can work a farm as good as your brother can, you'll soon be rich.
21. Milton had expected us to use the camera which he had given us and which we had lost.
22. The amount of hot dogs one boy can eat is almost unbelievable.
23. There is growing dissatisfaction among the students.
24. With three jobs offered to him, Paul could not decide which to except.
25. The dance on June 20 was sponsored by the high school alumni.

had of. The *of* is superfluous.

WRONG If I had of known him better, I'd have spoken to him.

RIGHT If I *had known* him better, I'd have spoken to him.

had ought, hadn't ought. Do not use *had* with *ought*.

WRONG You had ought to read more carefully.

RIGHT You *ought* to read more carefully.

WRONG You hadn't ought to stay out so late.
RIGHT You *ought not* to stay out so late.

hardly. See *Double negative* (page 179).

he, she, they, etc. Do not use unnecessary pronouns after a noun. This error is sometimes called the *double subject.*

WRONG My uncle he lives in California.
RIGHT My uncle lives in California.

here, there. See **this here, that there.**

hisself, theirselves. These words are sometimes incorrectly used for *himself, themselves.*

WRONG He did the work hisself.
RIGHT He did the work *himself.*

illusion, allusion. See **allusion, illusion.**

immigrate, emigrate. See **emigrate, immigrate.**

imply, infer. *Imply* means *to suggest something. Infer* means *to interpret* or *get a certain meaning from a remark or an action.*

EXAMPLES The speaker *implied* that he was a friend of the President's.
I *inferred* from the speaker's remarks that he was a friend of the President's.

in, into. In standard usage observe the difference in meaning between these words. *In* means *within; into* means *movement from the outside to the inside.*

STANDARD The meeting will be held *in* the principal's office.
At two o'clock we walked *into* the principal's office.

kind, sort, type. In standard usage the adjectives *this, these, that, those* are made to agree in number with the words *kind, sort, type; this kind, these kinds; that sort, those sorts.*

STANDARD I like *that kind* of orange.
I like *those kinds* of oranges.

kind of, sort of. In standard usage avoid using these expressions to mean *rather* or *somewhat.*

COLLOQUIAL I feel *kind of* tired.
STANDARD I feel *rather* (*somewhat*) tired.

kind of a, sort of a. The *a* is superfluous.

EXAMPLE What *kind of* (not *kind of a*) pen are you using?

lay, lie. See page 128.

leave, let. *Leave* (*left*) means *to go away. Let* means *to allow* or *permit.*

WRONG Leave me work by myself.
RIGHT *Let* me work by myself.

WRONG You should have left him go.
RIGHT You should have *let* him go.

The expressions "Leave me alone" and "Let me alone" are both correct and are commonly used interchangeably. Strictly speaking, "Leave me alone" suggests that you want somebody to go away, leaving you by yourself. "Let me alone" suggests that you want somebody to stop bothering you.

less, fewer. See **fewer, less.**

liable. See **apt, likely, liable.**

lie, lay. See page 128.

like, as. *Like* is a preposition and introduces a prepositional phrase. *As* is usually a conjunction and introduces a subordinate clause.

EXAMPLES He walks *like his father.* [prepositional phrase]
He walks *as his father walks.* [subordinate clause]

Like as a conjunction is commonly heard in informal speech, but it is not acceptable as a conjunction in standard usage.

COLLOQUIAL He arrived at ten like he said he would.
STANDARD He arrived at ten *as* he said he would.

like, as if. *Like* should not be used for *as if* or *as though*, which are conjunctions used to introduce clauses.

WRONG The boys played like they were tired.
RIGHT The boys played *as if* they were tired.

likely. See **apt, likely, liable.**

myself, ourselves. In standard English, pronouns ending in *–self*, *–selves* should not be used as personal pronouns. See page 111.

EXAMPLE Henry and *I* (not *myself*) did our homework together.

● EXERCISE 4. The sentences in this exercise cover usage problems explained in the glossary since the preceding exercises. Number on your paper from 1 to 20. Write after the proper number the correct one of the two words in parentheses.

1. In his novels Dickens (implied, inferred) that the poor were not responsible for their poverty.
2. As the procession came (in, into) the stadium, the crowd roared.

3. The Beals did all the work on the new house (theirselves, themselves).
4. Father objects to (those, that) kind of boys.
5. I merely asked them to (leave, let) me go along.
6. Parents (ought, had ought) to visit school more often.
7. For hours the troops had felt (like, as if) they could march no longer.
8. His comments (inferred, implied) that he did not believe in socialism.
9. Tom finished the job (hisself, himself).
10. (This, These) kind of exercises will drive you crazy.
11. Is an author to blame for what the public (infers, implies) from his work?
12. The team (oughtn't, hadn't ought) to object to playing on Saturday.
13. If you had behaved (like, as) you were supposed to, you would not be in trouble now.
14. The decision was left to Allan and (myself, me).
15. (These, This) (kind, kinds) will be expensive.
16. The coach (left, let) us use the gym after practice.
17. They ought to be home by now, (hadn't, oughtn't) they?
18. I did not mean to (infer, imply) that you are incompetent.
19. (Leave, Let) the girls come with us if they want to.
20. He sang (like, as if) he intended to shatter the windows.

none. *None* may be either singular or plural. See page 82.

of. Do not use *of* unnecessarily. See **could of, had of.**

off of. The *of* is unnecessary.

WRONG Never jump off of a moving train.
RIGHT Never jump *off* a moving train.

Do not use *off* or *off of* for *from.*

WRONG I got some money off Dad.
RIGHT I got some money *from* Dad.

WRONG I borrowed the book off of my English teacher.
RIGHT I borrowed the book *from* my English teacher.

or, nor. Use *or* with *either;* use *nor* with *neither.*

EXAMPLES *Either* John *or* Helen is mistaken.
Neither John *nor* Helen is mistaken.

ought. See **had ought.**

phenomena. If you use this word, use it correctly. *Phenomena* is the plural form of the word *phenomenon.* Do not use it as a singular noun.

EXAMPLES *These* (not *this*) phenomena *are* (not *is*) most interesting.
This *phenomenon* is most interesting.

politics, mathematics, athletics. For the number of these words and other similar words, see pages 89–90.

reason is because. See **because.**

respectfully, respectively. *Respectfully* means *with respect* or *full of respect. Respectively* means *each in the order given.*

EXAMPLES Although hostile, the audience listened *respectfully.*
David Copperfield, Vanity Fair, and *Adam Bede* were written by Dickens, Thackeray, and George Eliot *respectively.*

Reverend, Honorable. These titles should never be used with a person's last name alone. The word *the* commonly precedes the titles.

WRONG Reverend Hiller, the Reverend Hiller, Honorable Wagner
RIGHT the Reverend Kenneth Hiller, the Reverend K. H. Hiller, the Reverend Mr. Hiller, the

Reverend Dr. Hiller, the Honorable Robert F. Wagner

rise, raise. See page 133.

same, said, such. Avoid such artificial uses of these words as the following:

The crew worked all day on the boat and had *same* ready to sail by sundown.

We spent our summers at my uncle's ranch, and we became very fond of *said* uncle.

Jerry always wants me to let him copy my homework, but I don't approve of *such.*

says. Commonly used incorrectly for *said.*

WRONG Jane stopped me and says, "I know where you're going."

RIGHT Jane stopped me and *said,* "I know where you're going."

scarcely. See *Double negative* (page 179).

shall, will. The distinction between these words is no longer important. They are used interchangeably.

sit, set. See page 132.

so. Because this word is usually overworked, avoid it in your writing whenever you can.

POOR The weather cleared, so we put up the sail and headed out to sea.

BETTER When the weather cleared, we put up the sail and headed out to sea.

BETTER Because the weather cleared, we put up the sail and headed out to sea.

In writing, do not use *so* for *so that.*

EXAMPLE We worked hard in the morning *so that* (not *so*) we could go to the game in the afternoon.

some, somewhat. In standard usage use *somewhat* rather than *some* as an adverb.

STANDARD Conditions in Europe next year will be *somewhat* (not *some*) better.

strata. Plural form of the Latin word *stratum*. Use it as a plural.

WRONG This strata is sandstone.
RIGHT *These strata are* sandstone.

than, then. Do not confuse these words. *Than* is a conjunction:

Our new plan is better *than* our old one.

Then is an adverb telling when:

Then the car broke down.

them. Never use *them* as an adjective. Use *these* or *those*.

WRONG Have you seen them new dresses at Lloyd's?
RIGHT Have you seen *those* new dresses at Lloyd's?

this here, that there. The *here* and the *there* are unnecessary.

WRONG This here book is easy to read.
RIGHT *This* book is easy to read.

these kind, those kind. See **kind, sort, type.**

ways. Sometimes incorrectly used for *way* in referring to distance.

WRONG We decided to explore a little ways down the path.
RIGHT We decided to explore a little *way* down the path.

well, good. See page 155.

when, where. Do not use *when* or *where* in writing a definition.

WRONG A book report is when you write an essay on a book you have read.
RIGHT A book report is an essay written on a book you have read.

WRONG An atlas is where maps are printed.
RIGHT An atlas is a book of maps.

where. Do not use *where* for *that.*

WRONG I read where you are going to move away.
RIGHT I read *that* you are going to move away.

where . . . at. See **at.**

which, that, who. *Which* should be used to refer to *things only. That* may be used to refer to *both things and people. Who* should be used to refer to *people only.*

EXAMPLES This is a book *which* (*that*) you would enjoy.
There is a girl *who* (not *which*) has talent.
There is a girl *that* has talent.

who, whom. See page 106.

THE DOUBLE NEGATIVE

A double negative is a construction in which two negative words are used where one is sufficient. Most double negatives are poor English, in both colloquial and standard usage.

can't hardly, can't scarcely. The words *hardly* and *scarcely* are negatives. They should never be used with the negative *not.*

WRONG I can't hardly tell the difference between this year's cars and last year's.
RIGHT I *can hardly* tell the difference between this year's cars and last year's.

WRONG There wasn't scarcely enough food for everyone.
RIGHT There *was scarcely* enough food for everyone.

can't help but. In standard English avoid this double negative.

STANDARD I *can't help admiring* (not *can't help but admire*) his courage.

haven't but, haven't only. In certain uses *but* and *only* are negatives. Avoid using them with *not.*

WRONG We hadn't but a few cents in our pockets.
RIGHT We *had but* a few cents in our pockets.

WRONG We hadn't only a few cents in our pockets.
RIGHT We *had only* a few cents in our pockets.

no, nothing, none. Not to be used with another negative word.

WRONG Haven't you no ticket?
RIGHT *Haven't you a* ticket?
RIGHT *Have* you *no* ticket?

WRONG She hasn't nothing to do.
RIGHT She *has nothing* to do.
RIGHT She *hasn't anything* to do.

WRONG He didn't give me none.
RIGHT He *gave* me *none.*
RIGHT He *didn't give* me *any.*

● EXERCISE 5. The sentences in this exercise cover usage problems explained in the glossary since the preceding exercises. Number on your paper from 1 to 20. Write after the proper number the correct one of the two words in parentheses.

1. You may disagree with your teachers if you do so (respectfully, respectively).
2. You (can, can't) hardly afford to go to the movies every week.
3. Prospects for peace looked (some, somewhat) better.

4. Mary lives only a little (way, ways) from here.
5. (Them, Those) cars have two carburetors.
6. After he had heard our side of the story he (says, said) we were all wrong.
7. We (haven't, have) no reason to question your honesty.
8. Neither the steamship (or, nor) the railroad has been outmoded yet.
9. We were only a little (ways, way) from home when the accident happened.
10. (This, These) strange phenomena puzzled the geologists.
11. The refugees (could, couldn't) hardly find food and shelter.
12. True democracy has always been handicapped by (this, these) social strata.
13. I (have, haven't) only a short time for my homework.
14. Jack, Phil, and I had trouble with the ticket agent, the conductor, and the porter (respectively, respectfully).
15. He would neither let me go with him (or, nor) let me follow him in my car.
16. We (had, hadn't) but one choice to make.
17. I acquired a great respect for the Romans (whom, which) we studied in Latin class.
18. The superintendent said there wasn't (any, no) reason for closing school.
19. He never works any harder (than, then) necessary.
20. The boys insisted they (had, hadn't) nothing to do with the crime.

● EXERCISE 6. The sentences in this exercise cover usage problems explained in the entire glossary. Number on your paper from 1 to 25. If a sentence does not contain a usage error, write a + on your paper after the proper number. If a sentence does contain a usage error, write a 0. Your teacher may ask you to write the correct form after each 0.

1. Mr. Sims had told me he would take my letter to you.
2. Doris has made a large amount of friends.

3. War usually results from these causes and which the world seems powerless to remove.
4. The applause showed how deeply the music had affected the audience.
5. There are less reasons for alarm now than there were a year ago.
6. I can't hardly read your writing.
7. The trustees did not accept his resignation.
8. Driving in the mountains, you would of had a bad time with those brakes.
9. Order a gross of those kind.
10. His talk implied that he favored the Labor party.
11. It is later then you think.
12. Unfortunately, we cannot except your invitation.
13. Poetry is written in many forms such as the ballad, the sonnet, the ode, the elegy, the simple lyric, and etc.
14. The reason Charles resigned was because he did not see any opportunity for advancement.
15. Leave me give you a little good advice.
16. Beside his great interest in photography, Frank is an enthusiastic artist.
17. I have little sympathy for that kind of people.
18. Forty miles an hour is all the faster his jalopy will go.
19. The volcano had been acting like it might erupt.
20. Everywheres the king went he was welcome.
21. Dichotomy is when a thing is divided into two parts.
22. What effect will the new law have on taxes?
23. There isn't nothing else to do.
24. The mayor's speech inferred that the water shortage was serious.
25. Being as the winter is nearly over, the stores are having sales on heavy apparel.

PART THREE

WRITING CLEAR SENTENCES

CHAPTER 11

Co-ordination and Subordination

MAKE CLEAR THE RELATIONSHIP BETWEEN IDEAS IN YOUR SENTENCES

Co-ordinate Ideas

A single sentence usually contains more than one idea. The ideas in a sentence may be equal in rank or unequal in rank. Ideas that are equal in rank are *co-ordinate*. (*Co-* means "equal"; *-ordinate* means "kind" or "rank"; hence *co-ordinate* means "of equal kind or rank.")

CO-ORDINATE IDEAS **Mr. Carter is an architect, and Mr. Murphy is a contractor.**

When, as in the preceding sentence, co-ordinate (equal) ideas are expressed in clauses, the clauses are *co-ordinate clauses*.

When ideas in a sentence are unequal in rank, the ideas of lower rank are subordinate. (*Sub-* means "under" or "lower.") If the idea of lower rank is expressed in a clause, the clause is a *subordinate* clause.[1] The main idea of the sentence is expressed in a *main clause*.

[1] For a more detailed explanation of subordinate clauses see pages 47–56.

EXAMPLES **The pilot, who was a veteran flyer, brought his crippled plane down safely.** [Main clause: *The pilot brought his crippled plane down safely;* subordinate clause: *who was a veteran flyer.*]

After you have done your homework, you may listen to the radio. [Main clause: *you may listen to the radio;* subordinate clause: *After you have done your homework.*]

CLEAR RELATIONSHIP BETWEEN CO–ORDINATE IDEAS

The relationship between co-ordinate ideas (equal in rank) is made clear by means of the word used to connect the two ideas. Different connectives may be used to express different relationships. The common kinds of relationship between co-ordinate clauses are *addition*, *contrast*, *choice*, and *result.*

ADDITION I wrote to him, **and** he wrote to me.
CONTRAST I wrote to him, **but** he did not write to me.
CHOICE You write to him, **or** I will write to him.
RESULT I wrote to him; **therefore** he wrote to me.

A good writer chooses his connectives carefully. He makes certain that the connectives he chooses will express exactly the relationship he intends between the ideas in the sentence. In order to avoid a monotonous style he also uses a variety of connectives.

Study the following lists of connectives before attempting the exercises which follow.

1. *Connectives used to* **add** *one idea to another*

also	both . . . and	moreover
and	furthermore	then
besides	likewise	

2. *Connectives used to* **contrast** *one idea with another*

but	nevertheless	yet
however	still	

3. *Connectives used to express* **choice** *between one idea and another*

either . . . or	or, nor
neither . . . nor	otherwise

4. *Connectives used to express a* **result**

accordingly	hence
consequently	therefore

11a. Make clear the relationship between the ideas in co-ordinate clauses by using connectives which express the relationship exactly.

If the wrong connective is used, the relationship between the ideas will not be clear. The connectives in the following *not-clear* sentences were poorly chosen.

NOT CLEAR Mr. Bothwell took a long vacation, *and* his health did not improve. [Idea is *contrast*.]

CLEAR Mr. Bothwell took a long vacation, **but** his health did not improve.

NOT CLEAR The veterans spent a year in the hospital, *but* they emerged entirely well. [Idea is *result*.]

CLEAR The veterans spent a year in the hospital; **consequently,** they emerged entirely well.

● EXERCISE 1. Number on your paper from 1 to 20. Read each sentence thoughtfully. Determine the logical relationship between the two clauses and write after the proper number on your paper what this relationship is: *addition*, *contrast*, *choice*, or *result*. Then write the appropriate one of the two connectives given in parentheses — the word which will make unmistakably clear the relationship between the clauses.

Give the correct punctuation mark with each connective.[2]

EXAMPLE The demand exceeded the supply (furthermore, nevertheless) prices remained the same.
contrast ; nevertheless

1. School was dismissed at one o'clock (and, but) nobody went home.
2. Bill was seriously injured in yesterday's practice (moreover, therefore) he will not be able to play in the game today.
3. Jimmy played right end (and, but) I played left end on the varsity.
4. Deliver the shipment by the 25th (and, or) I will cancel my order!
5. Math has always been my hardest subject (and, but) I have never failed a math test.
6. In an auditorium of this size, you must speak louder (hence, otherwise) your audience will not be able to hear you.
7. My brother spent three years in the Navy (but, and) he never went aboard a ship.
8. The San Francisco airport reported that it was closed in by fog (however, accordingly) we had to stay overnight in Phoenix.
9. Paul hadn't written his theme (and, consequently) he failed the course.
10. The oil burner had stopped during the night (hence, but) the house was cold when we awoke.
11. We had heard the assignment (but, and) we hadn't understood it.
12. We were to be marked for neatness (nevertheless, therefore) we took greater pains than usual.
13. We returned late; the rented canoe was a wreck (con-

[2] When used to join co-ordinate clauses, the words *and*, *but*, *yet*, *or*, *nor* are usually preceded by a comma.

When used to join co-ordinate clauses, the words *besides*, *likewise*, *furthermore*, *moreover*, *however*, *nevertheless*, *otherwise*, *consequently*, *therefore*, *accordingly* are usually preceded by a semicolon.

sequently, but) the lifeguard said he'd like to see us after swim period.

14. Our hearts were in our boots (accordingly, nevertheless) we braved his wrath and took our medicine.
15. We had planned on going to town that afternoon (hence, furthermore) we were slightly annoyed at being kept in camp.
16. The head counselor warned us to take better care of the property of others (furthermore, but) he said he would send our fathers a bill.
17. The bill which Father received was quite unexpected (nevertheless, therefore) it took him some time to recover from the shock.
18. Sid's father received a bill too (and, but) he was just as surprised as my father.
19. We felt very lucky to be allowed to stay at camp (furthermore, however) our parents offered to buy us a canoe of our own.
20. Parents are put to a great deal of trouble and expense by their sons (accordingly, nevertheless) they are usually patient and generous with us.

Main and Subordinate Ideas

The subordinate ideas in a sentence are frequently given in adverb and adjective clauses. In writing, you must use these clauses in such a way that their relationship to the ideas in the main clause will be clear.

SUBORDINATE ADVERB CLAUSES

The relationship between the idea in a subordinate adverb clause and the idea in a main clause is made clear by the subordinating conjunction which introduces the subordinate clause. The common kinds of relationship between subordinate adverb clauses and main clauses are *time*, *cause* or *reason*, *purpose* or *result*, and *condition*.

TIME Several guests arrived **before** *we were ready.*

CAUSE OR REASON We stopped **because** *the light was red.*

PURPOSE OR RESULT **We came early so that *we wouldn't miss anything.***

CONDITION ***If you pass the examination,*** **you will pass the course.** [The clause states *under what condition* you will pass the course.]

Study the following lists of subordinating conjunctions before attempting the exercises which follow.

1. *Subordinating conjunctions used to express* **time**

after	until	whenever
before	when	while
since		

2. *Subordinating conjunctions used to express* **cause** *or* ***reason***

as	since
because	whereas

3. *Subordinating conjunctions used to express* **purpose** *or* ***result***

that in order that so that

4. *Subordinating conjunctions used to express* **condition**

although [3] provided unless if

11b. Make clear the relationship between subordinate adverb clauses and main clauses by selecting subordinating conjunctions which express the relationship exactly.

● EXERCISE 2. Number on your paper from 1 to 20. From the preceding lists choose a subordinating

[3] You will find it easy to use *although* correctly if you think of its meaning as "in spite of the fact that."

EXAMPLE Although (in spite of the fact that) it was raining, we went to the game. [The clause states the *condition* under which we went to the game.]

11b

conjunction to fill the blank in each sentence and write it after the proper number on your paper. Make sure the conjunction you choose fits logically the meaning of the sentence. After the conjunction tell what relationship it expresses: *cause* or *reason*, *condition*, *purpose* or *result*, *time*.

1. —— Jane wants to go with us, she must be ready to leave at 10 o'clock.
2. —— our team had not won a game all season, no one expected them to win their final game.
3. —— our holiday was a long one, we managed to do only half the things we had planned.
4. —— I had read his latest book, I changed my opinion of him.
5. —— many boys and girls do not know what to do after graduating, the guidance teachers help them to decide.
6. John was advised to take a post-graduate course —— he could prepare for West Point.
7. We ought to wait —— the boys get home.
8. We stood in line all morning —— we could get good seats for the game.
9. —— Colonel Brandon has traveled widely in the Orient, he knows a great deal about China and Japan.
10. I will write a letter to you —— I receive one from you.
11. —— George is older than I, he is in the same grade.
12. He said he would take the job —— the pay was high enough.
13. —— the rain was freezing on the windshield, we had to stop frequently.
14. We will eat dinner at the hotel —— you prefer some other place.
15. —— I had become better acquainted with Alex, I liked him very much.
16. Halstrom's store is being enlarged —— it will accommodate a cafeteria.
17. —— our train is going to be late, I will try to send you a telegram.

18. —— ground transportation was temporarily cut off by the storm, the city had to be supplied by air.
19. The President called a special session of Congress —— emergency legislation could be passed.
20. —— the judge had heard the testimony, he ordered a new trial.

● EXERCISE 3. Join the statements in each group into one sentence in which the relationship between the subordinate clause and the main clause will be shown by a logical subordinating conjunction. You will have to decide what the relationship is — *cause* or *reason*, *condition*, *purpose* or *result*, *time*. Be sure to place a comma after an adverb clause coming first in the sentence.

EXAMPLE Sally did her best.
She was unable to win the prize.
Although Sally did her best, she was unable to win the prize.

1. The bus broke down.
We were all tardy.
2. He will invest his money with you.
You can prove that the investment is safe.
3. We raised our prices.
Our business increased.
4. He wanted to graduate in January.
He could join the Navy.
5. The field was muddy and our team was very light.
We lost the game.
6. You train rigorously.
You will be able to do well in cross country.
7. We sat in the last row.
We were able to hear perfectly.
8. The school issued new uniforms.
The team would look well in the big game.
9. She was ill.
She insisted on going ahead with the show.

10. I had not had any foreign language.
    I was refused admission to the college of my choice.
11. The committee members could not agree.
    The whole matter was referred to the president.
12. The president took the responsibility.
    He wanted to settle the matter himself.
13. He decided to carry the issue before the entire club.
    Everyone could express an opinion.
14. There was a great deal of talk.
    Nothing was decided.
15. A decision is reached today.
    The donors will not give us the money.
16. The City Council offered to give us money for a club house.
    We would let the public use it.
17. We had never admitted the public to our meetings.
    We didn't want to admit them to our club house.
18. We would not lose the chance for a new club house.
    Some of us favored admitting the public.
19. I agreed with those in favor of admitting the public.
    I sympathized with the others.
20. No agreement was reached.
    The money went to another club.

SUBORDINATE ADJECTIVE CLAUSES

The subordinate clauses in the preceding exercises are *adverb* clauses. Subordinate *adjective* clauses are especially helpful in making clear the relationship between sentence ideas because they permit a writer to emphasize one idea above another.[4] A writer may, for instance, wish to express the following ideas in one sentence: *Abraham Lincoln became President of the United States; he was a self-educated man.* The writer, for his purposes, wishes to emphasize the fact that Lincoln became President. He emphasizes this idea

[4] Adjective clauses may begin with *who*, *whom*, *whose*, *which*, *that*, and *where*.

by placing it in the main clause of his sentence and by placing the other idea in a *subordinate adjective clause.*

Abraham Lincoln, who was a self-educated man, **became President of the United States.**

On the other hand, for a different purpose, the writer may wish to change his emphasis from one of these ideas to the other. He can do this by reversing the positions of the ideas.

Abraham Lincoln, who became President of the United States, **was a self-educated man.**

11c. Make clear the relative emphasis to be given ideas in a complex sentence by placing the idea you wish to emphasize in the main clause and by placing subordinate ideas in subordinate clauses.

● EXERCISE 4. Change the emphasis in each of the following sentences by placing in the main clause the idea which is now in the subordinate clause and by placing in the subordinate clause the idea which is now in the main clause.

1. Mr. Briggs, who was a famous lawyer, was defeated in the election.
2. Harvard University, which was founded in 1636, is the oldest university in the United States.
3. The plane which took us to Chicago was very comfortable.
4. Our friends, who had agreed to meet us at six o'clock, did not show up.
5. The old elm which stood at the edge of the park was destroyed by a hurricane in 1954.
6. The canoe trip, which was one of the highlights of our camping season, lasted two weeks.
7. The committee chairman, who was appointed by the president, presides over all meetings.

8. My dog, which is a beautiful Irish setter, was given to me by Uncle Al.
9. This classroom, which is the largest in the school, will accommodate nearly one hundred pupils.
10. The idea that was proposed by Jerry was liked most by the council.

CORRECTING FAULTY CO-ORDINATION

Faulty co-ordination occurs when two unequal ideas are placed in co-ordinate clauses as though they were of equal importance.

FAULTY CO-ORDINATION (ideas of unequal rank) **The Governor was a native of Ohio, and he was elected for a third term.**

The two ideas in this sentence are vastly different. It is unlikely that a writer would wish to give them equal rank. The faulty co-ordination can be corrected by placing one of the ideas in a subordinate position. Which idea the writer puts in the subordinate clause will depend on his purpose.

FAULTY CO-ORDINATION CORRECTED **The Governor,** who was a native of Ohio, **was elected for a third term.**

or

The Governor, who was elected for a third term, **was a native of Ohio.**

11d. Faulty co-ordination may be corrected by placing ideas of lesser emphasis in a subordinate position. An idea may be given less emphasis by being expressed in a subordinate clause or a modifying phrase or an appositive.[5]

[5] For the use of subordination in achieving sentence variety, see page 251. For the use of subordination in correcting stringy sentences and choppy sentences, see page 257.

(1) Subordination may be accomplished by means of a subordinate clause.

FAULTY CO-ORDINATION The books are on the new-book shelf, and they may be borrowed for a week.

CORRECTED BY AN ADJECTIVE CLAUSE **The books** which are on the new-book shelf **may be borrowed for a week.**

CORRECTED BY AN ADVERB CLAUSE If the books are on the new-book shelf, **they may be borrowed for a week.**

● EXERCISE 5. Clarify the relationship between ideas in the following examples of faulty co-ordination by placing one of the ideas in a subordinate clause, either an adverb clause or an adjective clause. Choose carefully the subordinating conjunctions which introduce your adverb clauses.

1. There are only two senators from each state, and the Senate is smaller than the House of Representatives.
2. Columbia University was originally King's College, and it is situated in New York City.
3. The constant roar of machinery nearly deafened us, and we enjoyed our trip through the factory.
4. The heavy fog made flying hazardous, and it did not lift until noon.
5. The highest respect is due the flag of our country, and it should be flown above all other flags on the same flagpole.
6. The school needs another driver-training car, and more students can learn how to drive.
7. A Future Teachers of America Club was formed at our school, and the number of students planning to be teachers nearly doubled.
8. Our milk is delivered at our door daily, and it comes from farms 500 miles away.
9. The junior college occupies the same building as the high school, and it has an enrollment of 300 students.
10. You do the work satisfactorily, and I will pay you handsomely.

11d

(2) Subordination may be accomplished by means of a modifying phrase.

FAULTY CO-ORDINATION The house is at the end of the street, and it is modernistic in design.

CORRECTED BY A MODIFYING PHRASE **The house** at the end of the street **is modernistic in design.**

(3) Subordination may be accomplished by means of an appositive.

An appositive is a word, with or without modifiers, which follows a noun or pronoun and helps to explain it.

FAULTY CO-ORDINATION Mr. Fitch is the manager of the store, and he is tall and handsome.

CORRECTED BY AN APPOSITIVE **Mr. Fitch,** the manager of the store, **is tall and handsome.**

● EXERCISE 6. Correct the faulty co-ordination in the following sentences in the ways prescribed.

Correct by a subordinate clause

1. Peter is going to college in the West, and he came in yesterday to say good-by.
2. Franklin was a scientist as well as a statesman, and he invented a new kind of stove.
3. I didn't understand how to do the assignment, and I didn't have my homework done.
4. A newspaper costs far more than the public pays for it, and it is supported by the sale of advertising space.
5. The American Constitution went into effect in 1789, and it is one of the great governmental documents of the world.

Correct by a modifying phrase

6. The car had red wheels, and it won the first race.
7. We were delighted to receive a bushel of oranges, and they came from Florida.
8. He told me to look in the unabridged dictionary, and it was on his desk.

9. The pocket knife had two dull blades, and it was the only weapon the shipwrecked men had.
10. The truck was full of explosives, and it narrowly missed a collision with an oil truck.

Correct by an appositive

11. Mr. Shapiro is the custodian of our building, and he came to this country only three years ago.
12. Uncle Bill is my favorite uncle, and he has invited me to spend the summer on his ranch.
13. The violin was an old instrument with a beautiful tone, and it belonged to my grandfather.
14. This plane is the fastest passenger plane in the world, and it will take you to Europe in record time.
15. His new book is a volume of poetry, and it received very favorable reviews.

SUMMARY

(1) Make clear the relationship between ideas in a sentence by using connectives which express the relationship exactly.

(2) Correct faulty co-ordination by placing ideas of lesser emphasis in a subordinate position. Use a subordinate clause or a modifying phrase or an appositive.

● EXERCISE 7. The relationship between ideas in the following sentences is not clear either because the conjunctions used are not exact, or because the sentences contain faulty co-ordination. Improve the sentences by rewriting them. Some may be improved in more than one way.

1. Mr. Greenberg was a high school coach for many years, and he is now coaching college teams in Ohio.
2. Representatives came from more than fifty countries, and they met in the United Nations Building in New York City.
3. The title of the book was very interesting, and the book itself was very dull.

4. Although our bus was late, we missed our train.
5. He wanted to go to college, and he studied hard during his senior year in high school.
6. Because their principal crop was potatoes and the potato season was poor, the farmers managed to avoid going into debt.
7. Miss Lang had not directed many plays, and she knew how to manage an inexperienced cast.
8. Helen may go to Wellesley next year, and she may go to Barnard.
9. Mitchel Field is on Long Island, and it is an Army air base.
10. Mr. Carter is a very fine man, and he is pastor of a very active church.
11. Carl has taken piano lessons for only three years, and he is already a good pianist.
12. You want me to help you with your homework, and you must help me with the dishes.
13. Mr. Stark has never paid back the money he borrowed, and he wants me to lend him more.
14. We waited on the corner for an hour, and the bus didn't come.
15. The Commercial High School is a large stone building on Market Street, and it is attended by students from all over the city.
16. Mr. Armstrong has been selling advertising for many years, and he has been made advertising director of the *Herald*.
17. Stewart Harrison was a famous detective, and he could not solve the arsenic murder case.
18. I am going to the airport to meet a friend, and he is coming from Chicago.
19. Professor Drake has been head of the chemistry department for twenty years, and he died yesterday.
20. The body of the new cars has been brought out flush with the fenders, and there is more room for passengers.

CHAPTER 12

Clear Reference

GIVE PRONOUNS CLEAR ANTECEDENTS

Sentence ideas are sometimes confused by the use of a pronoun which does not have a clear antecedent.

A pronoun is a word used in place of a noun. A pronoun has no definite meaning in itself; it has definite meaning only when the reader knows what noun it stands for. For instance, the pronoun *it* has no clear meaning in the sentence *It was too heavy for him*, unless the reader knows what noun *it* stands for. When the reader knows that *it* stands for a bag of cement, the pronoun has clear meaning: *When Harry tried to lift the bag of cement, he found it was too heavy for him.*

The word or idea to which a pronoun refers is its *antecedent*. In the following sentences the antecedents of the pronouns as well as the pronouns are in heavy type.

I invited **Jack** and **Katherine**, but **they** could not come.

The **work** was tedious, but **it** was not difficult.

The Masons bought a home in **Lake Park, which** is on the outskirts of the city.

Showing me a new **book** in a scarlet jacket, the clerk asked, "Have you read **this**?"

12a. A pronoun must refer clearly to the right antecedent. Avoid *ambiguous* reference, gen- 12a

***eral* reference, and *weak* reference. In formal writing, avoid indefinite use of the pronouns *it*, *they*, and *you*.**

AMBIGUOUS REFERENCE

(1) Avoid *ambiguous reference*. Ambiguous reference occurs when a pronoun refers confusingly to two antecedents so that the reader does not know at once which antecedent is meant.

AMBIGUOUS Helen told Marian that **she** was too young for college.

In this sentence, the pronoun *she* could refer either to Helen or to Marian. The fault can be corrected either by replacing the pronoun with a noun or by quoting Helen's exact words.

CLEAR Helen told Marian that **Marian** was too young for college.

CLEAR Helen said to Marian, "**You** are too young for college."

AMBIGUOUS George was talking to Bob, and **he** looked very unhappy.

CLEAR George was talking to Bob, **who** looked very unhappy.

CLEAR When he was talking to Bob, **George** looked very unhappy.

AMBIGUOUS As soon as the students had left the classrooms, the custodians cleaned **them**.

CLEAR As soon as the students had left, the custodians cleaned the **classrooms**.

There is no *one* way to correct ambiguous references. Any way is satisfactory, provided the meaning is made unmistakably clear and the sentence is not awkward. Sometimes the best way is to change the structure of the sentence.

AMBIGUOUS The President appointed Senator Moore as chairman of the new committee because **he** was interested in the committee's work.

CLEAR **The President**, who was interested in the committee's work, appointed Senator Moore as chairman.

CLEAR Because **Senator Moore** was interested in the committee's work, the President appointed him as chairman.

● EXERCISE 1. Find the ambiguous pronoun in each of the following sentences. Make the sentence clear either by revising it or by replacing the faulty pronoun with a noun.

1. Miss Barton told Jean that she might have to stay after school.
2. Phil was arguing with Jim about his English assignment.
3. The bus driver told one of the passengers that he didn't know the route very well.
4. We unpacked our dishes from the barrels and then returned them to the moving company.
5. When the accountant was studying the treasurer's report, he became very much alarmed.
6. The passengers on both trains were annoyed at being late. They had jumped the track just outside of Toledo.
7. Senator Mills conferred with the Secretary of State when he was touring the East.
8. Our job was to remove the labels from the old bottles and wash them.
9. The policeman chased the thief for several blocks; whereupon, he hid in an abandoned cellar.
10. International good will is essential to successful international trade. It will help to make a peaceful world.

GENERAL REFERENCE

(2) Avoid *general reference*. General reference occurs when a pronoun refers confusingly to a general idea

which is vague to the reader. The antecedent is expressed in terms which are too general to be clear.

The pronouns *which*, *this*, *that*, and *it* are commonly used in a general way.

GENERAL The boys wore ski boots to their classes **which** the principal disapproved of.

In this sentence the pronoun *which* refers to the general idea, *the wearing of ski boots to class;* furthermore, the pronoun is so placed that it appears to refer to *classes*. The writer did not mean that the principal disapproved of the classes. The sentence can be corrected by revision.

CLEAR The principal disapproved of **the boys' wearing** ski boots to their classes.

In the following example, the pronoun *this* does not have a clear antecedent.

GENERAL The trip to town was strenuous. The car broke down; a tire blew out; and Father sat on the basket of eggs. **This** put us in a poor frame of mind.

The pronoun *this* should be replaced with a definite noun, making clear the reference to a number of misfortunes.

CLEAR **These misfortunes** put us in a poor frame of mind.

In the next example, the pronoun *it* does not have a clear antecedent. A definite noun makes the meaning clear.

GENERAL Great ships were moving slowly up the harbor; tugs and ferryboats scurried in and out among them; here and there a white cabin cruiser sliced sharply through the blue water under the suspension bridge. **It** was thrilling to a farm boy.

CLEAR **The sight** was thrilling to a farm boy.

Although general reference can sometimes be corrected by merely substituting a noun for the unclear pronoun, as in the two preceding examples, the usual method of correction is to revise the entire sentence.

GENERAL **During class Tom tapped his pencil on the desk, scraped his feet on the floor, and dropped his books. This annoyed the teacher.**

CLEAR **Tom annoyed the teacher by tapping his pencil on the desk, scraping his feet on the floor, and dropping his books.**

● EXERCISE 2. The following sentences contain examples of the general reference of pronouns. Revise the sentences or replace the general pronouns with nouns. Make the meaning clear.

1. He is a conscientious, hard-working man with an engaging personality, but it doesn't make him any richer.
2. The end of the war finally came after Japan had been threatened with more atomic bombs, and after Russia had declared war on her. This proved to the Japanese the hopelessness of their plight.
3. A number of people gathered around the speaker and his microphone, which was due to curiosity.
4. I enjoyed the author's style and the type of characters he wrote about. It made me want to read his other books.
5. Father Meyer came to the house daily, from which a sturdy friendship grew.
6. A great deal of effort went into planning the expedition, hiring the right sort of men, and anticipating every emergency, which accounts for the success of the undertaking.
7. Chicago stretches along the shore of Lake Michigan, which makes a beautiful shore drive possible.
8. School gymnasiums will be open every Saturday during the winter, and school playgrounds will be supervised during the summer months. Other school facilities, such as the shops, the photography rooms, the little theater,

will be available to hobbyists. This will cost money, but the Board of Education thinks the public will be glad to meet the expense.

9. Even students with season tickets had to pay admission to the post-season games. We thought it wasn't fair.
10. Henry's mother forced him to have tea with the ladies when he would much rather have gone swimming and been spared the discomfort of the hot coat and tight necktie, which made him no social asset at all.

WEAK REFERENCE

(3) Avoid *weak reference.* Weak reference occurs when the antecedent has not been expressed but exists only in the writer's mind.

WEAK We spent the day aboard a fishing boat, but we didn't catch a single **one.**

In this sentence there is no antecedent of the pronoun *one*. The adjective *fishing* is not the antecedent, since it is fish, not fishing, that *one* refers to. The writer meant the pronoun to stand for the noun *fish.*

CLEAR We spent the day aboard a fishing boat, but we didn't catch a single **fish.**

CLEAR We spent the day aboard a fishing boat trying to catch some **fish**, but we didn't catch a single **one.**

In other words, the antecedent of a pronoun should be a noun. When the antecedent is "hidden" in a modifier or a verb form, the reference is weak.

WEAK The people want honest public servants, but **that** has not always been a virtue of politicians.

In this sentence the antecedent should be the noun *honesty*, but the noun is "hidden" in the adjective *honest.* The sentence may be corrected by replacing the weak pronoun with a noun.

CLEAR The people want honest public servants, but **honesty** has not always been a virtue of politicians.

In the next sentence, the antecedent of *it* should be the noun *writing*, which is "hidden" in the verb *wrote*.

WEAK Louis wrote whenever he could find the time, but none of **it** was ever published.

CLEAR Louis wrote whenever he could find the time, but none of **his writing** was ever published.

In the next sentence the pronoun *they* does not have an antecedent. The writer had *witches* in mind as the antecedent, but he did not use the word at all.

WEAK He is a great believer in witchcraft, but he doubts that **they** ride on broomsticks.

CLEAR He is a great believer in **witches**, but he doubts that **they** ride on broomsticks.

CLEAR He is a great believer in witchcraft, but he doubts that **witches** ride on broomsticks.

Weak reference may be corrected by replacing the weak pronoun with a noun, or by giving the pronoun a clear and sensible antecedent.

● EXERCISE 3. Correct the weak reference in each of the following sentences.

1. He owns several stables, but he never rides any of them himself.
2. The jewelry salesman tried to make us believe they were genuine.
3. He had written a great deal of poetry during his life, but he had never had any of them published.
4. After watching the fireman's daring exploits, all the little boys in the crowd decided that that is what they would be.
5. He is a very wealthy man, but he never spends any of it.
6. When we finally reached a gas station, the attendant told us he didn't have any.
7. She likes Indian lore although she has never seen one.
8. When we boarded the bus for Tulsa, we learned that it would take fourteen hours.

9. Although the soda jerker is a friend of mine, he won't give me any free ones.
10. Snow plows worked all night clearing the highway. In places it was several feet deep.

INDEFINITE USE OF PRONOUNS

(4) In writing avoid indefinite use of the pronouns *it*, *they*, and *you*.

The indefinite use of these pronouns in sentences like the following occurs in ordinary conversation but is not acceptable in writing.

INDEFINITE In the final chapter **it** implies that the hero died a martyr's death.

BETTER **The final chapter** implies that the hero died a martyr's death.

INDEFINITE On planes that are in flight at mealtime, **they** serve meals without charge.

BETTER On planes that are in flight at mealtime, **meals** are served without charge.

INDEFINITE In some countries, **you** don't dare express political views openly.

BETTER In some countries, **the people** don't dare express political views openly.

▶ NOTE: The expressions *it is raining*, *it seems*, *it is late* are, of course, entirely correct.

● EXERCISE 4. The sentences in this exercise contain examples of ambiguous, general, and weak reference. There are some examples of the indefinite use of *it*, *they*, and *you*. Correct the sentences either by replacing a faulty pronoun with a noun, or by revising the sentence. Make the meaning unmistakably clear.

1. Placing the rockets on planes will increase their effectiveness.
2. The radiator was leaking badly; it ran all over the garage floor.

3. Our new house is very much like our old one, which is what we asked the architect to do.
4. In the cabin he reloaded his gun. In those days this might mean the difference between life and death.
5. He overcame his hip injury which doctors had said was impossible.
6. His spelling and sentence structure are not good, but most of it is due to carelessness.
7. Ruth saw Jessie when she was in town last week.
8. In this morning's paper, it says we lost the game.
9. We talked with the other passengers as though we had had years of flying experience, but we had never been up in one before.
10. If the prospective buyer learns that the heating system in the house is unsatisfactory, he had better not buy it.
11. The witness testified that he had seen the accused when he was eating dinner in the dining car, which convinced the jury of his presence on the train.
12. The library does not have enough copies of some of the books in greatest demand by students writing research papers, which makes it hard for you.
13. In Washington they are skeptical about the success of the new farm program.
14. Stuart told John that the postman had brought two letters for him.
15. I pointed out the poor condition of the cover and the poor quality of the printing, but they insisted on charging ten dollars for it.
16. After being on their feet all day, the tired troops removed their boots and cooled them in a stream.
17. Since the children enjoy picnicking, we go on several every summer.
18. If a person intends to go to college, they should concentrate on getting a high scholastic average.
19. After installing the headlights in the cars, you are expected to clean them.
20. Speakers representing the new political party wished to address the villagers. They were extremely hostile, however, and soon told them to move along.

CHAPTER 13

Placement of Modifiers

PLACE MODIFIERS SO THAT THEY MODIFY THE WORDS THEY ARE MEANT TO MODIFY

Misplaced Modifiers

13a. Place phrase and clause modifiers as near as possible to the words they modify.

The purpose of a modifier is to make more definite the meaning of the word it modifies. If the modifier is too far removed from this word, the effect of the modifier may be either lost or diverted to some other word. Clear writing does not force the reader to stop for a second look at the sentence in order to figure out exactly what has been said. When a reader encounters sentences like the following examples, he may understand the writer's idea clearly; on the other hand, he may be momentarily puzzled and have to reread the sentence.

I

CONFUSING We were startled to see such a young boy exhibiting these poisonous snakes with bare hands.

The reader knows, of course, that "snakes with bare hands" is a ridiculous idea, and he need not be a genius to discover eventually what the writer was trying to say. Nevertheless, the reader is diverted from a train of thought by the misplacement of the phrase *with bare hands*. Placing the phrase next to *exhibiting*, which it modifies, will make the sentence clear immediately.

CLARIFIED We were startled to see such a young boy exhibiting with bare hands these poisonous snakes.

II

CONFUSING She was wearing a colorful scarf around her shoulders, which she had bought in Mexico.

On second reading, the reader understands well enough that the writer of this sentence did not mean what he said — that she had bought her shoulders in Mexico. Yet he was momentarily confused by the misplacement of the phrase. The sentence is perfectly clear when the phrase *around her shoulders* is moved next to *wearing* so that the clause *which she had bought in Mexico* comes next to *scarf*, the word it modifies.

CLARIFIED She was wearing around her shoulders a colorful scarf which she had bought in Mexico.

III

CONFUSING The President made some vigorous remarks about Communists rising from his desk during the news conference.

Since Communists are not likely to be rising from the President's desk at any time, this sentence should be clarified by placing the phrase *rising from his desk during the news conference* nearer to *President*, which it modifies.

CLARIFIED Rising from his desk during the news conference, the President made some vigorous remarks about Communists.

The point of this discussion of modifiers is that a careful writer recognizes the importance of making himself clear at first reading. He does not try to hide behind the weak explanation, "You know what I mean."

As you have seen, the way to correct a misplaced modifier is to place it as near as possible to the word it modifies. There are, however, some instances in which a slavish following of this rule would make the sentence even worse. Often, in such a case, you can solve the problem by putting the adverbial modifier at the beginning of the sentence. Indeed, regardless of how it may fit elsewhere in the sentence, an adverbial modifier is often better placed at the beginning.

MODIFIERS MISPLACED **The hero takes the heroine in his arms, after having rescued her three times in thirty minutes, at the end of the picture, with a he-man grip and plants an endless kiss upon her trembling lips.**

When corrected by placing modifiers as near as possible to the words they modify, this sentence would still be awkward.

MODIFIERS NEAR THE WORDS THEY MODIFY **The hero, after having rescued the heroine three times in thirty minutes, takes her at the end of the picture in his arms with a he-man grip and plants an endless kiss upon her trembling lips.**

Placing one of the modifiers at the beginning, however, makes the sentence smoother.

A MODIFIER AT THE BEGINNING **At the end of the picture, the hero, after having rescued the heroine three times in thirty minutes, takes her in his arms with a he-man grip and plants an endless kiss upon her trembling lips.**

● EXERCISE 1. The following sentences may be confusing on first reading because of a misplaced phrase or clause. Improve the sentences by so arranging them that modifiers are nearer to the words they modify. You may find that the best arrangement involves placing an adverbial modifier first in the sentence. Doing the exercise orally in class will save time.

1. We finally found the fire extinguisher we had been hunting for behind a pile of logs.
2. The causeway has a drawbridge to permit the passage of fishing boats from which all fishing is prohibited.
3. The mystery has been solved after ten years of the missing portrait.
4. The new house was built by Mrs. Borden, who later became Mrs. Gruber, at a cost of $200,000.
5. The notorious outlaw was found lying in the middle of his living room by his friend Harry James with a revolver at his side.
6. The suspect tried to make the police believe that he had found the wallet in his car that didn't belong to him.
7. Detectives narrowed down the houses where the robbers might strike by deduction.
8. Mike made the mistake one afternoon of running and diving when the pool was empty into the deep end.
9. I'll check the manuscript when you finish for accuracy.
10. He worked hard in his fields, raising crops that would bring in money without complaint.
11. Judge Hart asked for the submission of briefs before handing down a decision on the alleged criminal actions which were to be prepared by the opposing lawyers.
12. If what the directions say is true on the package, this is a powerful insecticide.
13. Mrs. Hudson helped Holmes by moving the wax dummy Holmes had made every fifteen minutes.
14. Father bought a gadget for his new car from a sharp salesman that was guaranteed to reduce gas consumption.
15. Mr. Simmons met a friend he hadn't seen for ten years in Grand Central Station.

16. In this book there are a million facts about reptiles which the librarian recommended very highly.
17. He wore a straw hat on the back of his head which was obviously much too small.
18. Mr. Buck, the explorer, described his trips through the jungle in our social studies class.
19. Uncle Jim brought a new carriage for the baby that was named "Boodle Buggy."
20. The Coast Guard admitted that it had received a report on the strange derelict from an airplane pilot that had neither masts nor a smokestack.

Dangling Modifiers

13b. A modifying phrase or clause must clearly and sensibly modify a word in the sentence. When there is no word that the phrase or clause can modify sensibly, the modifier is said to dangle.

EXAMPLE Reading in the library, the siren of a passing ambulance distracted me.

There is no word in this sentence which can be sensibly modified by the participial phrase *reading in the library*. A *siren*, which the phrase appears to modify, is not customarily found reading in a library. The sentence can be corrected in two ways:

1. *By adding to the sentence a word for the phrase to modify*

Reading in the library, **I** was distracted by the siren of a passing ambulance.

2. *By changing the phrase to an adverb clause*

While I was reading in the library, the siren of a passing ambulance distracted me.

Study the following examples of dangling modifiers and the ways in which they have been corrected.

WRONG **While watching television, the doorbell rang.**

RIGHT **While watching television, we heard the doorbell ring.**

RIGHT **While we were watching television, the doorbell rang.**

WRONG **To get a better view of the stage, our seats had to be changed.**

RIGHT **To get a better view of the stage, we had to change our seats.**

WRONG **While in the bowling alley, the car was stolen.**

RIGHT **While we were in the bowling alley, the car was stolen.**

It is only fair to point out that examples of dangling modifiers are to be found in the works of the best authors. These examples, however, are either so idiomatic as to be entirely acceptable, or they are so clear that no possible confusion can result. The following are not objectionable:

IDIOMATIC **Generally speaking, the cost of living has remained static for several years.**

CLEAR ENOUGH **To get the best results, the oven should be preheated.**

It is important, however, that you understand the absurd meanings into which danglers can lead you so that you will avoid them in your own writing.

● EXERCISE 2. Each of the following sentences contains a dangling modifier. Remove the danglers by revising the sentences.

1. By climbing to the top of the hill, the capitol dome could be seen in the distance.
2. Captured and held incommunicado, the police questioned him for hours.

13b

3. After spending Saturday morning working in the library, a feeling of righteousness possessed me.
4. After flying in darkness for two hours, the moon rose, and navigation became less difficult.
5. Although unfamiliar with currents and channels, the boat was brought safely into port by Captain Brandt.
6. While driving at high speed on a deserted highway, two deer leaped in front of our car.
7. Living in this coastal town for many years, the fishing boats and their skippers were well known to him.
8. After working in the fields all day, little strength was left for social activities.
9. When only a youngster in grade school, my father instructed me in the manly art of boxing.
10. While waiting for our plane to be announced, watching the other travelers was an interesting pastime.
11. Wearing nothing but a light sweater, the cold wind drove me indoors.
12. Yielding to the temptation to look at a classmate's paper, the proctor caught her cheating.
13. Swimming in the Gulf, his big toe was cut on a shell.
14. While working in California, his family was living in New York.
15. Having run off the road while passing a car, my father told me I did not know how to drive.
16. Having promised to be home by midnight, the family was annoyed when I came in at two o'clock.
17. While playing in the high chair, I was afraid the baby would fall out.
18. Riding in the glass-bottomed boat, hundreds of beautiful tropical fish could be seen.
19. Being very shy, strangers terrify my little sister.
20. After being wheeled into the operating room, a nurse placed a mask over my nose.

TWO-WAY MODIFIERS

A third way in which a careless writer sometimes confuses his reader is by placing a modifier in such a way that it may be taken to modify two words. As a result, the reader is not sure, at first, which of the two meanings is intended. For some unexplainable reason, grammar books have always called such a modifier a "squinting modifier."

EXAMPLE **Mary said *during the meeting* Helen acted like a fool.**

Since the phrase *during the meeting* may be taken to modify either *said* or *acted*, this sentence is not clear. Did Mary say this during the meeting, or did Helen act like a fool during the meeting? The sentence should be revised to make it say one thing or the other.

CLEAR ***During the meeting* Mary said Helen acted like a fool.**

CLEAR **Mary said Helen acted like a fool *during the meeting.***

Study the following examples of modifiers which modify two words:

NOT CLEAR **Mrs. Stewart asked us *before we left* to call on her.**

CLEAR ***Before we left,* Mrs. Stewart asked us to call on her.**

CLEAR **Mrs. Stewart asked us to call on her *before we left.***

NOT CLEAR **Tell Fred *when he comes home* I want to see him.**

CLEAR ***When he comes home,* tell Fred I want to see him.**

CLEAR **Tell Fred I want to see him *when he comes home.***

● EXERCISE 3. The sentences in this exercise contain misplaced, dangling, and squinting modifiers. Revise each sentence so that its meaning will be clear on first reading.

1. Having fallen heavily during the night, Sorenson found that the snow had reached the eaves of his cabin.
2. After urging many ridiculous reforms, the voters refused to re-elect Mr. Cooper.
3. It was a great pleasure to Grandmother to watch the unfamiliar countryside unrolling beside her from the back seat of our speeding car.
4. The auditors discovered upon their arrival at the bank the cashier had fled.
5. From talking to others, the prevalent opinion favors our cause.
6. While watching the ball game, Sid's horse ran away.
7. Hotels hold all articles for a year that are found on the premises.
8. I met another conference delegate on the train representing the Middle Western states.
9. Preferring the mountains to the seashore, the Great Smokies were chosen as our vacation spot.
10. After working in Washington for twenty years, the methods of lobbyists were familiar.
11. This bank approves loans to reliable individuals of any size.
12. I sat next to a man who had a wooden leg named George Carpenter.
13. Did you know when you were in Chicago I was living in Highland Park?
14. Rounding a sharp curve, a detour sign confronted us.
15. While lighting a cigar, the car swerved dangerously toward a telephone pole.
16. Being completely untamed, George warned us that the animals were dangerous.
17. One can see more than a hundred lakes, flying at an altitude of several thousand feet.

18. Jack bought a book of shorthand lessons with his new typewriter which he read and studied diligently.
19. Abandoned by my friends, loneliness overcame me.
20. Living constantly under the eyes of the police, his nervousness increased.
21. A new highway has finally been completed after three years of frustration through the mountains and across California by the federal government.
22. Phil wanted to know before the game began what the referees said to the two captains.
23. A sea robin, an unusual deep-sea creature, was caught by my father with stubby legs and enormous wings.
24. Believing that freedom was more important than security, homes, relatives, and countries were abandoned by these emigrants.
25. Ever changing color, ever forming new shapes, her eyes followed the clouds.

PART FOUR

WRITING SMOOTH SENTENCES

CHAPTER 14

Parallel Structure

EXPRESS PARALLEL IDEAS IN PARALLEL FORM

14a. Express parallel ideas in the same grammatical form.

KINDS OF PARALLEL STRUCTURE

(1) Co-ordinate ideas are parallel.

Co-ordinate ideas are equal in rank. They are joined by co-ordinate connectives. The co-ordinate connectives most often used in parallel structure are *and*, *but*, *or*, *nor*.

To express parallel ideas in the same grammatical form, pair a noun with a noun, an infinitive (*to* + verb) with an infinitive, a phrase with a phrase, a clause with a clause.

In parallel constructions do not mix these grammatical forms.

WRONG In summer school I studied *writing* and *how to increase my vocabulary*. [noun (gerund) paired with an infinitive]

RIGHT In summer school I studied how **to write** and how **to increase** my vocabulary. [infinitive paired with an infinitive]

WRONG The prisoners were accused of *robbery, assault*, and *forging checks*. [nouns paired with a phrase]

RIGHT The prisoners were accused of **robbery, assault,** and **forgery.** [nouns paired with a noun]

WRONG The superintendent recommended an *increase* in salaries and *that other expenses be decreased.* [noun paired with a clause]

RIGHT The superintendent recommended an **increase** in salaries and a **decrease** in other expenses. [noun paired with a noun]

RIGHT The superintendent recommended **that salaries be increased** and **that other expenses be decreased.** [clause paired with a clause]

(2) Compared and contrasted ideas are parallel.

WRONG He found *acting* in the theater more inspiring than *to act* in the movies. [gerund paired with an infinitive]

RIGHT He found **acting** in the theater more inspiring than **acting** in the movies. [gerund paired with a gerund]

WRONG *To play* fair is as important as *playing* well. [infinitive paired with a gerund]

RIGHT **To play** fair is as important as **to play** well. [infinitive paired with an infinitive]

(3) Correlative constructions are parallel.

Correlative constructions are formed with the correlative conjunctions *both . . . and*, *either . . . or*, *neither . . . nor*, *not only . . . but (also)*.

WRONG To gain entrance they tried both *persuasion* and *to force* their way in. [noun paired with an infinitive]

RIGHT To gain entrance they tried both **persuasion** and **force.** [noun paired with a noun]

WRONG The new clerk soon proved himself to be not only *capable* but also *a man who could be trusted.* [adjective paired with a noun]

RIGHT The new clerk soon proved himself to be not only **capable** but also **trustworthy.** [adjective paired with an adjective]

COMPLETED PARALLELISM

14b. Place correlative conjunctions immediately before the parallel terms.

WRONG Mr. Sayers is not only president of the National Bank but also of the Chamber of Commerce. [*Not only . . . but also* should precede the parallel terms *of the National Bank* and *of the Chamber of Commerce,* not the word *president.*]

RIGHT Mr. Sayers is president **not only** of the National Bank **but also** of the Chamber of Commerce.

WRONG The team both felt the satisfaction of victory and the disappointment of defeat.

RIGHT The team felt **both** the satisfaction of victory **and** the disappointment of defeat.

14c. In parallel constructions repeat an article, a preposition, or a pronoun whenever necessary to make the meaning clear.

Compare the sentences in each of the following pairs. Note that the omission or inclusion of a word changes the meaning.

1. Before the meeting I talked with the secretary and treasurer. [The sentence may mean that I talked with one person. He holds the double office of secretary and treasurer.]
   Before the meeting I talked with the secretary and **the** treasurer. [This sentence indicates that I talked with two persons.]
2. The weather was a greater handicap to the invading army than their enemy. [This sentence means that the invaders would rather fight the enemy than the weather.]
   The weather was a greater handicap to the invading army than **to** their enemy. [This sentence means that the invaders had the harder job.]
3. We feel certain that he is capable, he will succeed,

and you will be proud of him. [In a series of parallel *that* clauses, the meaning is usually clearer if the introductory word is repeated in each clause.]

We feel certain that he is capable, that he will succeed, and that you will be proud of him.

● EXERCISE 1. Improve the following sentences by putting parallel ideas into the same grammatical form. Correct any errors in the placement of correlatives and in the omission of a necessary article, preposition, or pronoun.

1. The doctor recommended plenty of food, sleep, and exercising.
2. Come to the meeting prepared to take notes and with some questions to ask.
3. Passing the oral test is usually more difficult than to pass the written test.
4. The politicians not only were convinced that their platform was sound but popular.
5. Our cabinetmaker did a better job on our furniture than theirs.
6. Tell me where you have been and an account of your activities there.
7. He regarded all natives as sly, ignorant, and not to be depended upon.
8. He thought it easier to listen to news on the radio than reading the newpaper.
9. The traffic judge told his teen-age audience that adolescents are selfish, they drive recklessly, and that they do not respect adults.
10. The audience neither understood the speaker's words nor what his purpose was.
11. Mud wasps had not only hung their cones under the porch but also the eaves.
12. The poem makes you feel the rolling of the cannon, the running of the horses, and how afraid the soldiers were.
13. His stories are exciting, fascinating, and they baffle me.

14. Parents of small children frequently find their evenings out reduced in number by either the expense of baby sitters or they can't get them.
15. I forgot that my book report was due on Monday and the teacher had said he would not accept late reports.
16. The new models will be costly to buy, but their cost of operation will be low.
17. Read the poems not only to get the moral but also an appreciation of our language and to enjoy the meter.
18. At one time Coleridge tried preaching but later turning to poetry and the fine arts.
19. In his lecture today Professor Hobbs both explained the causes of the war and what its results were.
20. Our life in the jungle was affected not only by the heat but the millions of insects, the poor living conditions, and rain.
21. The President not only is head of the nation but his political party.
22. I neither understood what she said nor was what she did clear to me.

INCOMPLETE PARALLELISM

Occasionally in your haste you may fail to include in one part of a parallel construction all the words necessary to make the construction complete.

INCOMPLETE She wore clothes that were better than the other girls.

COMPLETE She wore clothes that were better than **those of** the other girls.

In the first of these sentences you feel that something has been omitted because the sentence compares *clothes* with *girls*.

14d. Include in the second part of a parallel construction all words necessary to make the construction complete.

● EXERCISE 2. Correct the parallelism in each of the following sentences by inserting the words that have been omitted.

1. My experience was not half so exciting as the people who didn't get home until dawn.
2. As time passed, she was torn between her love for her parents and her husband.
3. This author's style is not much different from other writers of this time.
4. His strength was greater than his opponent.
5. Compare your grades for this quarter with last quarter.
6. Statistics prove that prices this year are lower than last year.
7. You will find the information in the second edition more up-to-date than the first edition.
8. Father said he was just as much pleased by the gift I gave him as you gave him.
9. The trail on the north side of the mountain is steeper than the south side.
10. The amount of money his wife received in the will was much smaller than the children.
11. The classrooms on the second floor are always cleaner than the first floor.
12. The inexpensive overcoat which I bought last week looks exactly like the more expensive stores.
13. Cats can catch rabbits as easily as dogs.
14. The damage done by this year's forest fires was greater than last year's.
15. The reaction of the students to the new regulations was more violent than the faculty.

● EXERCISE 3. The following sentences contain faulty parallelism. Rephrase the sentences so that the parallelism will be correctly and logically expressed. You will do well to review the various kinds of faulty parallelism before doing the exercise.

1. One of the accident victims suffered a broken arm, several broken ribs, and one of his lungs was punctured.

2. He not only was industrious but dependable.
3. That you are looking well does not necessarily mean you feel well.
4. A cloudy day is better for a game than sunshine.
5. The trip into the wilderness can be made by canoe, by powerboat, or flying, but not walking.
6. To the inexperienced soldier, war may be a romantic adventure, but a dull and dirty business is the way the combat veteran regards it.
7. He neither told me that I should attend the meeting nor make a report.
8. The skipper had a harsh voice, a weatherbeaten face, and was very stocky in build.
9. We were not sure that our request for a raise was fair or it would be granted.
10. Allan's success at the new school has been a greater surprise to me than his mother.
11. The public's attention has been centered on the need for more teachers, adequate classrooms, and there isn't enough new equipment.
12. This was a much harder assignment for me than Betty.
13. The ambassador did not know whether the President had sent for him or the Secretary of State.
14. His friends not only were shocked by his failure but they felt a great disappointment.
15. The players were annoyed not so much by the decisions of the officials as the hostile crowd.
16. The boys and girls in the junior high school display better manners than the senior high school.
17. The headmaster insisted that all boys return by ten o'clock and the housemasters must check them in.
18. High schools have been accused of being too closely tied in with college education and that they neglect the average teen-age boy or girl.
19. Pioneers came with hopes of being happy and free and to make their fortunes in the new world.
20. All delegates to the convention were advised that on their return they would both have to make a written and oral report.

CHAPTER 15

Unnecessary Shifts in Sentences

AVOID UNNECESSARY SHIFTS IN SUBJECT AND VERB

Smooth writing is writing in which the thought moves along easily without awkwardness or confusion. Smoothness is sometimes seriously affected by the writer's shifting needlessly from one simple subject to another.

WRONG A man should build his house to suit himself, and then you will be happy in it. [unnecessary shift from *a man* to *you*]

RIGHT A man should build his house to suit himself, and then **he** will be happy in it.

WRONG Two detectives went to the scene of the robbery, but no important clues were found. [unnecessary shift from *detectives* to *clues*]

RIGHT Two detectives went to the scene of the robbery, but **they** found no important clues.

Shifts in Subject

15a. Avoid unnecessary shifts from one subject to another.

UNNECESSARY SHIFTS IN SUBJECT

Fishermen from many states visit the Ontario lakes where *fish* are found in abundance and, in the cool, crisp air of the

15a

north woods, a welcome *relief* from summer heat is enjoyed. *Planes*, *trains*, or *automobiles* bring the fishermen to the edge of the wilderness. From there *boats* are used to penetrate the remoter waters where *trout*, *bass*, *pickerel*, *perch*, and fresh-water *salmon* are caught.

SHIFTS AVOIDED

Fishermen from many states visit the Ontario lakes where *they* find fish in abundance and, in the cool, crisp air of the north woods, enjoy a welcome relief from summer heat. After coming by plane, train, or automobile to the edge of the wilderness, the *fishermen* use boats to penetrate the remoter waters, where *they* catch trout, bass, pickerel, perch, and fresh-water salmon.

Shifts in Verb Form

Unnecessary shifts from one subject to another are usually accompanied by shifts from one verb form to another.

15b. Avoid unnecessary shifts from one verb form to another within one sentence.

(1) Avoid unnecessary shifts in the voice of verbs.

When the subject of a verb is acting, the verb is in the *active voice*. When the subject of a verb is acted upon, the verb is in the *passive voice*.[1]

ACTIVE VOICE **John won both events.** [subject acting]

PASSIVE VOICE **Both events were won by John.** [subject acted upon]

Note that if there is an unnecessary shift in voice there is also an unnecessary shift in subject.

[1] A fuller treatment of voice will be found on pages 144–47.

UNNECESSARY SHIFT Volunteers *made* (active verb) the dangerous journey after dark, but no wolves *were encountered* (passive verb).

SHIFT AVOIDED Volunteers **made** (active verb) the dangerous journey after dark but **encountered** (active verb) no wolves.

UNNECESSARY SHIFT Since *he knew* that ability to speak well before a group is important to success, a *course* in public speaking *was taken* by him.

SHIFT AVOIDED Since **he knew** that ability to speak well before a group is important to success, **he took** a course in public speaking.

(2) Avoid unnecessary shifts in the tense of verbs.

UNNECESSARY SHIFT At this point the President *reads* (present tense) a prepared statement but *refused* (past tense) to answer any questions.

SHIFT AVOIDED At this point the President **read** (past tense) a prepared statement but **refused** (past tense) to answer any questions.

SHIFT AVOIDED At this point the President **reads** (present tense) a prepared statement but **refuses** (present tense) to answer any questions.

UNNECESSARY SHIFT She *made* (past tense) some flippant remark and *rushes* (present tense) off down the hall.

SHIFT AVOIDED She **made** (past tense) some flippant remark and **rushed** (past tense) off down the hall.

SHIFT AVOIDED She **makes** (present tense) some flippant remark and **rushes** (present tense) off down the hall.

● EXERCISE 1. The following sentences contain unnecessary shifts from one subject to another or from one verb form to another. By revising the sentences orally in class, show how these shifts may be avoided.

1. Young people not only enjoy a few weeks away from home at a summer camp, but many valuable things are learned from the experience.

15b

2. Economists were aware of the country's dwindling oil reserves, and a steady rise in the price of fuel is predicted by them.
3. Students of engineering find many fields of specialization open to them. Civil, ceramic, chemical, automotive, marine, or electrical engineering may be chosen by them.
4. The seniors voted in favor of enlarging the Student Council, but the proposition to increase the number of freshman members of the council was voted down by them.
5. The flour and the butter should be mixed into a paste, and add a small amount of milk.
6. A high school student can often earn his own spending money, and his family is thus relieved of at least one of its financial responsibilities.
7. When the manufacturers find out how to use a new laboratory discovery, many changes will be made by them.
8. I read the newspaper from beginning to end, but the story I wanted couldn't be found.
9. The stringer first cut the old strings from the racket, and then the restringing begins.
10. When his father spoke to him about going to college, Walter says that he doesn't want to take so much money from the family at a time when living expenses were so high.
11. Since the proprietor had no room in his boathouse for our boat, we were permitted by him to anchor it near his dock.
12. Once a customer bites into one of our steaks, you will never complain about our bill.
13. The members of the audience were stirred by the martial music, and the words of the speaker inspired them to action.
14. Properly equipped men can survive for months in the Arctic and no ill effects will be suffered.
15. Although we could not see the planes, their motors could be clearly heard.
16. Ruth achieved fame as the home-run king, but a fine

record as a pitcher and an outfielder was also made by him.

17. If a person wishes to succeed in a writing career, you must have patience and the capacity for hard work.
18. Wholesale fruit and vegetable dealers are among the principal customers of the local weather bureau, and profitable use is made of the information they receive.
19. An artist must first sketch the rough outline of his picture before you begin to paint.
20. It was a clear December morning when my friend Joe called and asks me to go for a plane ride with him. I always liked Joe, and so you are glad to go anywhere with him. I accepted the invitation and Joe says he'd meet me at the airport in an hour. This was the simple beginning of the most frightening experience of my life.

● EXERCISE 2. In the following passage the tense of the verbs is frequently shifted from past to present and from present to past. Read the passage. Decide in what tense (past or present) it should be written. Prepare to read aloud in class, changing the verb forms to remove the unnecessary shifts in tense.

Mr. Sampson, who had been for ten years faculty adviser of the high school annual, sat calmly at his desk after school, watching the autumn sun light the empty room, while he waited for the first meeting of the new yearbook staff. A veteran like Mr. Sampson could hardly be expected to show much emotion over the repetition of an event he had taken part in so many times. He is not particularly disturbed when the door opens and Jane Billings led a noisy group of long-legged boys and heavily lipsticked girls into his room.

Following a general falling over desks and slumping into seats, Jane called the meeting to order. This year, she explains, the staff would produce the finest yearbook East High has ever had. Someone wanted to know, first of all, what kind of cover the book would have. A great preference is expressed for a thick and heavy leather cover, suitably embossed, and bearing the seal and colors of the school. Mr. Sampson smiles, for he had never yet known a new staff that did not begin with a discussion of the cover.

Complete agreement about the cover having been so quickly reached, Win Thompson wants to know why last year's book was so dull. Here Mr. Sampson smiles again. Everything's going to be just fine, he thought, remembering that no staff in the past had ever had a good word to say for its predecessors. "Let's have twice as many pictures, a bigger sports section, not so much writing that nobody ever reads." These weighty matters agreed upon, everyone wanted to know whether the seniors aren't entitled to more space in the book. "How about three or four instead of ten senior pictures to a page? After all, it's our book."

Mr. Sampson listened and said nothing. He is quietly thinking about next January, when the supply of snapshots will be disappointingly small, when the budget will be alarmingly inadequate, when compromise after compromise will be frantically made in order to get a yearbook out at all. But he doesn't say much. He knows it is better for the staff to find out for itself why last year's book and all the books before it had been such complete "failures."

● EXERCISE 3. The sentences in this exercise are awkward because of unnecessary shifts in the subject and in the verb. Revise the sentences so that these shifts will be removed.

1. The cement and sand are first mixed thoroughly; then add the water.
2. The experienced yachtsman is aware of the danger of fire, and, when filling the gas tank, great precautions are taken not to spill gasoline in the bottom of the boat.
3. As district attorney he successfully handled the Tam-

many Hall cases, and the backing of the Republican party was won.

4. Jimmy kept a careful record of all expenses and a complete report was submitted by him at the final club meeting.
5. As the bus careens toward the edge of the road, we thought our time had come, and our seats were grabbed in desperation.
6. Although Americans know that milk is a perfect food, much less milk is being drunk by them than they should drink.
7. The cost of meat has been rising while cattle raising has been going down in cost.
8. Many doctors recognize the value of health insurance, but the particular kind we should have is something they could not agree on.
9. Driven backward, Guy felt the ropes burning his back for a moment before he lunges forward with his right, and Hammer Joe's fighting days were brought to an abrupt end.
10. Sammy had just finished his bitter denunciation of all teachers and of one chemistry teacher in particular, when he turns around and Mr. Lerner was seen in the laboratory doorway.
11. Having learned not to pet strange dogs, Billy avoids all dogs whose acquaintance he hadn't yet made.
12. An explorer must study his maps very carefully so that you will be able to plan your trip efficiently.

CHAPTER 16

Sentence Conciseness

AVOID WORDINESS AND OVERWRITING

Students commonly confuse amount of writing with quality of writing. They mistakenly believe that the more words a theme contains the better it is. The professional writer who is paid according to the number of words in his articles may find wordiness profitable, but he would never claim that it improves his articles. Most good writing is effective because it is not cluttered with unnecessary words.

Do not think, however, that wordiness appears only in long compositions. A long piece of writing may contain no superfluous words, whereas a short piece may be full of them. Studying the principles in this section and doing the exercises will make you aware of wordiness in writing and help you to avoid it in your own compositions.

Superfluous Words and Unnecessary Repetition

The following example of wordiness was the opening paragraph of a high school student's composition about an overnight hike. Lines have been drawn through the superfluous words.

When ~~in the course of human events, when~~ a man finds it necessary to rest his weary bones, he packs up and goes on what is inappropriately called a vacation. Last summer I had the good fortune to go ~~during the summer~~ to a mountain camp in ~~the mountains of~~ eastern Pennsylvania. On the day that I arrived, ~~when I got to camp,~~ I found that the camp had been quarantined because of the measles that one of the younger campers had brought in, ~~and no one who was in the camp could leave.~~ After we had spent a week in camp, the prospect of an overnight hike in the mountainous wilds looked especially good to us campers who had been so long confined ~~to camp by the quarantine.~~

16a. Avoid wordiness by eliminating superfluous words and the unnecessary repetition of ideas.[1]

WORDY The game is played with tiny, little, round balls, which, in my opinion, I think are made of steel.

BETTER The game is played with tiny balls, which, I think, are made of steel.

WORDY After descending down to the edge of the river, we boarded a small raft which was floating there on the surface of the water.

BETTER After descending to the edge of the river, we boarded a small raft.

WORDY The first story in the book is a masterpiece in itself and quite a story.

BETTER The first story in the book is a masterpiece.

● EXERCISE 1. Revise the following sentences, eliminating superfluous words.

1. We watched the big, massive black cloud rising up from the level prairie and covering over the sun.
2. Far away in the distance, as far as anything was visible to the eye, the small, diminutive shapes of the settlers' huts were outlined in silhouette against the dark sky.

[1] Superfluous wording is known by several technical terms: *redundancy*, *tautology*, *pleonasm*. The terms are used interchangeably in dictionaries to refer to such expressions as the following: descend *down*, rise *up*, visible *to the eye*, repeat *again*, return *back*.

3. Modern cars of today, unlike the old cars of yesterday, can be driven faster without danger than the old ones.
4. When what the speaker was saying was not audible to our ears, I asked him to repeat again what he had said.
5. It was in this mountain fastness that the explorers found there the examples of wildlife for which they had been looking for.
6. During this year's current baseball season, all home games and many away games in other cities may be watched at home on your television screen as they are brought to you over station WPIX.
7. The mediator said that if both parties would give in a little that a satisfactory settlement could be reached that would satisfy both parties.
8. In spite of the fact that the danger was neither tangible to the touch nor visible to the eye, it was very real to all the dwellers and inhabitants of the village in the foothills which circled around the base of Mt. Wilson.
9. The drive over to Cross Village follows and winds along the top of a great, huge bluff above the lake.
10. When at last the pounding finally began to stop, I stretched myself out prone upon the bed and attempted to try to go to sleep.
11. The world in its present state of affairs today is in great and dire need of statesmen who will work hard to prevent the recurrence again of a disastrously destructive world war.
12. During the hours in the morning before noon, there is a variety of radio programs of different kinds to which you may listen to.
13. As you continue on in the book a little further, you will be surprised and amazed by the clever skill of the writer of the book in weaving in together the many previously unrelated threads of his story.
14. At the final end of the picture, the villain abruptly and suddenly does an about-face and changes completely into a good man with admirable characteristics.
15. His mental thought processes puzzled his school

teachers and made them despair of his future success in the years after his graduation from school.

16. I am always as a rule surprised to find out that a currently popular hit tune was also a popular number years ago in the past when my parents were in high school.
17. He was firmly determined to combine together both of the two divisions of the firm in order to achieve a stronger company eventually in the long run.
18. Circling around his adversary with a menacing look on his face, Broadhurst bided his time and waited for an opening through which he could connect up with his mighty right.
19. The President's struggle with Congress ended up in a victory for the President when the public voted at the November election to re-elect him again to the Presidency for another term of four years.
20. The final conclusion of the novel on which he had been working on for more than five years was disappointing to everyone who read the manuscript, and he decided to revise and change the story.

● EXERCISE 2. Revise the following wordy paragraphs. Eliminate all unnecessary words but keep the ideas of the paragraphs clear.

1

When we were two hundred yards away from our objective, which was a small little grove of pine trees on the sloping side of a hill, we were confronted by a vast, wet swamp. I remembered that during the last two weeks we had had, out of fourteen days, ten days of rain, and decided in my own mind to send out a few scouts who might discover a way by means of which we could reach the grove without getting our feet wet. Then, when the scouts reported back that their efforts to try to find a dry path through the swamp had been unsuccessful, we gave up and resigned ourselves to sloshing knee-deep through the muddy water.

2

When, after eight years of education in school, the student enters the ninth grade and becomes a freshman, then he begins to find out what seniors are really like. Up until this point, seniors have been heroes to him, admired from a respectful distance away as though they were gods, unless he has happened to know one personally, of course. But now, however, his conception undergoes a change. The senior becomes an ogre whose one and only purpose in life seems to the freshman to be to make life as miserable as possible for each and every freshman. Every way the freshman turns in the school corridors, a senior hall cop, with a great big letter on his chest, grabs him with huge talons and tells him with hot and fiery breath that he cannot go down an up stairway. He is enticed into joining clubs which are ruled over and presided over by seniors who use him mainly for the performance of unpleasant errands beneath the dignity of a senior. Whenever the freshman cannot be of use, he is ignored. His former ambition to be a senior fades out and wanes until one day he begins to think thoughts of getting his revenge. In his frenzied brain the idea dawns on him if he is patient, he too will someday enjoy the privilege of molding the lives and characters of ninth graders. This idea accounts for the fanatic fixed stare which is to be seen in the eyes of so many freshmen.

Conciseness Through Reduction

The opposite of wordiness is conciseness. In your effort to write well, you will profit from a study of some ways to make your writing more concise. Of course, there is a danger in being too economical in your use of words; writing which is too concise will not be clear and will not achieve its intended effect. Nevertheless, study of the following rule will call to your attention some helpful methods of avoiding wordiness.

16b. Avoid wordiness by reducing clauses to phrases and phrases to single words. This process is known as *reduction*.

1. *Clauses reduced to participial, gerund, or infinitive phrases*

CLAUSE *When he was left alone on the sinking vessel,* the captain made an inspection of the ship.

PARTICIPIAL PHRASE **Left alone on the sinking vessel,** the captain made an inspection of the ship.

CLAUSE *Since he believed the ship could be saved,* he called for volunteers to help him.

PARTICIPIAL PHRASE **Believing the ship could be saved,** he called for volunteers to help him.

CLAUSE *If you leave at noon,* you can reach Chicago at three o'clock.

GERUND PHRASE **By leaving at noon,** you can reach Chicago at three o'clock.

CLAUSE We decided *that we would get an early start.*

INFINITIVE PHRASE We decided **to get an early start.**

2. *Clauses reduced to prepositional phrases*

CLAUSE The teams *which had come from the Far West* were not scheduled to play the first day of the tournament.

PHRASE The teams **from the Far West** were not scheduled to play the first day of the tournament.

CLAUSE *When the sun sets,* the street lights come on.

PHRASE **At sunset** the street lights come on.

CLAUSE *After you have graduated,* you will be looking for a job.

PHRASE **After graduation,** you will be looking for a job.

CLAUSE My cousin *who lives in Mexico* speaks Spanish fluently.

PHRASE My cousin **in Mexico** speaks Spanish fluently.

3. *Clauses reduced to appositives*

CLAUSE Dr. Brown, *who is the chief surgeon,* will operate.
APPOSITIVE Dr. Brown, **the chief surgeon,** will operate.

CLAUSE His two dogs, *one of which is a collie and the other a spaniel,* perform different duties on the farm.
APPOSITIVE His two dogs, **a collie and a spaniel,** perform different duties on the farm.

4. *Clauses and phrases reduced to single words*

CLAUSE The troops *who had been captured* were sent to a prison camp.
WORD The **captured** troops were sent to a prison camp.

CLAUSE Henry is a runner *who never tires.*
WORD Henry is a **tireless** runner.

CLAUSE We met a man *who is a native of France.*
WORD We met a **Frenchman.**

PHRASE His career *in the movies* was brief.
WORD His **movie** career was brief.

PHRASE She greeted everyone *in a cordial manner.*
WORD She greeted everyone **cordially.**

From these examples of reduction you can see how to make your own writing more concise. Usually the time for such reduction is during revision of your papers. Revising the sentences in the following exercises will give you practice in writing more concisely.

● EXERCISE 3. The following sentences can be made more concise by reducing the italicized groups of words according to the directions given. Rewrite each sentence according to the directions.

1. (a) *When we had completed our homework*, we went downtown (b) *so that we could get a sundae.* [(a) Reduce clause to a gerund phrase (*–ing*); (b) reduce clause to an infinitive phrase (*to* + verb).]
2. (a) *After he had looked* everywhere for an old place

(b) *that he could renovate*, Mr. Dayton bought the house (c) *that was deserted* on the edge of town. [(a) Reduce clause to a gerund phrase (*–ing*); (b) reduce clause to an infinitive phrase (*to* + verb); (c) reduce clause to an adjective.]

3. The orchard (a) *of apple trees* which stood (b) *in the area behind the house* yielded no fruit during his first year there, but it bore bushels and bushels (c) *when the second season came.* [(a) Reduce phrase to an adjective; (b) reduce to one prepositional phrase; (c) reduce clause to a prepositional phrase.]
4. (a) *Since we were sitting in seats* (b) *which were near first base*, we were able to judge the accuracy of the decisions (c) *of the umpire.* [(a) Reduce clause to a participle (*–ing*), omitting *in seats;* (b) reduce clause to a prepositional phrase; (c) reduce phrase to a possessive.]
5. (a) *Because it was necessary for her to be away from home* (b) *in the afternoon and in the evening* for many days, Mrs. Stein (c) *who is the president of the Parent-Teacher Association*, hired a succession of baby sitters (d) *who were to take care of her children* (e) *while she was absent.* [(a) Reduce clause to a participial phrase (*Having to be . . .*); (b) reduce two phrases to two words telling when; (c) reduce clause to an appositive; (d) reduce clause to an infinitive phrase (*to* + verb); (e) reduce clause to a prepositional phrase.

● EXERCISE 4. The italicized clauses and phrases in the following sentences can be reduced. Revise the sentences, reducing the clauses to phrases or appositives or single words and the phrases to single words. You may omit unnecessary words, and you may occasionally find it necessary to change the order of ideas.

1. We took the bus *in order that we might save money.*
2. After I had read "A Tale of Two Cities," I read three other novels *which were written by Dickens.*
3. This small hotel, *which is situated in Connecticut*, is patronized mainly by *people from New York and Boston.*

4. *After he lost a leg in an accident which occurred while he was hunting*, Monty Stratton, *who was a pitcher for the White Sox*, made a comeback in professional baseball *which was amazing*.
5. Our seats *in which we sat at the Army-Navy game* were on the forty-yard line, *and they were at the top of the stadium*.
6. The poetry *of France* has had an influence *which is notable* on the poetry *of England*.
7. *While he was inspecting his new house, which is in the suburbs*, Mr. Doyle stumbled over a piece of flooring and fell down the stairs *leading to the cellar*.
8. Our days *that we spent in the north woods* would have been perfect if it had not been for the mosquitoes *that were enormous and hungry*.
9. Inez, *who is an ambitious young actress*, found that the acting *that she did in a stock company in the summer* gave her the experience *which she needed*.
10. The most common complaint *that is made by students* is that every teacher chooses Friday *on which to give examinations*.

● EXERCISE 5. The following sentences are unnecessarily wordy. Make them more concise by eliminating redundant expressions and by reducing clauses and phrases. In your revisions do not omit any ideas.

1. Arnold prefers to work alone by himself in his own room where he has combined together a study and a bedroom.
2. In spite of our efforts to try to keep the overturned boat afloat on the water, it sank down to the bottom.
3. We took the elevator up to the second floor and roamed up and down through the long aisles which extended endlessly between glass cases which were filled and bulging with most beautiful works of art.
4. The headmaster said that he hoped we would take and accept his suggestions which concerned the conduct of us boys when we are off campus and away from the school.

5. My brother he is taking golf lessons, but my sister, who is an expert swimmer, she is taking lessons in diving.
6. Johnny Long's six-piece orchestra will return again to play a repeat engagement at the Soph Hop which will be held in the gym at the high school this Saturday night of this week.
7. Proposed plans that have been suggested for a new field house which is to be constructed at the local college here have been approved and acted favorably upon by the legislature, which today voted funds that are necessary for the project.
8. Because of the fact that I can borrow free, without charge, the latest, most recent books from the public library, if I simply have patience enough to wait my turn, I do not usually as a rule use the lending library which is in the bookstore which charges a daily fee of so much per day.
9. I was just dialing his number on the telephone when he appeared in the doorway of my office and startled me so by his unexpected appearance that I just sat glued to my chair and gazed at him speechless, unable to get up or to say a word.
10. As June approached and the school year began to draw to a close, the seniors, who were concerned about graduation, became interested in their probable grades that they would be getting in their subjects and suddenly all at once showed a new and hitherto unnoticed interest in their studies.
11. After we had returned together again, my roommate and I decided that we would rush immediately to the bus station in the hope of catching up with and joining the rest of our group.
12. It was a wet, rainy day at the lake; the boats which were moored at the yacht club and which always looked so inviting to us looked forlorn and uncomfortable as they bobbed up and down on the water.

● EXERCISE 6. Combine the ideas in each group below into one smooth sentence. Show that you understand how to avoid wordiness by omitting superfluous words and expressions, and by reducing clauses and phrases.

EXAMPLE The afternoon paper was scattered over the yard.
The paper had been thrown carelessly by the newsboy.
The paper had become unfolded.
The paper had been caught up by the wind.

Thrown carelessly by the newsboy, the afternoon paper had become unfolded, been caught by the wind, and been scattered about the yard.

or

The afternoon paper, which had been thrown carelessly by the newsboy, had become unfolded and scattered about the yard by the wind.

1. Seniors should consult the guidance department.
   This applies to those seniors who are going to college.
   They should consult the department regularly.
   They will get suggestions.
   The suggestions will relate to their choice of college, to scholarships, and to their college expenses.
2. The school election was an imitation of local political elections.
   There was campaigning three days before the election.
   There were two parties.
   The parties offered slates of candidates.
3. A committee investigated the condition of play streets.
   The committee was appointed by the Woman's Club.
   The investigation showed that play streets were not being kept clean.
   It also showed that motorists did not obey the signs concerning traffic on play streets.
4. People sometimes judge a school by the actions of its students.
   I mean the way they act in public.

People watch the way students behave on the streets.
They observe student behavior at parties in the community.
They notice the way students drive a car.

5. My brother lives on Long Island.
His name is George.
He belongs to the Air Force Reserve.
He flies several hours a week.
He does his flying at Mitchel Air Force Base.
He does this flying to maintain his military rating.
6. A pig was being taken to market.
It was in the back of Mr. John Stover's truck.
While crossing the Savitt River Bridge, the pig escaped.
The bridge is a busy thoroughfare.
Traffic was held up for a half hour.
7. A gorilla and a tiger were locked in the same cage.
This was the result of a keeper's mistake.
The tiger won the battle.
He pulled an arm from the gorilla.
8. The natural resources of the Arctic have remained untouched because of lack of fuel for power.
Now these resources can be developed by atomic fuel.
An atomic furnace is small enough to be transported by plane into the remotest regions of the Arctic.
It is powerful enough to supply power for years without refueling.
9. Mr. Henry Dreyfus told about the subway of the future.
He is an industrial designer.
He said the future subway will be air conditioned.
It will be better lighted.
It will be equipped with ceiling maps and loudspeakers.
10. The majority of the American people do not continue their education beyond high school at the present time.
In the future they may continue in school two more years.
They will attend two-year community colleges.
They will get vocational training in the community colleges.

The Overwritten Style

In their efforts to write like Shakespeare, high school students sometimes produce a style of writing which is so artificial, flowery, and cumbersome that it is ineffective. Such a style is the result of the mistaken notion that big words, unusual words, and figures of speech, no matter how commonplace, are literary. Unlike mistakes made through carelessness or laziness, a mistake of this kind is made through trying too hard to sound like a great writer. The resulting style is said to be "overwritten." It is sometimes called "fine writing."

16c. Avoid an overwritten style (fine writing). Write naturally without straining after a "literary" effect.

The following example of overwriting will make you aware of the fault. Doing Exercise 7 on page 247 may help you correct overwritten passages in your own work.

HARBOR FOG

The fog slowly crept in and covered the metropolis with its sinister cloak of impressive quietude. An entire day of heavy rain had drenched the surrounding municipality, forming puddles in the thoroughfares which reflected the shimmering images of the gleaming street lights and the illumination emanating from multitudes of office windows.

As I stood on the magnificent man-made span which arched above the swirling waters, the mournful warnings of the anchored ships pierced the dense fog. The constant beat of the harbor bell buoys and the gentle lapping of the murky water on the piling of this bridge combined to permeate the night air with a mystic tenseness.

The harbor boats moved tediously through the night,

and their wakes left grotesque trails which slowly dissolved and enveloped themselves in the depths of the blackness.

Although it was late, the never-ceasing rumble of activity from the near-by city could still be apprehended. The penetrating night air was heavy with moisture and with each soft puff of breeze the salt of the sea could be detected.

During World War II Representative Maury Maverick, of Texas, became impatient with the overwritten style of some government writing and branded this sort of writing with the descriptive term "gobbledygook." Here is an example of the gobbledygook that troubled Mr. Maverick: "Illumination is required to be extinguished upon vacating these premises." You can see how much more effective would be, "Turn out the lights when you leave."

● EXERCISE 7. Each of the following sentences represents the fault of overwriting. In simpler words write your version of the idea which is here expressed in a forced and unnatural style.

1. In a vast explosion of frozen precipitation, Thor shot through the feathery drift, maintaining without apparent effort his equilibrium upon the fragile strips of ash strapped to his pedal extremities.
2. My exploration of the intriguing heights of the science of economics left me with the firm conviction that Homo sapiens is impotent when it comes to exerting any detectable influence on the fundamental operation of supply and demand.
3. The bitterest irony of our fevered time is the oft-repeated concept that only by creating more magnificent and more deadly instruments of explosive destruction can mankind bring to this whirling planet the era of tranquillity for which it has longed since the beginning of time.

4. The sharp impact of wood upon the little white sphere was followed by a sudden emanation of sound, like an explosion, from the throats of the assembled multitude in the tiered stands as the soaring pellet arched over the greensward and came to rest beyond the masonry in left field.
5. Nothing so impresses one with the warm security and pleasing restfulness of one's native surroundings as extensive peregrinations into foreign realms and among the exotic areas on the surface of our world.
6. Following our educational endeavors of the day, several of us conscientious seekers after knowledge relaxed our weary cerebrums by lending our ears to the latest discs at Jacobsen's music emporium.
7. Laying aside for the nonce the tomes of wisdom, I selected from the periodical rack the current issue of my favorite pictorial publication and, elongated upon the resilient davenport, slowly perused the photographic narrative of the week's outstanding occurrences.
8. In order to forestall the embarrassment of a refusal, I preceded my request for Helen's company upon an excursion to the local cinema by inquiring of her nearest of kin as to what Helen's social calendar held for the Friday evening in question.
9. Bent upon a week's tour by the time-honored expedient of thumbing accommodations from altruistic motorists, I bade a fond farewell to my anxious mater, and, with my earthly possessions ensconced in a cardboard brief case, embarked upon my great adventure.
10. Lifting the pigskin from the water-soaked gridiron with his trusty toe, Harvey booted it with mathematical precision directly between the white uprights silhouetted against the dying sun.

CHAPTER 17

Sentence Variety

VARY YOUR STYLE FOR INTEREST AND EMPHASIS

17a. Give variety to your writing by varying the beginnings of sentences, the structure of sentences, and the length of sentences.

Inexperienced writers tend to begin all their sentences with the subject. A sentence which begins with a modifier rather than with its subject is not necessarily any better than a sentence which begins with its subject, but a series of sentences all beginning in the same way will produce a monotonous style. Monotony may also result from exclusive use of simple and compound sentences or from overuse of short sentences.

Avoiding Monotonous Style

The first of the two paragraphs below is monotonous reading for three reasons. First, all the sentences begin in the same way — with the subject. Second, all the sentences are structurally alike — simple and compound. Third, the sentences are short. Read the paragraph through. Then read the second paragraph and note how much smoother the style is. The sentences begin in a variety of ways; the addition of subordinate clauses has brought in some complex sentences to relieve the monotony of so many simple and compound sentences; some of the short sentences have been combined to make a few longer sentences.

MONOTONOUS STYLE

The career of Marjorie Lawrence should be an inspiration to all of us. She was a starring soprano with the Metropolitan Opera Company. She was born in Australia and studied music first in Melbourne. She then continued her studies in Paris. She made her operatic debut with the Monte Carlo Opera Company. She came to New York in 1935 and sang her first role with the Metropolitan as Brunhild in Wagner's opera *Die Walküre*. She was nearing the height of her career in 1941. She went on a concert tour in Mexico and was struck down by polio. Doctors held little hope for her, but her husband was a doctor and polio specialist, and he helped her to regain her health. Marjorie Lawrence did not walk to any extent after her attack. Her beautiful voice, however, was not affected by the disease, and she appeared in opera and on the concert stage. She sang operatic roles in a sitting position, and she used a special movable platform in concerts. This enabled her to stand. Marjorie Lawrence overcame her handicap. The same handicap would have ended the career of a less courageous singer.

VARIED STYLE

The career of Marjorie Lawrence, who was a starring soprano with the Metropolitan Opera Company, should be an inspiration to all of us. Born in Australia, she first studied music in Melbourne. After continuing her studies in Paris, she made her operatic debut with the Monte Carlo Opera Company. In 1935 she came to New York, where she sang her first role with the Metropolitan as Brunhild in Wagner's opera *Die Walküre*. Nearing the height of her career, she was struck down by polio while on a concert tour in Mexico in 1941. Doctors held little hope for her, but her husband, who was a doctor and a polio specialist, helped her to regain her health. Marjorie Lawrence did not walk to any extent after her attack, but as her beautiful voice was not affected by the disease, she appeared in opera and on the concert stage. She sang operatic roles in a sitting position, but for concerts she used a special movable platform which enabled her to stand. Marjorie Lawrence overcame a handicap which would have ended the career of a less courageous singer.

Note the greater variety of the second paragraph as revealed in the following tabulation:

	1ST PAR.	2ND PAR.
Sentences beginning with the subject	15	5
Sentences beginning with a modifier	0	4
Simple and compound sentences	15	3
Complex and compound-complex sentences	0	7
Average sentence length	13 wds.	20 wds.

(1) Begin some of your sentences with a transposed appositive or with one of these modifiers: single-word modifier; phrase modifier; clause modifier.

Appositive

SUBJECT FIRST The president of the Board of Education, a frequent visitor to the schools, is well known to all students.

TRANSPOSED APPOSITIVE FIRST **A frequent visitor to the schools,** the president of the Board of Education is well known to all students.

Single-word Modifiers

SUBJECT FIRST Mr. Jackson is tall and handsome, and he makes an excellent doorman.

SINGLE-WORD MODIFIERS FIRST **Tall and handsome,** Mr. Jackson makes an excellent doorman.

SUBJECT FIRST A number of changes have been made here recently.

SINGLE-WORD MODIFIER FIRST **Recently,** a number of changes have been made here.

SUBJECT FIRST The house was deserted and dilapidated and made a depressing picture.

SINGLE-WORD MODIFIERS FIRST **Deserted and dilapidated,** the house made a depressing picture.

Phrase Modifiers

SUBJECT FIRST He was almost unbeatable on the tennis court.

PREPOSITIONAL PHRASE FIRST **On the tennis court,** he was almost unbeatable.

SUBJECT FIRST Joe tired rapidly during the second set and decided to save his strength for the third set.

PARTICIPIAL PHRASE FIRST **Tiring rapidly during the second set,** Joe decided to save his strength for the third set.

SUBJECT FIRST Pete worked in a hospital and acquired a great deal of medical information.

GERUND PHRASE FIRST **By working in a hospital,** Pete acquired a great deal of medical information.

Clause Modifiers

SUBJECT FIRST Investigators of the cause of the crash had to depend on evidence found in the wreckage because there were no survivors or witnesses.

CLAUSE FIRST **Because there were no survivors or witnesses,** investigators of the cause of the crash had to depend on evidence found in the wreckage.

SUBJECT FIRST Our leading lady, when she heard the orchestra playing the overture, suffered a severe attack of stage fright.

CLAUSE FIRST **When she heard the orchestra playing the overture,** our leading lady suffered a severe attack of stage fright.

● EXERCISE 1. This exercise will give you practice in beginning sentences in a variety of ways. Revise each sentence according to the instructions.

1. The college president stated at the alumni luncheon the immediate financial needs of the college. [Begin with a prepositional phrase.]
2. A university's primary responsibility is to its resident students, although it should encourage educational programs for its alumni. [Begin with a subordinate clause.]
3. This seems to be a highly technical book, to the casual reader. [Begin with a prepositional phrase.]
4. No American can ignore today the implications of international trade to American prosperity. [Begin with a single-word adverb modifier.]
5. The magazine will be published weekly during the winter months. [Begin with a prepositional phrase.]
6. The first ships of the expedition will sail in October, if present plans are approved. [Begin with a subordinate clause.]
7. Navy divers expertly and rapidly repaired the damaged hull. [Begin with single-word adverb modifiers.]
8. The Vice-President announced the make-up of the new committee after a meeting at the White House. [Begin with prepositional phrases.]
9. The legislature, according to the evening paper, will probably pass the Governor's bill to raise the tax on gasoline. [Begin with a prepositional phrase.]
10. Commencement exercises will be held in the stadium unless the weather is bad. [Begin with a subordinate clause.]
11. The firm lacked funds for expansion and so attempted to borrow the needed money. [Begin with a participial phrase: *Lacking* . . .]
12. Berra is the most impatient hitter in the league and frequently hits pitches that most batters wouldn't look at. [Begin with an appositive phrase: *The most* . . .]
13. The skin on the average adult weighs 8.8 pounds and occupies an area of 20 square feet. [Begin with a participial phrase]
14. The expedition was led by Colonel Walter H. Wood of New York and spent several weeks at its camp on Seward Glacier. [Begin with a participial phrase.]

15. One can see at first glance that this modernistic furniture uses as much metal as wood. [Begin with a prepositional phrase.]

● EXERCISE 2. Rearrange each sentence so that it will begin with a modifier or an appositive.

1. A bowling team was formed this winter for the first time in the history of the school.
2. A mysterious figure stepped cautiously into the darkened room.
3. Sally, a voracious reader, keeps the librarian busy supplying her with books.
4. Candidates for a driver's license must take a written examination to prove their knowledge of traffic regulations.
5. The children, when their mothers are working, are cared for in nursery schools.
6. The audience, tired and hot, soon became impatient.
7. We were frightened by the explosion and dared not move from our places.
8. More than half of the 90,000 acres under cultivation had been ruined by the recent drought.
9. Accept the plan we have proposed if you have nothing better to suggest.
10. Jim, a merchant sailor for ten years, knew every important port in the world.
11. There will never be a real compromise between such stubborn adversaries.
12. Resorters stand around the village store and chat with one another while waiting for the afternoon mail to be sorted.
13. The new houses, although they look exactly alike from the outside, have very different interiors.
14. Competition has been growing more and more intense between the railroads and the trucking companies.
15. A small boy, sobbing bitterly, ran toward me.

(2) By means of subordination vary the structure of your sentences. Avoid the exclusive use of simple

and compound sentences.[1] Skillful use of the complex sentence is an indication of maturity in style.

(3) Vary the length of your sentences. Avoid the choppy style caused by using too many short sentences. Combine short sentences into longer sentences.

Study the following examples to see how several short, simple sentences may, by subordination, be changed into one longer complex sentence.

SIMPLE SENTENCES William Halstead is a lieutenant colonel in the Air Forces Reserve. His plane crashed nineteen miles off Fire Island. He was rescued by a Coast Guard plane from Floyd Bennett Field.

COMPLEX SENTENCE *When his plane crashed nineteen miles off Fire Island,* William Halstead, *a lieutenant colonel in the Air Forces Reserve,* was rescued by a Coast Guard plane from Floyd Bennett Field. [In this sentence subordination was accomplished by means of an adverb clause and an appositive.]

SIMPLE SENTENCES The great earthquake in Ecuador in 1949 was caused by a shift in the Andes Mountains. It took over six thousand lives. It was the worst quake in South American history.

COMPLEX SENTENCE *Caused by a shift in the Andes Mountains,* the great earthquake in Ecuador in 1949, *which took over six thousand lives,* was the worst quake in South American history. [In this sentence subordination was accomplished by means of a beginning participial phrase and an adjective clause.]

SIMPLE SENTENCES The auditorium in the Cathedral Avenue School has not been used for several years. It has now been converted into classrooms and offices. These will house the art department and the reading clinic.

COMPLEX SENTENCE The auditorium in the Cathedral Avenue School, *which has not been used for several years,*

[1] For a review of subordination, see pages 192–97. For an explanation of the kinds of sentences, see pages 58–60.

has now been converted into classrooms and offices *which will house the art department and the reading clinic.* [In this sentence subordination was accomplished by means of adjective clauses.]

● EXERCISE 3. By using various means of subordination (participial phrase, appositive, subordinate clause, etc.) combine the short sentences in each group into one long, smooth sentence.

1. Engineers reported that a tunnel would be more practical than a bridge. The City Commission authorized the construction of a tunnel.
2. The students complained that they could not study in Miss Baker's study hall. There was too much confusion. They did not realize that they themselves were responsible for the confusion.
3. The cornerstone for the new post office in Meadbrook was laid on Monday. Politicians and federal and village dignitaries were present. The cornerstone was laid by Mayor James Fitzgerald.
4. Dr. Brown diagnosed the case as appendicitis. He called an ambulance, rushed the patient to the hospital, and removed the appendix. Dr. Brown is head surgeon at the Meadows Hospital.
5. Twenty-five students attended reading classes during the first term. All improved not only in reading but in spelling and vocabulary. Twenty raised their reading level two years.
6. Race officials decided to hold the races in spite of the rough water. Three boats were smashed. Two drivers were seriously injured. The officials were severely criticized.
7. Helen did not want another extracurricular job. She accepted the presidency of the Girls' Athletic Association. She was more interested in sports than in anything else.
8. The Pulaski Highway in Maryland and the Pulaski Skyway in New Jersey were named after General

Casimir Pulaski. He was an exiled Polish count. He served under Washington in the Revolution.

9. John heard that the city needed boys to cut grass and collect refuse. He applied at the City Hall. He was disappointed to learn that all jobs had been filled.
10. Mr. Sampson's will named his secretary as principal beneficiary and his business partner as executor. The will disappointed his relatives. They had expected to find themselves in one or the other of those positions.

Avoiding "Stringy" Style

17b. Give variety to your writing by avoiding the "stringy" style which results from the overuse of *and* and *so*.

In everyday conversation we tend to string our ideas out, one after another, by means of the simple conjunctions *and* and *so*. In writing, however, this sort of thing appears childish and monotonous. As you can see from the following examples, "stringiness" is an obvious fault which can be easily corrected. There are three ways to correct it.

(1) Correct a stringy sentence by subordination of ideas.

STRINGY SENTENCE Dad told me I could have the car, **and** I called Jane immediately **and** told her I would pick her up.

IMPROVED *As soon as Dad told me I could have the car,* I called Jane and told her I would pick her up. [*and* removed by subordination]

STRINGY SENTENCE Mr. Berg thought the bell had rung, **and** he dismissed his class early, **and** we used the extra time to get a coke.

IMPROVED *When Mr. Berg, thinking the bell had rung, dismissed his class early,* we used the extra time to get a coke. [*and* removed by subordination]

17b

The use of *so* as a conjunction is considered poor form. Its use can be avoided almost always by using a subordinate clause or a phrase expressing cause or reason.

POOR USE OF "SO" By this time it was dark, **so** we ended the game.

IMPROVED *Because by this time it was dark,* we ended the game. [*so* removed by subordination]

STRINGY USE OF "AND" AND "SO" Raymond was "going steady," **and** he found it was expensive, **so** he took an after-school job.

IMPROVED *When he found that "going steady" was expensive,* Raymond took an after-school job. [stringiness corrected by subordination]

(2) Correct a stringy sentence by dividing it into two sentences.

STRINGY SENTENCE The bag was too heavy to carry, **so** we dragged it, *and* eventually the bottom wore through, **so** we left a trail of cement up the sidewalk and across the lawn.

IMPROVED *Since the bag was too heavy to carry,* we dragged it. *When the bottom eventually wore through,* we left a trail of cement up the sidewalk and across the lawn. [stringiness corrected by subordination and by division into two sentences]

STRINGY SENTENCE We were in the middle of the bridge **and** the motor coughed, sputtered, *and* finally stopped, **so** Dad got out *and* looked under the hood, **but** he didn't find anything wrong, **so** he looked at the gas gauge **and** discovered that we were out of gas.

IMPROVED *When we were in the middle of the bridge,* the motor coughed, sputtered, and finally stopped. *After he had got out and looked under the hood without finding anything wrong,* Dad looked at the

gas gauge and discovered that we were out of gas. [stringiness corrected by subordination and by division into two sentences]

(3) Correct a stringy sentence by reducing co-ordinate clauses to a compound predicate.

STRINGY CO-ORDINATE CLAUSES Marvin entered into the spirit of the occasion, **and** he lost his usual shyness, **and** he became the life of the party.

IMPROVED Marvin *entered* into the spirit of the occasion, *lost* his usual shyness, and *became* the life of the party. [clauses reduced to a compound predicate]

● EXERCISE 4. This exercise consists of stringy sentences. Revise the sentences by one or more of the following methods: subordination, division into more than one sentence, and reduction of co-ordinate clauses to a compound predicate. Get rid of the monotonous use of *and* and *so*. You may add a few words of your own if the words will help you to improve the sentences.

1. The next morning most roads were impassable, so there was hardly anyone in school, so we were given a holiday.
2. Luckily at that time a tow truck came by, and we yelled to them, and they gave us a set of chains, and we put them on the car, and the chains helped us to get out of the snowbank and through the drifts on the way home.
3. You can follow Route 40 to Baltimore and cut straight south so you can reach Richmond without going to Washington, and you will have a beautiful drive.
4. The men began their search for the lost child at once, but they had no clues to follow, and the area was wild, so they sent for some bloodhounds, but the only ones near by were already busy trailing a bank robber.
5. Harry bowled a total of 600 in three games, and he tied

the alley's three-game record, and he broke the record for a single game, so he was hailed as alley champion.

6. It was my father's summer vacation, so we drove to Mt. Washington and left the car there and hiked for a week on the Appalachian Trail, and it was the best vacation of our lives.
7. There are small cabins and open shelters along the trail, so we felt sure of night quarters, but we were civilized hikers, and we always managed to be near an inn when evening came, so we could relax in luxury.
8. The story begins with a family that came over from Europe years ago, and they started West in a wagon train, but they had trouble with their wagon, so they told their friends to go ahead, but then it was hard to find the wagon train again out on the prairie.
9. You have an hour for lunch, so you plow through the crowds and finally get pushed into a cheap hamburger stand, and then you wait a half hour for a seat and another twenty minutes for them to kill and warm the meat, and you get back to work five minutes late, so you get a scolding from the boss.
10. I asked Sue for a date, but she had already accepted an invitation, so I asked Barbara, but she had heard that I had asked Sue first, so she wouldn't go with me.
11. Many displaced persons were people who had lost their homes and families, so they had no place to return to, and others had fled from their homelands during the war, and they didn't dare to return to live under a hostile government.

● EXERCISE 5. The style of the following items is choppy and stringy. Rewrite each item, making the style varied and smooth. Combine and subordinate ideas through phrases, appositives, subordinate clauses, and compound predicates. Vary the beginnings of sentences, the structure, and the length of sentences. You may add a few words of your own if the words will help you to improve the sentences.

1. Byrd's second expedition landed on Little America, and they proceeded to dig out the underground quarters left by the first expedition, but the buildings were twenty feet below the snow level, and so it took a lot of work to dig them out.
2. We took three empty oil drums for our raft and laid them in the water, and we took an old packing crate and made a frame to enclose the drums, and then the fun began. We slipped the frame over the drums and had visions of a leisurely sail down the river on our raft, but when we got aboard, the raft turned over, so we were wet and discouraged but patiently began rebuilding operations.
3. Two kinds of dream are very common. The first kind is the embarrassing-moment dream. You are walking down Main Street on Saturday afternoon, and you suddenly realize you are in your underclothes. The other kind is the can't-escape dream. A monster is chasing you, but you can't make your feet move. You face the grim and painful end with screams of horror, and then you awaken and shiver and stare at the ceiling and wonder at your close call.
4. Our group was scheduled for a mountain-climbing expedition. We drove thirty-five miles in the camp truck over bumpy roads, and we arrived at Mt. Kearsarge and put our bed rolls on the ground and started to tramp up the mountain, but we chose the harder trail at the branching-off place halfway up, so we got very tired and stopped to rest in a clearing.
5. It was Monday morning in history class, and I looked around at my classmates and saw that they were as sleepy as I was. Someone was reading, and she had the kind of voice that made me want to go to sleep, so I gave in and rested my forehead on my hand and closed my eyes. I was just settling down for a nap when the teacher's voice boomed out my name, and I was so startled that I dropped my book from my lap and looked up stupidly into his face.

CHAPTER 18

Appropriate Vocabulary

USE WORDS AND PHRASES WHICH ARE FRESH, CONSISTENT, IDIOMATIC, APPROPRIATE, AND SPECIFIC

In addition to the many methods of achieving correct, clear, and smooth writing which are discussed in other chapters in this book, the matter of word choice is an extremely important consideration in learning to write well. The whole subject of vocabulary building is too broad for treatment here, but the five cautions in this chapter concerning the words you use in writing will, if carefully observed, remove a few errors in word choice which are common in the writing of high school students.

Trite Expressions

18a. Use a vocabulary which is fresh — avoid trite expressions.

Trite expressions, sometimes called *clichés* or *bromides*, are expressions which have become stale through too frequent use. There is nothing inherently wrong with such expressions as *bolt from the blue*, *blanket of snow*, *doting parent*, *briny deep*, or such figures of speech as *fall into the arms of Morpheus* (go to sleep), *burn the midnight oil*, *busy as a bee;* but they have been used so much that they may bore your reader and weaken the effect of your writing. Trite expressions come to mind so readily that they will get into your writing unless you make a special effort to avoid them. A writer who relies on clichés does not long hold the respect of his readers, who soon conclude that he is either lacking in originality or too lazy to express his thoughts in his own words. The simple, straightforward statement of an idea is better than the use of a worn-out expression.

TRITE	SIMPLE, STRAIGHTFORWARD
beat a hasty retreat	retired quickly
burning question	important question
sumptuous repast	excellent dinner
green with envy	extremely envious
by the sweat of his brow	by hard work

The following list of trite expressions is only a sampling, but reading it through will make you aware of the fault of triteness. You and your classmates can add to the list.

TRITE EXPRESSIONS

a good time was had by all
accidents will happen
add insult to injury
after all is said and done
almighty dollar
beat a hasty retreat
beautiful but dumb
beyond the shadow of a doubt
blushing bride
budding genius
busy as a bee
calm before the storm
clear as crystal
demon rum
depths of despair
discreet silence
doomed to disappointment
each and every
easier said than done
fair sex
few and far between
fond parents
gala occasion
green with envy
Grim Reaper
hale and hearty
in no uncertain terms
in this day and age
irony of fate

last but not least
long arm of the law
make a long story short
momentous decision
nipped in the bud
none the worse for wear
point with pride
quick as a flash
ripe old age
sadder but wiser
silence reigned
straight and narrow path
supreme sacrifice
tender mercies
to the bitter end
trials and tribulations
view with alarm
viselike grip
weaker sex
wended our way
white as a sheet
word to the wise

● EXERCISE 1. Rewrite each of the following sentences, substituting fresh, simple, straightforward language for the trite expressions.

1. As I was burning the midnight oil, Stan bounded into the room like a bolt from the blue.
2. Cynthia shook her golden locks and scolded us in no uncertain terms.
3. Wreathed in smiles he met the Grim Reaper and, with heartfelt thanks, gave up the struggle for existence.
4. Wilbur beat a hasty retreat every time a member of the fair sex came into the room.
5. None the worse for wear at the close of the day, I wended my way home and dressed for a date with my one and only.
6. Out of a clear blue sky, the reason for my father's furrowed brow dawned upon me.
7. Hope springs eternal that my efforts will be crowned with success and that I shall earn a little hard cash this summer.
8. Looking out upon a sea of faces, the speaker advised each and every one of the assembled multitude that he had reached a momentous decision.
9. An alert detective nipped in the bud the crook's fond hopes of escaping the long arm of the law.
10. More dead than alive at the end of the gala occasion, Mrs. Parker sped the departing guests, bidding each a fond farewell.

Mixed Figures of Speech

18b. Use a vocabulary which is consistent — avoid mixed figures of speech.

A figure of speech is an expression in which words are used regardless of their true meaning to give a special effect. For instance, when we speak of "thunder growling behind the hills," we are implying that thunder is an animal and can growl. Whoever is listening to us knows well enough that thunder is not an animal capable of growling, yet our listener recognizes the effectiveness of our using *growl* in this way. *Growling thunder* is a figure of speech.

When, perhaps with a bow to the cliché expert, we refer to "muscles of steel," we know that no one actually has muscles of steel. We are using the word *steel* apart from its literal meaning, to create a figure of speech which, we hope, will express effectively the great strength of the muscles we are talking about. In our everyday speech and in our writing we use figures of speech so much that many of our commonest clichés fall into that category.

The following will serve to clarify what a figure of speech is:

milky sky [Literally, there is no milk in the sky.]
seas of bloom [A blossoming orchard is not literally a sea.]
galloping clouds [Animals, not clouds, gallop.]
her bespectacled beak [Is she really a bird?]

The most commonly used figures of speech are out-and-out comparisons: *feet like shovels*, *thin as a bookmark*, *the sun was a golden dollar*.

If you are at all imaginative, you should use figures of speech to give vividness and color to your writing. They are also an important means of gaining conciseness because they suggest much in a few words. You should be aware, however, of one error which is easily made in the use of figures of speech. This is the fault of mixing two different figures or comparisons; in other words, of failing to stick consistently to a comparison once you have made it. Examples will make clear the fault of inconsistency which results from mixed figures of speech, or *mixed metaphors*, as they are sometimes called.

MIXED Like a school of great fish plying the blue depths of the sea, the silver planes passed overhead, each dutiful bird following the leader of the flock. [The first figure likens the planes to fish; the second likens them to birds.]

BETTER Like a school of great fish plying the blue depths of the sea, the silver planes passed overhead, each dutiful **fish** following the leader.

MIXED His face reddened as mountainous waves of embarrassment broke over him, all but drying up the little confidence he had. [Mountainous waves are water; they would hardly "dry up" anything.]

BETTER His face reddened as mountainous waves of embarrassment broke over him, all but **washing away** the little confidence he had.

● EXERCISE 2. Seven of the following sentences contain mixed figures of speech. Revise the sentences to remove the mixed figures. If the figure is consistently maintained, write + after its number on your paper.

1. Finally taking the bit in its teeth, the team rolled through all opposition.
2. Like poisoned arrows, his words pierced our hopes.
3. Only recently the baby of the entertainment family, television is now the tail that wags the dog.
4. George dived into his studies, afraid that he would

never reach the top of the heap, but determined not to give up before the round started.

5. In this dull company his best joke sank like a soggy cake, and he sensed the futility of shooting a second time at a worthless target.
6. The hurricane sobbed about the house, clutched at the eaves with frantic fingers, and devoured the chimney in one bite.
7. Life is a worthy adversary for all of us; just when we think we are getting the better of him, he knocks us down; and as soon as we have again won the advantage, we find ourselves driven ashore on the rocks.
8. Mrs. Hepburn, like a cackling hen, fluttered into the room and bobbed eagerly about from one group of chickens to another.
9. He spent the morning of his career groping through the dark halls of obscurity until the publication of his third novel thrust him above the surface of the black waters into the brilliant noonday sun.
10. The productive field of psychiatry, once considered a pseudo science, has now achieved respectability and may become a most important branch of medical research.

● EXERCISE 3. Each item in the following exercise contains a figure of speech and a space where a portion of the sentence has been omitted. Beneath the sentence four wordings are suggested for this space, one of which is preferable if the figure of speech is to be consistently maintained. Number on your paper from 1 to 10. After the proper number write the letter of the wording which best fits the blank space.

1. I felt that the diagnosis was correct, but I doubted that the remedy offered would . . .
   a. smother the flame.
   b. solve the problem.
   c. cure the disease.
   d. overcome the opposition.

2. In middle age a man may look into the mirror of his past and . . .
   a. pat himself gently on the back.
   b. take a little pride in his achievements.
   c. congratulate himself.
   d. preen himself a bit.
3. Mr. Bowne behaves in the classroom like a tough top sergeant, . . .
   a. shouting from his pulpit and frightening even the most devout worshipers.
   b. calling all plays and carrying the ball himself.
   c. shouting out orders and brutally exaggerating the details of discipline.
   d. beating his slaves with the lash of long assignments and low grades.
4. In this green pasture of learning, my imagination . . .
   a. fed on the classics.
   b. turned into classical halls.
   c. built a classical house.
   d. was drawn to the shelves of classics.
5. Business enterprise disappeared in the wintry blasts of the depression, and capital . . .
   a. sank beneath the surface.
   b. melted from sight.
   c. hibernated.
   d. dwindled to nothing.
6. In the character of Willie Stark, fiction has been draped about the bones of fact, and, in places, . . .
   a. the truth emerges.
   b. one can recognize the original.
   c. the skeleton shows through.
   d. the model becomes clear.
7. The moon had just risen, very golden, over the hill, and like a bright, watching spirit . . . the bars of an ash tree's naked boughs.
   a. towered above
   b. rolled behind
   c. obscured
   d. peered through

8. All his life he struggled against the current of his time until eventually . . .
   a. the antagonistic forces destroyed him.
   b. he was driven downstream and drowned.
   c. the historic events drove him underground.
   d. he grew too weak to withstand the blows of Fate
9. The characters weave the pattern of the book, . . . of motives and cross-purposes, that looks like a triangle, but is in reality a quadrangle.
   a. an edifice
   b. a vehicle
   c. a fabric
   d. a structure
10. America is young. Her traditions are light bands around her heart and mind. She could easily . . ., make profound changes, and quickly adjust herself to new policies.
    a. part with them
    b. upset the applecart
    c. break them
    d. deny them

Unidiomatic Expressions

18c. Use a vocabulary which is idiomatic — avoid unidiomatic prepositions

An idiom is a particular combination of words with a generally understood meaning which has received the approval of custom. Idioms are not formed according to any rules. Each must be learned as a separate expression with a definite meaning. Because English is your native language, you usually experience little difficulty in speaking and writing idiomatically. You have learned English idioms by hearing them. You say, for example, **in** *Chicago* (not *at Chicago*), but **at** *home* (not *in home*). To reverse the prepositions in those expressions would be to use them unidiomatically. Certain words customarily (idiomatically) take certain prepositions. Even though your native tongue is English, you may at times be in doubt as to which of two or three prepositions is the idiomatic one. When such a doubt arises, consult a dictionary. Some of the words which are troublesome in this respect are listed below. The list is not complete; it is intended only to call your attention to the importance of idiom in the use of prepositions.

IDIOMATIC PREPOSITIONS

accompanied **by** (to be in the company of) The boys will be accompanied *by* a doctor and a guide.

accompanied **with** (associated with) He accompanied his demands *with* threats.

accused **of** (not *with*) We were accused *of* lying.

agree **to** or **on** (used usually for things) I agree *to* their proposal. We agreed *on* plans.

agree **with** (used for persons) I agree *with* Edna.

angry **at** (used for things) She is angry *at* the damage done to her garden.

angry **with** (used for persons) No one could stay angry *with* Jane.

at home (not *to*) Jane stayed *at* home all evening.

compare **to** (one thing is like another) She compared you *to* a squalling baby.

compare **with** (two things considered together and their qualities compared) The critics compared his earlier novels *with* his later ones.

comply **with** (not *to*) You must comply *with* the regulations.

frightened **by** (not *of*) He said he had been frightened *by* a ghost. [Note also: He is *afraid of* (*not* frightened of) dogs.]

part **from** (go away) Ted and I parted *from* the crowd.

part **with** (to give up something) He parted *with* his money reluctantly.

privilege **of** (not *to*) She asked for the privilege *of* staying out late.

wait on (to serve as a waiter or a clerk) No one in the store would wait *on* me.

wait for (to await the arrival of someone or something) We waited *for* (not *on*) Matthew almost an hour.

● EXERCISE 4. Number on your paper from 1 to 20. If the idiomatic preposition has been used, write a + after the proper number. If the unidiomatic preposition has been used, write the whole correct idiom (*accused of*, *wait for*, etc.) after the proper number.

1. The judge accused the prisoner with being armed and defying the law.
2. No one was frightened by my threats.
3. He asked for the privilege to leave school at noon.
4. Don't be angry with a situation you cannot change.
5. Each boy must be accompanied by his parents.
6. They refused to comply to our demands.
7. We were distressed when we were parted from our grammar school friends.
8. Don't be frightened of ordinary snakes.
9. He has often been compared with a bulldog.
10. Father hated to part with the old car.
11. I will not agree with these conditions.
12. Will the student body comply with such a request?
13. The essayist compared city life to country life.
14. She was living to home with her parents.
15. I don't know why you should be angry with me.
16. He accompanied his greeting by a bone-crushing handshake.
17. Why are you angry at me?
18. Teachers naturally compare me with my sister.
19. I guess they're not to home.
20. After waiting on Martin for twenty minutes, I decided he had forgotten our appointment.

Slang and Colloquialisms

18d. Use a vocabulary which is appropriate to the kind of composition which you are writing —

avoid slang in written composition: use colloquialisms sparingly in formal writing.

The following list of slang words will serve to make clear what slang is:

broke (no money)	nutty (crackbrained)
cagey	on the beam
corny	racket (fraudulent scheme)
cuckoo (crazy)	shebang
dumbbell (stupid person)	stinker
hep	swell
kick the bucket (die)	skip it

Slang is widely used in very informal conversation. It is particularly popular with high school and college students. Occasionally a slang expression finds its way up the usage ladder and becomes acceptable English, but most slang lasts but a short time. *Slang should not be used in writing, except in reproducing dialogue.*

A much broader category of informal expressions is the category of colloquial language. Colloquialisms are used in informal speaking and writing, but they must be carefully limited in composition of a serious nature. The following are typical colloquialisms: *jiffy*, *guy* (a person), *workout*, *slug* (heavy blow), *in a jam*, *out on a limb*, *exam*, *a kid* (child), *a sport* (gambler).

Although dictionaries label words *colloquial* or *slang*, you cannot rely on their arbitrarily drawn distinctions as a means of deciding whether a word is appropriate to your composition. You need to understand the basic point that any word which is inappropriate to the general *tone* of your composition should not be used, regardless of its dictionary label. You should control your natural tendency to use too many colloquialisms. The deciding factor is, of course, the degree of formality of your composition, which, in turn, determines the appropriateness of the words used. In a research paper colloquialisms should be used very sparingly. In an informal essay, they may be used as frequently as in conversation.

Read the following sentences taken from formal compositions and note the inappropriateness of the italicized words.

1. In any eighth-grade classroom where *kids* of the same chronological age are grouped together, we expect to find a physiological-age range of six or seven years.
2. There is a grave danger that we may expose far too many students of only medium ability to the long course of professional study in our universities. For the employment situation in some professional areas, we must admit, is *not so hot*.
3. Dickens was *hipped* on the idea that by revealing the social evils of the day he could destroy them one by one.

Meaning and Connotation

18e. Use a vocabulary which is specific. Select words with due regard for their varied meanings and their connotations.

A word is a symbol. A word has no meaning for you unless you know what it stands for. The thing or idea that a word stands for, or refers to, is known as its *referent* (rĕf′ĕr·ĕnt). You are able to understand a word only if you know what its referent is. The referent of a word should be the same for the person using the word as for the person reading or hearing it. When two persons have in mind different referents for the same word, the word is useless for communication between them.

If your teacher says, "Please give me the chalk," you immediately understand his request. You know what action *give* refers to, whom *me* refers to, and what the symbol *chalk* refers to. Had your teacher said, "Please give me the *glub*," however, you would have been confused. *Glub*, which looks and sounds like a word, is not customarily used to refer to anything. Since for you it has no referent, it is not, so far as you are concerned, a word at all.

CONCRETE WORDS AND ABSTRACT WORDS

Words may be divided into two groups — *concrete* words and *abstract* words. A concrete word is one whose referent can be touched or seen: *book*, *cloud*, *car*, *chalk*. An abstract word is one whose referent is an idea, something which cannot be touched or seen: *peace*, *need*, *love*, *freedom*.

(1) For clearness in description, choose the concrete word with the most specific referent.

Concrete words vary in definiteness. For example, the word *vehicle*, while its referent is something which can be seen and touched, is not at all specific. You probably do not have a clear mental picture of a *vehicle*. The word *car* is more specific; the word *convertible* is still more specific. "John was driving a dilapidated vehicle" will not convey as clear a picture as "John was driving a dilapidated convertible." As description, the second sentence is clearer. In all your writing, whenever you are considering several different words to express a particular meaning, select the one which is most specific.

● EXERCISE 5. Arrange the words in each group so that the word with the least specific referent will come first, and the word with the most specific referent will come last.

1. box, container, carton, hatbox
2. building, structure, bungalow, house

3. catastrophe, deluge, disturbance, storm
4. crack-up, plane crash, event, accident
5. globe, spheroid, baseball, ball
6. cigarette lighter, gadget, thing, mechanism

(2) For clearness, choose among synonyms the one word which expresses your meaning *exactly*.

Synonyms are words which are similar in meaning. Rarely, however, are they identical in meaning. A careful writer selects the word which has the exact referent that he has in mind. The following words are synonyms in that each is similar in meaning to the word *boat,* yet they are different, for each word calls up a special meaning not found in the others: *vessel, ship, craft.* "We found tied to the dock a —— which we used to rescue the tired swimmers." Your mental picture of this action will be different if the word *ship* is used from what it will be if the word *craft* is used. Synonyms, however, can go only so far. The *kind* of boat in this instance will be a more exact referent for *boat* than any of its synonyms. Try substituting *liner, yacht, cruiser, scow, canoe, speedboat, catboat* in the sample sentence and note how your mental picture changes.

● EXERCISE 6. Without using the dictionary, explain the difference in meaning of the words in each group. Describe the referent of each word.

1. highway, road, street, boulevard, thruway, path, trail
2. fire, flame, holocaust, conflagration, bonfire
3. gush, spurt, spout, swash, flow
4. laughing, giggling, snickering, guffawing
5. excursion, trip, jaunt, tour

(3) Make clear the referent of an abstract word by definition or example.

Abstract words, which usually refer to general ideas, must always be used with care. A great many misunderstandings are caused by abstract words which have not been carefully defined. Unless two persons agree on the meaning (referent) of an abstract word, communication between them may break down. An abstract word may have many referents.

The word *freedom*, for example, has only a very vague referent until you define it. To a prisoner behind bars, *freedom* means getting out of jail. To Mr. Barnes, who resents the neighbors' criticism of his noisy family, *freedom* means the right of his family to make as much noise as they wish. Franklin D. Roosevelt defined the freedoms in which America believes as freedom of speech, freedom of worship, freedom from want, and freedom from fear. Each of these definitions provides a more specific referent for the word *freedom*, and each, in turn, could be more narrowly defined.

Communist Russia's philosophy of government is different from that of the United States. Yet the United States is referred to as a *republic*, and Russia's full name is the Union of Soviet Socialist *Republics*. Clearly the word *republic* has different referents in these two uses.

Sometimes an example will help to clarify the meaning of an abstract word. In the following sentence, the word *character* is vague. "Only men of strong character have been appointed to the Board of Directors." An example helps to show what is meant by *character*. "Every member of the Board, for example, has demonstrated his power to control his fellow workers, and, as a result, has been promoted to a managerial position."

● EXERCISE 7. Without using a dictionary, write a one- or two-sentence definition of each of the following words. Compare your definitions with those of your classmates. In discussion, you may find it helpful to clarify your meaning by means of an example.

1. goodness
2. culture
3. progress
4. success
5. justice

(4) In reading and writing, distinguish between the denotative and the connotative meanings of a word.

Compare the meaning of the following sentences:

1. Roy's **persistence** surprised everyone.
2. Roy's **stubbornness** surprised everyone.

Of course, the meaning of the two sentences may be the same. *Persistence* is another word for *stubbornness*, the quality of not giving up easily. This is the "denotative" meaning of the words. But the *effect* of the words on reader or listener is very different. *Stubbornness* suggests that Roy is unreasonable, narrow-minded, unwilling to listen to others. This *suggestive* meaning of a word is its *connotation*, or *connotative* meaning. Many words have connotations. There is nothing wrong in using a word because of its connotations, but you must be aware of the connotations lest you say or write something you did not intend.

"LOADED" WORDS

A word which, through its connotations, carries strong feeling is said to be "loaded." The propagandist, the newspaper columnist, the political speaker are likely to use loaded words. They are trying to appeal to the emotions of people. When used deliberately, loaded words are a form of persuasion which clear thinkers disapprove of.[1]

● EXERCISE 8. Compare the following reports of the same speech. Both reports contain loaded words.

[1] For further help in developing your awareness of "loaded" words, see page 551.

One is loaded against Senator Blank; the other is loaded in his favor. List the loaded words and compare them with their counterparts in the other report.

1

Senator Blank today blasted opponents of his highway expansion program in a blistering attack from the Senate floor. In a long-winded tirade, the aging politician made a desperate bid for support but succeeded in frightening only a few senators into backing his program.

2

Senator Blank today criticized opponents of his highway expansion program in a powerful statement from the Senate floor. In a thorough discussion, the venerable legislator made another strong bid for support, which apparently convinced several senators that they should back the program.

● EXERCISE 9. Discuss with your classmates and teacher the connotations of the following words.

1. plump, fat, pot-bellied
2. advertising, propaganda, persuasion
3. liberal, radical, extremist
4. visionary, crackpot, idealist
5. crowd, gang, mob, assemblage

CHAPTER 19

Exercises in Sentence Revision

This chapter contains exercises only. The exercises will help you in two ways: (1) they will test your understanding of sentence correctness, clearness, and smoothness; (2) they will give you practice in repairing faulty sentence structure. The theory behind the inclusion of exercises in any textbook is that if you learn to criticize and revise the awkward sentences in the book, most of which have been taken from student compositions, you will be able to criticize and revise your own awkward sentences.

Use the exercises in this chapter to "keep your hand in" the skills of good writing. You may use the chapter as a review of the preceding chapters (Chapters 5–17), or you may turn to it from time to time as a refresher. The exercises are of various kinds, and every exercise is devoted to more than one kind of skill.

IDENTIFYING AND CORRECTING ERRORS

● EXERCISE 1. Immediately below these directions you will find a list of errors in sentence structure. Each faulty sentence in the exercise illustrates one of these errors. Some of the sentences are correct. You are to do two things: (1) write *before* the number of the sentence on your paper the letter of the error illustrated in the sentence; (2) write *after* the number of the sentence a revision which eliminates the error. How you remove the error is not important, provided your sentence is correct, clear, and smooth. If the sentence is correct as it stands, write a + before the number of the sentence.

A Lack of agreement (subject and verb, or pronoun and antecedent)
B Incorrect case of pronoun
C Dangling modifier
D Lack of parallelism or faulty parallelism
E Unclear reference of pronoun (ambiguous, general, weak)

EXAMPLE 1. Do you know whom it was?
B 1. Do you know **who** it was?

1. A person may disapprove of a law, but they should not violate it.
2. She is a splendid athlete, a beautiful dancer, and as a student receives excellent grades in school.
3. Watch the highway signs carefully. It will prevent your going wrong.
4. Before looking up material in the library, a knowledge of library tools should be had.
5. The editor of the paper, as well as many of its readers, was worried about recent attacks on its editorial policy.
6. When taking off from a long runway, the motors of the plane should not be strained by the pilot in his haste to be airborne.
7. Because the dishes burned his fingers, he dropped them.
8. Businessmen not only use airplanes to get ahead of competitors, but also they can have more time at home.
9. Do you think you and him can run as fast as Jack and me?
10. Jack is a boy who, I believe, will become a good student.

11. Neither the President nor the Secretary of Defense were willing to express their personal opinion.
12. When the child gets too big for the crib, fold it and make a wardrobe out of it.
13. While on duty in the children's ward, the hospital was bombed.
14. Playing without sufficient practice, the team had neither the necessary skill nor enough stamina to win the game.
15. My brother and me agreed not to tell anyone except you and she.
16. If students do not call for their notebooks this week, they will be destroyed.
17. Asking one absurd question after another, Bob's teacher was soon made to dislike him.
18. If you prefer to hire us boys, you will have to pay us more than them.
19. One of the nation's most serious concerns are the health and happiness of its citizens.
20. Europe was plagued by the lack of adequate production facilities, and unemployment was widespread.

● EXERCISE 2. Follow the directions for Exercise 1.

A Sentence fragment
B Run-on sentence
C Incorrect tense or verb form
D Misplaced modifier
E Unclear relationship between sentence ideas (lack of subordination, faulty co-ordination)

1. After I had laid there awhile, I begun to get restless.
2. Sally was not pleased by her B in English, having expected an A, she was disappointed.
3. The five junior high school buildings will cost eight million dollars, and they were approved by the taxpayers in yesterday's balloting.
4. The car was driven by a stunning girl with a convertible top and red wheels.
5. The band in its new uniforms and the high-stepping

majorette with her twirling baton as well as the stirring music.

6. Emma and Mr. Elton were driving back from a visit with Mrs. Weston in a carriage.
7. At lunch today, Pete told me that he was going to college next week.
8. She had intended to have gone to the dance with her brother.
9. At home we suffer the constant interference of our parents, at college we will be free to make our own decisions.
10. Tickets for matinees will cost $1.50, and matinees will be given on Wednesdays and Saturdays.
11. I studied nothing but chemistry for a week, and I failed the test.
12. I found that, except for different literature selections, each English course covered the same material I had the year before.
13. During negotiations between labor and management, work in the factory continued as usual.
14. Mr. Doubleday was voted the most popular teacher in school, and he is my English teacher.
15. We found several of the boys in the shop very busy. Learning how to take a motor apart and put it together again.
16. We discovered this valuable antique table in a corner of the shop supported by two broken legs.
17. In high school I have been unable to take some courses I wanted and have been required to take others I did not want.
18. Fifty-four per cent of the students said they wished they knew how to study more effectively, forty-nine per cent said they wanted work experience.
19. If you would have come earlier, you could have seen the first act.
20. The demand for good television material exceeds the supply, and some of the best material, important news events, is not being fully used, and the reason is that news telecasts are not profitable.

SELECTING THE BEST EXPRESSION

● EXERCISE 3. Number on your paper from 1 to 25. After each of the following sentences, the italicized part of the sentence is rephrased in two ways. If you consider one of these rephrasings an improvement, write the letter of the better one (*a* or *b*) after the proper number on your paper. If you consider the sentence correct as it stands, write + after the proper number.

1. Behind one of the doors waits a tiger, *and the other has a beautiful lady behind it.*
   a. . . . and behind the other waits a beautiful lady.
   b. . . . and a beautiful lady waits behind the other.
2. If you go on a trip, *it will give you an excellent chance to practice your camera technique.*
   a. . . . you will have an excellent chance to practice your camera technique.
   b. . . . an excellent chance to practice your camera technique will be yours.
3. When developing films, *a darkroom will be needed.*
   a. . . . one thing you will need is a darkroom.
   b. . . . you will need a darkroom.
4. Having acquired a ball club of my own, *a person would find me a very contented man.*
   a. . . . you would find me a very contented man.
   b. . . . I would be a very contented man.
5. This discovery had a bad effect on the mind of Usher, *he thought he buried his sister alive.*
   a. . . . because he thought he had buried his sister alive.
   b. . . . Usher. He thought he buried his sister alive.
6. *The "La Roch," a small Canadian vessel, made* the first complete voyage around North America.
   a. The *La Roch* is a small Canadian vessel, and it made . . .
   b. Being a small Canadian vessel, the *La Roch* made . . .
7. In this case taking a bus *will be easier and won't cost so much as to take the train.*
   a. . . . will be easier and cheaper than the train.
   b. . . . will be easier and cheaper than taking the train.

8. During the winter *Anderson both developed his skill in skiing and ice skating.*
   a. . . . Anderson developed his skill in both skiing and ice skating.
   b. . . . Anderson developed both his skill in skiing and in ice skating.
9. *Pat and him told Mike and I* the answers to the homework problems.
   a. Pat and him told Mike and me . . .
   b. Pat and he told Mike and me . . .
10. Ever since the accident, *driving past that spot*, the whole experience has returned.
    a. . . . while driving past that spot, . . .
    b. . . . as I have driven past that spot, . . .
11. As we had promised, *my friend and myself* went directly home.
    a. . . . my friend and me . . .
    b. . . . my friend and I . . .
12. *Was it him whom* you thought stole the money?
    a. Was it he whom . . .
    b. Was it he who . . .
    c. Was it him who . . .
13. When one of the girls *have completed their report, ask them* to bring it to me.
    a. . . . has completed their report, ask them . . .
    b. . . . has completed her report, ask her . . .
14. Don't expect *Paul and I to be as good as her* in English.
    a. . . . Paul and me to be as good as she . . .
    b. . . . Paul and I to be as good as she . . .
15. Plans for the P.T.A. party *include not only dancing but also a floor show and a buffet supper.*
    a. . . . not only include dancing but also . . .
    b. . . . include not only dancing, but also the guests will enjoy a . . .
16. Jim had been in jail for safe cracking *but because of good behavior was paroled.*
    a. . . . *but* because of good behavior had been paroled.
    b. . . . *but* had been paroled for good behavior.
17. To my surprise the students *accepted the new type of*

examination which the teachers had prepared without a complaint.

a. . . . accepted the new type of examination without a complaint, which the teachers had prepared.

b. . . . accepted without a complaint the new type of examination which the teachers had prepared.

18. The mayor's economy committee *has been investigating street-cleaning costs, and it has published a report on its findings.*

a. . . . , which has been investigating street-cleaning costs, has published a report on its findings.

b. . . . has been investigating street-cleaning costs, and a report has been published on its findings.

19. The result of the game *didn't hardly surprise nobody.*

a. . . . didn't surprise nobody.

b. . . . surprised hardly anybody.

20. The students received *the new yearbook*, which came out on the last day of school, *with enthusiasm.*

a. The students received with enthusiasm the new yearbook . . .

b. The students with enthusiasm received the new yearbook . . .

21. *The telegram reached me too late advising against going to Washington.*

a. Too late the telegram advising against going to Washington reached me.

b. The telegram advising against going to Washington reached me too late.

22. *It is not the cost of a gift but its appropriateness that matters.*

a. The cost of a gift does not matter, but the appropriateness of it does.

b. It is not the cost that matters of a gift, but its appropriateness.

23. After being reprimanded twice, *the teacher, for further punishment, sent Tom to the principal.*

a. . . . by the teacher, Tom was sent to the principal for further punishment.

b. . . . the teacher sent Tom to the principal for further punishment.

24. Public figures must learn to take *the reporters' questions and the flashing of camera bulbs calmly.*
    a. . . . the questions of reporters and the flashing of camera bulbs calmly.
    b. . . . calmly the questioning of reporters and the flashing of camera bulbs.
25. *Driving through the mountains,* we were impressed by the magnificent engineering achievements of road builders.
    a. We were impressed by the magnificent engineering achievements of road builders, driving through the mountains.
    b. We were impressed by the magnificent engineering achievements, driving through the mountains, of road builders.

REVISING AWKWARD SENTENCES

● EXERCISE 4. This exercise is composed of awkward sentences which you are to rewrite. The sentences may be rearranged in any way that will make them clearer and smoother. Your purpose is to express the same idea in a better way. The faults in a sentence may not always be specific errors; they may be generally clumsy constructions. You may add words or omit words wherever you wish, provided you do not alter the meaning. Remove wordy passages. Eliminate errors in usage. Each problem can be handled in a single sentence, but your teacher may allow you to divide some of the problems into two sentences.

1. The boys hid themselves behind the classroom door. Thinking their teacher would be the first person to pass through it, but the principal arrived to their surprise first.
2. It was a misty night, quiet but still, there seemed to be someone moving about in the garden, or maybe it was something.

3. The dean was more impressed by the candidate's scholastic record than his athletic record impressed him.
4. There are many persons who have jobs part of the year, and a job is not held by them the rest of the year, being among the unemployed.
5. There is a great deal of Franklin's philosophy which certainly everyone who reads it can benefit from in his *Autobiography*.
6. Soon many families will have helicopters just like cars today and able to go from place to place much more easier than by car since there will be a direct route and the traffic will be much less.
7. Since we hadn't no equipment to fix the tire with, the motorcycle was pushed to the nearest gas station where we had a patch put on it.
8. Trotter was an optimist, easygoing, and nothing ever seemed to trouble him no matter what happened.
9. Opening the curtain, an empty stage was revealed, but the stage crew arrived a moment later and, busily working and talking, the set was soon up for the first act.
10. As we were pulling the canoe up on the beach, a second clap of thunder followed by a downpour of rain came.

● EXERCISE 5. Follow the directions for Exercise 4.

1. Mrs. Turnbull is a good author and through experience has found out what a reader wants and has given them it in this book.
2. From my own standpoint, gardening, whether flowers or vegetables, is a lot of fun, good exercise, and the experience it provides is valuable.
3. There are many ways to show loyalty to a friend that you can use, and one of these is to stop talking about them behind their back.
4. The American people are spending more money on education than ever before, which shows the value of good schools are coming to be appreciated by them.
5. In the day of our parents or even in our grandparents'

day, there were quite different responsibilities given to teen-agers than today.

6. I don't see why I have to be waited up for by my mother, for I know most of the boys' mothers I go out with don't wait up for their older children to come in.
7. After the dances in the gymnasium, of which we have a reasonable amount, many couples go to some eating place which is not too far away to have a bite to eat.
8. I found out that shopping quickly weakens a man's patience as I was waiting outside a department store for Mother one day.
9. The clash between East and West of ideals were blocking world unity at a time when war might be led to if unity could not be achieved.
10. By the time you have got the children into bed, you are so exhausted that all ambition to study has been lost by you, and television is all that is left as the only entertainment until the return of the parents is made.
11. The force of prejudice is not only held by individuals but also groups of people, even nations as a whole.
12. Being the first author in our history to reach the whole American public, Paine's book was a big seller, and it was about American independence.
13. Going even further into the effects of not having any more petroleum would have on the world is the realization that the thousands of factories in the world which use oil would have to close down.
14. After graduating from high school the learning we have attained may be lost or become hazy in a year of military training and it also adds another year to the time we will graduate from college to get a job.
15. There should be required by the school a pre-season physical examination, and there should be enforced a law to prevent anyone from playing football with a history of heart abnormalities.

PART FIVE

USING THE LIBRARY

CHAPTER 20

Information in the Library

LEARN THE ARRANGEMENT OF THE LIBRARY AND HOW TO USE LIBRARY TOOLS

Libraries are sufficiently alike so that when you have become familiar with one library, you can easily find your way in others. You should learn:

1. The arrangement of books in the library
2. The uses of the card catalogue
3. The names and functions of the parts of a book
4. The use of the *Readers' Guide*
5. The use of the vertical file
6. The location of items in your library

Arrangement of Books in the Library

20a. Learn the arrangement of books.

FICTION

Books of fiction (novels and stories) are usually arranged on the shelves alphabetically by authors. By this time you know where in your library the books of fiction are located. It is a simple matter, if you know the author of a book, to go directly to the book on the fiction shelves.

You can find out whether or not the library owns a certain book by looking it up in the card catalogue (page 292). If the book you want is listed in the catalogue but is not on the shelf, ask the librarian about it. It may be "out" in circulation, or it may be "on reserve." If possible, the librarian will reserve the book for you by placing your name on the reserve list. When your name comes up, the librarian will notify you.

NONFICTION: THE DEWEY DECIMAL SYSTEM

The arrangement of nonfiction books is accomplished through an amazingly efficient system developed by Melvil Dewey, an American librarian.[1] Although only librarians need to know all the details of the Dewey system, every user of a library should understand the principle on which the system is based. If you are not familiar with it, study the description and outline below.

In the Dewey system, every nonfiction book receives a number. The number, which is written on the back of the book, is determined by the particular classification of the book in the system. There are ten subject classifications, and any book can be fitted into one of them.

Within these broad divisions there can be an unlimited number of subdivisions. Since a decimal point plays an important part in the numbering of books, the plan is called the Dewey Decimal System. A valuable feature of this method of classifying books is that all books on the same subject are given the same class number and may be placed together on the library shelves. Once you have learned the class number of the subject you are interested in, you can

[1] The Library of Congress system of cataloguing is not described here because it is not common in high school libraries.

find all the books in the library on this subject grouped together in one place.

000–099	General Works (encyclopedias, periodicals, etc.)
100–199	Philosophy (includes psychology, conduct, etc.)
200–299	Religion (includes mythology)
300–399	Social Sciences (economics, government, law, etc.)
400–499	Language (dictionaries, grammars, etc.)
500–599	Science (mathematics, chemistry, physics, etc.)
600–699	Useful Arts (agriculture, engineering, aviation, etc.)
700–799	Fine Arts (sculpture, painting, music, etc.)
800–899	Literature (poetry, plays, orations, etc.)
900–909, 930–999	History
910–919	Travel
920–929	Biography (arranged alphabetically by names of persons written about)

Books having the same class number may be distinguished from one another by the author's name. For instance, all books on aviation are given the number 629.1. This number appears on the back of the book. With the number appears the first letter of the author's name: if the author is Hood, the book's complete number is $\frac{629.1}{\text{H}}$. This number, including the first letter of the author's name, is known as the book's *call number*. To find the call number of a book, you look up the book in the card catalogue.

Locating Information in the Library

THE CARD CATALOGUE

Undoubtedly you have used the card catalogue in your school or town library. You may not, however, know as much about it as you need to know in order to get the most help from it.

20b. Learn the uses of the card catalogue.

The card catalogue is a cabinet containing drawers filled with alphabetically arranged cards. In most libraries, the catalogue holds three cards for each book in the library: the *author card*, the *title card*, and the *subject card*.

The Author Card

The *author card* has the name of the author at the top. You may look up any book in the library by looking under the author's name. Since the cards for all books by an author will be placed together, you have the additional advantage of being able to find out what other books by the author the library owns. Cards for books *about* an author follow the cards for books *by* an author.

797•2 **Poole, Lynn.**
P
Diving for science. Pictures by Jeanne Bendick. New York, Whittlesey House [1955]

160 p. illus. 21 cm.

1. Marine biology. 2. Ocean bottom. 3. Diving, Submarine. I. Title.

QH91.P58 797.2 55–9550 ‡

Library of Congress [30]

Author Card

The Title Card

The *title card* has the book's title at the top. The quickest way to find a book in the catalogue is to look it up under its title. Cards for books whose titles begin with *a*, *an*, or *the* will be arranged alphabetically by the second word in the title. For example, the title card for a book entitled *The Writing of Fiction* would be found under *W*.

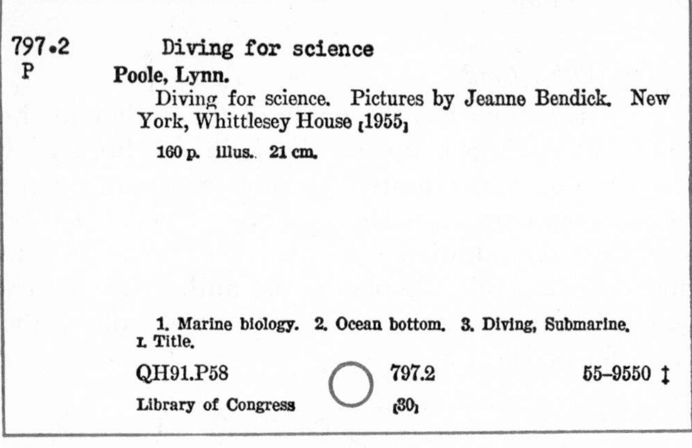

797.2 Diving for science
P Poole, Lynn.
Diving for science. Pictures by Jeanne Bendick. New York, Whittlesey House [1955]
160 p. illus. 21 cm.

1. Marine biology. 2. Ocean bottom. 3. Diving, Submarine.
I. Title.

QH91.P58 797.2 55-9550 ‡
Library of Congress [30]

Title Card

The Subject Card

The *subject card* has at the top the subject with which the book deals. Subject cards are invaluable when you wish to find a number of books on a subject but do not know specific titles or authors. Under the subject heading "Marine Biology," for instance, you will find a card for every book in the library on this subject. In fact, you may find a card for every book that contains as little as one article or chapter on marine biology, so thoroughly is the cataloguing done.

Information Given on a Catalogue Card

Brief study of one of the sample catalogue cards reproduced here will show you that a complete card

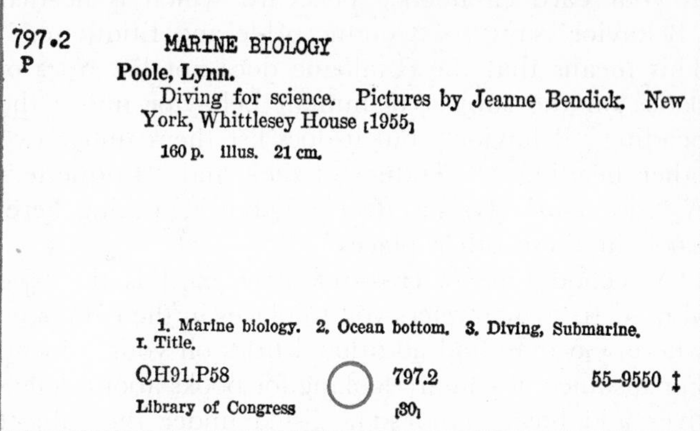
797.2
P
MARINE BIOLOGY
Poole, Lynn.
Diving for science. Pictures by Jeanne Bendick. New York, Whittlesey House [1955]
160 p. illus. 21 cm.

1. Marine biology. 2. Ocean bottom. 3. Diving, Submarine. I. Title.

QH91.P58 797.2 55-9550 ‡
Library of Congress [30]

Subject Card

gives a great deal of information. In addition to the title, author, and call number of a book, the card may give the following information:

1. *Facts about authorship:* full name of the author; names of joint authors and illustrators, if any. (When a book has several authors, there is an author card for each author.)

2. *Facts about publication:* the place of publication; the name of the publisher; the date of publication.

3. *Facts about the book:* number of pages; whether the book contains illustrations, diagrams, etc.; height of the book in centimeters.

"See" and "See Also" Cards

An important feature of a complete card catalogue is the cross-reference cards which it contains. These are of two kinds — "see" cards and "see also" cards. The "see" card refers you to a subject heading under which you will find the material you wish. For instance, suppose you have chosen to look up some books on human behavior. You look under "Behavior" in your card catalogue. The card which is headed "Behavior" says "see 'Conduct of life' and 'Etiquette.'" This means that the catalogue does not list titles of books on the subject of human behavior under the heading "Behavior," but it does list them under two other headings, "Conduct of life" and "Etiquette." A "see" card says in effect, "There is nothing here. Look in these other places."

A second type of cross-reference card is the "see also" card, which refers you to places in the catalogue where you may find additional titles on your subject. For instance, if you are looking for books about detectives and have found some listed under the subject heading "Detectives," you may find a "see also" card advising you to look also under the subject headings "Police" and "Secret service." A "see also" card says, "There is additional material in these other places."

```
    Behavior,   see
Conduct of life
Etiquette
```

```
    Detectives,   see also
Police
Secret service
```

"See" and "See Also" Cards

Summary

The card catalogue is a valuable library tool which may be used for the following purposes:

(1) To find the call number of a book
(2) To find out whether a certain book is owned by the library
(3) To find out what books by a certain author are in the library
(4) To find out what books on a certain subject are in the library
(5) To find out such facts about a book as may be given on a catalogue card: facts about authorship, publication, and the book itself

● EXERCISE 1. Using the card catalogue in your library, find the title, author, and call number of the following. Write them on your paper.

1. A history of American literature
2. A book about South America
3. A book by Samuel Clemens (Mark Twain)
4. A book giving information about Samuel Clemens
5. A book about baseball

Using the card catalogue, find answers to the following questions. Write the answers.

6. Does the library own any books by Stephen Vincent Benét? If so, give the title and call number of one of them.
7. Give the title, author, publisher, and publication date of a book about Franklin D. Roosevelt.
8. Does the library own the complete plays of Shakespeare in one volume? If so, give the exact title and the publisher of the book.
9. Give the title, author, and date of publication of a book of American poetry.
10. Does the library own a copy of Nathaniel Hawthorne's *The Scarlet Letter?* If so, give the publisher.

THE PARTS OF A BOOK

While on the general subject of books, you may wish to review the parts of a book. Not every book contains all the parts listed here, but as a person constantly working with books, you should know these parts, their names, and their functions.

20c. Learn the names and functions of the parts of a book.

The Frontispiece

The frontispiece is a full-page illustration. If the book has a frontispiece, it faces the title page.

The Title Page

The first important page in a book, the title page gives the complete title, the subtitle, if there is one, the name of the author or editor (sometimes his position, especially in a textbook), the name of the publisher, the place of publication, and sometimes the year of publication.

The Copyright Page

Following the title page is the copyright page. Here you find the year in which the book was copyrighted; i.e., registered in the government copyright office in Washington. Before a publisher releases a new book, he sends two copies to the United States Copyright Office along with certain required information. The office then issues a copyright which gives to the copyright owner exclusive right to print the book or any part of it for a period of twenty-eight years. At the end of that time the copyright may be renewed for another twenty-eight years. Sometimes publishers secure a copyright in their own name, sometimes in the name of the author.

The purpose of the copyright is to protect the author and publisher who have invested their work and money in the book. Reprinting copyrighted materials without the permission of the copyright owner is a criminal offense.

Often you will find more than one date listed on the copyright page: "Copyright 1946, 1949, 1955." This means that the first edition of the book was copyrighted in 1946. In 1949 and 1955 new material was added and a new copyright secured to cover the new material. The date of copyright is very important when you wish to know whether the material in a book is sufficiently up to date to be reliable.

Publishers sometimes indicate on this page which printing of the book this particular volume represents. Note the distinction between a new copyright date and a new printing date. The former tells when the book was last revised; the latter, when it was merely reprinted.

The Preface, Foreword, Introduction

These terms are now used interchangeably to refer to matter at the beginning of a book in which the author, editor, or publisher explains the purpose and scope of the book, gives information which aids the reader in understanding the book, acknowledges indebtedness, etc.

The Table of Contents

The table of contents appears at the front of the book and consists of a list of the chapters and subdivisions with their page numbers. It is useful for a quick view of the entire book, and a glance through it will often save you a great deal of time which might otherwise be spent thumbing pages.

List of Illustrations (Maps, Diagrams, Charts, etc.)

A list of illustrations with page numbers indicates how rich the book is in graphic materials, and provides a convenient place for the reader to look up the page number of a particular illustration.

The Appendix

The appendix contains additional material which the author did not wish to include in the body of the book. It may include long quotations from other works on the subject, lists, diagrams and tables, etc.

The Glossary

A glossary is usually a list of definitions of technical words used in the book. It is placed near the close of the book.

The Bibliography

The bibliography is a list of books consulted by the author in writing his book or recommended to the reader who wishes more information.

The Index

The index is an alphabetical list of topics treated in the book, given with page numbers. It is much more detailed than the table of contents.

The End Sheets

The pages pasted inside the front and back covers of the book are the end sheets. Sometimes they are used for a map or an illustration or to give a kind of summary of the contents.

● EXERCISE 2. Write answers to the following questions. You will notice that the last 6 items refer to this book (*English Grammar and Composition: Complete Course*).

1. List the parts of a book of nonfiction that you would not find in a book of fiction.
2. In a sentence or two distinguish between printing date and copyright date.
3. Explain the purpose of a glossary.
4. Distinguish between a table of contents and an index.
5. Write the date when this book was printed.
6. Write the date when this book was copyrighted.
7. By what firm was this book published?
8. Where is this firm located?
9. Skim the Preface of this book and in a sentence or two state its primary purpose.
10. What use has been made of the end sheets of this book?

THE *READERS' GUIDE*

A large part of the library reference work you will do in high school will deal with subjects of a contemporary rather than a historical nature. The best source of information, indeed very often the only source of information, on truly current subjects is the magazine. Without some sort of guide, you would have to spend hours hunting through magazines in search of articles on a subject. However, the *Readers' Guide* solves this problem for you.

20d. Learn how to use the *Readers' Guide to Periodical Literature*.

In the *Readers' Guide*, articles from more than 100 magazines are indexed alphabetically by subjects and by authors. You may look up the subject in which you are interested and find the articles that have been written on it and the magazines in which they appeared.

Magazine stories are listed by title and by author;

the complete entry is given with the author listing only. Poems and plays are listed by author and under the headings POEMS and DRAMAS. The complete entry is given with the author listing also.

Articles *about* moving pictures and plays are listed under the subject headings MOVING PICTURE PLAYS and DRAMAS, beneath the subheading **Criticisms, plots, etc.**

The *Readers' Guide* is published in paper-covered pamphlets twice a month from September to June and monthly in July and August. Occasionally during the year a cumulative issue is published including the articles listed in preceding months as well as those for the current month. At the end of a year, a large volume is published containing all entries for the year, and every two years a volume covering a two-year period is published.

You must remember, however, that the usefulness of the *Readers' Guide* is limited by the availability to you of the magazines to which it refers you. When you are taking down references from the *Readers' Guide*, you should know what magazines your library takes. You should know, too, whether the library has kept back issues of all these magazines or of only certain ones, and for how many years back it has the magazines.

A sample excerpt from the *Readers' Guide* is reproduced on the opposite page. You can probably understand the many abbreviations used, but if you cannot, you will find them explained in the front of the *Readers' Guide* itself.

● EXERCISE 3. Write answers to the following questions.

1. Is there in your library a list of the magazines to which the library subscribes? Does the list give the

Sample Excerpt from *Readers' Guide*[1]

CLERGY
Clergyman as hero in comics. Newsweek 47: 92 Mr 12 '56
2,300 Ohio pastors convene. il Nat Council O 6:21-2 Mr '56

CLEVELAND, Ohio

City planning

City shows how to fight decay. il Life 40: 62-3 Mr 12 '56

CLINCHY, Everett Ross
Prayer for a better world. Parents Mag 31: 87 Ap '56

CLINICS. See Business clinics

CLOCKS
Modern clock. R. Anderson. il Pop Sci 168:168 Ap '56

CLOTHES dryers
Automatic washer and clothes dryer. Consumers Res Bul 37:18 Mr '56

CLOTHIER, Robert C.
W. D. Scott, pioneer in applied psychology. Science 123:408 Mr 9 '56

CLOTHING and dress
For the feminine shopper. E. Bowen. il Holiday 19:90-1+ Ap '56
What to wear in London. Holiday 19:103 Ap '56

Men

Beau Brummell's town. R. Collier. il Holiday 19:92-7+ Ap '56
Light signs of spring. il Colliers 137:90-1 Mr 30 '56

CLOTHING industry

United States

Made in Hong Kong; Bell importing company. Fortune 53:238 Mr '56

CLOWNS
Ladeez and gentle-men. il Am Mag 161:52-3 Ap '56

CLUBB, Oliver Edmund
Power of China. Nation 182:202 Mr 10 '56

CLUBS
Success begins at forty plus. R. Schuessler. Am Mercury 82:54-7 Ap '56
Unique club activities: snake club; Dog training club, Reading, Pa. il Recreation 49: 124-5 Mr '56

COAGULATION of blood. See Blood—Coagulation

COAL mines and mining

Wages and hours

Wage chronology: bituminous coal mines; supplement no. three, 1952-56. tabs Mo Labor R 79:187-8 F '56

COASTAL waters. See Territorial waters

COBB, Margaret E.
Rice-paper paintings: trivialities of the China trade. Antiques 69:246-7 Mr '56

[1] Reproduced by permission of the H. W. Wilson Company.

dates of back numbers on file? If so, for what years does the library have back numbers of either the *Atlantic* or *Harper's Magazine?*

2. Where are the back numbers of magazines stored in your library? How do you get the particular number you want?
3. What is the date of the latest *Readers' Guide* in your library? What period does it cover?
4, 5, 6. Select one of the following subjects, look it up in the *Readers' Guide*, and list on your paper three articles *that you could get in your library* on the subject. Give the complete listing in the *Readers' Guide*. Show that you understand the abbreviations by spelling out all of them.

Housing	Aviation	Photography
Education	Taxation	Labor

7. Select a prominent person of today and look for an article about him in the *Readers' Guide*. Give the complete listing.
8. Find and copy a "see" reference from the *Readers' Guide*.
9. Copy from the *Readers' Guide* complete information about a poem.
10. Copy from the *Readers' Guide* the complete listing of a review of a motion picture.

THE VERTICAL FILE

20e. Learn the nature and proper use of the vertical file.

Useful information on current topics is often to be found in pamphlets, brief treatments of a subject usually bound in paper covers. They are published by government agencies, industrial concerns, museums, colleges and universities, radio stations, welfare organizations, etc. The librarian files pamphlets in a special cabinet, usually referred to as the vertical file, and can usually help you to find material on your subject, especially if it is of contemporary interest.

In the vertical file the librarian also stores interesting pictures and significant clippings from newspapers.

20f. Learn the location of items in your library.

Your use of a library will be more efficient if you know the exact location of the principal items you may wish to use. If you will remember the information the following exercise calls for, you will save both the librarian and yourself a great deal of time.

● EXERCISE 4. Be prepared to state the location in your school or public library of each of the following:

1. The desk where books are charged out
2. The card catalogue
3. The *Readers' Guide*
4. The magazine rack and the newspaper rack
5. The pamphlet file
6. The fiction shelves
7. The encyclopedias
8. The biography shelves
9. The unabridged dictionaries
10. The reserved-book shelf or the new-book shelf

CHAPTER 21

Information in the Dictionary

LEARN TO USE THE DICTIONARY

For anyone who reads and writes, a dictionary is indispensable. While it is used most often to look up the meaning or spelling of words, it has a great many other uses with which you should be familiar. Furthermore, you can greatly increase your understanding of the information given in a dictionary by a thorough knowledge of its organization and of the devices used to convey information.

21a. Know what kinds of dictionaries there are.

In general, dictionaries may be classified in three groups. In the first group are the unabridged (complete) dictionaries. These are so large and so expensive that they are found principally in libraries and schools. The best-known and most available of these are the one-volume dictionaries. You should find out whether your library has them.

Funk and Wagnalls New Standard Dictionary of the English Language, published by Funk and Wagnalls, New York.

Webster's New International Dictionary of the English Language, published by G. and C. Merriam Company, Springfield, Mass.

These unabridged dictionaries contain all the words in the language and give a great deal more information about each word than do the dictionaries of the second group, which may be called the "desk" dictionaries for general use.

There are many of these dictionaries of the second group; all are adequate for general use. The following are best known:

The American College Dictionary, published by Harper and Brothers, New York.

Funk and Wagnalls New College Standard Dictionary, published by Funk and Wagnalls, New York.

The Grosset Webster Dictionary, published by Grosset and Dunlap, New York.

Thorndike-Barnhart High School Dictionary, published by Scott, Foresman and Company, Chicago.

Webster's New Collegiate Dictionary, published by G. and C. Merriam Company, Springfield, Mass.

Webster's New World Dictionary, College Edition, published by World Publishing Company, Cleveland.

Webster's Students Dictionary, published by American Book Company, New York.

The Winston Dictionary (Advanced Edition), published by John G. Winston Company, Philadelphia.

The third group of dictionaries includes the small, often pocket-sized, books sold in book, stationery, and drug stores for a dollar or less. While these books may prove adequate for everyday use in looking up common word meanings and spellings, they should be taken for what they are intended to be — inexpensive condensations for quick, general reference; they are not dependable as scholarly, complete, up-to-date works.

During your study of the dictionary you should have a good dictionary to use, preferably one from the second group. Perhaps the most important considerations in evaluating a dictionary are the quality of the scholarship which produced it and the recency of its publication. A dictionary describes the language as it is. Because language is always changing (new words being added; other words taking on new meanings; spelling, pronunciation, and grammar conventions changing) a dictionary must be revised continually. Naturally, a dictionary published twenty-five years ago will not be so reliable as a newer one.

21b. Become familiar with contents and arrangement.

The dictionary is most commonly used as an authority on the spelling, pronunciation, and meaning of words. But to think of it in such simple terms is to ignore the many kinds of information it provides. Before making a detailed study of the treatment of individual words in the body of the dictionary, learn the kinds of information usually available in a good dictionary. The study materials and exercises on the following pages are intended to reveal to you the entire resources of your dictionary. Through your study of these pages, you should become so well acquainted with your dictionary that you will turn to it more often and use it more efficiently in the future.

Although all good dictionaries contain essentially the same kind of information, they may vary in their arrangement and in their manner of presenting the information. For instance, some dictionaries list such items as names of famous persons and places in the main body of the dictionary; others list them in separate sections. Some dictionaries list common abbreviations and foreign words and phrases in the main body, while others list these in separate sections. Familiarize yourself with your dictionary.

The exercises on the following pages apply to almost all conventional dictionaries. For your convenience an excerpt from *Webster's New Collegiate Dictionary* has been reproduced on page 312.

● EXERCISE 1. Using the dictionary with which you have been provided, write the answers to the following questions. This exercise is designed to familiarize you with the contents and the arrangement of the book. The table of contents will help you.

1. What is the full title of your dictionary?
2. Who is the publisher?
3. What is the latest copyright date?
4. What title is given to the introductory article explaining matters of pronunciation involved in the dictionary? On which pages does it appear?
5. Is there a section *explaining* the dictionary? What is it called? On which pages does it appear?
6. Are abbreviations listed by themselves in a separate section or are they listed in the dictionary proper? If they are in a separate section, write the exact title of the section and its page numbers.
7. Is there a section giving the meanings of commonly used signs and symbols? If so, write its title and page numbers.
8. Are spelling (orthography) rules given? If so, write the exact title of the section and its page numbers.
9. Are rules for capitalization and punctuation given? If so, under what title and on which pages?
10. Does the dictionary have a section on manuscript preparation and proofreading? If so, write its title and page numbers.
11. Are names of important persons and places listed in the main body of the book, or are they included in separate sections by themselves? If they are in separate sections, give the exact titles and the page numbers of the sections.
12. Are names of literary (Hamlet), mythological (Po-

seidon), and Biblical (Goliath) characters included in the main body of the book, or are they listed in separate sections? If they are in separate sections, give the exact titles of the sections and the page numbers.

13. Are foreign words included in the dictionary proper or in a special section? If they are in a special section, give the exact title of the section and the page numbers.
14. Does the dictionary give a list of colleges and universities? If so, under what title is the list given and on which pages?
15. List any other sections of your dictionary not included in the preceding questions.

● EXERCISE 2. Look up in your dictionary the answers to the following questions and write the answers in a column on your paper. *After each answer write the page number on which you found it.* If any of the items are not in your dictionary, write the number of the question and leave a blank space.

1. What does the abbreviation LL.D. mean? Give the English meaning.
2. What is the population of Londonderry?
3. What was the occupation of Joseph Jefferson?
4. Who was Europa?
5. Give the meaning of the French phrase *comme il faut.*
6. Give the spelling rule for retaining the silent *e* before an ending beginning with a consonant.
7. Where should commas and periods be placed with relation to quotation marks — inside the quotation marks or outside?
8. Give the meaning of the medical sign ℞.
9. In what play is Iago the villain?
10. Where is Prince Edward Island?

21c. Learn to use the vocabulary entries.

The words listed in alphabetical order in the main part of the dictionary are referred to as "vocabulary entries." The amount of information given about a word depends upon the size of the dictionary. For the most complete information, you should consult an unabridged dictionary. The examples and exercises which follow are based upon *Webster's New Collegiate Dictionary*. Frequent reference to the excerpt on page 312 will make clear the explanations.

DICTIONARY INFORMATION ABOUT A WORD

1. *Spelling*

Whenever you wish to know the correct spelling of a word, you turn as a matter of course to the dictionary. You can usually find the word even though you may not know exactly how to spell it.

When there are two acceptable spellings, the preferred spelling is given first. If the forms are of equal or nearly equal standing, they are separated by a comma or by the word *or:* **adviser, advisor.** If the spellings are not at all equal in their acceptability, the word "Also" will be given before the less acceptable spelling: **skeptic.** Also **sceptic.** On the sample page you will find that **loveable** and **loveably** are given as variant forms of **lovable, lovably.** This means that **lovable, lovably** are the most widely used and therefore the preferred spellings.

If the spelling of the various forms of a word is likely to present a problem, these forms are given. For instance, is the plural of *hero* spelled *heros* or *heroes?* Is the past tense of *refer* spelled *refered* or *referred?* The dictionary anticipates and answers such questions.

2. *Capital Letters*

Proper nouns and adjectives, which are capitalized, are given with capital letters in the dictionary. See **Louvre** in the excerpt on page 312.

Lou'vre (lo͞o'vr'), *n.* [F.] An ancient palace in Paris, now occupied by a museum of art and public offices.

lov'a·ble (lŭv'ȧ·b'l), *adj.* Having qualities that excite, or are fitted to excite, love; worthy of love. — **lov'a·bil'i·ty** (-bĭl'ĭ·tĭ), *n.* — **lov'a·ble·ness,** *n.* — **lov'a·bly,** *adv.*

Syn. Lovable, amiable mean worthy of liking. **Lovable** implies a definitely personal reaction; **amiable,** little more than an agreeable impression. — **Ant.** Hateful.

lov'age (lŭv'ĭj), *n.* [OF. *luvesche, leuesche,* fr. LL. *levisticum,* deriv. of L. *Ligusticus* Ligurian.] A European herb (*Levisticum officinale*) of the carrot family, cultivated in old gardens as a domestic remedy.

love (lŭv), *n.* [AS. *lufu.*] **1.** A feeling of strong personal attachment induced by sympathetic understanding, or by ties of kinship; ardent affection. **2.** The benevolence attributed to God as being like a father's affection for his children; also, men's adoration of God. **3.** Strong liking; fondness; good will; as, *love* of learning; *love* of country. **4.** Tender and passionate affection for one of the opposite sex. **5.** The object of affection; sweetheart. **6.** [*cap.*] Cupid, or Eros, as god of love; sometimes, Venus. **7.** [*cap.*] *Christian Science.* A synonym for God. **8.** *Tennis, etc.* Nothing; no points scored; — used in counting the score. — **Ant.** Hate. — *v. t.;* LOVED (lŭvd); LOV'ING (lŭv'ĭng). **1.** To have or manifest love for. **2.** To take delight or pleasure in; as, to *love* books. **3.** To show love for by caressing. — *v. i.* To have the feeling of love, esp. for one of the other sex; to be in love.

love'a·ble, love'a·bly, etc. Vars. of LOVABLE, etc.

love affair. An affair between lovers; an amour.

love apple. The tomato.

love'bird' (lŭv'bûrd'), *n.* Any of numerous small parrots (esp. genera *Agapornis* of Africa and *Psittacula* of South America) that show great affection for their mates.

love feast. Among the primitive Christians, a meal taken together to signify the Christian affection existing between members of the church; hence, among some religious denominations, a religious service in imitation of this.

love game. *Tennis, etc.* A game won without loss of a point.

love'-in-a-mist', *n.* A European garden plant (*Nigella damascena*) of the crowfoot family, having the flowers enveloped in a number of finely dissected bracts.

love'-in-i'dle·ness, *n.* The wild pansy. See PANSY.

love knot. A knot or bow of ribbon as a token of love.

love'less, *adj.* Without love; unloved or unloving. — **love'less·ly,** *adv.* — **love'less·ness,** *n.*

love'-lies-bleed'ing, *n.* Any cultivated amaranth.

love'lock' (lŭv'lŏk'), *n.* A long lock of hair; esp., that worn by men of fashion in the reigns of Elizabeth and James I.

love'lorn' (-lôrn'), *adj.* Forsaken by one's love.

love'ly (lŭv'lĭ), *adj.;* LOVE'LI·ER (-lĭ·ẽr); LOVE'LI·EST. **1.** *Archaic.* Loving; also, lovable. **2.** Beautiful; esp., having a delicate or exquisite beauty. **3.** Beautiful in refined moral or spiritual quality. **4.** *Colloq.* Very pleasing; as, a *lovely* view. — **Syn.** See BEAUTIFUL. — **love'li·ly,** *adv.* — **love'li·ness,** *n.*

love'-mak'ing (-māk'ĭng), *n.* Courtship.

lov'er (lŭv'ẽr), *n.* One who loves; specif.: **a** One held in affection by, or holding affection for, another; a friend. **b** One who is in love with one of the other sex; usually, *sing.,* a male lover; *pl.,* a pair in love with each other. **c** A paramour. **d** One who has a strong liking.

lov'er·ly (-lĭ), *adj. & adv.* Like or as a lover.

love seat. A double chair, or a settee or sofa for two persons.

love set. *Tennis, etc.* A set won without loss of a game.

love'sick' (lŭv'sĭk'), *adj.* Languishing with love; expressive of languishing love. — **love'sick'ness,** *n.*

love'some (-sŭm), *adj.* *Archaic & Dial.* **1.** Lovely; lovable. **2.** Loving; amorous.

love vine. The dodder.

lov'ing (lŭv'ĭng), *adj.* Feeling or expressing love or kindness. — **lov'ing·ly,** *adv.* — **lov'ing·ness,** *n.*

Sometimes a word is capitalized in only one of its many uses. In such instances, the dictionary indicates by the abbreviation [*cap.*] that when used in this sense, the word should be capitalized. An example of this is the sixth meaning of the word *love* on the sample page.

3. *Syllables*

When in your writing you wish to divide a word at the end of a line, you must divide it only between syllables. The dictionary indicates the syllables in a word by placing a centered period (·) between the syllables unless a syllable is accented. After an accented syllable the accent mark (′) indicates the division. For example, the word *lovable* is divided into syllables as follows: **lov′a·ble.**

4. *Pronunciation*

The correct pronunciation of a word is shown in the dictionary by means of accent marks, diacritical markings, and phonetic respelling. The method of indicating pronunciation is explained in detail in this book on pages 321–26. Your teacher may wish you to turn to these pages now and review your knowledge of diacritical marks. A thorough understanding of them is essential to efficient use of the dictionary.

If a word may be acceptably pronounced in two ways, the dictionary gives the most widely used pronunciation first: **acclimate** (*ă*·klī′mĭt, ăk′lĭ·māt). Each form entered, however, has the support of good usage, and in some cases this usage is equally divided.

5. *The Part of Speech*

The dictionary indicates the part of speech of each word by means of the following abbreviations:

n.	noun	*adj.*	adjective
pro.	pronoun	*adv.*	adverb
v.i.	intransitive verb [1]	*prep.*	preposition
v.t.	transitive verb	*conj.*	conjunction
	interj. interjection		

When a word is used as more than one part of speech, the meanings for each part of speech are grouped together. See **love** on the sample page.

6. *Inflected Forms of a Word*

As explained under *Spelling* (see page 311), the dictionary gives other forms of a word whenever there is an important reason for this information. These forms, representing a change in the word, are called *inflected* or *inflectional* forms. They may be of many kinds:

a. the plural of a word when formed irregularly: **hero;** *pl.* -ROES
b. the feminine form of a foreign word: **alumnus; alumna,** *fem.*
c. the principal parts of an irregular verb: **see;** SAW; SEEN
d. comparative and superlative forms of an adjective or adverb if formed irregularly: **good;** BETTER; BEST
e. case forms of pronouns: **who;** *possessive* WHOSE; *objective* WHOM

7. *The Derivation or Etymology*

Most dictionaries indicate the history of a word. They show by means of abbreviations what language the word originally came from and what its original meaning was. English is unusual among languages for the vast number of words it has taken from other

[1] An intransitive verb does not take an object. *Run* is intransitive in the sentence *Run as fast as you can.* *Run* is transitive in the sentence *Run the motor for twenty minutes.*

languages. The source of newly coined words is also given. Knowing the source and original meaning of a word is often a great help to you in understanding the word's present meaning and correct use.

The abbreviations used to indicate the languages from which words came are usually explained in a special section at the front of the dictionary. For instance, AS means Anglo-Saxon, the language of the early inhabitants of England; L. means Latin; F. means French; G. means German, etc. Dictionaries vary somewhat in their placing of this etymological information. As you will see by looking at the word *love* on the sample page, *Webster's New Collegiate Dictionary* gives the information in brackets immediately following the part of speech in the vocabulary entry. You will note that *love* is derived from the Anglo-Saxon word *lufu*. The history of *geography* is given in the dictionary as follows:

> [F. *géographie*, fr. L. *geographia*, fr. Gr. *geōgraphia*, fr. *gaia*, *gē*, the earth + *graphē* description.]

If written out, this etymology would read, "French *géographie*, from the Latin *geographia*, from the Greek *geōgraphia*, from *gaia*, *gē*, the earth + *graphē* description." *Geography*, then, according to its etymology, originally meant a description of the earth.

8. *The Meaning*

The principal function of a dictionary is to tell what a word means. Since a single word may have many different meanings, a dictionary gives all of them, numbering or lettering each one. Dictionaries differ in the order in which they list the various definitions. In *Webster's New Collegiate Dictionary* the definitions are listed in historical order — the earliest meaning first, the latest, last. Study the seven meanings of the noun *love* on the sample page. Some dictionaries list the meanings in the order of their use, the most common meaning at the present time being given first.

When you wish to find the definition of a word you have encountered in your reading, you may have to read through the list of definitions until you find the one which fits the particular context in which the word appeared. Failure to do this may result in your getting an entirely incorrect understanding of the word.

9. *Restrictive Labels*

In the dictionary many words are given so-called *restrictive labels*. These labels characterize the word in certain uses. They are of three kinds: *subject labels*, which specify the particular meaning given to a word in a special field: *Radio*, *Law*, *Bot.* (Botany), etc.; *usage labels*, which characterize the word as to its usage: *Slang*, *colloq.* (colloquial), *Dial.* (Dialectal), etc.; *geographic labels*, which indicate the region in which the word is principally used: *N.E.* (New England), *Western U.S.*, etc.

> *Slang* refers to words or expressions widely used, which have a forced or fantastic meaning, or a strange humor.
>
> *Colloquial* expressions are expressions used in informal conversation [and writing], but not in formal writing.
>
> *Dialectal* forms are forms which differ from the standard forms of a language and are used in particular localities.[2]

Examples of restrictive labels appear on the sample page with the fourth meaning of *lovely*, which is labeled *colloq.*, and with the word *lovesome*, which is labeled *Archaic & Dial.*

[2] From *Workbook* for use with *Webster's New International Dictionary*, Second Edition. Reprinted by permission of G. and C. Merriam Company.

10. *Synonyms and Antonyms*

As an aid to your understanding of word meanings the dictionary frequently gives synonyms and antonyms. Synonyms are words which are closely related in meaning to the word being defined. For *love* the synonyms given on the sample page are *attachment, affection.* Antonyms are words which have an opposite meaning from that of the word being defined. For *love* the antonym given is *hate.*

For a larger number of synonyms and antonyms than is found in the dictionary, you should consult a book of synonyms and antonyms. Several of these are listed on page 335 among the reference books. Even in a dictionary, however, fairly detailed explanations are sometimes given of the shades of difference in meaning between words commonly considered synonymous. For instance, under the vocabulary entry **lovable** on the sample page, the difference between *lovable* and *amiable* is explained.

11. *Illustrations*

Frequently the dictionary will give a picture to clarify the meaning of a word, usually a noun which cannot be easily described, such as the name of an animal, a plant, etc. Do not ignore the possibility of finding a picture illustrating the word you are looking up in the dictionary.

21d. Learn to use information entries.

IMPORTANT PERSONS

The dictionary usually gives the following biographical data about important persons:

1. *Name:* correct spelling, pronunciation, and the first name
2. *Dates of birth and death*

21d

3. *Nationality*
4. *Why famous*

The biographical information in a dictionary cannot always be up to date for contemporary figures. A more reliable source of information about contemporaries is *Who's Who* or *Who's Who in America* (see page 340).

IMPORTANT PLACES

In listing geographical place names the dictionary usually gives the following information:

1. *Name:* spelling, pronunciation
2. *Identification:* whether a city, country, lake, mountain, river, etc.
3. *Location*
4. *Size:* population, if a city or country; area in square miles, if a country or territory or body of water; length, if a river; height, if a mountain, etc.
5. *Importance:* If a city is capital of a state or country, this fact will be indicated, sometimes by a star or an asterisk. The capital of a country or state will also be given under the name of the country or state.
6. *Historical or other interesting information of importance:* thus, for Oak Ridge, Tennessee, *Webster's New Collegiate Dictionary* has the following entry:

> **Oak Ridge,** city, E Tennessee, W of Knoxville; site of research and training laboratories in nuclear studies; pop. 30,200.

7. *Governed or controlled by what country:* thus, for Madagascar the dictionary says ". . . French overseas territory."

● EXERCISE 3. This exercise is designed to test your knowledge of the information given about a word in the dictionary. With your dictionary before you, begin work at the teacher's signal. Look up the answers to the following questions. While your speed indicates to some degree your efficiency in using the dictionary, accuracy is the more important consideration.[3]

1. Which is the preferred spelling: *judgement* or *judgment?*
2. Which is the preferred pronunciation: *re′search* or *re search′?*
3. Copy the correct pronunciation of the word *comely,* including diacritical marks. Be able to pronounce it correctly.
4. Are the comparative and superlative forms of *comely* shown to be *more comely* and *most comely,* or *comelier* and *comeliest?*
5. Copy the word *automatic,* dividing it correctly into syllables.
6. How many different meanings are given in your dictionary for the word *run* as an intransitive verb?
7. Is the use of the word *swell* as an adjective classed as *dialectal, slang,* or *colloquial?*
8. Which of the meanings of the word *shank* is described as *colloquial?*
9. What are the past and past-participle forms of the irregular verb *burst?*
10. Distinguish between the meaning of *councilor* and *counselor.*
11. What restrictive label is given to the adjective *erstwhile?*
12. What restrictive label is given to the word *gyp?*
13. What was the original meaning of *candidate?*
14. In what literary work does the character Mrs. Malaprop appear? For what was she noted?
15. Tell the story of Hero and Leander as given in your dictionary.

[3] The questions in the dictionary exercises have been checked against several dictionaries. Because of major differences among dictionaries, it is not possible to make exercises which will fit every dictionary equally well. Before assigning the exercises, the teacher will do well to check them with the dictionary his students are using.

● EXERCISE 4. Like the preceding exercise, this exercise will test your knowledge of the information given in a dictionary and your familiarity with the location of this information in the dictionary. At the teacher's signal look up the answers to the following questions. Accuracy is more important than speed, but speed is important.

1. Find two synonyms for the word *covetous.*
2. Write the plural of *analysis.*
3. Write the comparative and superlative forms of *ill.*
4. What city is the capital of Burma?
5. What is the population of Dallas, Texas?
6. When did Queen Victoria reign?
7. For what is Johann Gutenberg famous?
8. What was George Eliot's real name?
9. What is the meaning of the abbreviation ROTC?
10. Which is the preferred pronunciation of *hospitable: hos'pitable* or *hospit'able?*
11. What symbol is used in mathematics for the word *therefore?*
12. Write the plural of *crisis.*
13. Should you or should you not use a comma before the *and* joining the last two items of a series; for instance, *At the beach we swam, played* (,) *and fished?*
14. Give the rule for the formation of the plural of nouns ending in *o* preceded by a vowel. Give two examples.
15. What is the meaning of the Latin phrase *caveat emptor?*

CHAPTER 22

Pronunciation in the Dictionary

LEARN HOW TO READ DIACRITICAL MARKS FOR CORRECT PRONUNCIATION[1]

22a. Learn the names and the meanings of the common diacritical marks.

Diacritical marks are the marks used by dictionary makers to show the pronunciation of vowels: *a, e, i, o, u,* and sometimes *y.* The names and uses of the common diacritical marks are described on the following pages.

NAMES AND USES OF DIACRITICAL MARKS

The Macron (mā′krŏn)

The macron (¯) is used to mark a long vowel. A long vowel is pronounced as the vowel itself is named. For instance, long *a* (*a* marked with a macron) has the sound of *a* in the words *ale* (āle) and *fate* (fāte). Long *e* (*e* marked with a macron) is pronounced as in the words *eve* (ēve) and *senior* (sē′nior). How should you pronounce the following letters when they are

[1] There are important differences among dictionaries in their systems of indicating pronunciation. The system described here is the Webster system. Naturally, the exercises and explanations in this chapter will not apply in every respect to dictionaries whose pronunciation system is radically different from the Webster system.

long: ī, ō, ū? Note that long *u* (ū) is pronounced "yew" as in *cube* and *pure*, not o͞o as in *moon*.

The macron with a vertical mark on top (ˆ) indicates a "half-long" sound. When pronouncing a "half-long" vowel, you hurry a little more than when pronouncing a long vowel. This is clearly shown by the word *vacation*, in which both the half-long ǡ and the long ā sounds are present: vǡ·cā′tion. Other uses of the half-long mark are seen in the words *event* (ē̇·vent′) and *unite* (ū̇·nite′).

The Breve (brēv)

The breve (˘) tells you that the sound of the vowel is "shortened" or "flattened." The following list shows the pronunciation of letters marked with a breve:

ă	ădd	ĭ	ĭll	ŭ	ŭp
ĕ	ĕnd	ŏ	ŏdd		

The Dieresis (dī·ĕr′*ĕ*·sĭs)

The dieresis, or double dot (¨), is placed over an *a* to indicate the broad sound: cälm, härm.

The Dot

The dot (˙) is placed over an *a* to indicate a short sound halfway between ă and ä: ȧsk, pȧth. When it is placed over an italicized *a* (*ȧ*), the dot indicates the sound of *a* in *sofa* (so′f*ȧ*) and *abound* (*ȧ*·bound′).

The Tilde (tĭl′dĕ)

The tilde (˜) is used over an *e* in an unaccented *er*, as in *maker* (mak′ẽr) and *ever* (ev′ẽr).

The Circumflex (sûr′kŭm·flĕks)

The circumflex (ˆ) has three important uses. Over an *o* it gives the letter the sound of *o* in *or:*

lôrd, ôr′der; over a *u* it gives the sound of *u* in *urn:* ûrn, hûrt; over an *a* the circumflex indicates the sound of *a* in *care* (câre). The circumflex over a *u* is the accented equivalent of the unaccented tilde (ẽr). The dictionary gives the pronunciation of *observer* as ŏb·zûr′vẽr, which has ûr in the accented syllable and ẽr in the unaccented syllable.

o͞o *and* o͝o

The sound of the double *o* in *stoop* is indicated by a double *o* marked with a macron (o͞o). The sound of double *o* in *book* is indicated by a double *o* marked with a breve (o͝o). Thus — sto͞op, lo͞op; bo͝ok, lo͝ok.

The Italicized Vowel

An italicized vowel occurs only in an unaccented syllable. It is pronounced hurriedly.

COMPLETE KEY TO VOWEL MARKINGS

āle, chǡotic, câre, ădd, *ă*ccount, ärm, ȧsk, sof*ȧ*; ēve, hẹ̄re, ė̄vent, ĕnd, sil*ĕ*nt, makẽr; īce, ĭll, char*ĭ*ty; ōld, ō̇bey, ôrb, ŏdd, sô̇ft, c*ŏ*nnect; **oi**l, fo͞od, fo͝ot, **ou**t; cūbe, ū̇nite, ûrn, ŭp, circ*ŭ*s, ü = German grün.

● EXERCISE 1. Only the experts who make our dictionaries can mark vowel sounds authoritatively; however, try your hand at marking the vowels in the simple words in the list on the next page. Write the words on your paper and place the mark above each vowel. Final silent *e*, of course, cannot be marked. Check your answers with the dictionary. They will probably not be 100 per cent correct.

1. sun
2. bad
3. state
4. smite
5. dope
6. use
7. lorn
8. hit
9. lot
10. can
11. i de a
12. came
13. part
14. a lone
15. se quel
16. curt
17. bit ter
18. cook
19. June
20. spoo k

22b. Learn the dictionary method of showing the pronunciation of consonants.

Since consonants do not have so many different sounds as vowels do, they do not require diacritical marking. Most consonant sounds are sufficiently indicated simply by the consonant itself; thus *k* is always pronounced the same, *n* is always pronounced the same, etc. There are some consonant sounds, however, which must be shown by a system of re-spelling.

PRONUNCIATION OF CONSONANTS

Study carefully the methods of indicating pronunciation of both vowels and consonants in these words.

crouch krouch
documentary dŏk′û·mĕn′tȧ·rĭ
finger fĭng′gẽr
characteristic kăr′ăk·tẽr·ĭs′tĭk
knowledge nŏl′ĕj
conjunction kŏn·jŭngk′shŭn
judgment jŭj′mĕnt
mother mŭth′ẽr

COMPLETE KEY TO CONSONANT SOUNDS

but; **ch**air; **d**ay, ver**d**ûre; **f**ill; **g**o; **h**at; **j**oke; **k**eep, K = **ch** in German **ich;** **l**ate; **m**an; **n**od; N = French boN; si**ng;** **p**en; **r**at; **s**it; **sh**e; **t**o; **th**in, **th**en; na**t**ûre; **v**an; **w**in; **y**et; **z**one, **zh** = **z** in a**z**ure.

By permission. From Webster's New Collegiate Dictionary

● EXERCISE 2. The Webster key for the pronunciation of consonants is reprinted above. Use this key *and your dictionary* to find the answers to the following questions:

1. How is "soft" *c* as in *cereal* distinguished from "hard" *c* as in *connect?*
2. How is *th* in *thin* distinguished from *th* in *those?*
3. How is the *ng* sound in *sing* distinguished from the *ng* sound in *anger?*
4. How is *ch* in *machine* distinguished from *ch* in *chapter* and *character?*
5. How is the *z* sound in *zone* distinguished from the *z* sound in *azure?*
6. How is the *g* sound in *good* distinguished from the *g* sound in *geranium?*
7. How is the *d* sound in *door* distinguished from the *d* sound in *tripped?*
8. How is the *s* sound in *soap* distinguished from the *s* sound in *advertise?*

22c. Learn the dictionary method of indicating accent.

In words of several syllables, one syllable is usually given greater prominence or stress than the others.[2] This stressed or accented syllable is shown by an accent mark placed immediately after the syllable: be·long′, im·por′tant, a·bout′, vig′or·ous.

ACCENT

In long words there may be two accented syllables, but one of them is accented more than the other. The one receiving the heavier stress is marked by the heavier accent mark — the primary accent. The other is marked by a light accent mark — the secondary accent. *Examples:* cat′er·pil′lar, lab′o·ra·to′ry.

[2] A syllable is a letter or group of letters which can be pronounced by itself.

Observe that a shift in accent sometimes accompanies a change in the meaning of a word.

trans′port [noun]	trans·port′ [verb]
com′pact [noun]	com·pact′ [adjective]
es′cort [noun]	es·cort′ [verb]
con′tent [noun]	con·tent′ [adjective]
ref′use [noun]	re·fuse′ [verb]

● EXERCISE 3. Copy the following words on your paper, leaving space between syllables as shown here. Place the primary accent mark after the proper syllable in each word. You are expected to know the correct pronunciation of these words without looking them up in the dictionary. The exercise is a test of your understanding of accent. Show that you know the meaning of accent by reading the words aloud.

1. dis turb
2. no tice
3. class y
4. dis gust ed
5. re lieve
6. paint er
7. con di tion
8. care less
9. de ny
10. cor rect ly
11. car pen ter
12. at trac tive
13. man ag er
14. con sid er
15. mem ber ship
16. res er va tion
17. gen er os i ty
18. de pos it
19. con tri bu tion
20. pro nun ci a tion

● EXERCISE 4. Copy from the dictionary the correct pronunciation of each of the words in the following list. Be especially careful to copy accurately. Indicate an italicized letter by putting a line under it: ȧ or ă. Prepare to pronounce the words in class.

1. coupon
2. nicely
3. hamburger
4. demise
5. neither
6. linger
7. addition
8. mischievous
9. authentic
10. wonderful
11. extraordinary
12. gesticulate

● EXERCISE 5. By respelling and adding accent and diacritical marks to the following words as you think the dictionary would mark them, show your understanding of the dictionary's methods of indicating pronunciation. You will not be 100 per cent correct, but the exercise will be a good preparation for your reading of pronunciation. The division into syllables has been done for you. Check your results with the actual dictionary methods.

1. a rise
2. both
3. breathe
4. chem is try
5. cute
6. cause
7. flood
8. un tie
9. through
10. feath er
11. chick en
12. mer cy
13. Chi nese
14. chol er a
15. beau ti ful
16. pop corn
17. po si tion
18. par ties
19. wrought
20. rep u ta tion

WORDS COMMONLY MISPRONOUNCED

If you have understood the discussion of pronunciation on the preceding pages, you should be able to "read" the correct pronunciation of the words in the following list of commonly mispronounced words. Perhaps you already know how to pronounce these words. However, you should read the list through, pronouncing aloud each word according to the pronunciation shown. Whenever you find a word that you have been mispronouncing, jot it down to fix the correct form in your mind. The exercises on pages 330 to 333 are based on the words in this list.

Errors may be of three kinds:

1. *Accenting the wrong syllable* — *prefer′able* for *pref′erable*.

2. *Mispronouncing a letter* — *bāde* for *băde; gesture* for *jesture* (Spelled *gesture*).

3. *Enunciating incorrectly*. Errors in enunciation are the result of either carelessness or a wrong idea

of the spelling of a word. They may result from the omission of letters or syllables — *probaly* for *probably;* they may result from the addition of sounds not in the word — *athalete* for *athlete.*

When you are studying the following list, you may encounter some words whose meaning you do not know. Look up in the dictionary the meaning of all such words.

acumen ă·kū′mĕn
across ȧ·krŏ̂s′

acoustics ȧ·ko͞os′tĭks
across ȧ·krŏ̂s′
acumen ă·kū′mĕn
admirable ăd′mĭ·rȧ·b'l
adversary ăd′vẽr·sĕr′ĭ
alias ā′lĭ·ăs
almond ä′mŭnd
alumnae ȧ·lŭm′nē
alumni ȧ·lŭm′nī
antipathy ăn·tĭp′ȧ·thĭ
archipelago är′kĭ·pĕl′ȧ-gō
architect är′kĭ·tĕkt
archives är′kīvz
arctic ärk′tĭk
athlete ăth′lēt
attaché ăt′ȧ·shā′
attacked ă·tăkt′
auxiliary ôg·zĭl′yȧ·rĭ
awry ȧ·rī′
bade băd
because bē̇·kôz′
beneficent bē̇·nĕf′ĭ·sĕnt
benevolent bē̇·nĕv′ō̇·lĕnt
bicycle bī′sĭk·'l
biography bī·ŏg′rȧ·fĭ
blackguard blăg′ärd
bravado brȧ·vä′dō
cabaret kăb′ȧ·rā′
cache kăsh
café kă·fā′
cello chĕl′ō
cement sē̇·mĕnt′
champion chăm′pĭ·ŭn
chasm kăz'm
chastisement chăs′tĭz-mĕnt
clandestine klăn·dĕs′tĭn
column kŏl′ŭm
combatant kŏm′bȧ·tănt
commandant kŏm′ăn-dănt′
communiqué kŏ·mū′nĭ-kā′
comparable kŏm′pȧ·rȧ·b'l
contrary kŏn′trĕr·ĭ
coupon ko͞o′pŏn
creek krēk
cuisine kwē̇·zēn′
deaf dĕf
deficit dĕf′ĭ·sĭt
demonstrative dē̇·mŏn′-strȧ·tĭv
diphtheria dĭf·thēr′ĭ·ȧ
dirigible dĭr′ĭ·jĭ·b'l
discretion dĭs·krĕsh′ŭn

docile dŏs′ĭl
drowned dround
elm ĕlm
err ûr
extraordinary ĕks·trôr′-dĭ·nĕr′ĭ
facsimile făk·sĭm′ĭ·lē
faucet fô′sĕt
film fĭlm
finale fē·nä′lā

forbade fŏr·băd′
formidable fôr′mĭ·dȧ·b'l
futile fū′tĭl
genuine jĕn′ū·ĭn
geography jē·ŏg′rȧ·fĭ
geometry jē·ŏm′ē·trĭ
gesture jĕs′tūr
gibberish jĭb′ẽr·ĭsh
gigantic jī·găn′tĭk
gondola gŏn′dō·lȧ

government gŭv′ẽrn-mĕnt
grimy grīm′ĭ
height hīt
hyperbole hī·pûr′bō·lē
ignominy ĭg′nō·mĭn·ĭ
ignoramus ĭg′nō·rā′mŭs
impious ĭm′pĭ·ŭs
impotent ĭm′pō·tĕnt
incomparable ĭn·kŏm′-pȧ·rȧ·b'l
indefatigable ĭn·dē·făt′-ĭ·gȧ·b'l

indicted ĭn·dīt′ĕd
inexorable ĭn·ĕk′sō·rȧ·b'l
inexplicable ĭn·ĕks′plĭ-kȧ·b'l

infamous ĭn′fȧ·mŭs
influence ĭn′flōō·ĕns
irrelevant ĭr·rĕl′ē·vȧnt
irreparable ĭ·rĕp′ȧ·rȧ·b'l
irrevocable ĭ·rĕv′ō·kȧ·b'l
Italian ĭ·tăl′yăn
italics ĭ·tăl′ĭks

just jŭst
lamentable lăm′ĕn·tȧ·b'l
length lĕngth
library lī′brĕr′ĭ
longevity lŏn·jĕv′ĭ·tĭ
long-lived lŏng′līvd′
mischievous mĭs′chĭ·vŭs
mortgage môr′gĭj
municipal mū·nĭs′ĭ·păl
museum mū·zē′ŭm

naïve nä·ēv′
naphtha năf′thȧ
often ŏf′ĕn
omnipotent ŏm·nĭp′ō-tĕnt
pathos pā′thŏs
perhaps pẽr·hăps′
perspiration pûr′spĭ·rā′-shŭn
poem pō′ĕm
poignant poin′yănt
posthumous pŏs′tū·mŭs

precedent prĕs′ē·dĕnt
preferable prĕf′ẽr·ȧ·b'l
prevalent prĕv′ȧ·lĕnt
probably prŏb′ȧ·blĭ
protégé prō′tĕ·zhā
pyramidal pĭ·răm′ĭ·dăl
recognize rĕk′ŏg·nīz

recuperate rē·kū′pĕr·āt
relapse rē·lăps′
remonstrate rē·mŏn′-strāt

reputable rĕp′ū·tȧ·b'l
respite rĕs′pĭt
robust rō·bŭst′
sacrilegious săk′rĭ·lē′jŭs
sagacious sȧ·gā′shŭs
sanguine săng′gwĭn
schism sĭz'm
scion sī′ŭn
simile sĭm′ĭ·lē
solace sŏl′ĭs

stipend stī′pĕnd
stomach stŭm′ăk
strength strĕngth
succinct sŭk·sĭngkt′
suite swēt
superfluous sū·pûr′flōō-ŭs
theater thē′ȧ·tẽr
ultimatum ŭl′tĭ·mā′tŭm
vehement vē′ĕ·mĕnt
vehicle vē′ĭ·k'l

vigilante vĭj′ĭ·lăn′tē
viscount vī′kount′
zoology zō·ŏl′ō·jĭ

● EXERCISE 6. Number on your paper from 1 to 40. Pronounce each of the following words, accenting the syllable marked with an accent mark. If the word is correctly marked, write a + after the proper number on your paper. If the word is not correctly marked, write a 0. If you are not sure, consult the preceding list. In any case check your answers with the list before doing the next exercise.[3]

1. im pi′ous
2. gon do′la
3. ad′mi ra ble
4. in′flu ence
5. om nip′o tent
6. chas tise′ment
7. bi cy′cle
8. prev′a lent
9. pre fer′a ble
10. a wry′
11. de fic ′it
12. la men′ta ble
13. mis chie′vous
14. su per′flu ous
15. an tip′a thy
16. ac′u men
17. com bat′ant
18. post hu′mous
19. in′fa mous
20. fi na′le

[3] An exercise of this kind may be read to the class, the teacher pronouncing the words as marked and the students marking a + for words correctly pronounced and a 0 for words incorrectly pronounced.

21. in com par′a ble
22. im po′tent
23. com par′a ble
24. ben e fic′ent
25. dir′i gi ble
26. bra va′do
27. res′pite
28. ir re voc′a ble
29. re mon′strate
30. mu ni ci′pal
31. py ram′i dal
32. hy per′bo le
33. for′mi da ble
34. com man′dant
35. re put′a ble
36. con tra′ry
37. de mon′stra tive
38. clan des′tine
39. in ex plic′a ble
40. be nev′o lent

● EXERCISE 7. Copy the following words on your paper, adhering to the syllable division. Insert the accent mark after the proper syllable.

1. su per flu ous
2. bi cy cle
3. lam en ta ble
4. in fa mous
5. a cu men
6. im pi ous
7. gon do la
8. be nef i cent
9. hy per bo le
10. com bat ant
11. ro bust
12. ad mi ra ble
13. in flu ence
14. com man dant
15. in com pa ra ble
16. fi na le
17. prev a lent
18. chas tise ment
19. re mon strate
20. post hu mous

● EXERCISE 8. Copy the following words on your paper, adhering to the syllable division. Insert the accent mark after the proper syllable.

1. a wry
2. res pite
3. def i cit
4. a li as
5. an tip a thy
6. mis chie vous
7. com pa ra ble
8. be nev o lent
9. in ex pli ca ble
10. im po tent
11. bra va do
12. py ram i dal
13. clan des tine
14. ir rev o ca ble
15. ig no min y
16. de mon stra tive
17. mu nic i pal
18. in de fat i ga ble
19. con tra ry
20. for mi da ble

● EXERCISE 9. Number on your paper from 1 to 30. Study the pronunciations indicated for each word in the following pairs. Pronounce the word aloud as it is marked. Select the correct pronunciation and write, after the proper number on your paper, the letter (A or B) of the column in which the correct form appears.

		A	B
1.	alumnae	*ȧ*·lŭm′nē	*ȧ*·lŭm′nī
2.	arctic	ärk′tĭk	är′tĭk
3.	blackguard	blăk′gärd	blăg′ärd
4.	cache	kăsh	kăsh·ā′
5.	champion	chăm′pĭ·*ŭ*n	chăm·pēn′
6.	chasm	kăz'm	chăs'm
7.	column	kŏl′*ŭ*m	kŏl′yŭm
8.	communiqué	kŏm′ū·nēk′	k*ŏ*·mū′n*ĭ*·kā′
9.	coupon	kū′pŏn	kōō′pŏn
10.	deaf	dĕf	dēf
11.	diphtheria	dĭp·thēr′ĭ·*ȧ*	dĭf·thēr′ĭ·*ȧ*
12.	discretion	dĭs·krĕsh′*ŭ*n	dĭs·krē′sh*ŭ*n
13.	docile	dŏs′ĭl	dō′sĭl
14.	err	ûr	âr
15.	extraordinary	ĕks′tr*ȧ*·ôr′dĭ·nâr·ĭ	ĕks·trôr′dĭ·nĕr′ĭ
16.	futile	fū′tĭl	fū′tīl
17.	genuine	jĕn′ū·ĭn	jĕn′ū·īn′
18.	gesture	jĕs′tūr	gĕs′tūr
19.	gibberish	gĭb′ẽr·ĭsh	jĭb′ẽr·ĭsh
20.	gigantic	jī·găn′tĭk	gī·jăn′tĭk
21.	grimy	grīm′ĭ	grĭm′ĭ
22.	indicted	ĭn·dīk′tĕd	ĭn·dīt′ĕd
23.	Italian	ĭ·tăl′y*ă*n	ī′tăl·*ă*y*ă*n
24.	often	ôf′*ĕ*n	ôf′t*ĕ*n
25.	pathos	păth′ŏs	pā′thŏs
26.	perspiration	prĕs·pĭ·rā′sh*ŭ*n	pûr′spĭ·rā′sh*ŭ*n
27.	poignant	poig′n*ă*nt	poin′y*ă*nt
28.	posthumous	pŏs′tū·mŭs	pōst·hū′m*ŭ*s
29.	prevalent	prē·vā′l*ĕ*nt	prĕv′*ȧ*·l*ĕ*nt
30.	probably	prŏb′*ȧ*·blĭ	prŏb′*ȧ*·lĭ

● EXERCISE 10. Number on your paper from 1 to 33. Study the three pronunciations given for each word and select the correct one. Write, after the proper number on your paper, the letter (A, B, or C) of the column in which the correct form appears.

	A	B	C
1. adversary	ăd·vẽrs′ȧ·rĭ	ăd′vẽr·sâr′ĭ	ăd′vẽr·sĕr′ĭ
2. alias	ă′lĭ·ŭs	ā′lĭ·ăs	ȧ·lī′ŭs
3. almond	äl′mŭnd	ăl′mŭnd	ä′mŭnd
4. alumni	ȧ·lŭm′nē	ȧ·lŭm′nī	ăl′ŭm·nī
5. archipelago	är′kĭ·pĕl′ȧ·gō	ärch·ĭ·pĕl′ȧ·gō	är′kĭ·pĕl·ā′gō
6. archives	är′chīvs	är′kīvz	är′chĭvs
7. athlete	ăth·lēt′	ăth′ȧ·lēt	ăth′lēt
8. auxiliary	ôg·zĭl′ȧ·rĭ	ôks′ĭ·lâr′ĭ	ôg·zĭl′yȧ·rĭ
9. biography	bī·ō·grăf′ĭ	bĭ·ŏg′rȧ·fĭ	bī·ŏg′rȧ·fĭ
10. cabaret	kăb′ȧ·rā	kăb·ȧ·rĕt′	kăb·ȧ·rā′
11. café	kāf	kăf	kă·fā′
12. cello	chĕl′ō	sĕl′ō	kĕl′ō
13. government	gŭv′ẽr·mĕnt	gŭv′mĕnt	gŭv′ẽrn·mĕnt
14. ignoramus	ĭg′nȯ·rā′mŭs	ĭg′nȯ·ră′mŭs	ĭg′nȯ·rä′mŭs
15. impious	ĭm·pī′ŭs	ĭm′pĭ·ŭs	ĭm′pi̇·ŭs
16. inexorable	ĭn·ĕg′zȯ·rȧ′b′l	ĭn·ĕk′sȯ·rȧ·b′l	ĭn·ĕg·zō′rȧ·b′l
17. lamentable	lȧ·mĕn′tȧ·b′l	lăm′ĕn·tā′b′l	lăm′ĕn·tȧ·b′l
18. library	lī′brĕr·ĭ	lī·brĕr′ĭ	lī′bĕr·ĭ
19. longevity	lông·gĕv′ĭ·tĭ	lông·ȧ·vĭt′ĭ	lŏn·jĕv′ĭ·tĭ
20. mischievous	mĭs′chĭ·vŭs	mĭs·chē′vŭs	mĭs·chēv′ĭ·ŭs
21. mortgage	môrt′gāj	môr′gĭj	môrt′gĭj
22. naïve	nāv	nā′vē	nä·ēv′
23. recognize	rĕk′ŏg·nīz	rĕk′ŭn·īz	rė·kŏg′nīz
24. reputable	rė·pū′tȧ·b′l	rĕp·u̇·tā′b′l	rĕp′u̇·tȧ·b′l
25. schism	schĭz′m	skĭz′m	sĭz′m
26. sacrilegious	săk′rē·lĭj′ŭs	săk′rĭ·lē′jŭs	săk·rĭl′ė·jŭs
27. scion	skī′ŏn	sī′ŭn	skē′ŏn
28. solace	sō′lĭs	sŏl′ĭs	sŏl′ās
29. ultimatum	ŭl′tĭ·mā′tŭm	ŭl′tĭ·mă′tŭm	ŭl′tĭ·mä′tŭm
30. vehement	vē′ĕ·mĕnt	vė·hē′mĕnt	vā′ĕ·mĕnt
31. vehicle	vē′ĭ·k′l	vē′hĭk′l	vē·hĭk′′l
32. vigilante	vĭj′ĭ·lăn′tė	vĭj′ĭ·lănt′	vĭg′ĭ·lȧnt
33. viscount	vĭs′kount	vīs′kount	vī′kount′

CHAPTER 23

Reference Books

LEARN TITLES AND USES OF IMPORTANT REFERENCE BOOKS

Libraries vary in the number and kinds of reference books they own, but almost any library will have some, if not all, of the standard reference books described here. Familiarity with these useful books will increase your efficiency in looking up information. You may be surprised to find how easily you can acquire the information you need simply by knowing that there is a reference book that is specifically designed to provide it.

Studying the descriptions given on the following pages will not be an adequate substitute for actually having the books in your hands and working with them. If possible, go to the library and spend a few minutes with each book. One member of the class may be assigned to each of the reference works listed on the following pages. Have him find out whether the work is in your school or public library. If it is, have him skim the preface and read here and there in the book in order to report to the class any additional information about it. If practical, have him bring the book (one volume of a many-volumed work) to class so that everyone may see it.

Every class member should study carefully the

descriptions of the books given here and do the exercises on pages 345–49. Even though you do not have access to a particular reference work now, you should know that the book exists and what its principal uses are.

23a. Learn the use of special dictionaries.

In addition to the general dictionaries of the English language, there are many "word books" which are useful to anyone who does much writing. These are the books of synonyms. They help you to find just the right word when you are in doubt as to which word to use, and they help you to vary your choice of words so that you do not have to keep using the same words over and over. Three of the best known of these books of synonyms are listed below.

Fernald, James C., *Funk and Wagnalls Standard Handbook of Synonyms, Antonyms, and Prepositions*

This standard book lists in alphabetical order most of the words you would wish to use, and gives synonyms and antonyms for them.

Roget's Thesaurus of the English Language in Dictionary Form

Roget's Thesaurus has long been the best known of the synonym books. In its original form it was arranged in a rather complicated manner, which made its use time-consuming. Words in the new editions, however, are arranged in alphabetical order, an arrangement which has greatly increased the book's usefulness. Although arranged in the old manner, the abridged Pocket Book edition makes the Roget material available to every student at a small cost.

Webster's Dictionary of Synonyms

This book of synonyms and antonyms is especially valuable for its detailed explanations of the distinctions among words of similar meaning. It is, of course, like the Fernald and Roget books, a handy reference volume for authors in search of a word.

23b. Become familiar with the content and organization of encyclopedias.

Probably you have already used encyclopedias in your schoolwork. You know that an encyclopedia is a collection of articles on every phase of knowledge. Makers of encyclopedias are very careful to publish only authoritative articles written by eminent scholars. Encyclopedias contain helpful illustrations, diagrams, and bibliographies. The bibliographies tell you where to look for further information.

Although encyclopedias are arranged alphabetically like a dictionary, they also have an index. The reason for this is that a topic may be discussed in several widely separated articles. To find in one place a list of all the articles containing information on a topic, use the index (usually in the last volume).

For example, suppose that you were looking up information about the Olympic games. If you looked in the *Encyclopædia Britannica* volume containing the entry "Olympic Games," you would find an article several columns long. Then, if you looked in the index, you would find the volume and page number of ten other entries in the *Britannica* giving additional information about the games. Without the index you might not have known of these other entries.

Most encyclopedias are kept up to date in two ways First, they are constantly being revised as the world's knowledge expands, so that each printing represents some revision. Second, they are kept up to date through the publication of an annual, or yearbook, giving the important events, statistics, and developments in each phase of knowledge during that year.

ENCYCLOPEDIAS IN MANY VOLUMES

Collier's Encyclopedia
20 volumes
Bibliography and index in Volume 20
Publishes *Collier's Yearbook*

Encyclopedia Americana
30 volumes
Index in Volume 30
Publishes the *Americana Annual*

Encyclopædia Britannica
24 volumes
Index and atlas in Volume 24
Publishes the *Britannica Book of the Year*

FOR YOUNGER READERS

Compton's Pictured Encyclopedia
15 volumes
One third of space is devoted to pictures
Fact index (an index which itself gives information) at end of each volume

World Book Encyclopedia
19 volumes
Reading and Study Guide in Volume 19
Publishes an annual supplement

ONE-VOLUME ENCYCLOPEDIAS

Very often you may wish a brief, handy account of a subject. To meet this need, the one-volume "desk" encyclopedias are adequate. There are three well-known works of this kind. The *Columbia Encyclopedia* and the *Columbia-Viking Concise Encyclopedia* are arranged alphabetically like a dictionary. The

Lincoln Library of Essential Information is arranged in broad divisions of knowledge with many subdivision articles, and an index. Typical of the broad divisions covered are "The English Language," "Literature," "History," etc.

23c. Learn to use biographical reference books.

The reference shelves of your library will contain many, if not all, of the following biographical reference books. Since these books vary in their functions, you should be acquainted with the particular purpose served by each.

Biography Index (1946 to date)

This work contains no biographies. It tells you where you can find biographical accounts of almost anyone about whom a book or an article has been written. It indexes current biographical books in the English language and biographical material in more than 1,500 periodicals. Like the *Readers' Guide*, the *Biography Index* is published regularly and in cumulative editions. Specifically, it appears quarterly (November, February, May, and August). One bound volume annually includes the year's listings. Arrangement is of two kinds: (1) straight alphabetical listing of persons written about, and (2) alphabetical listing of names under broad divisions of professions or occupations. Remember that this is an *index* to biographical books and articles, not a book of biographies.

Current Biography

As indicated by its own slogan, "who's news and why," this regularly published reference work prints each month about 100 biographies of persons prominent in the news. It is international in scope and informal in style. As often as possible, the biographical articles are accompanied by a picture of the person written about. Published monthly in paper covers, the year's issues are cumulated in one bound volume. By using the cumulative index in each issue, you can find biographies that have appeared in other issues and in other years. Biographies are also indexed by professions.

The Dictionary of American Biography (20 volumes)

Comprehensive and authoritative, this monumental reference work contains the lives of important Americans no longer living. The articles are of varying length, but they are, in general, somewhat more detailed than the biographies in the large encyclopedias. The work covers a far greater number of Americans than does an encyclopedia. Entries date back to pre-Colonial times.

The Dictionary of National Biography

The British counterpart of the *Dictionary of American Biography*, this work contains lives of important Englishmen no longer living.

Webster's Biographical Dictionary

In this book more than 40,000 concise biographies are arranged in alphabetical order. Special care has been taken to give the correct pronunciation of each name. This book is useful for the same kind of information given about important persons in the general dictionaries; it contains, of course, more details, but it is not intended to provide the complete life of any person. The biography of Abraham Lincoln, for instance, occupies less than one column.

Who's Who and *Who's Who in America*

These standard books found in all libraries give the essential facts about famous *living* persons. It should be noted that the books are books of facts; they do not give a subject's life in any detail. Typical items of information to be found about a person in the *Who's Who* volumes are parentage, date of birth, positions held, principal achievements, writings and their dates, names of members of family, membership in clubs and societies, present address.

Who's Who gives information about famous British persons and some world figures in other countries. It is published annually.

Who's Who in America gives information about famous Americans. It is published every two years.

BOOKS ABOUT AUTHORS

Although the lives of authors are included in all the biographical reference books and in the encyclopedias, the following books are devoted exclusively to them. The articles are informally written, full of interesting information, and, whenever possible, accompanied by the author's picture. Each article gives a list of the author's works with their dates, and a bibliography for further reading.

American Authors 1600–1900 by Kunitz and Haycraft
British Authors Before 1800 by Kunitz and Haycraft
British Authors of the Nineteenth Century by Kunitz and Haycraft
Twentieth Century Authors by Kunitz and Haycraft
Twentieth Century Authors: First Supplement 1955

23d. Become familiar with several yearbooks.

World Almanac and Book of Facts

Most popular of the desk reference books on the world today, the *World Almanac* gives, in one handy volume, facts and statistics which are frequently in demand. Typical items in the *Almanac* are sports records, exports and imports of principal countries, statistics of population, officials of the governments of the world, Nobel and other prize winners, a summary of important events of the year, etc. Although the *Almanac* is published annually to cover one year at a time, many of its statistical tables cover data for preceding years. Remember that the *Almanac* for a certain year covers the year before; thus the 1957 issue covers the year 1956. The *Almanac* has its index in the front.

Information Please Almanac

The contents of the *Information Please Almanac* are arranged somewhat differently from those of the *World Almanac*, but by using the index at the back, you can find much of the same kind of information. The book is written in an informal style, easy to understand, and discusses in a more leisurely way a smaller number of subjects than the *World Almanac*.

Statesman's Year-Book

Self-characterized as a "statistical and historical annual of the states of the world" the *Statesman's Year-Book* gives the kind of information that is of interest to government officials, diplomats, and statesmen. Beginning with accounts of important *international* governing bodies, the *Year-Book* takes up each country, giving facts about each under the following headings: government, area and population, religion, education, welfare, finance, production and industry, commerce and communications. The index is at the back of the book.

Other Yearbooks

Several encyclopedias publish annual yearbooks. For example, see page 337, where the *Americana Annual*, the *Britannica Book of the Year*, and *Collier's Yearbook* are listed.

23e. Learn how to use atlases.

An atlas is much more than a book of maps. It gives valuable data about the topography and climate of countries, important places of interest, crops, exports and imports, and historical information. There are many excellent atlases. Find out which ones are in your library and where they are located. Since in our uncertain world the international scene changes so rapidly, the date of publication of an atlas is of great importance. Before relying on the accuracy of an atlas, look at its copyright date.

The following atlases are commonly found in high school libraries:

Collier's World Atlas and Geography
The Encyclopædia Britannica Atlas
Goode's World Atlas
Hammond's Universal World Atlas
Rand McNally Cosmopolitan World Atlas

23f. Know several literature reference books.

Benét's *The Reader's Encyclopedia*

Self-characterized as "an encyclopedia of all the things you encounter in reading," *The Reader's Encyclopedia* provides a great variety of information. In it you will find plots and characters in fiction, summaries of poems, brief biographies of writers, mythological, classical, and Biblical allusions, literary terms, descriptions of works of art, musical compositions, etc.

Books of Quotations

Everyone, at some time or other, wishes to locate the source of a quotation. There are many books of quotations; you may find three or four in your school library. Since they are arranged in various ways, you should ascertain the particular arrangement of the book you are using and its fitness for your purpose.

Bartlett's Familiar Quotations is probably the best-known source of information about quotations. The book may be used to find the following four kinds of information: (1) the author of a quotation; (2) the source or literary work in which a quotation appeared; (3) the complete quotation of which you know only a part; (4) a few famous lines from any author.

To find the author and source of a quotation, you must use the index at the back of the book. This index is arranged alphabetically according to "key words" in the quotation. To find the source of

> "Ill fares the land, to hastening ills a prey,
> Where wealth accumulates, and men decay."

you could look under any one of the "key words" *ill*, *fares*, *land*, *wealth*, *men*.

Since *Bartlett's Quotations* is arranged by authors in chronological order, you can find a great many famous quotations from a well-known author simply by turning to his name in the author index and then to the page on which quotations from his works appear.

Stevenson's *Home Book of Quotations* and *Home Book of Proverbs, Maxims, and Familiar Phrases*

Representing another kind of arrangement, these books group quotations according to the subjects with which the quotations deal. This makes the book especially helpful if, for an essay or a speech, you wish to find quotations on a particular subject — love, happiness, beauty, etc.

Stevenson's *Home Book of Verse* and *Home Book of Modern Verse*

When you wish to find a popular poem, you will do well to look for it first in one of these large anthologies. The poems are arranged by subjects; for instance, Poems of Youth and Age; Love Poems; Poems of Nature; Familiar Verse; Poems, Humorous and Satiric; etc. Since the books are indexed in three ways — by author, by title, and by first line — you should have no difficulty finding the poem you want, if it is in the book.

Granger's Index to Poetry and Recitations

Granger's Index tells you where you can find almost any poem or recitation (popular prose selection) published prior to the *Index*. Suppose, for instance, that you wish to find the poem "Casey at the Bat," but you do not know in which book in the library the poem appears. In *Granger's* you may look for the poem in the title index and find a number of abbreviations, each of which stands for an anthology of poetry containing the poem. By checking these books against the card catalogue, you will discover which of them are in your library, and then find the poem. *Granger's* is also a good book to use to find out who wrote a certain poem, because it contains an index of authors and an index of first lines. Bear in mind, however, that unlike the Stevenson books, *Granger's* contains no poems; it is only a list of poems and the books in which you may find them.

23g. Learn about other reference books.

Your teacher may assign members of the class to report on some of the following reference works sometimes found in high school libraries.

American Universities and Colleges, edited by A. J. Brumbaugh
Book Review Digest
Cambridge History of American Literature
Cambridge History of English Literature
Century Cyclopedia of Names
College Blue Book, edited by Christian E. Burckel
Encyclopedia of the Social Sciences
Essay and General Literature Index
Fowler's *Dictionary of Modern English Usage*
Grove's *Dictionary of Music and Musicians*
Langer's *An Encyclopedia of World History*
Oxford Companion to American Literature
Oxford Companion to English Literature
Oxford Companion to Music
Short Story Index
Webster's Geographical Dictionary

● EXERCISE 1. The following library tools and reference books have been described in this and the preceding chapters. Be able to explain the principal uses of each.

Library tools
  The card catalogue
  The Readers' Guide to Periodical Literature
  The vertical file
Dictionaries
  A dictionary of the English language
  Special dictionaries
  Funk and Wagnalls Standard Handbook of Synonyms, Antonyms, and Prepositions by J. C. Fernald
  Roget's Thesaurus of the English Language in Dictionary Form
  Webster's Dictionary of Synonyms
An encyclopedia

Biographical reference books
Biography Index
Current Biography
Dictionary of American Biography
Webster's Biographical Dictionary
Who's Who and *Who's Who in America*
British Authors Before 1800
British Authors of the Nineteenth Century
American Authors 1600–1900
Twentieth Century Authors
Twentieth Century Authors: First Supplement

Yearbooks
World Almanac and Book of Facts
Information Please Almanac
Statesman's Year-Book
Americana Annual
Britannica Book of the Year
Collier's Yearbook

An atlas

Literature reference books
Bartlett's Familiar Quotations
Benét's *The Reader's Encyclopedia*
Stevenson's *Home Book of Quotations*
Stevenson's *Home Book of Proverbs, Maxims, and Familiar Phrases*
Stevenson's *Home Book of Verse* and *Home Book of Modern Verse*
Granger's Index to Poetry and Recitations

● EXERCISE 2. Answer in writing the following questions.

1. Distinguish between *Who's Who* and *Who's Who in America.*
2. Explain the difference between the *Biography Index* and *Current Biography.*
3. For what kind of information is *Webster's Dictionary of Synonyms* especially valuable?
4. Name 3 important differences between the *Dictionary of American Biography* and *Who's Who in America.*

5. List 4 books that contain information about events of the past year.
6. Which literature reference book would you use to find the author of a poem whose title you know?
7. Which literature reference book would you use to find the title of a book containing a poem you want?
8. Arrange the following titles in order according to the length of their biographical articles, listing the one with the longest articles first, etc.: the dictionary, *Dictionary of American Biography, Webster's Biographical Dictionary.*
9. Arrange the following titles in order according to the frequency of their publication, listing the most frequently published first: *Readers' Guide, Biography Index, Who's Who in America, Who's Who, Current Biography.*
10. Explain the difference in arrangement between *Bartlett's Familiar Quotations* and Stevenson's *Home Book of Quotations.*

● EXERCISE 3. Number from 1 to 20 on your paper. From the books and reference tools given in brackets, select the one you would use to get the specified information. Write the title after the proper number on your paper. Be prepared to explain your choices.

1. Names of the senators in Congress from your state. [encyclopedia, *Who's Who in America*, *World Almanac*]
2. Synonyms for *calm.* [*Bartlett's Familiar Quotations*, dictionary, *Roget's Thesaurus*]
3. Books in your library about reptiles. [*Readers' Guide*, card catalogue, vertical file]
4. A description of the present government of France. [encyclopedia, dictionary, *Statesman's Year-Book*]
5. The life of Thomas Jefferson. [*Biography Index*, *Twentieth Century Authors*, *Dictionary of American Biography*]
6. A list of magazine articles on education published during the past few months. [*World Almanac*, *Readers' Guide*, card catalogue]

7. Life of the Secretary-General of the United Nations. [*Current Biography*, *Dictionary of American Biography*, *Webster's Biographical Dictionary*]
8. Which book would probably contain Poe's poem "The Raven"? [*Granger's Index*, *Bartlett's Familiar Quotations*, Stevenson's *Home Book of Verse*]
9. The origin of the word *jeep*. [encyclopedia, dictionary, *Information Please Almanac*]
10. A description and history of the rubber industry. [*Britannica Book of the Year*, *World Almanac*, encyclopedia]
11. International records in track events. [*Information Please Almanac*, *Statesman's Year-Book*, *Readers' Guide*]
12. The source of the common expression "All the world's a stage." [Stevenson's *Home Book of Verse*, *Webster's Dictionary of Synonyms*, *Bartlett's Familiar Quotations*]
13. Titles and authors of biographies of the President. [*Biographical Index*, *Who's Who in America*, *Webster's Biographical Dictionary*]
14. A quotation about youth. [*Bartlett's Familiar Quotations*, *Information Please Almanac*, Stevenson's *Home Book of Quotations*]
15. The copyright date of any book in your library. [encyclopedia, card catalogue, *Readers' Guide*]
16. The body of water into which the Suwannee River flows. [*Statesman's Year-Book*, *World Almanac*, atlas]
17. The location and height of Mt. Everest. [dictionary, *Americana Annual*, *Readers' Guide*]
18. A picture of an author who came into prominence during the past six months. [encyclopedia, *Current Biography*, *Who's Who*]
19. Leaflets recently published by the National Safety Council. [card catalogue, *Readers' Guide*, vertical file]
20. Educational background of the president of an American university. [*Who's Who*, *Biography Index*, *Who's Who in America*]

● EXERCISE 4. Which library tool or reference book, including the dictionary and encyclopedia, would you use to find the following items of information?

1. A number of magazine articles on the latest fashions in dress.
2. For what power was the mythological character Aeolus important?
3. What books does the library own on conservation of natural resources?
4. An account of climatic conditions in Tahiti.
5. The life of the author of a best-selling first novel, recently published.
6. A discussion of differences in meaning among words of similar meaning.
7. Biographies (books and articles) of a famous person in today's world.
8. The latest magazine articles about automobile accidents.
9. The capital city of Australia.
10. The native state of the Vice-President of the United States.
11. The publisher and copyright date of a book in the library.
12. The ten largest cities in the United States.
13. An illustrated article on the American Indian.
14. A history of the past year in sports.
15. Leaflets published by America's Town Meeting of the Air.
16. Does the library have any books on stamp collecting?
17. Officials of the present government of Pakistan.
18. An illustrated article on Italian art.
19. The derivation of any word.
20. A picture of Robert Sherwood, modern dramatist.

PART SIX

WRITING COMPOSITIONS

CHAPTER 24

The Effective Paragraph

LEARN HOW TO DEVELOP UNIFIED, COHERENT PARAGRAPHS[1]

24a. A *paragraph* is a series of sentences developing one topic.

A paragraph is a carefully organized unit of writing. Although brief, it is built on the same plan as a long composition. It has an introduction, which usually states its point; a second part, which develops the point; and, sometimes, a conclusion or summary. When you have learned to write a good paragraph, you will have learned most of the principles of organization required in all writing.

The Topic Sentence

24b. The topic of a paragraph should be stated in a single sentence somewhere in the paragraph. This sentence is the *topic sentence*.

In the paragraph at the top of the next page, the topic sentence is in bold type. The author develops the idea in this sentence by listing supporting details. Most paragraphs are developed in this way.

[1] This chapter is concerned primarily with the paragraph in relatively formal, expository writing. The student should realize that the rules for paragraph organization and development given here do not apply to the paragraph in narrative writing or in very informal personal essays.

The interpretation of words is a never-ending task for any citizen in modern society. We now have, as the result of modern means of communication, hundreds of thousands of words flung at us daily. We are constantly being talked at, by teachers, preachers, salesmen, public officials, and moving-picture sound tracks. The cries of the hawkers of soft drinks, soap chips, and laxatives pursue us into our very homes, thanks to the radio — and in some houses the radio is never turned off from morning to night. Daily the newsboy brings us, in large cities, from thirty to fifty enormous pages of print, and almost three times that amount on Sundays. The mailman brings magazines and direct-mail advertising. We go out and get more words at bookstores and libraries. Billboards confront us on the highways, and we even take portable radios with us to the seashore. Words fill our lives.[2]

24c. In general, place the topic sentence at or near the beginning of the paragraph.

A topic sentence may be placed at any point in a paragraph, but the most effective position for it in most paragraphs is at or near the beginning. Placing the topic sentence at the beginning helps the reader by giving him a clear idea of what is going to be said; it helps the writer by requiring him to formulate clearly his main point before going on to develop it.

In a composition of several paragraphs it would, of course, be unwise to begin every paragraph with the topic sentence; to do so might give a monotonous effect.

If you should try to find a topic sentence in every paragraph of a magazine article or a book, you would

[2] From *Language in Action* by S. I. Hayakawa. Copyright 1941 by Harcourt, Brace and Company. Reprinted by permission of the publishers.

soon discover that experienced writers do not always state in any one sentence the topics of their paragraphs. They may *imply* the central point so strongly that they do not need to give an out-and-out statement of it. But as an inexperienced writer, you should actually include a topic sentence in your paragraphs.

The preceding sample paragraph about the interpretation of words illustrates the placement of a topic sentence at the beginning of a paragraph. Placement of the topic sentence in other positions is illustrated by the two paragraphs which follow.

PARAGRAPH WITH THE TOPIC SENTENCE IN THE MIDDLE

Future generations, if there are to be future generations, may look upon the harnessing of atomic energy as the greatest single milestone in man's material progress, in the course of the everlasting battle to harness nature's forces to make possible a decent life for himself on this earth. **But while this development may mean man's greatest scientific triumph, it may also mean the most tragic moment in his history — a moment in which we may be standing on the brink of the great abyss.** For all man's recent ills have been brought about by the misuse of the products of man's genius. If mankind sees to it that atomic energy is properly controlled, this new cosmic fire can bring him new light and new warmth and new freedom. If he allows it to get out of control, as was the case with man's other inventions, it will mean a conflagration that will engulf the earth and all its inhabitants, leaving abysmal chaos and ruin.[3]

PARAGRAPH WITH THE TOPIC SENTENCE AT THE END

Let us see just what one of these reptiles may be worth to a farmer. Hishaw and Gloyd fed a lot of bull snakes and kept accurate track of the amount of food that they ate. A typical snake weighed 2.5 pounds and consumed

[3] From *Dawn over Zero* by William L. Laurence. Reprinted by permission of Alfred A. Knopf.

in six months 6.7 pounds of food. Now this would be about the weight of twelve pocket gophers or the number ordinarily found on an acre and a half of alfalfa. The snake would scarcely be active for more than six months in a year, so we can conclude that a bull snake for every acre and a half might solve the pocket gopher problem. Since this problem is estimated to cost the farmer $3.75 per year for every acre and a half, it is obvious that bull snakes should be valued highly instead of slaughtered ruthlessly. Killing them is not unlike tearing up five-dollar bills because they frighten you or seem disgusting. The snake is in truth cleaner and more beautiful than the money. **Every time a bull snake is butchered a farmer has lost several dollars.**[4]

THE CONCLUDING OR CLINCHER SENTENCE

At the end of a paragraph, particularly a long one, a writer will sometimes summarize by restating, in different words, the topic sentence he used at the beginning. In the sample paragraph on page 353, the final sentence "Words fill our lives" is such a summarizing sentence. A concluding sentence of this kind is sometimes called a "clincher" sentence because it clinches the point made in the paragraph.

You should be warned against overuse of the clincher sentence and against tacking it on artificially when it is not of any value. Avoid such weak and unnecessary concluding sentences as "Those are the three reasons why I like baseball" or "Now I have told you why I like baseball."

Of all the subjects I have studied in high school, Latin has proven most valuable to me. It has increased my knowledge in many fields. Through the intensive study of Latin words and forms, I have been able to expand my English vocabulary, for many of our English words are derived from Latin. I have also learned grammar and sentence construction

[4] Adapted from *Snakes Alive* by Clifford H. Pope. Reprinted by permission of the Viking Press.

since the study of Latin involves concentrated work on both of these subjects. Latin has given me an understanding of ancient Rome, which has had a great influence on our own civilization. Through Latin, I have become familiar with the lives and accomplishments of great Roman orators, poets, and generals such as Cicero, Vergil, and Caesar. I have also gained a knowledge of mythology, a subject which is all around us in the form of paintings, statues, operas, and even current Broadway plays. **Although many consider the study of Latin a waste of time, I believe that I could not possibly have put my time to better use than I did in learning Latin.**

● EXERCISE 1. Each of the following subjects can be treated in a paragraph. Select 3 subjects from the list; think through your ideas on each of the 3, and write a topic sentence you could use to introduce a paragraph on it. You will write 3 topic sentences.

1. The most important decision you ever made
2. Your worst defect
3. A common cause of unpopularity
4. An animal that you find interesting
5. Description of a favorite place
6. Rules for safe driving
7. Qualities of a successful teacher
8. Physical requirements for a basketball player
9. Overcoming a handicap
10. How to judge a used car

● EXERCISE 2. Develop one of the topic sentences written for Exercise 1 into a paragraph of approximately 150 words.

Development of the Topic Sentence into a Paragraph

24d. A paragraph is usually developed by means of additional, detailed information given in

support of the idea expressed in the topic sentence.

No skill acquired in your English course is more important in the improvement of your writing than the ability to develop a topic sentence into a good paragraph. An effective paragraph cannot be made out of nothing. You must have in mind the details with which to develop it. These details may be of many kinds. They may be facts or examples or incidents or arguments. The kind of details is not especially important, but the details themselves are all-important.

Study the following sample paragraphs. Each of them is developed by a different kind of details.

(1) A topic sentence may be developed by *facts*.

In the following paragraph, note that the details used to develop the topic sentence are facts which give meaning to the opening statement.

Baseball demands intelligence, especially behind the plate — because the catcher is the quarterback of baseball. He runs the team and is the only man who sees every player on the field and every move that takes place. He calls the pitches and sometimes directs much of the defensive play. He is the one person on the team who can never for a moment relax, whether his team is in the field or at bat. He must know wind conditions in every ball park, and his duties vary from studying the opposing batteries, the mental condition of his own pitcher, and the spacing of the outfielders, watching runners on base, keeping track of the tactical situation and seeing that the rest of the team knows it also, to backing up third and first except when a runner is in a scoring position.[5]

[5] From "Who's Catching?" by John R. Tunis. Reprinted by permission of *The Atlantic Monthly*.

(2) A topic sentence may be developed by *examples.*

Sometimes a topic sentence may be developed by giving one or more examples of the truth it expresses. In the following paragraph the author gives two examples to support his opening statement.

The amazing feats of master chess players show that real expertness requires a unique talent, a particular kind of imagination and memory. Many champions have been able to play one hundred good opponents simultaneously, spending no more than three or four minutes at each board and usually winning every game. Even more extraordinary is the ability of a master to play "blindfold" chess, in which he is told his opponent's moves by an umpire, then reports his own moves without ever seeing the board. He must keep in mind the positions of all thirty-two chessmen, his plan of attack for several moves in advance, and the possibilities of his opponent's counter-attack.

(3) A topic sentence may be developed by an *incident.*

As in the following paragraph, a brief story, an incident, is sometimes used in support of the topic sentence. An incident is, of course, a particular type of example. To show what he means by his statement "Not all police stories are bloody," Mr. Arm, a newspaper reporter, tells a police story about some elephants.

Not all police stories are bloody. One day in the 1920's three elephants wandered away from a circus in Harlem and entered the West 123rd Street Station House. They tramped ponderously past the desk lieutenant, whose eyes widened in amazement, and on into the back room where a group of patrolmen were filling in reports. The policemen took one look and dived into the courtyard from nearby windows. The lieutenant called the emergency squad and when he told them why he wanted them, they laughed and refused to answer his appeal. Finally, he convinced them, and the emergency squad found it had quite a job on its hands. It took three tubs of lard and the combined efforts of ten patrolmen to coax and push the pachyderms out of the precinct.[6]

(4) A topic sentence may be developed by *arguments* in a line of reasoning.

A paragraph which states and then explains a point of view or one side of an argument may be developed by a logical train of thought, one point leading to another until the position of the writer has been effectively supported. In a paragraph of this kind, the details used to develop the topic sentence are the reasons for, or arguments in favor of, the author's point. These reasons and arguments, of course, may themselves be supported by facts, examples, or incidents.

Study the following paragraph. Note that the argument is advanced by a line of reasoning logically presented.

Now, to be properly enjoyed, a walking tour should be gone upon alone. If you go in a company, or even in pairs, it is no longer a walking tour in anything but name; it is something else and more in the nature of a picnic. A walking tour should be gone upon alone, because freedom is of the essence; because you should be able to stop and go on, and follow this way or that, as the freak takes you; and because you must have your own pace, and neither trot alongside a champion walker, nor mince in time with a girl. And then you must be open to all impressions and let your thoughts take color from what you see. You should be as a pipe for any wind to play upon. "I cannot see the wit," says Hazlitt, "of walking and talking at the same time. When I am in the country, I wish to vegetate like the country" — which is the gist of all that can be said

[6] From "Police Reporter" by Walter Arm in *Late City Edition*, by Joseph G. Herzberg. Reprinted by permission of Henry Holt and Company.

upon the matter. There should be no cackle of voices at your elbow to jar on the meditative silence of the morning. And so long as a man is reasoning he cannot surrender himself to that fine intoxication that comes of much motion in the open air, that begins in a sort of dazzle and sluggishness of the brain, and ends in a peace that passes comprehension.[7]

● EXERCISE 3. Read carefully each of the following paragraphs. Find the topic sentence in each and write it on your paper. After each topic sentence indicate by the rule numbers — (1), (2), (3), (4) — the kind or kinds of details the writer used to develop the paragraph:

(1) facts
(2) examples (one or more)
(3) incidents (one or more)
(4) arguments or reasons

1

There are certain phrases which through constant use have become standard decoration for textbook covers of drab brown paper. Among these is "In case of fire, throw in!" a command which is often found on English grammars. I know of one case where a student was harshly criticized for such a remark on the cover of his English text, and was asked by the teacher to remove it at once. The next day when the student came to class he had a brand new cover on which was printed "English Is a Wonderful Subject" — this remark being decorated with flowers and little angels peeping out from behind the letters. Another stand-by is, "Don't open until Christmas," which is invariably followed by a detailed picture of Santa Claus, whose beard usually extends the whole length of the cover by Christmas time, since each day the student absent-mindedly sketches on a few more whiskers. Recently there has been a movement underfoot to change this expression to "Don't open until a week before mid-terms!" which sounds more logical. This expression is usually found on biology and chemistry books.

[7] From "Walking Tours," by Robert Louis Stevenson.

2

Until the moment the referee steps into the ring, no one knows that he will even be at the fight. Except for the actual punches, he works almost as hard as the boxers. The fairness with which a match is judged, even its pace and cleanness, rests largely with him. Yet in the melee that follows, he is remembered only by those who disagreed with his verdict. And when it comes time to divide up the gate he will be lucky, if it's a title bout, to get as much as $300 as his share. No wonder the referee considers himself the forgotten man of prizefighting.[8]

3

Luck is sometimes the deciding factor in a game. In the eighth inning of the deciding game of the World Series of 1924, the Giants were leading the Senators by the fairly comfortable margin of 3–1. A hard-hit ground ball struck a pebble, bounded over the head of third-baseman Fred Lindstrom, and two runs came in, tying up the game. The contest went into extra innings. In the last of the twelfth, the Giant catcher, about to dash for a pop fly behind the plate, caught his foot in his mask and, unable to free himself, missed an easy out. The batter, given another chance, then doubled. The next man up hit another grounder toward third base. The ball again struck a pebble, soared over the third baseman, and the game and series were won by the Senators.

4

The old essays on friendship tell you that your friends should have about the same education, the same kind of home, the same mentality, and the same financial standing as you do yourself. I don't entirely agree, although in general I *do* think it is a mistake to have friends who live in a fashion very much more expensive than you can afford. But if you are the kind of girl who wants to keep on growing, you will find it more congenial to have friends

[8] From "Man in the Middle — The Referee" by David Dempsey. Reprinted by permission of the *New York Times Magazine.*

who know more than you do, and who are a little ahead of you in some, if not all, particulars. No girl can develop beyond her environment if she surrounds herself with friends who have exactly the same, or less, education than she has. The friends you will value most in the long run (unless you are too lazy, or too vain, to want to improve yourself) are the friends who stimulate you to be up-and-coming, well informed, and entertaining, the friends who make you stretch yourself intellectually. That's different from "keeping up with the Joneses." Keeping up with the Joneses, you know, means pretending to have something you haven't got, spending money that you cannot afford (bad manners, of course), while stretching yourself intellectually is merely using to the full those talents you really possess.[9]

5

A native of the Nile, the Egyptian mouthbreeder is a translucent brown in color. The largest specimens are rarely over two and one-half inches in length. At breeding time the male scoops up the eggs and places them in a small indentation in the sand. As soon as the spawning is completed, the female scoops all the eggs into her mouth. For the next fifteen days she carries them about, going without food to avoid swallowing her future children. When the eggs hatch, the children are allowed to swim out of their mother's mouth, but at the first sign of danger, all of them rush back. This behavior continues until the children grow too large to fit in. The mouthbreeder is truly an exotic fish.

● EXERCISE 4. Number on your paper from 1 to 20. Read the topic sentences listed below and after the proper number indicate by the rule numbers — **(1), (2), (3), (4)** — the method or combination of methods you would use to develop a paragraph from

[9] From *It's More Fun When You Know the Rules* by Beatrice Pierce. Reprinted by permission of Rinehart and Company.

each of the sentences. Class discussion will reveal that the same sentence can be developed in more than one way.

(1) facts
(2) examples (one or more)
(3) incidents (one or more)
(4) arguments or reasons

1. Teen-agers are conformists.
2. Some restrictions placed on teen-agers do more harm than good.
3. High marks should not be the only basis for evaluating a student's success.
4. First impressions of people are often proved wrong.
5. I have learned an infallible formula for failure.
6. The day was full of surprises.
7. The United States is aiding many underdeveloped countries.
8. Honor students should be excused from examinations.
9. Students should be given a stronger voice in the operation of the school.
10. In basketball, skill is more important than strength.
11. Clothes do make a difference.
12. The church deserves our support.
13. I am grateful for that course in public speaking.
14. A slip of the tongue may be embarrassing.
15. Prejudices are acquired at home.
16. Every high school student should be required to take the course in driver training.
17. That one mistake was disastrous.
18. To avoid war, prepare for war.
19. Preparedness leads to war.
20. Regardless of his sport, an athlete must follow certain training rules.

● EXERCISE 5. Choose one topic sentence from the preceding list and, using the kinds of details you think best suited, develop it into an interesting paragraph of about 150 words.

ADEQUATE DEVELOPMENT OF THE TOPIC SENTENCE

Since a paragraph is the development of an idea, it must give enough details to make the idea clear and convincing. A common fault in one-paragraph compositions, such as you are writing in your study of this chapter, is the failure to provide enough information. Although there can be no strict rule as to paragraph length, a one-paragraph composition of only two sentences or of less than 100 words is likely to be thin. Because most students have difficulty in expanding rather than in limiting their paragraphs, it is hardly necessary to set a maximum number of words; but if you find your paragraph running above 300 words, you are taking the risk of destroying its unity. Long paragraphs are likely, in other words, to contain details not closely related to the topic sentence.

24e. In developing a paragraph, supply enough information to insure adequate development. Avoid the thinness which results from merely repeating in different words the idea in the topic sentence.

THIN PARAGRAPH LACKING SUFFICIENT DEVELOPMENT

Every student should engage in some extracurricular activity. A student needs experience in such an activity if he is to succeed in life. If you include athletics, there are enough activities to provide everyone with something to do in addition to his regular schoolwork. No boy or girl should leave school every day when the final bell rings and have no definite interest to follow in the after-school hours. Everyone can benefit educationally and socially by extracurricular work. No one should think of school as solely a matter of subjects to study and classes to attend.

PARAGRAPH MORE ADEQUATELY DEVELOPED

Every student should engage in some extracurricular activity because from extracurricular work you learn a great many valuable things that you won't learn in a classroom. School is not just a matter of learning the difference between *lie* and *lay*, or what caused the War Between the States; it is learning to live and work with others. You learn to work and play with others harmoniously, to give and take, win and lose. When, as a member of a club, you are given a job to do, you learn to assume responsibility and to work unselfishly for the good of the group. In a radio club or a photography club you get additional knowledge which may be more valuable in the long run than the knowledge you get from doing homework or attending classes. Furthermore, if you work hard in dramatics or in musical organizations you will develop talents which will be satisfying to you all your life, talents which might never have been discovered had you thought of school as confined to the hours of the daily schedule. Finally, extracurricular activities broaden your circle of acquaintances. No amount of ordinary schoolwork can take the place of friends acquired in the informal familiarity of activities.

Unity in the Paragraph

24f. A paragraph should be unified. Unity is achieved by discussing only one topic in a paragraph, the topic stated in the topic sentence.

● EXERCISE 6. The unity of the paragraphs which follow has been weakened by inclusion of ideas not closely related to the topic of the paragraph. The topic sentences are in bold type. Point out which sentences in each paragraph should be omitted because they do not deal with the topic.

1

The first tee is a place of perpetual embarrassment. It seems there is always an audience on the first tee. When the golfer steps up to hit his shot, he is certain that everyone is watching. The nervous golfer will invariably dub his shot miserably. Though power helps, great strength is unnecessary in golf. The player must have good timing in his hands. There is nothing funnier to the first-tee audience or more embarrassing to the player himself than a two-hundred-pound football player who takes a vicious swing and misses the ball completely. The discreet silence which follows this futile stroke is almost too much to bear.

2

A dishonest newspaper may warp the day's news either by hiding a story or by slanting headlines. A paper with a strong political bias may hide a story favorable to the opposing party by placing it in an inconspicuous position. On the other hand, it may give large headlines and a front-page position to news favorable to its own party. Although newspapers do not change the facts in the stories which come to them, they may, if it serves their political purpose, change the total effect of a story by giving it a headline which is deliberately misleading or slanted. Headlines are written by the paper's copyreaders, men highly skilled in their jobs. Once the drudges of the newspaper office, these men in recent years have been accorded greater respect as reflected in easier hours and higher pay. A headline may be made misleading simply by means of the words used. MAYOR JONES REPLIES TO CRITICS gives a quite different impression from MAYOR JONES CRACKS DOWN ON CRITICS.

3

During the first days of September, my friends spend their time complaining about having to go back to school. They say they are going to miss the carefree summer days, the free evenings, the lying in bed on Monday mornings. The summer looked endless back in June when it all lay ahead of them. **As for me, I don't mind going back to school because the experience has always been interesting to me.** I like the atmosphere of confusion and excitement in the halls and the fun of greeting old friends again. I am full of curiosity about my homeroom, my schedule, and my teachers. Just before entering a class on the first day, I wonder who else will be in the class, whether I will meet any new students, what the teacher will be like. I like to let my first impressions of a new teacher sink into my memory, so that I can recall them after a few months to see if my original opinion was correct. The teachers always try to look as though they are glad to be back. Maybe teachers like school all the time, or they wouldn't be teachers. I enjoy, too, the helpless way the freshmen wander around the building, without a friend, trying to find their way to unfamiliar classrooms. Their gratitude for the slightest help or the merest show of friendliness is amusing. Even the building looks good with its freshly painted, spotless interior. Yes, I enjoy going back to school — for the first day, at least.

4

The book-buying habits of the American people reflect the human desire to be "in the know." The woman who would rather stay at home than go out in last year's hat will also rather read, or have read, the latest popular book, regardless of its quality, than a better book published a year ago. She wants to impress others with the fact that she is up to date in her reading. The weekly publication of best-seller lists stems from this desire, and the widespread membership in such standardizing influences as the Book-of-the-Month Club and the Literary Guild fosters the custom. Lending-library employees are always being rushed by avid seekers of the latest novel, who wish to be the first to spring it at the next tea party. Lending libraries can now be found in drug and stationery stores as well as in bookstores. Of course, the demand for twenty-five cent books, which are not current best sellers, is attributable to another human characteristic, the desire for a bargain.

● EXERCISE 7. Select one of the following topic sentences and develop it into a paragraph of approximately 150 words. Insure adequate development of the topic by (1) gathering enough ideas, (2) avoiding commonplace ideas, and (3) resisting the tendency to restate the topic sentence again and again in different words. Insure unity by including only ideas which support the topic sentence.

1. As a literary experience, a long novel has advantages over a short novel.
2. I have chosen ——— as my life work for several reasons.
3. ——— is an ideal vacation spot.
4. Training a dog (horse) requires patience.
5. A "mutt" makes a better pet than a pedigreed dog.
6. Many of our school assignments are wasteful busy work.
7. Parents should spend more time with their children.
8. Teachers are sometimes responsible for their students' misconduct.
9. Teen-agers should be permitted to make their own decisions.
10. Leisure time should be devoted to self-improvement.

Coherence in the Paragraph

ARRANGEMENT OF DETAILS

A paragraph is coherent when its ideas are logically and clearly related to one another, and the total effect of the sentences is the clear development of the paragraph idea. One way of achieving coherence is by arranging the details in a paragraph in a clear and logical order.

24g. To insure that the details in a paragraph will follow one another logically and smoothly, arrange them in order according to some definite plan.

Three plans, or orders, for the arrangement of the details in a paragraph are *the order of time*, *the order of importance*, and *the order required to bring out a comparison or contrast.*[10]

(1) The details in a paragraph may be arranged in the order of *time*.

The order of time is followed in two kinds of paragraph. It is followed in the *narrative* paragraph, in which events are given in the order in which they happened; and it is followed in the *expository* paragraph, in which a *process* is described from beginning to end. The paragraph on page 358 about the elephants in the police station will serve as an illustration of the time order in a narrative paragraph. The following paragraph illustrates the time order required in explaining a process, in this case the process by which a river deposits in its bed the products of erosion.

All the products of erosion which reach the coast finally settle down on the sea floor, but rivers also deposit in their beds a great deal of the material they bring down from the mountains. What usually happens is that frost and rain conspire to wash in the sides and form a valley, and the vast bulk of rock disintegrated by these agents is carried away as mud, sand, and pebbles by the stream at the bottom. As the valley gets older it grows wider and may presently be so wide in its lower reaches as to have a virtually level bottom, over which the river slowly winds toward the sea. The river has now lost speed, and begins

[10] The "order of space," in which the parts of a word picture are arranged according to their location in the picture (right to left, foreground to background, etc.) is sometimes useful in descriptive writing. However, discussion of this kind of arrangement has been omitted here because slavish adherence to it usually produces an artificial style. It is not, as a rule, followed in the best descriptive writing.

to distribute its mud and sand over its widened valley floor. Once a river begins to flow in a curve, a cycle of events is started which results in a steady and systematic covering of the whole valley floor with sediment. The water naturally moves most rapidly round the outside of the curve, where its increased speed causes it to remove a quantity of mud from its bank. It may actually scoop out a little cliff for itself. But on the inside of the curve the water is moving extra slowly, and because mud settles down in still water it is here that some of the mud it is already carrying is deposited. As the river goes on scooping out mud from one bank and depositing it on the other, so it moves sideways across its valley, leaving a carpet of alluvium in its train.[11]

(2) The details in a paragraph may be arranged in the order of *importance*.

Order of importance usually means proceeding from the least important to the most important. This order may be profitably followed in any paragraph which presents evidence in support of an opinion or an argument. For instance, in the following example, the author, after stating her preference for a coeducational college, gives three reasons for her opinion. You will note that the reasons are given in the order of importance, the least important coming first, the most important last.

In spite of the many arguments offered by those who favor women's colleges, I have decided to go to a coeducational school. There are three main reasons for my decision. The first, and admittedly the least important consideration, is that I think I will have more fun at a coeducational college. I have always enjoyed mixed company more than "hen parties," and I'm afraid that I'd be bored in the company of girls four or five days a week for four years.

[11] Adapted from *Science Marches On* by Walter Shepherd. Copyright 1939 by Harcourt, Brace and Company. Reprinted by permission of the publishers.

Also, I think that we ought to have the male viewpoint in our classes. It's one thing to read what men say and what their attitudes are toward a subject, but it's quite another to hear it firsthand. In high school the boys have always contributed the most original ideas to our class discussions. Mixed classes are more interesting and more enlightening. Finally, education is supposed to be a preparation for life. How can you prepare for life in a world where both sexes are constantly together, by living largely in a woman's world all through college?

(3) The details in a paragraph may be arranged to bring out a *comparison* or a *contrast*.

Occasionally a writer wishes to use a paragraph to compare or contrast two things or ideas. Naturally he will arrange his details in such a way as to bring out clearly the nature of the comparison or contrast.

In bringing out a comparison or a contrast, a writer may follow one of two arrangements: (1) details supporting one point of view may be presented first, followed by details supporting the opposite point of view; (2) details of similarity or difference may be compared or contrasted one by one, rather than being grouped into two complete parts as in the first method. These two arrangements are illustrated by the following sample paragraphs.

In the first paragraph, one point of view is presented first, followed by the other.

The similarity between the human body (or any animal body) and a machine is really rather superficial. It can be summed up in the statement that both require fuel and oxygen, and obtain energy by slow or rapid combustion; both require systems of elimination for the waste products of combustion and the ashes of the fuel; the moving parts of each consist of mechanical levers, if we consider the wheel as a continuous lever, and each contains secondary structures which can be crudely described as "tubes," "triggers," "straps," and "wires," some of which are by no means indispensable to the healthy working of the whole. Beyond that, comparison fails. No machine grows in size; no machine sees, hears, or feels; no machine reproduces its kind or repairs its own broken and worn-out parts; no machine thinks. The points of difference far outweigh the points of resemblance, which are, indeed, almost the minimum consistent with the round statement that bodies and machines exist in the same universe.[12]

In the paragraph below, details of difference are contrasted one by one.

The difference between democracy and communism in practice is clearly shown by the differences between the United States and Russia. In the United States the people are supreme, and the government is their servant. In Russia, the government is supreme, and the people are its servants. The United States Constitution guarantees to American citizens the right to choose their leaders. The two-party system insures them a choice. Control of the government in Russia rests in the hands of a small group of leaders. Voting is a farce because there is only one party — the Communist party, and any citizen who dares to oppose the ruling group receives harsh treatment. In America the government guarantees the people complete freedom to worship as they please, but in Russia the leaders discourage religion and religious worship. Freedom of speech in America gives everyone the privilege of saying exactly what he thinks, even to the point of criticizing his government. Freedom of speech does not exist in Russia. The people, living in constant fear of their government, are afraid to express any views contrary to those of the party.

● EXERCISE 8. Each of the following items suggests a comparison or contrast that can be developed

[12] From *Science Marches On* by Walter Shepherd. Copyright 1939 by Harcourt, Brace and Company. Reprinted by permission of the publishers.

into an interesting paragraph. Select one and fashion a topic sentence stating your point. Using one of the three methods of arranging material in a paragraph of this kind, write a paragraph of about 150 words which will bring out clearly the point in the topic sentence. You will be developing a paragraph by means of comparison or contrast.

1. Our new car and our old car
2. Country life and city life
3. Intramural sports and interscholastic sports
4. The book version of a novel and the movie version
5. Appearance and personality
6. Life in a foreign country and life here
7. Independent school and public school
8. A baseball crowd and a tennis crowd
9. Boys' manners and girls' manners
10. Mother and Father

LINKING EXPRESSIONS AND CONNECTIVES [13]

24h. Strengthen the coherence of a paragraph by the use of linking expressions and connectives which help the reader to follow the line of thought from one idea to the next.

The linking expressions are usually pronouns which refer to words or ideas in the preceding sentences. They serve to carry the reader back to what has just been said. The pronouns commonly used in this way are *he*, *they*, *this*, *that*, *these*, *those*, *them*, *it*. When they are used as adjectives, the words *this*, *that*, *these*, and *those* serve as linking expressions just as well as when they are used as pronouns.

[13] Methods of making smooth transitions from one paragraph to another are described on pages 388–93 in the chapter on "The Whole Composition."

(1) Keep the thought of a paragraph flowing smoothly from sentence to sentence by using pronouns which refer to words or ideas in preceding sentences.

EXAMPLE Gary made a number of suggestions to the student council. Although **they** were not new, **they** were impressive enough to stir the council to action. **This** result was in itself a good thing. About half of Gary's suggestions were placed on the agenda. **These** pertained to financial matters. The most interesting of **them** was a suggestion to make the yearbook a school, rather than an exclusively senior class, publication.

(2) Keep the thought of a paragraph flowing smoothly from sentence to sentence by the use of connectives.

The use of connectives (words and phrases) is a common means of maintaining a clear line of thought from one sentence to the next. You may help yourself to more coherent writing by studying the following lists of connectives. You will note duplication in the various lists because many connectives are useful in more than one kind of writing. Naturally, you must not overuse them, for too many connectives will make the style wordy and cumbersome. Their judicious use, however, will improve the coherence of your paragraphs.[14]

CONNECTIVES FOR DESCRIPTIVE WRITING

above	beyond	on my left
across from	further	on my right
adjacent to	here	opposite to
also	in the distance	to the left
before me	near by	to the right
below	next to	

[14] For work on the careful selection of the proper connective, see pages 185–89.

CONNECTIVES FOR EXPLANATORY WRITING

also	for example	on the other hand
another	for instance	otherwise
as a result	for this purpose	second
at last	furthermore	similarly
consequently	likewise	such
finally	next	then
first	on the contrary	thus

CONNECTIVES FOR ARGUMENTATIVE WRITING

accordingly	for example	on the contrary
again	for instance	on the other hand
although	furthermore	otherwise
another	hence	second
as a result	if this be true	such
at the same time	in addition	then too
besides	in fact	therefore
consequently	in short	thus
equally important	moreover	to sum up
finally	nevertheless	whereas
first		

EXAMPLES Many complaints have been leveled against the secondary schools. **For instance,** they have been accused of being too closely tied in with college education and of neglecting the "average" teen-aged boy or girl of the community. At present, most of the high schools in the United States gear their curriculum to the college program. **However,** only 20 per cent of the high school students go on to college. **Another** 20 per cent take vocational or technical courses.

When you buy a car, examine carefully the important features of the model you are considering. One of **these** features is the size of the car. Many a buyer of the latest models has made trouble for himself by buying a car too broad or too long for his garage. **Further-**

> more, a long car is much harder to maneuver in traffic and much more difficult to park. Another feature is the comfort afforded. Are the seats wide and durably upholstered? Is there enough glass area to give the driver a good view in all directions, particularly to the rear? It should be remembered, too, that the heavier and more powerful a car is, the more expensive it will be to operate. High-powered motors require expensive high-octane gasoline. Replacement parts are more costly. The greater weight means greater tire wear and enlarged brakes. The old cliché is still true — it's not the initial cost but the upkeep!

● EXERCISE 9. Select one of the following topics and write a paragraph of approximately 150 words on it. Begin with your topic sentence. Then develop it, paying special attention to such matters as having enough details to develop the idea adequately, sticking to the subject, following a definite arrangement, and using linking expressions and connectives to keep the thought running smoothly.

1. Factors to consider in selecting a college
2. Recreational facilities for youth in this community
3. The qualities of a good quarterback
4. Basic causes of family quarrels
5. Valid criticisms of this school
6. The meaning of sportsmanship
7. Advantages and disadvantages of being left-handed
8. Impractical high school courses
9. The book-report burden
10. Father's moods
11. Regional differences in the United States
12. Privileges carry responsibilities
13. Ways to entertain children
14. How a prejudice starts
15. My favorite road

CHAPTER 25

The Whole Composition

LEARN THE TECHNIQUES OF WRITING AN INTERESTING, WELL-ORGANIZED COMPOSITION

You have been writing compositions for many years. It is only by requiring you to write them that your teacher can help you to write better. Although the advice given in this chapter may seem familiar to you, you should study the chapter carefully. The basic steps involved in writing are almost always the same, regardless of what you are writing; and these steps must be so thoroughly understood that you will follow them habitually. The main steps in the planning and writing of a composition are listed below in the order in which they are performed. Each of these steps is important if you are to write a well-organized and coherent composition.

1. Selecting and limiting the subject
2. Assembling materials
3. Organizing materials — outlining
4. Writing the first draft
5. Revising
6. Writing the final draft

Selecting and Limiting the Subject

25a. Select a subject that can be adequately treated within the limits of your composition.

Unless your teacher specifies what you are to write about, your first problem is the choice of a subject. Of course, you will choose one in which you are interested. You will choose one, too, on which you either have or can find enough information to make a worth-while composition. You should know before you select your subject how long your composition is going to be. On this basis you must limit your subject so that you will be able to cover it adequately in the space at your disposal. Study the following examples of how a subject may be limited for treatment in compositions of different length.

1

UNLIMITED Transportation
SLIGHTLY LIMITED The history of transportation
MORE LIMITED The history of transportation in the United States
LIMITED FOR A 2,000-WORD TREATMENT The growth of the trucking industry in the United States
LIMITED FOR A 1,000-WORD TREATMENT Long-distance trucking today
LIMITED FOR A 500-WORD TREATMENT Driving a long-distance truck

2

UNLIMITED Conservation
SLIGHTLY LIMITED Conservation of natural resources
MORE LIMITED Conservation of natural resources in the United States
LIMITED FOR A 2,000-WORD TREATMENT Soil conservation in the United States
LIMITED FOR A 1,000-WORD TREATMENT Soil conservation in the Dust Bowl

LIMITED FOR A 500-WORD TREATMENT Two methods of soil conservation

State your purpose. Limiting your subject must always be done with reference to your purpose. The purpose of your composition, in fact, determines its scope. Your teacher may ask you to precede your composition with a statement of your purpose, or, at least, to state the purpose in the introductory paragraph. In any event, you will do well to write the purpose in a one-sentence statement so that you will be able to keep it clearly before you as you plan and write. "My purpose in this composition is ———"

Assembling Materials

25b. List all the ideas you think you may wish to use in your composition.

Some compositions can be written "out of your head" without recourse to the library or to the opinions of others. Many compositions, however, will send you on a hunt for information.[1] In both cases Step 2 is the same. It is the listing of the ideas you think you can use in your paper. In this step, it does not matter in what order you list the ideas; the important thing is to get them down where you can look at them, evaluate them, and arrange them.

In order to illustrate the steps in planning and writing a composition, the next few pages are devoted to showing you, through a specific example, how the steps should be followed.

Imagine that, following a class discussion of the good and bad qualities that high schools possess,

[1] For detailed discussion of writing a long research paper, see Chapter 29.

including your own school, you have decided to write a composition giving your concept of the ideal high school. Your teacher has asked for a paper about 500 words in length. Since the ideas to be expressed are drawn from your experience and presently exist in your mind, you can perform Step 2 without having to look up material. You begin the step by listing your ideas just as they occur to you.

LIST OF IDEAS FOR A COMPOSITION ON "MY CONCEPT OF THE IDEAL HIGH SCHOOL"

democratic spirit
friendly spirit
loyalty to school
no cliques
self-government
student government with real power
understanding teachers
friendly teachers
a curriculum fitting needs of every student
small classes *
good discipline
competent teachers
an athletic program for every student
an extracurricular program for every student
modern buildings *
modern equipment *
adequate cafeteria and auditorium *
good school newspaper *
plenty of social affairs *

After the list has been completed, you should go over it carefully and remove any items which, on second thought, seem unrelated to the subject, or which, if included, would make the composition too long. For example, in going over this list, you decide to eliminate certain items (marked by an asterisk). You decide that a worth-while discussion of the building and equipment for a high school would make your paper much too long; you realize, furthermore, that the physical plant of the school (cafeteria and auditorium) is not really the most important consideration. You decide also that three other items can be omitted because they do not relate importantly to the principal points you have in mind. These items are the following: small classes, good school newspaper, plenty of social affairs.

Having eliminated the items you will not use, you next perform the all-important step of organizing the remaining ones logically.

Organizing Materials — Outlining

25c. Group related ideas together. Arrange the groups in a logical order. Make an outline.

As you group the related ideas, you are really making an outline. In making an outline, you must make major decisions concerning the content and the organization of your composition. It is no exaggeration to say that more than half the work on a composition has been done when the outline has been completed.

THE TOPICAL OUTLINE

Two kinds of outline are in common use: the topical outline and the sentence outline. In a topical outline each item is merely a topic to be discussed in the paper; it is not a sentence. For most of the outlining that you will do, the topical outline will be adequate; in fact, it will be preferable because it is easier to make and is clear enough to serve its purpose. The following outline of the first part of the essay on an ideal high school is done in topical outline form.

I. The spirit of the school
   A. Friendly
   B. Democratic
   C. Loyal
II. The government of the school
   A. Democratic
   B. Respected

THE SENTENCE OUTLINE

There are some occasions, however, when you may prefer to use the sentence outline, which is always clearer because it gives in more detail the exact meaning of each topic. A sentence outline is the better kind if you are outlining for someone else who may not grasp the full meaning of the short headings in a topical outline. A comparison of the sentence outline below with the topical outline above will indicate the advantage of the sentence form.

I. The spirit of the school is friendly, democratic, and loyal.
  A. Students are friendly to one another and to visitors.
  B. Students do not tolerate undemocratic cliques and exclusive social clubs.
  C. Students show their loyalty by their good behavior as well as by supporting the school teams.

II. The government of the school is democratic and respected.
  A. The students elect their own officers and governing bodies.
  B. The elected officers are respected because they have real power to govern.

RULES FOR FORM IN MAKING AN OUTLINE

25d. Observe rules for form in making an outline.

(1) Place the title above the outline. It is not one of the numbered or lettered topics.

(2) The terms *Introduction, Body, Conclusion* should not be included in the outline. They are not topics to be discussed in the composition. They are merely organizational terms in the author's mind as he plans.

(3) Use Roman numerals for the main topics. Subtopics are given letters and numbers as follows: capital

letters, Arabic numerals, small letters, Arabic numerals in parentheses, small letters in parentheses.

CORRECT ARRANGEMENT OF NUMBERS AND LETTERS

I.
  A.
  B.
    1.
    2.
      a.
      b.
        (1)
        (2)
          (a)
          (b)
II.

(4) Indent subtopics so that all letters or numbers of the same kind will come directly under one another in a vertical line.

(5) Begin each topic with a capital letter. Do not capitalize words other than the first unless they are proper nouns or proper adjectives.

(6) In a topical outline do not follow topics with a period.

(7) There must never be, under any topic, a lone subtopic; there must be either two or more subtopics or none at all. Subtopics are divisions of the topic above them. A topic cannot be divided into less than two parts.

(8) As a rule, main topics should be parallel in form, and subtopics under the same topic should be parallel in form. If in a list of topics, the first is a noun, the others should be nouns; if it is an adjective, the others should be adjectives, etc. Topics in the form of phrases should not be mixed with topics in the form of nouns or a noun and its modifiers.

The second half of the topical outline for the essay on an ideal high school is given below to indicate parallelism of topics.

Parallel main topics — noun and modifiers

III. The faculty of the school
   A. Friendly
   B. Understanding
   C. Competent
   } *adjectives*
IV. The program of the school
   A. Courses for every student
   B. Activities for every student
   } *nouns and modifiers*
      1. Clubs
      2. Sports
      } *nouns*

A violation of the parallelism of topics is illustrated by this part of the outline, incorrectly phrased.

IV. The program of the school
   A. Offers courses for every student [verb and object with modifier]
   B. Activities for every student [noun and modifier]
      1. Joining clubs [gerund phrase]
      2. Sports [noun]

(9) Do not mix the topical and sentence forms of outline.

In the outline below topics and sentences have been mixed.

IV. The program of the school [topic]
   A. Courses are offered for every student. [sentence]
   B. Activities for every student [topic]
      1. Students may join clubs. [sentence]
      2. Sports [topic]

(10) For each number or letter in an outline there must be a topic. Never place an *a*, for instance, next to *1* like this: *1a*.

The complete outline for the composition on an ideal high school is given on page 385. Note that all ten points about correct outlining have been carefully observed.

Compare this outline with the original list of topics on page 380. The changes in wording are necessary to make the outline clear and consistent in form.

MY CONCEPT OF THE IDEAL HIGH SCHOOL

I. The spirit of the school
  A. Friendly
  B. Democratic
  C. Loyal
II. The government of the school
  A. Democratic
  B. Respected
III. The faculty of the school
  A. Friendly
  B. Understanding
  C. Competent
IV. The program of the school
  A. Courses for every student
  B. Activities for every student
    1. Clubs
    2. Sports

● EXERCISE 1. From the incorrect outline below, make a correct topical outline. Write in parallel form the subheadings under each main heading. Eliminate sentences and the subtopic standing by itself.

ON TARDINESS

I. Causes of tardiness
  A. You oversleep
  B. Laziness
  C. Being indifferent
  D. You have home responsibilities.
II. Results of tardiness
  A. Loss of time from classes
  B. Getting a bad reputation
  C. Punished
    1. Being kept after school

● EXERCISE 2. Arrange the items in the following list in a correct topical outline. Begin by placing the title, which is included in the list, at the top of your paper. Then select the major topics, those to be given Roman numerals. Finally, place and letter the subtopics correctly and copy the outline neatly in perfect arrangement.

cartoons	controversial subjects
personalities	special columns and columnists
complete coverage	attractive features
clear	correct
characteristics of a good school paper	organizations
events	competent writing
interesting	

Writing the First Draft

25e. With the outline before you, write the first draft of your composition. Include an introduction and a conclusion. Pay careful attention to the division into paragraphs.

THE INTRODUCTION

Before you present the first point in your composition, you will introduce the subject. Whether or not the introduction is a separate paragraph depends upon the length of the entire paper. In a composition of 500 words, you will probably devote the first paragraph to introducing the subject.

(1) Write an introduction which will make clear the purpose of your composition and arouse the interest of the reader.

A good introductory paragraph should include a statement of the purpose of the composition. It may give facts that will explain the choice of subject, and it may give information necessary to the understanding of the subject. It should, if possible, arouse the interest of the reader so that he will want to read further. The following is the final form of the introductory paragraph in the composition on the ideal high school.

Seven million boys and girls attend high school in this country. In brick buildings full of square rooms with blackboarded walls, they attend classes and study halls, work in shops, laboratories, and libraries, participate in sports and other activities. While the pattern of high school life is generally the same everywhere, it does vary in its details from school to school. There are important differences between schools. After our class discussion of what some of these differences are, I decided to write my concept of the ideal high school.

Write the first draft rapidly. Do not worry about details of punctuation and sentence structure. These can be taken care of later in your revision.

PARAGRAPHING

(2) Paragraph a composition in such a way that the various phases of the subject will stand out clearly.

As you write the first draft, you must decide at what points new paragraphs should be started. By paragraphing you indicate to your reader the main divisions of your composition. By indention of the first line and by spacing, you set apart each paragraph as a unit developing a single aspect of your subject. Whenever you begin a paragraph, you notify the reader that you are taking up another phase of your subject. In a brief composition you may find it advisable to devote one paragraph to each of the major (Roman numeral) topics in your outline. This is the method followed in the sample composition about the ideal high school. There were four main topics in the outline; hence there are four main paragraphs in the final composition. With an introductory paragraph and a concluding paragraph, this makes a six-paragraph composition (see page 394).

In a longer paper, a research paper, for instance, you cannot follow any such simple formula for paragraphing; indeed, you may wish to devote several paragraphs to a subtopic.

(3) Avoid the overlong and the very short paragraph.

When paragraphing your writing, bear in mind the fact that your reader will be able to follow you more easily if your paragraphs are not too long. Paragraphs of 300 words are probably too long for high school writers to handle effectively. On the other hand, a number of paragraphs of less than 100 words may indicate poor planning. Such paragraphs show that the writer is not taking time to support his topic sentence, and they give the composition a broken-up appearance which is confusing because it does not emphasize the major ideas.

(4) Make the transition between paragraphs clear and smooth by using a transitional device at the beginning of a paragraph.

Because the beginning of a paragraph signifies a shift to another phase of your subject, you should make your train of thought clear to the reader by showing the relationship between this new phase and the phase discussed in the preceding paragraph. There are several devices for accomplishing this transition between paragraphs. These devices help to keep the thought flowing smoothly from paragraph to paragraph in the same way that linking words and connectives (see the section beginning on page 373) keep the thought flowing from sentence to sentence. Four transitional devices are explained and illustrated on the following pages.

1. *Use a pronoun which refers to a person or an idea just mentioned in the preceding paragraph.*

The pronouns most commonly used in this way are *he*, *they*, *this*, *that*, *these*, *those*, *them*, *it*. The use of these words carries the reader back to their antecedents, helping him to bridge the gap between the two paragraphs. *This*, *that*, *these*, *those*, when used as adjectives, are used in the same way.

EXAMPLE .... When Casey finally departed, he left behind him an appalling number of debts, which, in one way or another, he had charmingly contracted among the simple villagers.

Although not one of **these** was ever paid, the people not only held no resentment, but actually delighted in telling story after story about Casey's kindness and generosity. .... [The pronoun *these*, referring to *debts* in the preceding paragraph, accomplishes the transition between paragraphs.]

Each of the five sentences below is the opening sentence of a paragraph. Note how the word in bold type reflects something in the preceding paragraph.

In all **this** he invariably gave the credit to others.

The public was quick to show its approval of **this** new development.

It was because of **these** careful preparations that the expedition was able to cope with every emergency.

Since **that** was the purpose of the undertaking, we kept our plans secret.

Unfortunately, **they** did not look upon my proposal with any enthusiasm.

2. *Repeat a key word used in the preceding paragraph.*

Consider the first sentence in each of the following pairs as the final sentence of a paragraph, and the second sentence as the opening of the next paragraph.

1

. . . . In short, the Board of Education felt rebuffed, almost insulted, by his **refusal** of the principalship.

Several reasons for his **refusal** were suggested, but not one of them was convincing. . . . . [The repetition of the word *refusal* carries the thought across the gap between paragraphs.]

2

. . . . A boy should be given as much **independence** as possible, for once he has left home, he will not have his **parents** to fall back on.

Parents often find it difficult to give their child **independence.** . . . .

3

. . . . Deprived in this way of their only recreation area, the children have nowhere to play but in the **streets.**

Unfortunately, the **streets** in this congested section are used principally by heavy trucks. . . . .

3. *Refer directly to the preceding idea.*

Sometimes, at the risk of being repetitious, you can achieve a strong transition by referring, in the same words previously used, to the idea left in the reader's mind at the end of the preceding paragraph.

1

. . . . At the end of the third quarter the score stood 18–0 in our favor.

Not only was the score in our favor, but after the change in goals **at the end of the quarter,** we once again had the advantage of the wind at our back. . . . .

2

. . . . For more than a year the convoy route to Murmansk was the most dangerous voyage in the world.

The voyage was dangerous because of its vulnerability to attack by land-based planes, and the extreme cold of the northern seas through which it passed. . . . .

4. *Use transitional expressions.*

Most of the connectives listed for use in linking sentences (see page 373) will serve also as transitional expressions between paragraphs. The following connectives are commonly used in this way:

accordingly	for example	otherwise
also	for instance	similarly
another	furthermore	such
as a result	in fact	then
at last	likewise	therefore
at this time	moreover	thus
consequently	nevertheless	too
finally	on the other hand	

1

. . . . At the end of a day like this on the ski run, we look forward blissfully to an early bed hour.

The attraction of good talk before a roaring fire, **however,** often proves stronger than sleepiness, and we find ourselves staying up later than is good for us. . . . .

2

. . . . From this I concluded that there had been foul play of the most terrible kind.

Moreover, Addison had more than once warned me that a great capacity for evil-doing lay very near the surface in some of these people. . . . .

● EXERCISE 3. Each of the following sentences is the opening sentence of a paragraph. The sentences were selected at random from the same textbook.[2]

Point out the device or devices used in each sentence to effect a transition from what had been discussed in the preceding paragraph.

1. Nevertheless, the idea that heat was an actual substance was still clung to by many physicists, though it now rejoiced in the name of "caloric."
2. One of the most remarkable of these is the story of the flood . . .
3. What we have said of the oak and amoeba is found to be characteristic of all types of life . . .
4. Another discovery of almost equal importance was that of cocaine . . .
5. This brings us to the age of X-ray diagnosis and treatment, radium therapy, and other recent methods of tackling the problems of disease.
6. A great deal of scientific work is, however, concerned with the description of immeasurable things . . .
7. The Babylonians seem also to have been aware at an astonishingly early date that the stars are in the sky by day as well as by night . . .
8. Pythagoras knew all that, and he also knew of the phenomenon known as "resonance," to which we now turn.
9. Thunder and lightning were similarly not connected with electricity till the time of Benjamin Franklin . . .
10. At about this time John Canton paved the way for a new type of electrical machine by his discovery of the principle of "induction."

● EXERCISE 4. Examine a daily newspaper or a current magazine to find further examples of transitional devices used by professional writers. Copy onto your paper 5 paragraph openings which contain such devices. Underline the transitional expressions.

[2] From *Science Marches On* by Walter Shepherd. Copyright 1939 by Harcourt, Brace and Company. Reprinted by permission of the publishers.

THE CONCLUSION

(5) Write a conclusion which will summarize or re-emphasize the major point of the composition.

A whole paragraph of summary or conclusion may not be necessary. But you should make an effort to remind the reader at the end of the composition what it is that you have said. In a short paper one or two concluding sentences will usually be enough. Read the conclusion to the sample composition on page 396.

Revising the First Draft

25f. Read over the first draft. Eliminate or add ideas; change the order of ideas if advisable; revise sentences to improve their structure; check spelling and punctuation.

The revision of your first draft is extremely important. The student who lazily chooses to hand in this draft as a completed composition is doing himself a great injustice. Professional writers are thorough revisers. They are rarely satisfied with the first draft of their work. A student should not claim an ability which an experienced writer would never claim.

A study of the first draft may reveal faults in the original outline. Do not hesitate, in such a case, to change the outline. *No aspect of the composition should be considered unchangeable until the final draft has been completed.*

As you revise, ask yourself the following questions:

1. Have I made my purpose clear at the start?
2. Is the paragraphing correct? Does it reveal the major points in the composition? Is each paragraph unified and coherent? Are the paragraphs clearly related to one another by transitional devices?

3. Are the sentences varied in structure? Can more complex sentences be used?
4. Is the style wordy? What expressions can be eliminated?
5. Are all words spelled correctly?
6. Where is punctuation needed to make the meaning clear?

Preparing the Final Draft

25g. When the revision has been completed, copy the composition neatly. If you can, typewrite this copy.

The final draft of the composition you have seen taking shape throughout this chapter is given below. Read it through, noting the general organization, the adherence to the outline (page 385), the paragraphing, the transitions, the introduction, and the conclusion.

MY CONCEPT OF THE IDEAL HIGH SCHOOL

Introduction Seven million boys and girls attend high school in this country. In brick buildings full of square rooms with chalkboarded walls, they attend classes and study halls, work in shops, laboratories, and libraries, participate in sports and other activities. While the pattern of high school life is generally the same everywhere, it does vary in its details from school to school. There are important differences between schools. After our class discussion of what some of these differences

Purpose are, **I decided to write my concept of the ideal high school.**

Transition **In the first place,** the spirit in **such a school** is a friendly one. The atmosphere is cheerful. A stranger entering the building senses this friendliness in the cordial greeting of a student receptionist. He hears it in the laughter in the halls. Could he delve deeper into the life of the school, he would discover that there is, among the students, a strong loyalty to the school, not only the kind that shows itself in cheering for the team, but also the kind that results in good behavior and hard work. He would discover, too, that there are no self-centered, exclusive cliques. There are no social clubs to draw the line between the privileged and the underprivileged, the socially acceptable and the supposedly unacceptable. Everyone treats everyone else as an equal. The spirit is democratic.

Transition **Also democratic** is the government of the ideal school. A wise faculty has placed real power in the hands of the students, who elect their officers and their governing bodies. Problems of school business — discipline, assembly programs, social events, clubs, and athletic contests — are handled by the students themselves. Except for the bigger matters, like serious infractions of discipline or the planning of the program and curriculum, the students govern themselves without faculty interference.

Transition Largely **free of disagreeable disciplinary duties,** the teachers in the ideal school are able to treat their students as friends. Not only is there a friendly atmosphere of working together to get the job done, but the teachers understand their pupils. Each teacher is aware that his students take several subjects, not just the one he happens to teach. The teachers know that boys and girls are not perfect, that they are sometimes lazy and sometimes confused. The teachers are willing to give more than just the minimum amount of time required of them. They are competent teachers who know their subject and how to teach it; moreover, they are firm in their control of classes without being mean or ruling with an iron hand.

Students respect them because, while they are not "easy," they are considerate.

Transition **Finally,** the program of the **ideal school** meets the needs of all the students. Those who are going to college are adequately prepared. Those who are going to get jobs after graduation are taught vocations. The slow pupil and the bright pupil are equally well provided for. Extracurricular activities are provided to fit everyone's taste. Dramatics, music, hobby clubs, language clubs, and publications are sponsored. Every boy and girl is urged to take part in at least one sport, and the athletic program is broad enough to make this possible. The ideal high school provides equal opportunities for all.

Conclusion No school, I suppose, is ideal. Yet a school is what its teachers and students want it to be. If a friendly spirit prevails and if the opportunity is given for everyone to follow a course suited to his needs and abilities, a school will be as nearly ideal as a school can be.

SUMMARY

Follow these steps in preparing a composition:

(1) *Selecting and limiting the subject.* Select a subject that can be adequately treated within the limits of your composition. State your purpose.

(2) *Assembling materials.* List all the ideas you think you may wish to use in your composition.

(3) *Organizing materials.* Group related ideas together. Arrange the groups in a logical order. Make an outline. Observe rules for form in making an outline.

(4) *Writing the first draft.* With the outline before you, write the first draft of your composition. Include an introduction and a conclusion. Pay careful attention to the division into paragraphs.

(a) Paragraph a composition in such a way that the various phases of the subject will stand out clearly.

(b) Avoid the overlong and the very short paragraph.
(c) Make the transition between paragraphs clear and smooth by using at the beginnings of paragraphs a transitional device.

(5) *Revising the first draft.* Read over the first draft. Eliminate or add ideas; change the order of ideas if advisable; revise sentences to improve their structure; check spelling and punctuation.

(6) *Preparing the final draft.* When the revision has been completed, copy the composition neatly. If you can, typewrite this copy.

SUGGESTED TOPICS FOR COMPOSITION

Put into practice the techniques described in this chapter as you write compositions assigned to you. If you are not assigned a definite subject on which to write, the topics in the following list may provide suggestions. Many will require limiting if you are to treat them in a composition of two or three pages.

The arts

1. Classical vs. popular music
2. Color combinations
3. The use of water color
4. What to look for in a painting
5. How to appreciate good music
6. How to refinish furniture
7. Qualities of a good orchestra conductor
8. My favorite poet (artist, musician, etc.)
9. Good music on the radio
10. Opera — grand or comic?
11. Features of modern houses
12. Leatherworking
13. Ceramics
14. Advertising layouts
15. Music and moods
16. Understanding modern art
17. What poetry means to me
18. Designing and building a stage set
19. Effective poster making
20. Ballet or modern dance?

Family life

1. On saving money
2. Moving day
3. How to influence parents
4. On being an apartment dweller
5. Mistakes parents make
6. Why families quarrel
7. Mother and I and the supermarket
8. Television and family life
9. On being the oldest (youngest) member

People

1. My father
2. The social climber
3. The school politician
4. Teachers as they really are
5. A great sports figure
6. My little sister
7. People who have influenced me
8. The big wheel
9. Our doctor
10. My favorite fictional character

Personal

1. Overcoming an inferiority complex
2. On being an outsider
3. My frustrations
4. Traits I wish I didn't have
5. On being plain
6. On being average
7. How to be unpopular
8. On being left-handed
9. On being spoiled
10. On being an only child
11. Beliefs changed by experience
12. Rules I could do without
13. My after-school jobs
14. On choosing one's own name
15. The art of bluffing
16. The meaning of "well dressed"
17. On being gullible
18. My biggest mistake
19. My frustrations
20. On problem solving
21. What teen-agers value most
22. A teen-ager's observations on love
23. Living up to or living down a reputation

School

1. My high school course — an evaluation
2. Good and bad study habits
3. Too much extracurricular work
4. Needed improvements in this school
5. The ideal teacher
6. Teachers' faults
7. Why students leave school

8. An opinion of the honor system
9. Senior worries
10. How to get an A
11. A formula for failure
12. Movies in the classroom
13. Our high school manners
14. Bookworm vs. playboy
15. Glamour in high school
16. College life as a high school student sees it
17. Coeducation or not?
18. How to choose a college
19. Large college vs. small college
20. Four-year college vs. junior college
21. My experiences with guidance
22. Book reports
23. Why students "cut up"
24. On homework
25. My first dramatic role
26. Make-up for the stage
27. The fraternity system
28. Education by television

Science

1. A conservation project
2. Prevention of soil erosion
3. Science aids the hunter and fisherman
4. Peacetime uses of radar
5. New drugs and their uses
6. Products of petroleum
7. Kitchen chemistry
8. The cook as guardian of family health
9. New uses of plastics
10. Varied-crop vs. one-crop farming
11. The scientist aids the detective
12. Photography, a scientific tool
13. The use of blood tests with dairy animals
14. The scientist looks at cosmetics
15. Uranium — the new "gold rush"
16. A scientist looks at the comics
17. Tornado, cyclone, hurricane, and typhoon
18. Chemical aids to agriculture
19. Predicting the weather
20. Effects of science on our amusements
21. Sunspots
22. The geography of our town
23. Household insects
24. Television vs. movies
25. Field trips: educational fun
26. Rules for success in farming
27. Lengthening the span of life
28. On science fiction
29. Man-made satellites
30. Hi-fi

Social life

1. Having fun without money
2. On following the crowd
3. Dating at home vs. going out
4. Party stags — help or hindrance
5. The disappearance of chivalry
6. The definition of a gentleman
7. Dates, steady and unsteady
8. Dutch-treat dating
9. On being a joiner
10. How to plan a party
11. A successful youth center

Social studies

1. Propaganda techniques
2. A threat to international peace
3. Tolerance in our school
4. The importance of the minority
5. If we had no Bill of Rights
6. Some lessons of history
7. Our dependence on other nations
8. States' rights vs. federal rights
9. Socialized medicine
10. Pan-Americanism
11. One world
12. The United States as others see us
13. Facts about the population of our community
14. Cleaning up the slums
15. The menace of installment buying
16. The importance of a free press
17. The cause and cure of juvenile delinquency
18. Characteristics of a good citizen
19. The meaning of democracy
20. The making of a criminal
21. How to vote intelligently
22. Government support of farm prices
23. History in movies
24. Is America imperialistic?
25. Should 18-year-olds vote?
26. Our overstuffed and understaffed schools
27. The UN must succeed
28. A news event of the past week
29. A cause of international tension

Sports

1. The breaks of the game
2. Is a varsity position worth it?
3. Refereeing
4. Professional vs. amateur sports

5. Good sportsmanship
6. Bench warming
7. Grandstand manners
8. My best performance
9. Winter fishing
10. The hunter's equipment
11. Tennis tips
12. Coaches' nightmares
13. My favorite team
14. A great sports figure
15. On sports predictions
16. How to sail
17. How to train
18. Reliability of sports statistics
19. Growing up in TV tastes
20. What is success?
21. Living your religion
22. My encounters with prejudice
23. My chosen vocation
24. The importance and the dangers of habit

General

1. Popular superstitions
2. On being a time waster
3. Gifts
4. Cafeteria meals
5. Experiences as a tourist
6. On teaching a Sunday School class
7. High school slang
8. Growing up in reading tastes
9. Living on a budget
10. The life of a camp counselor
11. On friendship
12. The bells in my life
13. A definition of happiness
14. An even break for girls
15. Humor and corn
16. Why I prefer farm life (*or* city life, suburban life, etc.)
17. Growing up in TV tastes
18. What is success?
19. Living your religion
20. My encounters with prejudice
21. My chosen vocation
22. The importance and the dangers of habit
23. Supermarket vs. small grocery
24. Values of 4–H club work
25. Values of Scouting
26. Our gadget civilization
27. The duties of the chairman of a meeting
28. On being a salesman
29. On orthodontia
30. The drugless drugstore
31. Furnishing a room
32. Causes of highway accidents
33. The teen-age driver
34. Considerations in buying a car
35. A character sketch of our town
36. How to train a dog
37. How to judge a newspaper
38. The case for (against) early marriage
39. Our dependence on machines
40. My life one year hence
41. American speech mannerisms
42. American life as revealed by the movies

CHAPTER 26

Clear Thinking

LEARN TO AVOID PITFALLS IN REASONING

Your purpose in argumentative writing is to persuade your reader to accept your point of view on a debatable subject. Since you wish to present the strongest possible support for your ideas, you must be sure that your reasoning is clear and logical. Study the kinds of reasoning described on the following pages, and note the pitfalls into which unclear thinking may lead you.

INDUCTIVE REASONING

In inductive reasoning you begin with evidence — facts, statistics, instances, etc., and after studying the evidence, you arrive at a conclusion or generalization. For example, suppose that you have a box of chocolate creams all of which are identical in appearance. You bite into one of the chocolates and find it to be a peppermint cream. You taste a second and find it to be peppermint, too. You try a third which is also peppermint. Now, reasoning inductively, you are about to say, "This box contains only peppermint creams." Of course, your generalization may be wrong because you have not tested every piece of candy in the box. The chances are, however, that you may be right. The more creams you sample, the more reliable your generalization becomes. You can easily see that the more evidence you have in favor of your generalization, the more likely it is that the generalization will be true. This basic fact about inductive reasoning is stated in the following principle:

26a. A generalization is as sound as the evidence supporting it is complete. Avoid generalizations based on insufficient evidence.

Hasty Generalization

When you make a generalization on the basis of insufficient evidence, you are committing a major error in reasoning. This error is called "hasty generalization." All your life you will hear people make it.

An understandably angry motorist wrote the following letter to his newspaper:

> About midnight Saturday I was going through the intersection of Haven Boulevard and Elm Street on a green light when my car was rammed at a right angle by a car which had obviously passed through the red light. The driver of this car was 17 years old. He had six other teen-agers in the car with him, one of whom was badly injured in the collision. A month ago I was forced off the highway by a car driven by a high school student who insisted on passing even though there was not enough room to pass. To avoid a sideswipe, I drove into the ditch. These experiences have convinced me that teen-age drivers are a menace and that the driving age in this state should be raised to 21.

The truth of this motorist's generalization is highly doubtful because the generalization is based on only two instances. It could be true, but it certainly has not been "proved" true by the evidence given.

Now suppose that a large insurance company

26a

decides to find out whether teen-age drivers, in proportion to their number, are involved in more accidents than are adult drivers. The insurance company has access to a vast amount of information. Its research department conducts an extensive investigation. If, after studying thousands of accident reports, the company finds that the percentage of teen-age drivers involved is greater than the percentage of adult drivers involved, the company may draw a generalization which will probably be true. There is always the possibility that further research may disprove the generalization, but until that happens, the company would be justified in making a generalization on the basis of its research.

DEDUCTIVE REASONING

The opposite of inductive reasoning is deductive reasoning. You reason deductively when you are able to begin with a generalization that can be accepted as true. You may yourself have arrived inductively at this generalization, or it may be one that others have arrived at and which has become generally accepted. You then apply it to a particular situation and draw a conclusion.

A deductive argument may be stated in a three-part form called a *syllogism*. The first part is the generalization with which the argument begins. It is called the *major premise*. The second part states the particular situation to which the major premise is to be applied. It is called the *minor premise*. The third part states the *conclusion*.

SYLLOGISM All sweet apples are ripe. [major premise]
This apple is sweet. [minor premise]
(Therefore) This apple is ripe. [conclusion]

If the major and minor premises in this syllogism are true, the conclusion is sound. There are many complicated ways of testing the soundness of a syllogism, but for ordinary purposes, you may test a syllogism by asking three questions.

26b. Test a syllogism by asking:

(1) Are the premises true? That is, has the major premise been arrived at inductively from enough instances? And is the fact stated in the minor premise true?

(2) Does the major premise ignore any significant fact?

(3) Does the conclusion follow logically?

False Syllogisms

When you apply the three-question test to the following false syllogisms, you will see why they are false.

1. All ripe apples are sweet. [major premise]
   This apple is ripe. [minor premise]
   (Therefore) This apple is sweet. [conclusion]

This syllogism is false because it does not stand up under the test of the first question. It is not true that all ripe apples are sweet.

2. Red apples are ripe. [major premise]
   This apple is green. [minor premise]
   (Therefore) This apple is not ripe. [conclusion]

This syllogism can be shown to be false when the second test question is applied to it. The generalization (major premise) ignores a very significant fact, which is that some green apples are also ripe.

3. All sweet apples are ripe. [major premise]
   This apple is ripe. [minor premise]
   (Therefore) This apple is sweet. [conclusion]

The syllogism is false because it does not pass the test of the third question. The conclusion does not follow logically. It is based on a misunderstanding of what the major premise says. The major premise does not say that all ripe apples are sweet.

The falseness of these simple "apple" syllogisms is easy to understand. Yet deductive reasoning of the kind they illustrate is all too common. Have you ever heard arguments like this:

> Communists believe in government ownership of natural resources.
>
> Mr. Doe believes in government ownership of the coal mines.
>
> (Therefore) Mr. Doe is a Communist.

Here the premises are true, but the major premise *ignores* the important fact that some people who are not Communists also believe in government ownership of coal mines.

An unsound deductive conclusion reached in this way is like a hasty generalization in inductive reasoning. It is too quickly arrived at. We call it "jumping to a conclusion," for the argument literally "jumps" over (ignores) an important fact.

● EXERCISE 1. This exercise is a series of examples of both inductive and deductive reasoning. Number in a column on your paper from 1 to 10. After studying each item, write after the corresponding number on your paper the kind of reasoning it represents (inductive or deductive). If the reasoning is sound, add a plus (+); if it is unsound, add a zero (0). Be able to explain your answers.

1. Both my brother and my sister thought Mr. Hare was a boring teacher. I do not want to have Mr. Hare for math because I do not want to be bored.
2. To get his working papers a boy must be fourteen

years old. Since Joel has his working papers, he must be at least fourteen.

3. Only members of the club were allowed to attend last night's meeting. Since Betty attended the meeting, she must be a club member.
4. After the sophomore class meeting, I asked ten sophomores whether they planned to vote for Jerry Straight for class president. Seven of the ten said they did intend to vote for Jerry. He will be elected.
5. Socialists believe in socialized medicine. Mr. Cross believes in socialized medicine. Mr. Cross must be a socialist.
6. In three recent train wrecks, the engineer at the controls was over sixty years of age. A law should be passed prohibiting employment of engineers over sixty.
7. Citizens of the United States may enter Canada without a passport. Since I am a United States citizen, I will not need a passport when I go to Canada.
8. I am through watching television because the four shows I watched Saturday night ranged from very bad to terrible.
9. People who attend church are religious. Since Mr. Doe never attends church, he is not a religious man.
10. When the Salk Vaccine against polio was given to 440,000 school children, it was reported to be 60%–90% effective in preventing paralytic polio. The Salk Vaccine is an effective means of preventing polio.

REASONING BY ANALOGY

Sometimes during an argument a person, in order to clarify a point, will use an analogy. An analogy is a comparison. Reasoning by analogy is the kind of reasoning that compares one situation with another. Suppose, for example, that the president of the Student Council of a school is impatient with the students for not co-operating with their student monitors, who are charged with keeping order in corridors, cafeteria, assembly, and at athletic events. In an address before the school he tries, by drawing an analogy, to persuade the students to be more co-operative. He says that a school is like an army. Just as soldiers must obey their officers, students must obey their monitors. If soldiers ignore their officers' orders, the battle may be lost. If students ignore their monitors' orders, the school will not function smoothly and its educational and social programs will be affected. It is the function of an army to win battles; it is the function of a school to provide effective educational and social programs for its students. The success of a school, like the success of an army, depends upon discipline and respect for authority. Like good soldiers, all students should obey orders.

By drawing this analogy between a school and an army, the speaker hoped to persuade his listeners to be more co-operative, more obedient. Since discipline is essential in both an army and a school, there is some point in the analogy, and this point may have been persuasive. However, you will recognize at once that the analogy is really very weak because there are many more dissimilarities than similarities between an army and a school. Is military discipline the kind we want in a school? Is the job of an army officer like that of a school monitor? Is winning a battle really much like furthering an educational program? The analogy grows weaker the longer you study it, a fact which is true of most analogies.

Remember that an analogy never proves anything. Its only value lies in its ability to clarify an argument. Also, the further you carry an analogy, the weaker it becomes.

26c. The soundness of an analogy depends upon the number of points in common between the things being compared.

The False Analogy

When an analogy will not stand careful examination, it is called a false analogy. That is, when the points of similarity are found to be very few or even nonexistent, the analogy is false.

● EXERCISE 2. Discuss the following examples of argument by analogy. How strong are the analogies?

1

A nation is like a family. The citizens are the children who need guidance and discipline. Children do not always know what is best for them, and parents, who are wiser and more experienced, must force them at times to do things they do not want to do. Similarly, citizens do not always know what is best for them, and so there must be a ruler to dictate to them for their own good. This shows that a dictatorship is a better form of government than a democracy. Just as a family could not last very long if the children voted on every rule of discipline that the parents imposed, so a nation will not last if the citizens are given the power to decide what is right for the country.

2

The state requires that its citizens pass a test and be licensed before permitting them to engage in activities that may affect other citizens. For instance, one must be licensed to drive a car, sell real estate, practice law, etc. Nothing has a greater effect on citizens than their family upbringing. The state ought to require all married people to pass a test on how to raise children and to be licensed before they can have a family.

3

It is an axiom of good sportsmanship that every member of a team should think first of the victory of the team and not of his desire to make a spectacular individual showing. In the same way, it is more important that the state should be strong than that the citizens should be happy. Just as a sportsmanlike player will sacrifice himself for a team victory, individuals should sacrifice themselves, even their happiness, for the state.

4

In the adult world, a man who does not do a good job is either fired or denied a promotion. School is a preparation for adult life. If a student does not do his work well, he should either be expelled from school or be denied promotion to the next grade.

THINKING CLEARLY ABOUT CAUSE AND EFFECT

The purpose of much of our discussion and writing is to find remedies and preventive measures for existing evils. As any physician knows, the first step in assigning a remedy for an illness is to find the cause, and it is important that the true cause be found. In our effort to explain an event or a situation, we naturally examine the events which preceded it. We look for the cause. In so doing, however, we must not make the mistake of assuming that just because one event preceded another, it caused the second event. A Latin phrase is commonly used to describe this kind of thinking: *post hoc, ergo propter hoc*, which means "after this, therefore because of this."

A simple example of this kind of error in thinking derives from our superstitions. For instance, you may slip on the stairs and sprain your ankle so badly that you are on crutches for weeks. Looking back on events preceding the accident, you recall that when you were on your way home from school earlier in the day, a black cat crossed your path. You say, "Now that explains it. That cat was the cause of my bad luck."

26d. The fact that an event or a condition follows another event or condition does not neces-

sarily mean that the second was caused by the first. Before ascribing a result to a certain cause, consider other possible causes.

Suppose that the basketball team at your school has won the regional championship and is therefore going to the state tournament, a day's journey away. The team travels by bus and must play its first tournament game the same night. It loses the game to a team which eventually wins the tournament. The sports columnist in your school paper, looking for the cause of the defeat, seizes upon the bus ride which preceded the game: "If the boys hadn't been exhausted from the tiring trip, they would have won the game and the championship." Of course, the columnist could be right, but there were other factors which he should have considered before deciding on the cause of defeat. The winning team also made a long trip the day of the game. The winners won by a margin of 16 points. The winning team had a better season record than the losing team. Finally, they went on to win the tournament. In the light of these considerations, it looks as though the columnist was guilty of *post hoc, ergo propter hoc* thinking.

THE IRRELEVANT FACT — "OFF-THE-SUBJECT" ARGUMENTS

The word *relevant* means "related to." A relevant argument is one which is related to the issue being argued. An *irrelevant* argument is one which is not related to the issue. When introduced into a discussion, irrelevant facts or arguments may throw the discussion "off the track." You have probably heard the chairman of a meeting accuse the participants of "getting off the subject." Clever but dishonest people may deliberately try to sidetrack a discussion when they find the argument going against them.

A common form of irrelevant argument is the one which attacks the person offering an argument rather than attacking the argument itself.

FATHER (at 2:00 A.M.) Is that you, son?

SON Yes.

FATHER It is after two o'clock. You know you were to be home by midnight. Explain yourself!

SON Well, you used to come in later than this when you were in high school. Grandmother told me about it

26e. Do not let an argument or discussion be confused by an irrelevant point.

An irrelevant point is one which simply has no bearing on the discussion. For example, a Democrat and a Republican are arguing the merits of their party platforms in an election year. The Republican says, "The American people have elected more Republican Presidents than Democratic Presidents." You can see, of course, that this statement, although true, is irrelevant so far as the merits of the current party platforms are concerned.

● EXERCISE 3. A student-faculty committee is discussing the question, "Should boys trying out for varsity sports be excused from last-period study halls?" Arguments presented by both sides are listed below. Study the arguments and identify those which are irrelevant, likely to lead the discussion off the subject.

Arguments in favor of excusing the boys:

1. It will relieve locker-room congestion after school.
2. Outdoor exercise is better for the boys than studying in a stuffy classroom.
3. Recently four boys on the varsity were sent to the office from last-period study because they created a discipline problem.

4. The boys will have more time for practice. The more they practice, the better the varsity teams will be.
5. Study halls should be eliminated anyway so that the school day can be shortened.
6. Athletics are as important as studies.
7. Last year our teams were the worst in years.

Arguments against excusing the boys:

1. The boys would waste the extra time because the coaches cannot join them until after school.
2. Those who are excused would have an unfair advantage over those who have a class the last period.
3. Sometimes the weather is bad, and the boys could not go outdoors.
4. It is better for the boys to study in school before practice because they will be too tired after practice to study at home.
5. We don't excuse students for other outdoor activities like fishing or playing golf, or playing outdoors at home.
6. Girls need athletics just as much as boys.

● EXERCISE 4. Each of the following items is based on an error in thinking. Number in a column on your paper from 1 to 12. Analyze the thinking in each item and after its corresponding number write the letter of the kind of unclear thinking it represents.

A hasty generalization
B unsound deductive reasoning (false syllogism)
C unclear thinking about cause and effect
D weak or false analogy
E irrelevant (off-the-subject) argument

1. Americans do not get enough physical exercise. This is shown by the fact that 4 out of 10 men called by Selective Service are rejected for physical reasons.
2. When I visited the Lirones, Mrs. Lirone served lasagna for dinner. I know now that I do not like Italian dishes.
3. Ina Glamor and Sally Smart have beautiful complex-

ions. They use Radiant face cream. If I use Radiant face cream, I will have a beautiful complexion.

4. Jack wrote a short story which his classmates selected as the best short story written during the school term. Allan objected to the vote on the ground that Jack's stories were always chosen as best. He said no one else ever had a chance.
5. Dr. Kimball advised me not to smoke because, he said, it is bad for my health. I didn't pay any attention because I noticed that he smokes all the time.
6. Both Jim and Tom, who graduated from the same high school, failed their freshman English course in college. Instruction in English at their high school was inferior.
7. Our cat did not come home this morning. Dad said he saw the Lloyds' dog cross our yard about 11 o'clock last night. We are going to ask the Lloyds to get us another cat.
8. JANE No, Joe, you can't have my homework paper to copy. If you don't do the assignments yourself, you won't be able to pass the tests.

   JOE Well, I remember seeing you copy Helen's paper one morning last week.
9. BILL I think students with a B average should be excused from study halls. They could have more freedom, and it would give all students something to work for.

   PRINCIPAL We can't excuse students unless we have a place for them to go. They can't just wander around the school.

   BILL Why not? Teachers can wander around the school during their free periods.
10. Automobile mechanics do not need to know good English. I intend to become an automobile mechanic. Teaching me correct English makes as much sense as teaching a polar bear how to catch an alligator.
11. Agricultural surpluses cause the price of food to drop. Since all consumers like low prices, we should encourage agricultural surpluses.

12. People who are so conscientious that they always do more work than the teacher assigned make it hard for the rest of us to get good grades. If it weren't for these people, I'd be getting an A instead of a C in English.

● EXERCISE 5. The principal arguments in the following essay are bracketed and numbered. Keeping in mind the types of thinking described in the preceding pages, name the type represented by each argument. Decide whether the thinking is sound or not sound.

COLLEGE ENTRANCE REQUIREMENTS

According to our guidance department, the entrance requirements of some colleges include two and a half years of mathematics and three years of a foreign language. These requirements do not make sense.

In most high schools, the requirement of two and a half years of mathematics means that a college-bound student will have to labor his way through algebra, plane geometry, and a half-year course in advanced algebra or trigonometry. [1. These subjects are useless to the majority of boys and to practically all girls. The future scientist or engineer will need them, but students destined for business or farming or such professions as teaching and law will find them of no value. My sister, who graduated from one of the best women's colleges in the East, told me that she had absolutely no use in college for any of the math she learned in high school.]

Geometry, I know, is sometimes defended on the ground that it teaches us to think logically. [2. The trouble is that it teaches us to think logically about unimportant things like lines, angles, and arcs, but not about important things like world problems or how to make a living. A good course in how to think or a course in modern problems would be a lot more valuable.]

[3. Studying a foreign language like Latin or French is a waste of time for most students because they will never use what they learn. No one today reads or speaks or writes Latin.] [4. It's more important to know your own language, which you use all the time, than a language you will never use. I know a boy who failed freshman English in college. He had had to spend so much time in high school learning Latin and French that he couldn't learn his English.] [5. Mr. Johnson, our principal, advised me to take Latin, but he's an old Latin teacher himself and besides he's always handing out advice about something.]

[6. Knowing a modern language like French is useless because most students will never use it. Even if a person goes to France, he will find that he can get along very well without knowing the language. A friend of mine who went to Europe last summer told me that whenever she tried to speak French in Paris, the French would answer her in English.] [7. Learning French because you might go to France someday is like learning to fly an airliner because you will sometime travel on the airlines.]

Some people say that you should study a foreign language to learn about the country in which it is spoken. [8. A half-year course in French history and culture would accomplish the same result as two years of hard work on French irregular verbs.] [9. I know that foreign language study will enlarge your vocabulary, but so will the study of English. It would be better to study more English than to waste years on the grammar of a language you won't ever use.] [10. School courses should have practical value. Since, as I have shown, high school math and foreign languages do not have practical value for English-speaking students, they should not be required for college entrance.]

CHAPTER 27

Exercises in Composition

The exercises in this chapter will provide valuable practice in composition. In many of them the subject matter for writing has been supplied for you so that you may concentrate entirely on the writing. Do not attempt to work straight through the chapter in one stretch of a few weeks, for that plan would soon grow tiresome. Use the exercises from time to time during the year as your teacher assigns them, working on one type of exercise for a while and then on another. This plan will afford regular reviews of writing skills.

Although it is quite possible that you may do well on these composition exercises without having studied other chapters in this book, you will certainly get more help from the practice they provide if you bring to the work an understanding of the composition principles presented in Chapters 11 through 18 and especially in Chapters 24 and 25.

The kind of writing required by these exercises is rather formal expository writing. This is the kind of writing you are most often expected to do in your other classes, and the kind expected of you in business and in college.

Since in doing these exercises every member of the class faces the same composition problems, you will find it to your advantage to compare papers and, in class discussion, to evaluate the various methods of solving these problems.

THE GARBLED PARAGRAPH

In the garbled-paragraph type of exercise, you are given a paragraph in which the style has been garbled (mixed up, made awkward) and asked to rewrite the paragraph in a form as nearly perfect as you can achieve. The garbled paragraph has been so designed that revising it will test your ability to write in a clear, smooth style. The rewriting provides excellent practice in many composition skills.

In each of the following paragraphs the first sentence is satisfactory. The other sentences may or may not be faulty. Follow these steps in rewriting the paragraph:

1. Read the paragraph through thoughtfully several times. You must have a clear idea of the meaning which the author intended.
2. The order in which the ideas are arranged may not be the best. Study the order and decide whether it should be changed and in what respects. Note any points at which ideas may be profitably combined into one sentence, or one sentence divided into two sentences.
3. On scrap paper, copy the opening sentence exactly as it stands. Write the idea which, in your opinion, should come next, revising the style as you think advisable. Then turn to the idea which you think should come next in order, and continue in this way.
4. You may make changes in style and word choice but *do not omit any ideas* and *do not add any ideas of your own.*
5. Copy the revised paragraph neatly in ink.

Before beginning work, read the following list of composition skills. Not every paragraph will require all of these skills, but you may be expected to use many of them. Refer to the list occasionally as you work.

1. Arranging ideas in logical order
2. Writing complete sentences
3. Supplying proper links (connectives) between ideas
4. Subordinating ideas
5. Expressing parallel ideas in parallel form
6. Avoiding shifts in subject and verb forms
7. Improving the choice of words
8. Using correct grammar
9. Eliminating vague pronouns
10. Avoiding wordiness
11. Varying sentence structure
12. Punctuating for clearness
13. Placing modifiers clearly

● EXERCISE 1. As your teacher directs, use the following paragraphs for practice in composition skills.

1

Above all else what society needs is parents who will seek to create better home environments for their children. To raise boys and girls on the part of parents not only requires sacrifice and patience and you have to have understanding but real work. On the responsibility of parents in the case of juvenile delinquency too much emphasis cannot be placed. Boys and girls whose parents teach them to respect them rarely need to be taught respect of the laws of the land. It is a matter of adult delinquency in a way. Because the way parents frequently shirk their duties is the way in which they are frequently delinquent.

2

Some experts believe that before we can develop an adequate program for the reduction of crime, we must change our criminal codes to conform to new concepts of punishment. Here is an illustration. Assume that two men are charged with the same offense. Assault with a ball bat. The record reveals that

Smith is a drunkard who beats his wife and his family is not supported by him. Jones, the other defendant, is clean-living; he works steady and his home life is excellent. Smith also provokes brawls and fights in liquor taverns. Should Smith and Jones receive equal punishment? The idea of making punishment fit the crime by "giving the criminal what's coming to him" is the old eye-for-an-eye concept. The reports of social workers reveal that these two men have different personalities and it should be taken into account. The new scientific approach is that punishment should fit the person. For both the good of Smith and society the treatment Smith receives should be of a different nature from Jones.

3

The adolescent has three psychological problems. First, he wishes to become self-directing. He wants to get himself mentally free from dependence on his parents. The achievement of a satisfactory relationship with the opposite sex is the second thing he wants. There is too the desire to become self-supporting or at least prepared for it. On the one hand he enjoys being watched over by his parents and supported by them. He faces these problems and he is torn between the desire to remain a child and the fact that he has a strong desire to be an adult and treated in that way. On the other hand he craves to be independent, to escape from parental restraints and so that he can prove he is grown up. His wishes pull him in opposite directions. His behavior is not consistent. He wavers between acceptance and rejecting responsibility and independence and depending on adults.

4

One of the reasons coal is wasted is that in bad times it is uneconomic to mine poor deposits. The sides of the abandoned mines cave in, the roofs fall down, water fills up the beds with water. Making it impossible to reclaim the thinner veins of coal. Only the best veins are mined. Large quantities of it being left underground. Many of these pits will never be reopened again. Through wasteful practices the United States Bureau of Mines estimates that one-third of our mined bituminous coal is lost by us. Two-thirds of this coal that is wasted could be salvaged by methods of mining that are more efficient. It is estimated that we waste 150,000,000 tons of coal annually. In anthracite mining the loss is greater. For every ton of coal which is mined, one ton is lost. A recovery of only 50 per cent. The waste of coal in western European countries from mining practices results in a loss of only 5 to 10 per cent. We need to conserve our anthracite or other resources must be found to take its place. It is estimated that our bituminous (soft) coal supply should last for 4,000 years; moreover our anthracite (hard) coal may not continue for more than 200 years.

5

Poe's stories deal with mysterious situations and with the still more mysterious effects that situations have upon the mind. The detective story was created by him long before Sherlock Holmes was born or Arsène Lupin. His interest in what it is now the fashion to call psychological was an absorbing interest with him. Whether a criminal was caught and punished was not at all to him the important question in a detective story, it was wholly a question of how the logical part of the mind acts in the presence of a fact. Poe was very vain of his own power of ratiocination as he called it. Believing and proving that any puzzle which one mind can contrive another mind can disentangle. It not mattering whether the puzzle is mechanical or not. Poe invented not only detective stories like "The Purloined Letter" and "The Murders in the Rue Morgue" and these are the best of their kind, but an actual case which at the time when he wrote remained unsolved was taken by him and he turned it into a piece of fiction "The Mystery of Marie Roget" and the plot later was proved to be almost an exact parallel of the real events.

6

Queen Victoria died early in 1901, after a reign of sixty-three years, perhaps the happiest reign in England's history. By her the royal dignity had been restored and enhanced. It had been besmirched by the rulers before her. In the course of her reign the country had accepted a revolution far more profound than 1688. Without civil strife or grave suffering. While the kingdom was not only becoming in name but in fact an empire. Thanks to Victoria, constitutional monarchy had become an accepted form of government which had been tested and desirable. She had always been wise enough to yield to her ministers, except in the far-off days of her girlhood, but she retained her three essential rights in which she insisted upon, that she should be consulted, to encourage and warn. Early in her reign and again in 1870 when as a "professional widow" she seemed to lose interest in her realm, waves of republican feeling rose here and there, but when Victoria died however the country's attachment to the monarchy was as firm as the days of Elizabeth.

THE PRÉCIS

A précis is a brief summary. Writing a précis is valuable training in composition. Since the writing requires you to be clear and concise, you must choose your words carefully and arrange them skillfully to get the maximum amount of meaning into the minimum space.

In addition to its value as a writing exercise, précis work is excellent reading practice. In order to summarize another's ideas in your own words, you must understand the ideas thoroughly.

In school and in life after school, there are many situations that call for the writing of a brief, accurate summary of your reading. You are frequently asked to prepare a summary of what you have read in your textbook or in the library. Answers on examinations often require a brief summary. People in business, in club work, and in social work must prepare short digests of articles and reports.

Study the following facts about a précis and the basic steps in précis writing.

1. *A précis is a* **short** *summary.* It is not a paraphrase, which merely says in different and simpler words exactly what the passage being paraphrased has to say. A paraphrase may be as long as the passage itself. A précis rarely is more than one-third the length of the original selection and may be only one-fourth as long.

2. *A précis gives only the "heart" of a passage.* It omits repetitions and such details as examples, illustrations, and adjectives unless they are of unusual importance.

3. *A précis is written entirely in the words of the person writing it, not in the words of the original selection.* Avoid the temptation to lift long phrases and whole sentences from the original.

4. *A précis is written from the point of view of the author whose work is being summarized.* Do not begin with such expressions as "This author says" or "The paragraph means." Begin as though you were summarizing your own writing.

In writing a précis proceed as follows:

1. Read carefully, sentence by sentence, the passage to be summarized. Try to grasp the writer's main point. Spotting the topic sentence will help.

Look up in the dictionary any words whose meaning is not absolutely clear. As you read, take brief notes to be used in your writing.

2. When you have finally decided what the author's main point is, write it out in your own words. Do not use the wording of the original except for certain key words which you may find indispensable. If you cannot translate the ideas into language of your own, you do not understand them very well. Be especially careful not to rely too much on the topic sentence. Do not add any opinions or ideas of your own.

3. Revise your writing until you are sure that you have given an accurate summary.

4. Usually you will find your précis is too long — more than one-third the length of the original. Continue your revision until you have reduced the précis to the proper length. In this careful revision lies the principal value of the précis as a composition exercise. The work on "reduction" on pages 238–45 will be helpful to you in shortening your précis. Don't try to get the précis into a single sentence unless the passage you are summarizing is very short.

● EXERCISE 2. Read the following paragraph two or three times. Then read the four précis of it given below. Each of them illustrates one major error in précis writing. Tell what this error is.

Any bobsled run is a masterpiece of engineering skill, Lake Placid probably being more artfully devised than most. From the top of the hill to the bottom there is an invisible driving line, the line of safety and the line of greatest speed. One cannot come into the giant horseshoe turns of Whiteface and Shady Corner, each some twenty-five feet high, in haphazard fashion. The invisible driving line has to be found and followed. Centrifugal force has to be fought all the way. If a sled approaches too low, it never will swerve down in time. If it comes in too high, that force will throw it over the top. The right line will take it in at the proper angle, carry it safely up near the lip of the wall and send it darting precipitously down the far slope.[1] [138 words]

1. Any bobsled run is a masterpiece of engineering skill, Lake Placid being more artfully devised than most. An invisible driving line of safety and greatest speed runs from top to bottom of the hill. This line has to be found and followed to counteract centrifugal force, which has to be fought all the way. [53 words]

2. The Lake Placid bobsled run has an invisible driving line which a driver should follow to get the greatest speed and safety on the horseshoe turns of Whiteface and Shady Corner. These turns are twenty-five feet high and cannot be approached haphazardly. A sled should go to the top of the wall and then should swerve down the far slope. [58 words]

3. The bobsled run at Lake Placid is skillfully devised so that an invisible line runs through it from the top of the hill to the bottom. This is the line of greatest safety and speed, and a driver must find it and follow it, or his sled won't go through such dangerous horseshoe turns as Whiteface and Shady Corner safely. What will happen is that if a driver comes into a turn below the line, the centrifugal force which he is constantly fighting will prevent his sled from swerving down in time, and if he comes in above the line, the force will throw him over the top. [106 words]

4. The Lake Placid bobsled run, where the Olympics were held, is a marvel of engineering skill. It has an invisible line from top to bottom along which is the path of greatest speed and safety. Bobsledding is a dangerous sport, and unless a driver can follow this line, he may be killed. [51 words]

[1] From "Duel with Death" in *Sports of the Times* by Arthur Daley, from the New York *Times*, February 16, 1949. Reprinted by permission of the New York *Times*.

These précis, as you noticed, illustrate major faults as follows:

1. The précis has merely lifted sentences from the original.
2. The précis missed the point of the original paragraph, emphasizing unimportant details.
3. The précis is too long — two-thirds as long as the original.
4. The writer has injected his own ideas into the précis.

The following précis may be considered satisfactory.

The Lake Placid bobsled run was so skillfully designed that an invisible line of greatest speed and safety extends from top to bottom. In the struggle against centrifugal force, a driver must follow this line or risk not swerving down in time or going over the top. [46 words]

● EXERCISE 3. A satisfactory précis of the following passage is given on the next page. Before reading it, try your hand at writing a précis of the passage. Then compare yours with the one on the next page. Yours may very likely be better.

The coach does not always open up to the visiting reporter and acquaint him with the full potentialities of his new men. The tendency is rather to minimize their ability. The coach has a mortal fear of overconfidence in the squad. He particularly dreads the effect of too much publicity on his younger players. He does not like to have his team elevated to the position of favorite. It's a matter of psychology, and also he doesn't want to put himself on the spot. If his team or his players individually get a big build-up, the public and especially the alumni expect big things of them. If they don't come through, the criticism is all the more severe. It looks as though he has failed to make the most of his material, and he begins to worry about keeping his job.

So the coach would rather the reporter didn't say too

many nice things about his squad until after the big game is won or the season is over. Then there is no danger of overconfidence and the pressure is off the men. You can't blame him for this attitude. Even when he has the makings of a great team, so many things can happen to wreck the season — the setting-in of overconfidence, the loss through injury of one or two key players, a missed signal or the failure to throw a block on a vitally important play, the development of the opponents, who may have just as good material and better luck.[2] [263 words]

PRÉCIS

When talking to a reporter early in the season, a coach tends to talk down the abilities of his new men. He does not want his team to become known as a favorite because, if the team loses, he will be criticized for not making the most of his material. Even when he knows he has a great team, a coach avoids favorable publicity. He realizes that overconfidence, injuries, an error on the field, or the better luck of his opponents may wreck any season. [85 words]

● EXERCISE 4. As your teacher directs, use the following passages for practice in précis writing.

1

Rapidity in reading has an obvious direct bearing on success in college work, because of the large amount of reading which must be covered in nearly all college courses. But it is probably also a direct measure of the special kind of aptitude which I am calling bookish, because rapidity of reading usually correlates with comprehension and retention. Generally speaking, the more rapidly a reader reads, the more effectively he grasps and retains. The median reading speed of college freshmen has been found to be around 250 words a minute on ordinary reading matter, and a student who reads more slowly than that will certainly have difficulty in completing his college

[2] "Football" by Allison Danzig, from the New York *Times*, May 1, 1950. Reprinted by permission of the New York *Times*.

tasks within reasonable study periods. To be a really good college risk under this criterion one should readily and habitually cover not fewer than 300 words a minute on ordinary reading matter.[3] [143 words]

2

One feature of snowblindness is that each attack predisposes to another. People who have never been in snow countries are likely to remain immune and not suffer until the eyes have been excessively exposed, but people such as the Eskimos who are subject to the predisposing conditions every year are very readily affected. Some of them have a sort of fatalistic idea that snowblindness is inevitable and for that reason do not take enough precautions, although they nearly always take some precautions. I have known the severest cases of snowblindness chiefly among Eskimos. Men whom I have reason to consider as stoical as the ordinary lie moaning in bed with a skin or blanket over their heads, sleepless for as much as twenty-four hours. The period of considerable pain seldom extends over more than three days if one is in a darkened room or wears black or amber glasses. After complete recovery a second attack is not likely to come in less than a week, no matter how the eyes are exposed, but careless persons will have attacks every week or ten days.[4] [183 words]

3

In the minds of these self-reliant pioneer farmers certain ideas began to take root and grow. They were free men, who by their own efforts had created homes in the wilderness. They were individualists, for a man's success depended on his own strength and skill. They believed in the value of co-operation, for only by helping each other could they clear the enormous trees from their land and

[3] From "Who Should Go to College?" by Max McConn, in *Our Children*, edited by Dorothy Canfield Fisher and Sidonie Matsner Gruenberg. Reprinted by permission of the Viking Press.

[4] From *The Friendly Arctic* by Vilhjalmur Stefansson. Reprinted by permission of The Macmillan Company.

raise their houses. They felt themselves to be the equal of other men, for in looking about them they saw most of their neighbors living the same kind of lives that they were living. Finally, they were optimists, for all about them they saw the forests yielding to their axes, homes and villages springing up, and men who had started with nothing raising families in security and growing comfort. And many of the children of these pioneer farmers looked to the west, where they knew their futures lay. Those of English descent still thought of themselves as Englishmen, but the ties between this group of settlers and the mother country were few and far between. Like the frontiersmen, their minds were open to the ideas of democracy and a rising American self-consciousness, or nationalism.[5] [203 words]

4

There are human beings who wish the visible trappings of success, the automobile, the applause, the servility of hotel employees, the consciousness of opulence and distinction in the world's eyes. How shortsighted are these people! They may have all these blessings, may carry them everywhere, but they may never know the love and respect of their fellow creatures. As soon as their backs are turned they may be forgotten. As soon as their purses are empty they may lack even hospitality. They may have toadies, but they may never have friends. What a world to live in!

The reason I do not want wealth is that money is only useful in so far as it buys ease and comfort and the regard of those whose regard is not worth having. As for ease and comfort — once one has attained a reasonable degree of comfort, the rest is a superfluity. Luxury is good for nobody except the manufacturers of luxuries. And habitual luxury is a bore, for it kills enjoyment of the occasional rare treat.

Wealth has no value in itself. It has no real value as the means of helping others, because sporadic charity is one of the most uncertain of all benefits to the unfortunate.

[5] From *America's History* by Lewis Paul Todd and Merle Curti. Copyright 1950 by Harcourt, Brace and Company. Reprinted by permission of the publishers.

I have known some rich men, some "successful" men, and I have been shocked by the sight of their friends and beneficiaries. These friends and beneficiaries are deferential, flattering, even boastful of acquaintance with the great; but this is not the friendship I covet. I will explain in a little while what I require of friendship. It is certainly not deference or flattery. I can say at once that I have never enjoyed deference or flattery, except from strangers. My own friends are the reverse of flattering or deferential. They would not understand any suggestion that they should behave otherwise than naturally. Most of them are extremely caustic. I need say no more.[6] [318 words]

5

The core and the essence of democracy is the active participation of the people in governmental affairs. The atom has not changed this proposition. It has indeed heightened its importance. When the people do not participate, when they are uninformed or uninterested, when they cannot or will not make their voices heard or felt, when in short they default, the spirit of democratic action will soon die and, indeed, if all this has occurred, already is on its way to extinction. But when the people individually and through their institutions and organizations are active watchmen and participants in the governmental activities of their communities and region and nation, then we have that fertile soil in which democracy flourishes and grows in strength and in fruitfulness.

This democracy of ours is founded upon a faith in the over-all judgment and good sense of the people as a whole. Note that I am not speaking of "majorities," but of "the people as a whole." The magic lies not in the literal arithmetic of majority vote, but in the people's oft-proven sense of what is right and what is fair, that "sense of the meeting" that has at times so profoundly affected the course of American life.

We believe that when the people are honestly and

[6] "A Happy Man" by Frank Swinnerton. Reprinted by permission of Frank Swinnerton and his agent, Richard Steele and Son.

clearly informed their conscience and their common sense can be relied upon to carry the nation safely through any crisis. This is not only our faith; by and large it is the actual practice of our American way of life.[7] [253 words]

6

Ever since a group of men first developed a government, there have been two opposing ideas of the relation between the state and its members. One view puts the state above the individual. The individual has no existence except as a member of the community, carrying out its will, living for its welfare, ready to die in its service. He is not supposed to separate his identity or his personal profit from that of the nation. The community has a right to interfere in all of his affairs; he has no private life in which it is bound not to interfere. The state is more than the sum of its members. Its continuance must be assured at whatever cost to them. The state is a *totality* in which they are completely submerged. This view of the state is held by all absolute rulers, including modern dictators. We usually speak of it today as *totalitarianism* or *fascism.* It prevails over a large part of the world.

The other view puts the individual above the state. The state exists for the individual, not the individual for the state. The government has no other purpose than to serve the people; they may alter its form or, if need be, revolt against it, should it fail to carry out their wishes. Public and private life are quite distinct. The state may not interfere with the individual's private life so long as he does no injury to others. The individual has numerous rights which the state may not restrict except to protect the rights of other individuals. This view came to be widely held in England and northern Europe in the 1600's and 1700's; from there it spread to the New World. It took shape in the democratic form of government.[8] [319 words]

[7] From *This I Do Believe* by David E. Lilienthal. Reprinted by permission of Harper and Brothers.

[8] From *Our Changing Social Order* by Ruth Wood Gavian, A. A. Gray, and Ernest R. Groves. Reprinted by permission of D. C. Heath and Company.

7

The value of culture is its effect on character. It avails nothing unless it ennobles and strengthens that. Its use is for life. Its aim is not beauty but goodness. Too often, as we know, it gives rise to self-complacency. Who has not seen the scholar's thin-lipped smile when he corrects a misquotation and the connoisseur's pained look when someone praises a picture he does not care for? There is no more merit in having read a thousand books than in having plowed a thousand fields. There is no more merit in being able to attach a correct description to a picture than in being able to find out what is wrong with a stalled motorcar. In each case it is special knowledge. The stockbroker has his knowledge too, and so has the artisan. It is a silly prejudice of the intellectual that his is the only one that counts. The True, the Good, and the Beautiful are not the perquisites of those who have been to expensive schools, burrowed in libraries, and frequented museums. The artist has no excuse when he uses others with condescension. He is a fool if he thinks his knowledge is more important than theirs and an oaf if he cannot comfortably meet them on an equal footing.[9] [213 words]

THE ESSAY OF OPINION

The essay of opinion supports one side of a controversial issue; the writer's purpose is usually to state his point of view and to reveal weaknesses in opposing points of view. It is a kind of written debate. Editorials in newspapers and magazines are often essays of opinion. The "Letters to the Editor" columns in the larger newspapers also belong in this class. Sometimes you are asked by a teacher or an organization to look up facts on a debatable subject and, after evaluating these facts, to submit a report giving your conclusions, your opinions. Such a report is really an essay of opinion.

[9] From *The Summing Up* by W. Somerset Maugham. Reprinted by permission of Doubleday and Company.

In the exercises which follow you are given all the data you need for writing an essay of opinion. Study these data carefully. After weighing the facts and arguments, draw your own conclusions and write an essay making as strong a statement of your opinion as you can.

In preparing your essay follow the six steps in writing a composition as outlined in Chapter 25. Remember that only a clearly written, logical, well-organized composition will be convincing. Show that you understand the kinds of thinking described in the chapter on clear thinking, pages 402–16. Check your arguments to be sure that they do not represent any of the common errors in reasoning: hasty generalization, false syllogism, false analogy, false cause-and-effect thinking, and irrelevant argument.

● EXERCISE 5. In a four-year high school of 1,600 students, the seniors have been agitating for special privileges to be granted to them because they are seniors. The school authorities have shown some reluctance to grant these privileges.

The specific privileges the seniors want are given in the following list. After the list you will find a number of facts and considerations pertinent to the problem. Study these lists. Form your opinion, which will undoubtedly be affected somewhat by whether or not you are a senior, and in an essay of at least 300 words state and support this opinion. Be extremely careful not to *copy* the various items listed below. Use the information, but give it in your own words. If other considerations occur to you, by all means include them in your essay.

PRIVILEGES REQUESTED BY THE SENIORS

1. A "Senior Lounge" will be provided and furnished by the school for the exclusive use of seniors. The sen-

iors themselves will provide a radio-phonograph and automatic dispensing machines — cokes and candy. The room will not be intended as a study hall, but merely as a lounge. It will be supervised entirely by the seniors.

2. Seniors will not be required to attend study halls. They will be permitted to spend their "free" periods as they wish — in a study hall, in the library, or in their lounge.
3. Seniors having no class in the periods preceding or following their lunch period and in the final period of the day will be allowed to leave the building at these times.
4. Seniors with an 85 average will be excused from semester and final examinations.

FACTS AND CONSIDERATIONS

In favor of granting the privileges:

1. Being a senior should really mean something. Underclassmen should look forward to their senior year as something special. The prospect of someday enjoying these special privileges would improve the morale of the whole school.
2. Since seniors are about to be sent out on their own, they should be given more freedom during their senior year to teach them how to use wisely the great freedom they will have after graduation. Teaching this sort of self-discipline is an important educational responsibility of the school.
3. The privileges will benefit all students who stay in school until their senior year. It is not just the present seniors who will benefit.
4. The Board of Education can afford the small expense of furnishing the room. A classroom now used as a study hall can be turned over to the seniors for their lounge without any loss of room space because, with seniors excused from study, fewer study halls will be needed.

Against granting the privileges:

1. Even seniors cannot be trusted to make good use of the extra free time. Their grades, which are important to the school as well as to individual seniors, will suffer. The fact that a student is a senior does not mean that he can afford to waste his time. The seniors will create a disturbance if not required to be in study halls.
2. The building is crowded. A "senior room" would deprive the school of a needed classroom.
3. Two years ago senior study halls under senior supervision were a failure. No one could study in them.
4. It is undemocratic to single out one group as a privileged class. Seniors are too full of their own importance already.
5. Excusing the better students from examinations is unwise because these are the students who will probably go to college, where they will have to write final examinations.

● EXERCISE 6. The student council of a high school faces the following problem: the art students, represented by the Brush and Palette Club, have asked the council for $500 to equip a room in the school as a permanent art gallery. At the same time the school band has asked for $700 for uniforms for their recently organized drill corps. How should the student council act on these requests? The facts and the arguments on both sides are given below. Study these facts and arguments, draw your own conclusion from them, and write an essay of about 500 words expressing your opinion on this subject. Do not copy the various items as given here, but write in your own words. You may add any further ideas in favor of your opinion if they are not at variance with the facts.

The facts:

1. A drill corps is a group of girls who, through practice, have become highly expert in intricate drilling. Their

only function is to present a colorful spectacle at football games.

2. As the result of an unusually profitable year, the student council has a surplus of $850 in its treasury. The council's funds are derived from two sources: the sale of General Organization books, containing tickets to school functions and subscriptions to school publications, provides two-thirds of the money; the gate receipts from school musical, dramatic, and athletic events provide the other third.
3. The council funds are apportioned according to need among all school organizations. Those not able to make money are subsidized from the general fund. A few organizations thus support the others. In its concerts this year the band cleared $700. It was given $100 for traveling expenses to the state music contest and $200 for band uniforms. Two years ago the band was allowed to spend for band uniforms all the money it took in at its concerts.
4. The principal has promised to let the art club have an extra classroom, but he has no funds for transforming it into a gallery.

Arguments in favor of giving $500 to the Brush and Palette Club:

1. An art gallery is needed. There is no good place in the school in which art work may be displayed. Exhibitions have to be held in the art rooms, which are crowded, and visitors always interrupt the work of art students Very few students ever have a chance to see the work done in the art department.
2. The job of a high school is education. An art gallery could be used to display borrowed exhibits of a cultura nature as well as exhibits of student work in all the arts Such exhibits are educational.
3. Cultural values are more important than mere enter tainment by a pretty drill team at football games.
4. The band is not contributing its share to the schoo because it keeps asking for almost as much money a it contributes.

5. An art gallery is less expensive and does not wear out as uniforms do.
6. With a gallery, art students will have a better chance of selling their pictures and other creations. One-half of the money from such sales will be turned over to the council.

Arguments in favor of giving $700 to the band for uniforms:

1. The student council represents the entire student body. It should spend its money where it will benefit the most people. Thousands of students and townspeople will enjoy the drill corps in their new uniforms. Hardly anyone will go to an art exhibit.
2. The drill corps, properly dressed and trained, is an excellent advertisement for the school. Other high schools have drill corps; ours should be as good as theirs.
3. Since this has been an unusually prosperous year, there is enough money now for the uniforms. There may not be enough money in other years. But the smaller amount required for the art gallery may be available in other years. Let the gallery wait.
4. The girls in the drill corps have worked hard this year, believing they would have uniforms next fall. They deserve not to be disappointed.
5. The band made most of the money it is asking for. The art club is thus asking the band to pay for its gallery.
6. The athletic department, which contributes more money to the council than any other school activity, would rather have the money given to the drill corps.
7. If the art club can make money by selling its work, let it do so now and, in this way, help to finance its gallery.

● EXERCISE 7. Choose a subject of current controversy in your school, gather the facts and arguments in support of both sides, and write an essay of 500 words giving your opinion on the subject. A class discussion of the subject will be helpful before planning your essay.

THE ONE-PARAGRAPH FACTUAL REPORT

The two exercises which follow will give you practice in summarizing factual material in a brief and clear paragraph. The material is presented graphically. You are to study the graphs and write out the significant facts which they present. You must support convincingly whatever conclusions you draw.

To insure clear organization, make a brief outline of your paragraph before you write. Fashion a topic sentence. You will find it advisable to write two drafts. In the first you will be primarily concerned with getting the facts down on paper; in the second

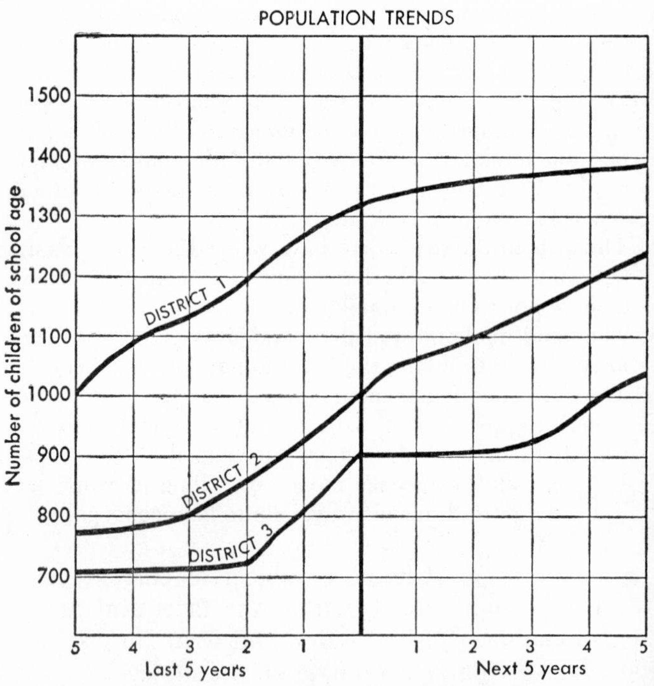

Which District Needs a Larger School?

(Compare the above with graph on facing page.)

you will be concerned with matters of style. This kind of writing must be especially clear and concise.

● EXERCISE 8. School facilities in the city of Elmhurst must be expanded. As part of a unit on education in your social studies class, you have decided to investigate the problem, which boils down to the question of which of three districts is in most immediate need of new building facilities. In your research you have found two graphs prepared by a citizens' committee. Study the graphs and write a one-paragraph summary of the information they convey, giving your own conclusion as to which district needs an enlarged building and why. Write approximately 150 words.

AVERAGE CLASS SIZE AT PRESENT

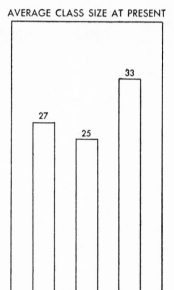

District 1	District 2	District 3
27	25	33

● EXERCISE 9. In this exercise you are not confronted with a specific problem to be solved by the study of graphs, but rather with data from which certain conclusions of interest to the public can be drawn. Study the two graphs on the next page. Draw whatever conclusions they warrant. Write a paragraph of approximately 150 words stating and supporting your conclusions.

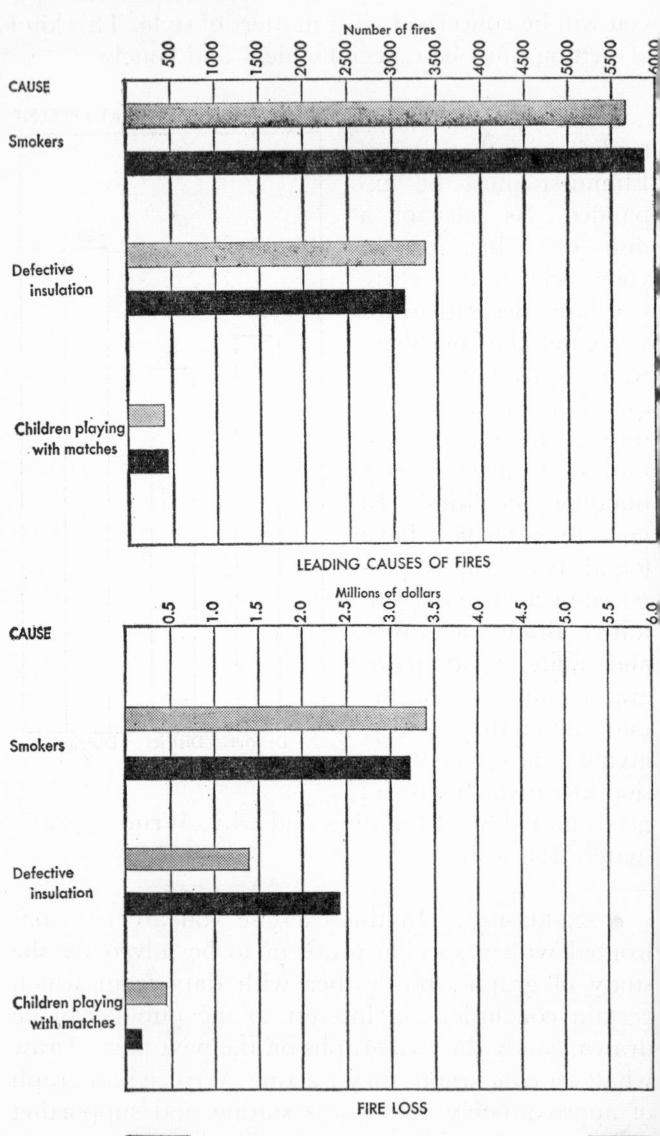
Number of fires
500
1000
1500
2000
2500
3000
3500
4000
4500
5000
5500
6000
CAUSE
Smokers
Defective insulation
Children playing with matches
LEADING CAUSES OF FIRES
Millions of dollars
0.5
1.0
1.5
2.0
2.5
3.0
3.5
4.0
4.5
5.0
5.5
6.0
CAUSE
Smokers
Defective insulation
Children playing with matches
FIRE LOSS
Last year
Year before last

CHAPTER 28

Narrative Writing

LEARN TO WRITE INTERESTING NARRATIVES

Narrative writing is writing which tells what happened. Whether you write a complicated, carefully plotted short story or a simple account of an incident that occurred on your way to school this morning, you are writing narrative.

Most students find narrative writing more fun than expository writing. A story is not only more interesting to read than a formal essay, but it is also more interesting to write. A story writer experiences the same kind of satisfaction as that enjoyed by the artist, the composer, the sculptor — he *creates* out of his experience and imagination.

For many years you have been writing "stories" in school. In elementary school you undoubtedly wrote a gripping account of the most exciting thing that happened during vacation, or you told a story about your dog, or you made up a thrilling tale about two boys who caught the bad men and turned them over to the police — all in the fine tradition of the Western. As a high school senior you may, if you wish, use these same materials, but you will write your story differently. Because you are more mature, your planning will be more skillful, your style will be more effective, your purpose may even go beyond merely trying to entertain, and reach the realm of ideas. Although you may never become a professional author, you will write more like one.

28a. Recognize the story material around you.

The successful professional author rarely lacks something to write about. He has trained his eyes and ears to recognize story material wherever he is. To a degree, you can do the same. The subject matter for your writing lies all around you — in the school corridors, on the athletic field, at "hen parties" and "bull sessions," at dances, even at home, not to mention the less common adventures of vacation and travel. In fact, wherever there are people there are stories, for people are stories. Of course, you do not write about people in general, but rather about a person, an individual.

28b. Write about that which you know well.

Although you need not confine yourself to writing about your own experiences or those of people your age, you should not at first stray too far from what you know firsthand. It is possible for a high school senior to write a good story about college life or about espionage in a foreign country, but success with subjects of that kind is the exception rather than the rule. Unless you have extraordinary talent, you had better begin with subjects close to your everyday experience.

Several approaches to narrative writing are suggested below. They may help you to recognize usable material already in your possession.

(1) Select an incident which actually occurred.

You can write interestingly without a plot. The essential element in narrative is a happening; an incident is a happening. Your daily life is a series of incidents, some trivial and dull, others important and even exciting. Of course, you are expected to use your imagination to "improve" a real experience, to make it more interesting, if necessary, than it actually was. You may have seen the coach stop Bill Jones in the hall this morning and, pulling him out of traffic, disappear with him into the principal's office. This is the incident; this is all you saw, but when you start imagining what the incident might mean and what might have occurred in the office, you are thinking like an author.

In searching for an incident to use as the basis for a narrative sketch, do not confine yourself to recent events. One fertile field is childhood. You can write well about the experiences of many years ago because you are far enough away from them to see them in perspective.

(2) Select a character and make up an incident involving him.

Many stories have had their inception in a character, someone interesting enough to inspire a writer to put him in motion or place him in a predicament from which he must extricate himself. This person, while he should be interesting, need not be a "character" in the sense of being eccentric. He may be a typical teen-ager, even your closest friend. You will probably find it easier, in the beginning of your literary career, however, to write about someone unusual. An old fisherman, a courageous invalid, a conceited "big wheel" at school, a bully, a student from another country, an unusual teacher — these can put your narrative train of thought in motion.

(3) Select a common human problem and fashion an incident to illustrate it.

A specific incident can exemplify a general problem. The problem of being accepted by a congenial group in school is uppermost in the minds of teenagers. You can probably imagine rather quickly an incident illustrating specifically this general problem.

Study the following list and try to imagine incidents illustrating each item.

- Problems at school
  - Pupil-teacher relationships
  - Cliques, gangs, fraternities
  - The outsider; breaking into a new school
  - Tests, grades, and keeping up scholastically
- Problems at home
  - Relations with parents, and brothers and sisters
  - Money, allowances, and home duties
  - Relatives
  - Family occasions — trips, weddings, reunions, funerals
- Social problems
  - Boy-girl relationships — dates, steadies, love
  - The struggle for popularity
  - The inferiority feeling
  - Breaking into a new community
- Problems of society in general
  - Prejudices — religious, racial, class, political
  - Poverty and wealth
  - Divorced parents — broken homes
  - Following the crowd — conformist and nonconformist
  - Morality — cheating, lying, hypocrisy, juvenile delinquency
  - The struggle for success
  - The struggle for survival
  - War and peace

(4) Select an incident from the newspaper.

Newspaper reporters are skilled at finding unusual incidents. Every day your paper contains material for a dozen pieces of interesting narrative, provided you have enough imagination to see the possibilities in a news article. You realize, of course, that a news story is usually written in a way opposite to the way good narrative is written. It tells the whole story briefly in the beginning, then adds details. News and not suspense is the business of a daily paper. Sometimes, however, a feature story will approximate narrative form. You can easily see the possibilities of an amusing incident in the following newspaper account.

TICKING PACKAGE DRAMA

Police Find Clock in Pail at American Stock Exchange

None of the employees of the public relations office for the American Stock Exchange at 86 Trinity Place knew the boss was expecting a clock yesterday.

Just after 1 P.M. it arrived, addressed to John J. Sheen, public-relations director. The 4-by-4-inch package was signed for by Rosemarie Matise, a stenographer. She put it on Mr. Sheen's desk, heard the ticking, and became alarmed.

The security-police force in the building sent a guard to the eleventh-floor office. He called for a bucket of water.

The city police were notified. Two radio cars, an emergency truck, and the bomb squad rushed to the building.

In the midst of the commotion Mr. Sheen walked into the office and asked if he had received a package.

All hands looked into the bucket where the package was soaking. It was opened and proved to be a traveling clock.[1]

The basic ingredients of an interesting narrative are here. As an author, you have complete freedom to develop the incident in any way you wish. Change the location — suppose the incident happened in the school principal's office. Build up the boss's character to add to the humor — how did he take the surprise? Add to the importance of the clock — it could have been a promised gift to his wife on an important occasion. Was the clock damaged by its bath? Change the story completely: The clock contains a fortune in smuggled jewels. Or, it really was a bomb disguised as a clock!

[1] From the New York *Times*, September 22, 1956. Reprinted by permission.

28c. Learn to write by writing.

It is trite to say that the only way to learn to write is to write, but it is true. Reading about writing will never produce a story. In fact, until you have had some experience, even the elementary advice on these pages will mean very little. Before studying the next section on planning a narrative, turn to Exercises in Narration on page 460. After trying your skill at one or two of these, you will be more ready to study planning.

28d. Learn how to plan a narrative.

Having chosen a happening to relate, you face the problem of working out a story plan. If you were writing a short story, this plan would be the plot, but you do not need a plot in the usual sense. All you need is a happening which you wish to make vivid and interesting through your manner of narrating it. Even a very simple incident, however, must be carefully planned. In planning you will probably have to answer the following questions:

1. What is to be the end of the story?
2. Where should the story begin?
3. How can I work in events that happen before the beginning?
4. Should the story be told in the first person or the third person?
5. Which parts or scenes will be written in the greatest detail?

(1) Determine the end first.

Beginning with the ending may seem to be reversing the logical way to proceed, but in narration, if you are to have any plan at all, you must know exactly where you are going. Every effective piece of narration should lead to a high point, a point toward which you carry your reader and at which the interest is greatest. Not until you know what this point is can you decide where to begin.

While you are planning the conclusion of your story, you should realize that the conclusion must grow logically out of the events preceding it. Three types of unrelated endings should be avoided.

The most obvious and the worst type of unrelated ending is the "then-I-woke-up" or "then-he-fell-out-of-bed" ending, which is simply a cheap trick to get the character out of the impossible dream-predicament in which you have placed him.

Another type of unacceptable ending is the accident ending, in which an unexpected, purely accidental event solves everything. Suppose, for example, that a story is about a girl who has made two dates for the same dance. The story is a description of her frantic reactions to this embarrassing situation. Since she likes both boys, she cannot decide which one to break the date with. However, two days before the dance, while she is still procrastinating, she gets the flu and has to spend a week in bed. Her problem is thus handily solved, but not by her. A flu germ has been brought in by the author to rescue his heroine. This kind of accidental ending is always unsatisfactory, whether it takes the form of an illness, an automobile accident, a hurricane, or a roving police car.

A third type of ending to avoid is the ending which leaves the story glaringly unfinished. In other words, it is not an ending at all. If, for example, the story just described had ended before the girl had made a decision, leaving it up to the reader to guess which date she would break, the reader would certainly feel that he had been shortchanged. As a mere literary trick which is the only reason for the story's existence, this type of ending may be acceptable. A few famous stories have ended in just this way, but they are clever tricks rather than good narrative.

(2) Begin the story as near the end as possible.

When you have decided on the ending, you should ask yourself, "What is the latest point before the end at which I can begin and still have a story?"

Suppose, for example, that after her third-period class an eighth-grade girl has been asked to go to the ninth-grade dance, the big social event of the year, by a boy whom she likes very much. She has lived for days in hope that this would happen, and she can hardly wait for school to let out so that she can tell her friend Betty. When she does find Betty, she learns that Betty had been asked by the same boy and turned him down because she already had a date.

This is the material of your story. With what scene will you end it? Probably you will end it when the girl, to her great disappointment, finds out that the boy had asked Betty first. Now where will you begin? Should you begin with the preceding days during which she kept wondering whether she'd have a date or have to go "stag" with the other girls? Should you begin with the opening of school on the day the boy asked for the date? Should you begin in the third-period class or with the invitation itself or even later? Following the advice "Begin as near the end as possible," where should you start your story? Read the following narrative account of this incident as written by a senior.

LET DOWN

For the tenth time in five minutes, Jan looked at the clock above the classroom door. The last period, she thought, is always the longest. Quietly she closed her book, stacked it with the others on her notebook, laid her pencil case — the new one she'd got for her thirteenth birthday — on top of the whole pile, and looked at the clock.

What a day! she dreamed. It might have been better if Bert Phillips hadn't asked her until after school; then she wouldn't have wasted every period just thinking about Bert and the ninth-grade dance next week. Not every girl had a date for the dance. Sue and Helen and Louise would be going by themselves, their mothers probably driving them to the gym. But Jan had a date — and with Bert Phillips, too! Won't Betty be surprised, and won't she be jealous? Jan gloated. Betty, who was always so popular with the boys, well, with *some* boys, anyway. Jan could hardly wait the two long minutes for the bell and freedom and the chance to tell Betty.

As she had been doing all afternoon, Jan recalled how it had happened. At the time, she had been too surprised to think. Bert had come out of English right behind her. "Jan, wait a minute."

"Oh, hi, Bert!"

"Jan, you know the dance next week — well, would you go with me? My father'll drive us over."

And there she was, Jan Miller, with a date. She felt almost grown-up.

At last the bell! Why does that big Bill Corwin always have to walk so slowly? Jan pushed by him into the crowded hall.

"Betty, hey, Betty! I've got to tell you something. I . . ."

Betty breathlessly appeared at Jan's side. "Jan, where've you been all day? I've got something too exciting for words. You know what? Last night I got *two* invitations to the dance next week — *two!* First Harry called, and then Bert Phillips. I had to say no to Bert, of course, but wasn't that great to be asked *twice?*" She beamed in expectation of Jan's envy.

Jan hiked her books up a little higher in front of her, took a deep breath, forced a smile, and said, "Oh, Betty, that's swell, really swell. Mom wants me home early — I have to go now. 'By."

Note that the actual duration of this incident was only a few minutes. The story is built on a common narrative device, the flashback. Through the girl's remembering and thinking about them, the events which preceded the actual opening of the story are made clear. The flashback is a good way to shorten the time of a story.

(3) Use flashbacks but don't overuse them.

In the preceding example, the flashback was a useful device for condensing the story.

Since this story is primarily one of mental state (excitement, surprise, anticipation, disappointment), it was properly told through Jan's thoughts, which made the flashback relatively natural and easy. Stories, however, which contain primarily physical action are likely to be most effective when given in straight chronological order. A writer may, if he is not careful, get into the flashback habit and find it a difficult habit to break

(4) Decide whether to tell the story in the first person or the third person.

Most narratives are told in the third person, but for many stories, first person is preferable. There is a closeness, an intimacy, about an "I" story which makes the author's task easier and makes the reader feel the story more personally. However, the advantage of the third person is that the writer becomes an onlooker rather than a character in the story. As an onlooker, he can know the thoughts and motives of all the characters and can follow them wherever they go. In many stories this freedom of the all-seeing eye is essential. As one of the characters himself, he cannot know the unspoken thoughts of the others and he cannot describe happenings at a place where, as a character, he could not be.

Frequently you may tell in the third person an incident which actually happened to you. In this way, you look at yourself through the eyes of an outsider and are able to write more frankly because the story apparently involves someone other than you.

(5) Select the parts (scenes) of the narrative which will be shown in detail.

Suppose you know how your story will end, where it will begin, what use, if any, you will have for flashbacks and which person you will use. Now you must, like a playwright, decide which parts of the story should be emphasized. In other words, which scenes will you present fully and in detail? Different writers, telling the same story, may choose different scenes to emphasize. The choice should be made in relation to the effect the author wishes to produce and in relation to the author's own experience, for a writer writes best about things with which he is most familiar.

As an exercise in planning, decide how you would tell the story described below. Prepare to tell your class how you would end and begin the story, what flashbacks you would use, whether the story calls for first or third person, and to which scenes you would give detailed treatment.

Hal Winter, son of a wealthy real-estate broker and member of the "country-club crowd," decides to spend the summer following his high school graduation working for a construction company in order to get practical experience before taking an engineering course in college. Through his father's influence, he gets a job with a construction gang building concrete foundations. Tony, the foreman, takes a liking to the rich man's son, and the other workmen gradually grow to accept him and enjoy having him on the crew.

Mary Jane Spencer, a siren-like girl in the club set, finds Hal a desirable conquest and during the summer succeeds in attaching herself to him. She is constantly critical of his working, unable to understand his preferring to haul cement all day long when he could be swimming and playing golf with her at the club. Mary Jane gets Hal to help her arrange a picnic for the "crowd" on a Friday afternoon. Hal helps her with plans and arrangements, and guests are invited for five o'clock. On the day of the picnic, however, Hal's crew is given a job which must be done in one day. As the hours pass, it is clear that several hours of overtime will be necessary. At four o'clock, Tony announces that the entire crew will work until the job is finished, even if it means working until dark. Hal must decide whether to stick with the crew or walk off the job at 4:30, the usual quitting time, to keep his date with Mary Jane and the crowd. Tony and the crew watch with disappointment and some bitterness as Hal, at 4:30, drops his wheelbarrow and walks away to keep his date, leaving the tired crew shorthanded to complete the job.

28e. Develop an interesting narrative style.

The development of an interesting narrative style is, by all odds, your most important concern as a beginner. You may have an abundance of story material and be a genius at planning, but your story will fail if you have not learned the rudiments of good narrative style.

(1) Be natural.

It is possible to learn to write well by imitating good writers. However, you must be very careful not to *force* yourself into a language which is obviously unnatural to you. Don't try to be "literary." Don't strain for big words or figures of speech which may give the impression that you are trying to show off your literary ability rather than trying to tell a good story. Use a thesaurus, a book of synonyms, if you wish, but don't let your thesaurus show. A good rule for a beginner to follow is "Write your first draft in the style of your natural speech, as though you were telling the story orally." Later you can polish your style as much as you wish. Try to develop a style that will make the story vivid and real without itself attracting attention.

For examples and exercises on the too literary, overwritten style, see pages 253–56.

(2) *Show* the action; don't summarize it. Keep yourself out of the way.

The fundamental principle of narrative writing is that the characters through their actions must tell the story. This means, first, that you must *show* the characters actually in action. You must not merely summarize for the reader what they did. Second, it means that you, as the author, must keep yourself out of the way.

Amateurs are too often inclined to summarize action instead of showing it. In the following passage the summarizing lines are italicized. Note that they convey no clear picture, and they sound as though the author preferred to draw a curtain across his scene and then step out and tell the reader what happened behind the curtain.

Nancy, right arm outstretched, hesitatingly approached the tethered goat, which eyed her suspiciously but held his head up as if fondly showing her his dirty yellow beard. "Nice goat," she said softly as she held out the bright red apple. *But Nancy was in for a surprise. Breaking loose, the goat, which apparently was not securely tied, gave her a glancing blow with his horns, and she found herself sprawled on the grass, more frightened than hurt.*

In his haste, the writer of this passage has not really *shown* what happened; he has summarized it. Furthermore, by saying "Nancy was in for a surprise," he has pushed himself between the action and the reader, who would have drawn this conclusion himself if the action had been described in detail.

Read the following paragraph. Can you tell where the author stops "showing" and turns to "summarizing"?

1

Mike dug his cleats in hard, lurched violently to the right, twisted his hips instinctively, and found himself abruptly in the clear with the white goal posts forty yards ahead across the bright green field. He streaked toward the goal. Bits of turf flew out behind his pounding feet. "Run, run, don't look back," he gasped to himself, stretching his sore leg painfully. But Mike didn't make it. He was tackled from behind as he crossed the 20-yard line. He heard the referee's whistle, felt the heavy breathing of his tackler and the steel grip still tight on his knees.

Now read the following version of the same action, noting how the author *shows* the tackle instead of merely summarizing it with the announcement that it happened.

2

Mike dug his cleats in hard, lurched violently to the right, twisted his hips instinctively, and found himself abruptly in the clear with the white goal posts forty yards ahead across the bright green field. "Run, run, don't look back," he gasped to himself, stretching his sore leg painfully. Feet pounded behind him faster, faster. Thirty yards, twenty-five, twen— Mike felt himself leave the ground. For a moment, he saw the blue sky, the spinning crowd, the green grass. A stab of pain cut through his shoulder. He heard the heavy breathing of his tackler and felt the steel grip still tight on his knees.

(3) Do not shift the point of view unnecessarily.

The point of view in a narrative is that of the character through whose eyes the events are seen. It is occasionally necessary to shift the point of view, especially in a long story. In a short narrative, however, one point of view should be maintained if possible.

In the first of the two accounts of the football player, you may have noticed that the point of view shifted. As you reread the first passage, notice that the first part is told from the point of view of the player. Then the point of view is shifted to that of a spectator. "He streaked toward the goal. Bits of turf flew out behind his pounding feet." The runner could not have seen these things. Later the writer returns to Mike's point of view. In the second passage, one point of view is maintained, as it should be. We experience the entire action from the point of view of Mike.

Can you detect the shift in point of view in the following example?

> On our way back from the drive-in, Jack started talking about the game. Bored, I settled down in my corner, leaning against the door, to listen to his alibis. Each time he wanted to emphasize a point, he angrily stepped on the gas, and I felt the car surge. It was a dark streak against the white pavement as it roared toward the big intersection near Maury's hamburger stand.

Wait a minute, author! You're inside the car; you can't see the car as a dark streak unless you're watching it from a distance. This is an unnecessary shift in point of view.

(4) Accompany narrative action with an abundance of detail.

Vividness in narration comes from the details of action and scene which the author chooses. The difference between a brief, straightforward statement of what happened and an interesting, artistically written story lies in the greater amount of detail the creative writer uses. Any incident can be told briefly and simply as a bare outline. It does not become narrative until details are added. The selection about Mike, the football player, could be told without accompanying detail, but it would lose all its interest. Compare the following statement with the second version on page 454.

Mike broke loose and raced for the goal but was overtaken and tackled on the 20-yard line.

Point out the accompanying details in the following passages, which were written by students.

1

Ling Han gave his horse a slap as they reached the flat plain country that stretches for miles away from the Rockies. He glanced back at his saddlebags, in which he had carefully placed his books only an hour before. A smile crossed his lips, and his light brown skin laughed its way into wrinkles at his eyes, and the corners of his mouth turned up. He crossed the small brook and started up the trail toward the school. His horse's muscles rippled at the shoulders, and the saddle droned out a squeaky, crunchy sound.

They passed the Bar J ranch and took the left fork, which led to the spring below. The water had cut deeply into the rock surrounding it, and the small waterfall ten feet downstream sent up spray in which a rainbow formed. Ling dismounted and knelt on one of the overhanging rocks. He plunged his hands into the icy water and smoothed back his jet black hair. Small rivulets of water made their way down his forehead and flowed on to his laterally projecting cheekbones. He raised a yellow-shirted arm and wiped off his face. It felt good to be outdoors in the early morning. A red-winged blackbird was singing nearby in an aspen tree, and as the sun broke away from an early cloud, Ling mounted up again to ride the remaining half mile. — C. KENDALL

2

House-party week end! It was just the same as always, the last quarter-hour going up on the train. There were about a dozen girls left in the car, no one else, because everybody else gets off before the last stop. They all had the same smooth veneer of calm. The nonchalant exterior must never be broken; but down inside there was a sort of Christmas-morning atmosphere — you know, the way you used to feel when you were little, during those few delicious moments of anticipation just before you opened your eyes to look at the tree. You could see it — the same breathless quality — shining in everybody's eyes, while we powdered our noses. Light conversation floated gently through the coach like milkweed, borne on soft, expectant laughter. Then the low wail of the train whistle sounded and broke the spell. Everyone stood up, took a final glance in mirrors, and began yanking bags off the racks with little bouncing thuds. I pulled my two pieces down and put them in the aisle, trying to control the butterflies fluttering in my breast, and the smile on my face, remembering last year's house party. — J. WHITE

(5) Write realistic dialogue.

Good dialogue must above all be natural This means that it must sound the way you would expect the speaker to sound. The speeches must be brief, for we do not give orations when we are conversing. A dialogue also carries action with it. Ask yourself what your characters are doing as they talk. They surely are not standing motionless and speaking without expression.

Don't worry about always naming the speaker — "said Mary," "said John," etc. — unless there is danger of confusion as to who is speaking. If only two characters are involved, you show when the speaker changes simply by starting a new paragraph; you do not need to identify them each time they say something.

The following is skillful dialogue written by a high school student. It is the beginning of a story. Note that both action and accompanying detail are given with the dialogue. Note, too, that the speeches are not more than three or four short sentences long. "He said" tags have been used occasionally but not every time.

I heard the door open behind me, and Marve ambled around to the front of my desk. His stupid grin showed he was in a disgustingly good mood. He'd stuck me with an editorial on student-faculty relationships, and there I was in the office pounding away on it when I wanted to be anywhere else.

"Hiya, Jody," he said, swinging one leg over the table. "How are the student-faculty relationships coming along?"

I looked up at him with distaste.

"Look, Star Editor, old boy," I said, "if you don't mind my saying so, I wish you'd write your own editorials."

He regarded me sadly.

"Jody, I don't think you're properly grateful to me. Who was it that got you on make-up when you were just a lousy little cub? Who was it that made you associate editor? Who was it that put you in line for the editorship next year? Me!"

I snorted politely. "Being associate editor's sort of a doubtful privilege when I have to associate with you. And this typewriter ought to be counted in the next census as the oldest inhabitant of Riverhead High."

By this time I was good and sore. He grated me, coming in and making a nuisance of himself when I wanted to finish and go home.

"Stop crabbing," he said. "If it's good enough for the greatest newspaperman since Horace Greeley, it's good enough for you."

"Yeah!" I tried to sound surprised. "Who's that?"

I grinned up at him. That had really gotten his goat.

"Who's that? You'll know who when I'm managing editor of the New York *Times* and magnanimously forgive your previous offenses to grant you a position as third copy girl."

"O. K., Horatio Alger, Jr., only I'll be over in Moscow doing foreign news, and if you cut so much as a line out of my stories I'll go over to the *Tribune*."

Marve unwound from the table and started for the door.

— M. LOVELACE

28f. Learn to build a plot — problem, struggle, climax.

Having practiced some of the techniques of narrative writing, you may enjoy the more exacting experience of writing a short story. The element of a short story which your narrative sketches probably have lacked is the element called plot.

A short story has a plot. The story is more than just a simple incident. It is a series of incidents so related that together they succeed in making a single definite impression on your reader. This single impression is closely related to the problem with which the story is concerned. To have a plot, you must have a problem which a character in your story tries to solve. His attempt to solve the problem makes up the narrative thread of the story. Typical problems might include the following: to win the affection of a member of the opposite sex; to break off a romance; to acquire money or property; to take revenge on someone; to win a fight; to survive in a flood; to convince a parent; to gain acceptance by a group; to avoid capture by one's foes; to catch a criminal; to carry aid to the suffering. Of course, if a character can do what he wishes without encountering any opposition, he has no problem. It is only when he finds obstacles in his way that his problem makes a story. The plot of a short story, then, is the struggle of a character to overcome opposing forces in his effort to solve a problem. The struggle need not be physical; it may be emotional or mental.

The end of a short story is usually the point at which the leading character either succeeds in solving his problem or definitely fails to solve it. The period of the struggle is called the "rising action." The point at which the struggle ends is called the "climax." In a short story there is very little writing beyond the climax. The action rises; the suspense increases steadily until the climax is reached. As soon as the climax has been described, the problem solved or not solved, the story ends.

Write and bring to class for discussion a plot outline for an original short story. Include the following in your outline:

1. List and characterize briefly each character in your story.
2. Give the setting — time and place.
3. State the problem and the obstacles to its solution.
4. State the climax or high point with which the story will end.
5. List the events, the incidents, you will include.
6. Write the opening scene — about a half page.

After hearing the suggestions and criticisms offered by your classmates and your teacher, revise your outline and write your story. Demonstrate throughout that you have learned the principles of narrative writing in this chapter.

EXERCISES IN NARRATION

The following suggestions for practice in narrative writing may help you get started. Do not, however, feel confined to them. If they suggest a subject, use it. If not, use one of your own.

● EXERCISE 1. Select an incident which you saw in which emotions were apparent. Using your imagination, expand the happening into a brief story illustrating the emotion: anger, fear, disappointment, disgust, embarrassment, discouragement, frustration, affection, etc.

● EXERCISE 2. Take any common object and imagine a story involving it. An inkwell, a lunchbox, a wallet, a knife, a notebook, a doll, a car — anything will do. The object may or may not be of major importance, but it will serve to start a train of thought.

● EXERCISE 3. Write an interesting incident to reveal the outstanding quality of a person's character. By describing the person in action in a clearly imagined situation, show that he is a bully, a coward, a conceited person, a shy person, a generous person, girl-crazy, boy-crazy, a flirt, lazy, etc.

● EXERCISE 4. Write an incident which illustrates a social problem — prejudice, unpopularity, juvenile delinquency, international understanding.

● EXERCISE 5. Cut from a newspaper a human-interest story which you could expand into a narrative. Plan and write your story. Clip the newspaper story to your own imaginary account.

● EXERCISE 6. Read the material for a story that appears at the top of the next page. Plan how you would tell this story. Answer the following questions:

1. With what event will you end?
2. Where will you begin?
3. What incident, if any, will you cover by means of a flashback?
4. In what person will you tell your story?
5. To which parts will you give the most detailed treatment?

A girl has for a long time looked with admiration and envy upon a certain clique or crowd, desiring to be a member of the group. To her surprise, she is invited by one of the boys to go to a party given by this group. She tries too hard to be one of them — to be like them — and as a result makes a bad impression. She talks too much, shows too much animation, expresses the wrong opinions, monopolizes the other girls' boys, comes to the party overdressed. As she thinks it over after the party, she realizes what a mistake she has made.

Plan this story, with obvious variations, with a boy as the central character.

● EXERCISE 7. Watch someone carefully in class or study hall. Jot down *all* his actions. Write a *complete* description, omitting nothing, of his every movement, his every reaction. The result will not be great literature, but it will show you how much you ordinarily let go unnoticed.

● EXERCISE 8. Write a sketch to reveal a single atmosphere. Use only those details which will bring out the atmosphere — the library, the office, the church, etc. Sense impressions — sound, smell, touch — will be important.

● EXERCISE 9. Build a narrative around an incident in which a character faces a specific problem and solves it by deciding on an action which he carries through.

● EXERCISE 10. Write a "snapshot" sentence for each of the following actions. A snapshot sentence is a descriptive sentence which gives a clear, interesting picture of a single action or a character.

1. Back-parking a car in heavy traffic
2. A baseball player making a fast play
3. A dog begging for food

4. A girl "making an entrance" at a formal dance
5. A television personality in a typical action
6. A basketball coach watching his team in a tight game
7. A high school boy waking up in the morning
8. An expert diver making a high dive
9. A typical high school student taking his seat in class
10. An angry parent at the head of the stairs as his son (daughter) slips in at 2 A.M.

● EXERCISE 11. Select one of the following lines and write an incident in which the line will be used. You may wish to use the line as the high point, perhaps as the end of the story. However, you may place it anywhere, even at the beginning.

1. Now get out of here! I don't ever want to see you again.
2. I couldn't believe my eyes.
3. Why didn't you tell me?
4. You'll never get away with it.
5. You can't do this to me.
6. Do you think I'm made of money?
7. I never forget a face.
8. A child could assemble it.
9. You owe it to yourself.
10. What was that?

● EXERCISE 12. Select two or three characters, place them in a specific setting and write their dialogue. Try to reveal their personalities through their speech and manner. Suggestions: two girls on the school bus; the principal and a truant boy; gossip in a small group at a party; whispers in the back row in class; parents at the bridge table; a salesman and an argumentative customer.

CHAPTER 29

The Research Paper

LEARN THE SPECIAL TECHNIQUES OF WRITING A RESEARCH PAPER

A research paper is an extensive, formal composition giving information gleaned from reading in a number of sources. The preparation of a research paper requires several weeks and provides a valuable review of the following skills: using the library and reference tools; note taking; organizing and outlining; paragraphing; footnoting; compiling and writing a bibliography; writing correct, clear, and smooth sentences. Before beginning work on your research paper, study Chapters 20 and 23, which deal with the library and reference books.

Consider your research paper one of the most important composition assignments of the year. Plan to devote to the paper enough time to insure that your work will be thorough and unhurried. Research work is careful work. Do not be satisfied with a paper that will merely "get by." Take pride in the amount of information you can give in approximately 1,500 to 2,000 words (or whatever length your teacher specifies); take pride in the accuracy of your work, and in the neatness of its appearance.

From the experience of thousands of students, a standard method of preparing a research paper and a standard form for the paper have been developed.

This method and this form are described on the following pages, which you should read through rapidly before starting work on your paper in order to get some idea of the nature and the proportions of the job ahead; then begin work, following the seven-step method.

THE SEVEN STEPS IN WRITING A RESEARCH PAPER

1. Selecting and limiting the subject
2. Preparing a working bibliography — a list of available sources
3. Preparing a preliminary outline
4. Reading and taking notes
5. Assembling notes and writing the final outline
6. Writing the first draft
7. Writing the revised final draft with footnotes and the bibliography

SELECTING AND LIMITING THE SUBJECT

29a. Select a subject which is interesting to you and suitable for research in the libraries at your disposal.

Since you are to do a large amount of reading, you owe it to yourself to choose a subject you really want to know more about. In a small way, you are to become an authority on this subject; the least you can do to prevent your own boredom is to choose a topic which will hold your interest.

Two other considerations are involved in the selection of a subject. The subject must lend itself to research in several sources, and the sources must be available in the libraries you use. Your autobiography would not be a suitable subject for a research paper because you could not look up material on it. It is not a research subject. Even the life of a famous person in whom you are interested would be of doubtful value for research because a complete life has probably already been published in one book, and you would tend to rely too much on just this one source. The best kind of subject is one on which information can be found in many different sources. No matter how interesting to you a subject may be or how suitable for research, it will not be usable unless you can get the source material. If you find that your library does not have enough information on your chosen subject, you will have to choose another.

It should be obvious that your subject must be sufficiently limited so that it can be adequately treated within the scope of your paper. Your paper will be a better piece of work if you go deeply into a narrow subject rather than treat superficially a broad one. How a subject may be limited is explained on page 378.

High school research papers have been written on limited subjects from within the following *general areas*. The lists are intended only to give you some idea of the kind of subject matter which is suitable for research. Most of the examples are much too broad for a research paper title.

TYPICAL AREAS FOR RESEARCH

Social History: Social customs in the eighteenth century; costume in Elizabethan England; medieval arms and armor; amusements in the Middle Ages; family life in the Victorian period; American colonial life; child labor in the nineteenth century.

Political History: The Crusades; early invaders of England; early history of the Republican party; the French Revolution; the pioneer in American history; Pan-Americanism; the United Nations; the League of Nations; the Monroe Doctrine in American history; India's struggle for independence; socialism; communism.

Literary History: Poetry of John Masefield; modern American essayists; experimental theaters; Shakespearean playhouses; satire in eighteenth-century literature; the frontier in literature; romanticism and realism.

Modern Problems: Juvenile delinquency; modern race problems; labor unions; education; social security; conservation of natural resources; the farm problem; NATO; rise of nationalism.

Science: Medieval medicine; history of anesthesia; peacetime uses of atomic energy; electronics; chemistry in agriculture; dairying; the manufacture of steel; plastics; synthetic clothing; interplanetary travel; prolonging life.

Art: The Pre-Raphaelite painters; Gothic architecture; abstract art; modern sculpture; new home designs; history of opera; furniture materials and design; the story of jazz; art in advertising.

PREPARING A WORKING BIBLIOGRAPHY

29b. Use library tools to look up available sources of information. Prepare a working bibliography on cards.

When you have selected a subject for your research paper and had it approved by your teacher, you are ready to look over the field. You begin by equipping yourself with a package of 3 × 5-inch cards. With these in hand, you go to the card catalogue, the *Readers' Guide*, the vertical file, and appropriate reference books, and compile a list of all books and articles in the library which promise to be useful to you. Record each book or article on a card — one source to a card. For reasons which will be clear later, you must write on the card complete information about the source. For books, this information can be obtained from the card catalogue; for magazines, it can be obtained from the *Readers' Guide*. A working-bibliography card should contain the following information:

BOOKS

1. Call number in upper left-hand corner
2. Author or editor (Indicate editor by placing *ed.* after his name.)
3. Title (volume, if necessary)
4. Place of publication
5. Publisher
6. Year of publication

MAGAZINE ARTICLES

1. Author
2. Title of article
3. Name of magazine
4. Volume and page number
5. Date

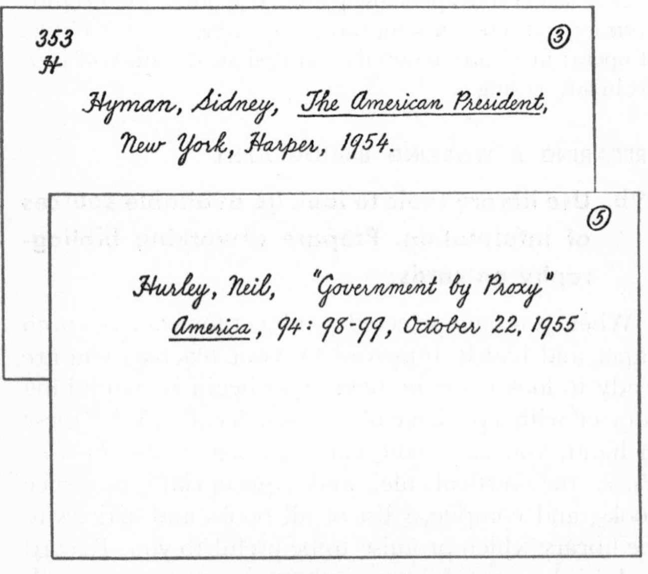

353
H
③
Hyman, Sidney, The American President,
New York, Harper, 1954.
⑤
Hurley, Neil, "Government by Proxy"
America, 94: 98-99, October 22, 1955

Cards in a Working Bibliography

At the conclusion of Step 2, you will have a stack of cards — a working bibliography — representing the sources you plan to read. *Number the cards clearly in the upper right-hand corner.* The card numbers will be used later, when you are taking notes, to save you the task of copying details about the source with each note you jot down from that source. Instead of the complete source, you will merely write the number of the source.

PREPARING A PRELIMINARY OUTLINE

29c. Prepare a preliminary outline to guide you in note-taking.

Before you can take notes in an organized way, you must have some idea of the topics on which you will need information. To formulate a list of such topics, begin your reading with a few general articles which give an over-all survey. If your subject is treated in an encyclopedia, the article there will be excellent for this purpose. Another way to approach such an outline is to try to anticipate the important questions your paper will have to answer. Jot down what seem to be the major divisions of the subject. A list of these constitutes your preliminary outline.

The preliminary outline is not an outline of your paper as it will finally be organized. It is, rather, a guide for use in your reading and note-taking. It represents the topics which, at this point in your work, you think you will want to cover eventually. As your reading suggests new topics, insert them in the outline; as you find that some of your topics cannot or should not be treated in your paper, remove them from the outline.

PRELIMINARY OUTLINE FOR A RESEARCH PAPER

Needed Changes in the Role of the Vice-President

I. The problem
   A. Succession to the Presidency
   B. Factors which govern selection of candidates
   C. The lowered prestige of the office

II. The original concept of the office
 A. Opinions of early statesmen
 B. Powers granted by the Constitution
III. Causes of the decline in prestige of the office
 A. Two-party system
 B. Twelfth Amendment
 C. Caliber of our Vice-Presidents
IV. Methods of raising the prestige of the office
 A. Improvement in method of nomination
 B. Improvement in method of election
 C. Changes in the powers of the Vice-President
  1. More important powers
  2. Experimental changes already made

READING AND TAKING NOTES

29d. Read and take notes on cards.

With a package of 4 × 6-inch index cards, your working bibliography, and your preliminary outline, you are ready to turn to the major task of reading your sources. The notes you take should fall under one or another of the topics in your outline. At the top of each note card write the outline topic with which the notes deal. This topic is called a "slug." See the sample note card on page 472.

Use a separate card for each source. In the upper right-hand corner of the card write the number of the source as you have indicated it on the card in the working bibliography. Always write the page number after every idea you jot down. You will need this page number for the footnotes in your paper.

The best way to acquire skill in note-taking is to start right in jotting down information which you think may be usable. As you progress, you will develop judgment as to what you are likely to use. You will develop judgment, too, as to when you should copy word for word from your sources and when you should write the information in your own words. *In general you should do very little copying. A research paper should not consist of a mere list of quotations. You are expected to gather facts and ideas from your sources, digest them thoroughly, and write them in your own words.* Quote verbatim only when the words of the source are especially important and especially well chosen.

No fault is more common and more serious in high school research papers than the use of quotations without acknowledging the sources. Teachers are quick to detect quotations that are not enclosed in quotation marks, and they are impatient with papers written not in your own style, but in the style of your sources. The danger here is that, in spite of good intentions, you may be led into copying the style of your sources without realizing that you are doing so. A "derived" style is caused by the habit of copying word for word everything you place on your note cards. The cure for this fault is always to take notes in your own words. Don't copy unless you intend to quote exactly. The use of the words of others as though they were your own is called plagiarism, and it is a serious offense. When you do copy, be sure to copy accurately and to enclose the copied material in quotation marks.

As a high school student, you are not able to judge very well the reliability of the various sources you are using. Experienced scholars know that sources vary greatly in their reliability and are able to judge among them. However, you should develop a critical attitude, especially when you are writing on a controversial subject Ask yourself these questions: What do I know about this author? By what right does he claim to be an authority? Is there any ulterior motive behind his writing? When was this book or article published? Since newspaper stories and magazine articles vary widely in quality, you should be particularly careful in relying on them.

Every idea or fact jotted down on your note card must be followed by the number of the page from which it was taken.

Slug — from preliminary outline

Number of working bibliography card

> Succession to the Presidency (6)
>
> Seven times "catapulted" into prominence by the death of a President.
>
> Three – T. Roosevelt, Coolidge, and Truman – were later elected President in their own right.
>
> page 121

Sample Note Card

The reading and note-taking will continue over a period of a few weeks. It is impossible to overemphasize the importance of beginning your reading early and continuing it regularly. A research paper need not be an exhausting task if the work is properly organized so that it can be completed within the specified time.

● EXERCISE 1. This exercise is included to give you practice in making out a note card before you begin your actual note-taking. Suppose you are writing a research paper on the FBI. One of your topics is "Character of the FBI agent." From the excerpt opposite take notes on this topic. In your working bibliography the source number is 10, and the page number is 6. Be sure to put the slug at the top of the card and to give the page number. Submit your card to your teacher for criticism. Compare your notes with those taken by others in the class.

One of the Bureau's principal wartime achievements has been the protection of the nation's war industries from sabotage. Special agents have entered 2,300 such plants, made a thorough study of their individual faults, outlined a plan for overcoming these, explained these plans to the managers and owners, and persuaded them, often against their preconceived ideas, to spend their own money — sometimes a great deal of money — in carrying them out. This business of going into the plants of some of the world's biggest industrialists and making suggestions as to how they should run their own businesses was no task for the ordinary flatfoot. It was accomplished however by the FBI type of law-enforcement officer with the minimum amount of friction.

The G-men have two duties as Hoover sees them: to protect the innocent and to convict the guilty. As a lawyer, he knows that there is only one kind of evidence worth getting and that is evidence that will stand up in court. He has to have agents who know that kind of evidence when they see it, who can not only catch criminals but convict them. To get that kind of evidence the agent must be able to meet every kind of person who can help. If cheapness of manner is essential, which it very seldom is, he can assume it if he has it not. "Class," on the other hand, is not assumable. But nowhere is this indefinable quality of more value than in the courtroom. Juries, even judges, are suspicious of expert testimony, a commodity which is notoriously bought and sold. Expert testimony by the clean-cut, impartial, and obviously honest young men Hoover sends into court to clinch his carefully prepared cases is believed. The truth of this statement is shown by the fact that approximately 97 per cent of the cases prepared by the FBI for prosecution have resulted in conviction, a record unequaled and unapproached by any other law enforcement body in the world.[1]

ASSEMBLING YOUR NOTES AND WRITING THE FINAL OUTLINE

29e. Assemble your notes and write the final outline.

When you are satisfied that you have enough notes to insure adequate treatment of your subject, you should undertake the task of arranging the notes in the order in which you will use them. Since each note card has a slug, your first step is to assemble in one pile all cards bearing the same slug. This simple mechanical task actually carries you a long way toward the organization of your paper. You will have before you a number of piles of information, each pile treating one division of your subject as represented in the preliminary outline. You have now to consider such matters as the order of topics in your paper and the possibility of various subdivisions of the slug topics.

You will find it necessary at this point to prepare your final outline in rough form. This final outline will take shape readily as you skim through your note cards. Before writing the outline, review the techniques of outline-making described on page 382. You will find that many of your slugs will become subtopics, while others may become major topics. Some may be discarded. You should probably have no more than six major topics. Using too many of these Roman numeral divisions suggests poor organization.

[1] From *The FBI in Peace and War* by Frederick L. Collins. Reprinted by permission of G. P. Putnam's Sons.

WRITING THE FIRST DRAFT

29f. Write the first draft.

With your outline to guide you and your notes on each topic conveniently arranged, you are ready to write. This first draft of your paper is a step in the whole process of creating a research paper; it is not a draft for anyone to read. Do not worry unduly over details of style and mechanics. Do not delay your work trying to think of a clever introduction. You may start anywhere you wish; the important thing is to make a start, to put your ideas on paper, even though eventually you may revise the style completely.

As you incorporate in your paper the ideas on your note cards, be very careful to indicate their source on your manuscript, *whether you are giving the ideas in your own words or quoting the wording of the source.* You do not need to give the source of information which is a matter of general knowledge. For instance, it would not be necessary to give a source for the fact that the Vice-President is elected every four years. In writing this rough draft it will be sufficient to indicate the source of material by simply writing down after each idea the source number from the working-bibliography card, and the page number. You need not bother to copy long quotations into this rough draft; merely jot down enough information to help you find the quotation later when writing your final draft. Write rapidly. Put the entire paper together.

WRITING THE FINAL DRAFT

29g. Write the revised final draft with footnotes and a bibliography.

If you have planned your work so that you are not pressed for time, the writing of the final draft should be relatively easy. Having already solved troublesome problems of organization and expression, you are now concerned primarily with form. The following matters must be carefully handled.

1. *Style*

Revise and punctuate your sentences so that they are correct, clear, and smooth.

2. *Appearance*

Allow ample margins on both sides and at the top and bottom of each page. If you are typing your paper, type it double space and on only one side of the paper. Long quotations (paragraph length) should be typed single space and set off by wider margins than the rest of the paper.

3. *Transitions*

Use transitional devices to keep the thought moving smoothly from paragraph to paragraph and from one major division to another. See pages 388 to 393.

Do not divide your paper into chapters. Chapter divisions in a 2,000-word paper tend to break it up and destroy its unity. The paper becomes five or six research papers instead of one.

4. *Footnotes*

To avoid constantly interrupting your paper with the citation of sources, you use footnotes. To the right of and above the final word in a quotation or an idea taken from one of your sources, you will write a number. Write number 1 for the first source on a page, 2 for the second, etc. These numbers refer the reader to their counterparts at the foot of the page, where the source is given. Each page must be so planned that there will be enough space at the bottom to accommodate the footnotes for sources cited on that page.

You must give footnotes for all ideas taken from sources even though the ideas are, as they should be, written in your own words. Do not make the mistake of using footnotes only for quoted matter.

The footnote for a book gives the name of the author (first name first), the title of the book (underlined), and the page number. Underlining in a manuscript is the equivalent of italicizing in print. Since you will have a complete bibliography (list of sources used) at the end of your paper, you need not give facts about publication in the footnotes.

The footnote for a magazine article gives the author (unless the article is anonymous), the title of the article (in quotation marks), the name of the magazine (underlined), the volume and page numbers, as in the *Readers' Guide*, (142:15–17), and the date of the magazine. All items in a footnote are separated by commas. The following are sample footnotes.

[1] Sidney Hyman, The American President, p. 190. [book]

[2] James M. Burns, "New Look at the Vice-Presidency," New York Times Magazine, p. 11, October 9, 1955. [magazine article]

[3] "Dangerous Oversight," Newsweek, 47:29, March 12, 1956. [anonymous magazine article]

In order to avoid repeating the same author, title, etc., each time the same source is referred to, writers use Latin abbreviations in their footnotes.

Ibid. This abbreviation represents the Latin word *ibidem*, meaning "in the same place." It is used instead of repeating the identical footnote immediately preceding it. Suppose, for example, that you have referred three times in succession to the same source; you have, however, referred to a different page each time. Your footnotes will appear as follows:

[1] Sidney Hyman, The American President, p. 190.
[2] Ibid., p. 192.
[3] Ibid., p. 193.

Op. cit. This abbreviation represents the Latin words *opere citato*, meaning "in the work cited." It is used to avoid repeating a reference, but only when another reference has intervened. For instance, had the footnotes listed above been separated by another footnote, the result would appear as follows:

[1] Sidney Hyman, The American President, p. 190.
[2] Neil Hurley, "Government by Proxy," America, 94:98-99, October 22, 1955.
[3] Hyman, op. cit., p. 192.
[4] Ibid., p. 193.

You should be familiar with *op. cit.* so that you will understand it in the writing of others, but you may, according to the most modern practice, omit it. The third footnote in the examples above would then read:

[3] Hyman, p. 192.

▶ NOTE: Both *Ibid.* and *op. cit.* must be underlined and followed by a period. The last name of the author must always precede *op. cit.*, and the page number must follow.

The question may arise as to how to footnote a quotation or an idea which the author you were reading had, in turn, taken from another author. The following sample will indicate how to give credit to both sources.

```
    1 Arthur M. Schlesinger, "Historians Rate
U. S. Presidents," Life, November 1, 1948, quoted
in Monroe E. Deutsch, "Veeps Can Become Presi-
dents," Nation, 175:579-80, December 20, 1952.
```

EXERCISE 2. Each of the following 5 items contains complete information for a footnote. Write the footnotes in correct form in the order in which they are given. Use *Ibid.* and follow your teacher's instructions as to whether he wishes you to use *op. cit.* or to omit it.

1. Magazine article entitled Responsible Government, When? Written by David Lawrence. Appeared in United States News and World Report for November 4, 1955, volume 32, page 92.
2. The same article as above, same page.
3. Book by Joan Coyne MacLean, The President and Congress, page 50.
4. Magazine article in Time for January 18, 1954, volume 63, page 26. No author. Title of article: Bridgebuilder.
5. Same as item 3 above, page 53.

▶ NOTE: Footnotes are sometimes used for comments by the author or for additional, interesting information which is not important enough to be included in the paper. This kind of footnote should be sparingly used.

5. *The Bibliography*

In order to give the reader complete information as to your sources, you must attach to your paper a bibliography, a list of the sources you used. This final bibliography differs from the working bibliography, which you prepared first, in that it includes only the books and articles you actually used. The bibliography is an important part of a research paper

Prepare it with great care. Be sure that it is complete and accurate.

In a bibliography the following information is given for each item:

BOOK	MAGAZINE
Author (last name first)	Author (last name first)
Title (underlined)	Title of article (in quotation marks)
Place of publication (city)	Name of magazine (underlined)
Publisher	Volume and page numbers
Year of publication	Date

PAMPHLET

Author (last name first)
Title underlined
Series, if any, quoted and followed by series number; enclosed together in parentheses
Date, if given

EXAMPLES

Hyman, Sidney, The American President, New York, Harper, 1954.

Hurley, Neil, "Government by Proxy," America, 94:98–99, October 22, 1955.

Hoyt, E., Freedom from Want: A World Goal ("Public Affairs Pamphlet," No. 80), 1943.

In writing a bibliography, observe the following details of form:

1. Items are arranged in alphabetical order according to the last names of authors. It is not necessary to number the items. Anonymous items are placed alphabetically by the first word of their titles, unless the first word is *the*, *an*, or *a*, in which case the second word determines the alphabetical position. Alphabetizing can be done easily

by arranging the working-bibliography cards in alphabetical order.

2. If the bibliography includes more than one work by the same author, it is not necessary to repeat the author's name with each. Use a long dash in place of the name in all listings after the first.

3. When an item occupies more than one line, the second line should be indented so that the names of authors will stand out on the page.

4. Commas are used between all parts of a bibliographical item. A period at the end is optional.

Study the following bibliography. The items in it were selected from a longer bibliography to illustrate the correct form for various kinds of listings.

BIBLIOGRAPHY

Bailey, H. M., Lazare, E.L., and Hawkins, C. H., Your American Government, New York, Longmans, Green, 1951

Corwin, E. S., and Koenig, L. W., The Presidency Today, New York, New York University Press, 1956.

"Dangerous Oversight," Newsweek, 47:29, March 12, 1956.

Gould, K. M., "Job for the Veep," Scholastic, 63:21, November 4, 1953.

——— "When a President Is Ill," Scholastic, 67:13, October 20, 1955

Hyman, Sidney, The American President, New York, Harper, 1954.

Moley, Raymond R., "Vice Presidents," Newsweek, 43:84, January 11, 1954

● EXERCISE 3. Each of the items in this exercise gives complete bibliographical information about a book or an article. Revise the items so that they are correct in form and write them in the proper order and arrangement as in a bibliography.

TEEN-AGE DRIVING

Bibliography

1. Magazine article by S. Kessler entitled "Teenicide, Who Is to Blame?" appeared in *Today's Health*, volume 28, pages 38–39, March, 1950.
2. Magazine article "Don't Teach Your Son to Drive" in the *Farm Journal* for October, 1955, volume 79, page 145. Written by L. Campbell.
3. A book *Driving Today and Tomorrow* by M. O. Hyde, published by Whittlesey House, New York, in 1954.
4. Magazine article, anonymous, entitled "Road Behavior." Appeared in *Consumer Reports* for April, 1956, volume 21, pages 165–67.
5. Magazine article, anonymous, "Will Teen-Age Curfews Curb Crashes?" in the September 12, 1955, issue of *Scholastic*, volume 67, pages 7–8.

6. *Charts, Diagrams, and Illustrations*

Charts and diagrams may be included in your paper where they are of real value. Always give with each the source from which you copied it. Illustrations cut out from sources may be looked upon with suspicion as attempts at padding, or as evidence of vandalism in the treatment of source material.

7. *The Complete Paper*

The complete paper will consist of the following:

1. *Cover.* Give your research paper a stiff cover, bearing the title of the paper. Make it attractive.

2. *Title page.* The title page should give the title, your name, the name of the course, and the date. The first two will occupy the center of the page; the last two will be placed at the bottom, either centered or at the right.

3. *Final outline.* This, in its revised form, is the outline you followed in writing your paper.

4. *The paper itself.*

5. *The bibliography.*

ABBREVIATIONS USED IN SOURCE MATERIALS

In your reading you may encounter some of the abbreviations listed below. The meanings are given here as an aid to your understanding of your sources. Learn to recognize them at once.

c or © *copyright;* used before a copyright date (c1935) to distinguish copyright date from the date on the title page of a book.

c., ca. *about* (from the Latin *circa*, *circum*); used with dates — "*ca.* 1732" means "about 1732."

cf. *compare* (from the Latin *confer*); "*cf.* the Atlantic Treaty" means "compare with the Atlantic Treaty."

ed. *editor*, *edited*, *edition*

e.g. *for example* (from the Latin *exempli gratia*)

et al. *and others* (from the Latin *et alii*); also *and elsewhere* (from the Latin *et alibi*)

f., ff. *following page*, *pages;* "p. 25f." means "page 25 and the following page"; "p. 25ff." means "page 25 and following pages."

ibid. *in the same place* (from the Latin *ibidem*)

id. *the same* (from the Latin *idem*)

i.e. *that is* (from the Latin *id est*)

l., ll. *line*, *lines*

loc. cit. *in the place cited* (from the Latin *loco citato*)

ms., mss. *manuscript*, *manuscripts*

N.B. *note well* (from the Latin *nota bene*)

n.d. *no date;* publication date not given in book

op. cit. *in the work cited* (from the Latin *opere citato*)

p., pp. *page*, *pages*

q.v. *which see*, *whom see* (from the Latin *quod vide*)

sic *thus* (from the Latin); when a writer quotes a passage containing an error (wrong date, misspelling, etc.) and he wishes to make clear that he has copied the original accurately, he inserts [*sic*] beside the error.

vide *see* (from the Latin)

-5-

Even though Tyler established a precedent when, following the death of Harrison, he declared himself President, there is still some dissatisfaction with this practice, which puts into the Presidency for as many as three or four years a man who probably was not very carefully selected for the great office. One suggestion for a change in this procedure is the Fulbright-Smathers proposal.

> They would divide the four-year tenure of a President into its two phases, corresponding to Congressional elections. If the President died within the first phase, the Vice-President would complete only what remained of the two years. An election of a new President for the four-year term could then be held coincident with the election of a new Congress. If the President died within the second phase, the Vice-President as now would complete what remained of his term. In this method, the nation would have a direct and early voice in the choice of a Presidential replacement.[1]

Another proposal states that "when a Presidential vacancy occurs, it should be filled by the Vice-President until the next Congressional election when a new President should be elected."[2] This proposal, like the Fulbright-Smathers proposal, presents difficult problems. If a President were to die a week before the next Congressional election, a new President would have to be elected immediately. The country would be thrown into a state of confusion, for no political party could sponsor a major election in such a short time. The man in office, the former Vice-President, would probably be nominated anyway.[3]

---

[1]Sidney Hyman, <u>The American President</u>, p. 193.

[2]Monroe E. Deutsch, "Veeps Can Become Presidents," <u>Nation</u>, 175:479-80, December 20, 1952.

[3]<u>Ibid</u>., p. 579.

Sample Page from High School Research Paper

CHAPTER 30

Letter Writing

WRITE FRIENDLY AND BUSINESS LETTERS ACCORDING TO STANDARD PRACTICE

The Friendly Letter

You have been taught letter writing since your days in elementary school. You have had experience in writing friendly letters. Probably you have noticed that the letters you write to, or receive from, your family and closest friends bear little resemblance to the model letters in your English textbooks. A book cannot and should not try to tell you what to say in an intimate letter, or how to say it, any more than it can tell you how to chat with your friends on the way home from school. A friendly letter is as natural, informal, and intimate as a conversation. Even details of form, like the three-line heading with its two essential commas, may in many instances be safely ignored. If, for example, you are writing to your sister who is away at college, a carefully inscribed heading telling her your street address and the city in which you live is quite superfluous, although the date may be of importance. Like standard usage in grammar and punctuation, standard practice in the writing of friendly letters recognizes a difference between informal and formal situations. While you need not observe all details of standard letter form in writing the more intimate of your letters, you will surely want to observe them carefully in writing to a new acquaintance or to your aunt in Alaska whom you have never seen, for such persons may judge you very largely by your letters.

Just as you have learned the characteristics of standard English even though you use colloquial English most of the time, so you should learn the characteristics of the more formal type of friendly letter, even though most of the letters you write are very informal. Of course, a friendly letter, like any social contact, should reveal an understanding of good manners. Considerations of neatness, attractive arrangement, and proper stationery are important in all letters.

30a. Observe standard practice in writing friendly letters.

(1) Use appropriate stationery and ink.

Appropriate stationery is stationery which displays good taste. The fact that white stationery is always in good taste need not rule out tinted varieties. If you feel the need to express your personality in purple or green ink, do so only in letters to friends who know you well. Never write letters in pencil, and never use ruled paper as letter stationery.

If you know how to typewrite, you may type friendly letters. Do not, however, subject your reader to the arduous task of reading a letter which has been badly typed. Unless you have had experience in typing, use longhand.

(2) Make the letter neat.

Even the most informal letters, like the most informal dress, should be neat. Avoid cross-outs, ink blots, uphill writing, crowded lines. A messy letter is an insult to its receiver.

(3) Make the margins equal.

A letter always looks better when the margins are wide and equal. Remember that the margins at the top and bottom of the page are just as important as those at the sides.

(4) Make the page order follow standard practice.

If your stationery is a folded sheet and your letter will be three or four pages long, follow the regular order of book paging, writing the second page on the back of the first page. If the letter is to be only two pages long, use the third page of the stationery for the second page of the letter.

(5) Make the five parts of the letter conform to standard practice.

While you are studying the following descriptions of the five parts of a friendly letter, refer frequently to the model form on page 489.

1. *The Heading*

Placed usually in the upper right-hand corner of the first page, the heading gives in three lines three pieces of information in which your correspondent may be interested: your street address; your city and state, separated by a comma (placed after a zone number); the date, with a comma between the day and the year. In order to afford an attractive margin, do not crowd the heading. It should not be placed at the very top of the page nor should it reach to the right-hand edge of the paper.

An alternative position for the heading is flush with the left-hand margin just below the signature, as shown below. The same considerations of margins and spacing apply.

Sincerely yours,
Helen

14 Hathaway Drive
Mount Royal, Colorado
October 3, 19—

The indented form shown in the example below and the block form, as in the model letter on page 489, are equally acceptable.

EXAMPLE 14 Hathaway Drive
Mount Royal, Colorado
October 3, 19—

2. *The Salutation*

The salutation is placed a short distance down the page from the heading, and it is begun at the left-hand margin. It is usually followed by a comma, not a colon. In a friendly letter almost any salutation is permissible, but *Dear* —— is always proper.

3. *The Body*

The body of a friendly letter, the letter itself, should begin either directly below the end of the salutation, or after an indention of an inch. Subsequent paragraphs should be indented uniformly with the first paragraph. At the end of the letter avoid such outmoded formalities as "Hoping to hear from you, I remain," or "I am," etc.

4. *The Closing*

The closing, or leave-taking, follows just below the final line of the letter. It is begun just to the right

Heading	14 Hathaway Drive Mount Royal, Colorado October 3, 19—
Salutation	Dear Barbara,
Body	
Closing	Sincerely yours,
Signature	Helen

Model Friendly Letter

of the middle of the page and is usually followed by a comma. Although you may use whatever closing you wish, *Sincerely*, or *Sincerely yours*, is always proper. *Yours truly*, and *Very truly yours*, should be used only in business letters.

5. *The Signature*

Write your name below the closing. Since you usually sign only your first name, center it under the closing.

(6) Make the envelope conform to standard practice.

Note in the following model that your name and address are placed in the upper left-hand corner of the envelope and the name and address of the person to whom the letter is going are placed just below the middle and begun a little to the left of the center. The person's name should be preceded by a title (Mr., Miss, Mrs., Dr., etc.). Always include the initials or the first name: *Mr. G. H. Bryce* or *Mr. George Bryce*, not *George Bryce* or *Mr. Bryce*. Your own name is not preceded by a title.

Helen O'Neill
14 Hathaway Drive
Mount Royal, Colorado

Miss Barbara Blomquist
336 East High Street
Grand Rapids 6
Michigan

● EXERCISE 1. On a page of personal stationery, lay out a friendly letter as the model on page 489 is laid out. Use your own address in the heading; arrange the five parts of the letter attractively according to the instructions given above. Use neatly drawn lines for the body of the letter.

Place the letter in its envelope and write correctly on the envelope the return address and the address. Do not seal the envelope.

Social Notes

Social notes are written to meet the demands of certain social situations. Four types are described on the following pages: the informal invitation; the reply to an informal invitation; the thank-you note; the "bread-and-butter" note.

Social notes are written on personal stationery (preferably white) or, if they are very brief, on correspondence cards. They generally follow the form of a friendly letter. Usually the name of the state is known to the receiver of the letter and may be omitted from the heading of a social note.

THE INFORMAL INVITATION

The telephone and the increased informality of modern living have reduced the number of social occasions calling for written invitations; nevertheless, there are still some occasions for which a written invitation is desirable. When an organization like a school club or class wishes to invite a number of guests to a social event, the invitations are written. When you are giving a party at your home and you wish your invitations to be somewhat more formal than they would be if given over the telephone or passed casually in the corridors at school, a brief note is appropriate.

When you write an invitation to a married faculty member and you wish him to bring his wife, or her to bring her husband, you should make this clear either by addressing the invitation to both or by saying in the invitation that you would like to have them both come. It is not, as a rule, good manners to invite a married faculty member to a dance or other affair to which guests come in couples, without including the husband or wife in the invitation.

THE INFORMAL REPLY

Whether you can accept an invitation or not, you must answer it promptly — the day you receive it. Your reply, if you can accept, need not be long and

Room 22
Cranford High School
November 10, 19—

Dear Mr. and Mrs. Smith,

The Library Club is giving a tea in the library from three to four-thirty on Tuesday afternoon, November 16. We should be pleased to have you come.

Sincerely yours,

Jean Thomas
Secretary

Room 22
Cranford High School
October 10, 19—

Dear Mr. Long,

The French Club cordially invites you to attend its meeting on Monday afternoon, October 22, at three o'clock in Room 301 to hear an illustrated lecture by M. René Mosher, secretary of the French Consulate in New York City.

Sincerely yours,

Sarah Gilbert
Secretary

---

160 Locust Street
May 3, 19—

Dear Sue,

Mother and I are giving a buffet supper on Sunday May 10, at six o'clock in honor of my aunt Mrs. John Lamberg and my cousin Julia Lamberg from Denver. We hope that you can come.

Sincerely yours,
Betty Hamilton

Model Informal Invitations

chatty. Your acceptance should indicate to your hostess, however, that you have understood correctly the time, place, and nature of the occasion. If you must decline the invitation, you will wish to give some explanation.

● EXERCISE 2. Assume that you are secretary of a school club which is giving a social affair to which you wish to invite certain members of the faculty. Write on appropriate stationery an informal invitation. Then, imagining that you are the faculty member receiving the invitation, write a reply.

---

125 Cambridge Avenue
Cranford
November 11, 19—

Dear Jean,

Thank you for your invitation to the Library Club tea from three to four-thirty on Tuesday afternoon, November 16. Mr. Smith and I are delighted to accept.

Sincerely yours,
Grace Smith

Dear Betty,

Thank you for your invitation for Sunday evening. Unfortunately, I shall be out of town with the family that week end and Dad says we will not be home until late at night. I hope I shall have another opportunity to meet your aunt and cousin.

Sincerely yours,
Sue Wright

13 Meadbrook Road
Stamford
May 4, 19—

Model Informal Replies

THE THANK-YOU NOTE

After Christmas, your birthday, and, if you are lucky, at other times when you receive gifts from friends and relatives who live some distance away, you must write thank-you notes. A thank-you note becomes more formidable every time you put it off. Write it promptly and save yourself worry. In many instances you should use the occasion to write a full letter; it will be appreciated. On the other hand, a brief thank-you note is often sufficient.

A thank-you note should not be gushy. Make it sound enthusiastic and sincere, even though you may not have been exactly thrilled with the gift. Here is an example of an adequate thank-you note.

April 2, 19—

Dear Uncle Ned,

Thank you for the copy of "Times at Bat." I took it to bed with me last night and read it slowly so that it would last longer — that's how good a book it is. Dad says if I could learn my schoolwork as easily as I can learn all the unimportant facts about ball players, I'd be bringing home all A's instead of you know what!

The only celebration of my birthday was a special dinner and a cake. Dad and Mother promised me tickets for the opening game of the season next week.

You couldn't have chosen a book I'd enjoy more than Arthur Daley's.

Sincerely yours,

Bill

THE BREAD-AND-BUTTER NOTE

The bread-and-butter note is the note you write to your hostess to thank her for her hospitality. Often such a note becomes a full-length letter but, depending on the circumstances, it may or may not be long.

A bread-and-butter note is a "must" after you have been entertained out of town in someone's home overnight or longer. Like the reply to an invitation, it should be written promptly, immediately after your return home. It is good manners to tell your hostess that you enjoyed your stay. Make her feel that you appreciate the things she did to insure your comfort and enjoyment. Be specific. You may appropriately mention your return trip, which will be of interest to your hostess. Study the following example of a bread-and-butter note.

621 Roosevelt Street
Boonton, New Jersey
July 1, 19—

Dear Mrs. Kingsbury,

Since my wonderful three days at your cottage I have spent my time remembering the good fun we had. I am sure that you and Mr. Kingsbury could have had no doubt about how very much I enjoyed my visit. I appreciated especially the trouble you took to arrange the big fishing trip on Saturday and the party Saturday night. You'll understand how I envy Jimmy his summer at such a grand place and with such a good crowd of friends.

The bus trip was hot but otherwise all right. I kept wishing all the way home that I was in the surf at Seaside.

Sincerely yours,
John Taylor

A bread-and-butter note always goes to your hostess. You may have been the guest of her son or daughter, and while you should write to your friend, too, you should write a note to his mother first.

THE FORMAL INVITATION AND REPLY

The formal invitation is used for formal social affairs and customarily for commencements and weddings. Since it is usually printed or engraved, you can rely on the printer to use the proper form. There is little likelihood of your having to write one yourself, but if you should have to do so, look up the correct form in a handbook or book of etiquette.

Mr. and Mrs. James Carter Jones
request the pleasure of your company
at a dinner dance for their daughter
Shirley Anne
on Friday evening, the eleventh of June
at seven o'clock
at the
Bay View Country Club
Fairfield, Ohio

R.S.V.P.

The letters *R.S.V.P.* stand for the French phrase *répondez s'il vous plaît*, which means "please reply."

Although it is unlikely that you will ever have to write a formal invitation, it is entirely possible that you will receive one and have to reply to it. Your reply will be handwritten in a special form as illustrated on the opposite page. It must always follow the exact wording of the invitation. The acceptance should repeat the time and place; it is always written in the third person; numbers are spelled out.

> *Mr. Arnold Bennett*
> *accepts with pleasure*
> *Mr. and Mrs. James Carter Jones's*
> *kind invitation to be present at*
> *a dinner dance for their daughter*
> *Shirley Anne*
> *on Friday evening, the eleventh of June*
> *at seven o'clock*
> *at the*
> *Bay View Country Club*
> *Fairfield, Ohio*

The date and hour are repeated in the regret, but the place is not repeated.

> *Mr. Arnold Bennett*
> *regrets that a previous engagement*
> *prevents his accepting*
> *Mr. and Mrs. James Carter Jones's*
> *kind invitation for*
> *Friday evening the eleventh of June,*
> *at seven o'clock*

The Business Letter

Whether formal or informal in tone, the business letter is always written according to a standard procedure.

30b. Observe standard practice in the writing of business letters.

(1) Use appropriate stationery.

Standard business stationery comes in two sizes, either of which is subject to slight variations by individual firms. The larger of the standard sizes is $8\frac{1}{2} \times 11$ inches; the smaller is $5\frac{1}{2} \times 8\frac{1}{2}$ inches, used for very short letters.

(2) Make an attractive "letter picture."

The "letter picture" is the over-all picture a letter presents to the reader at first glance. Businessmen insist that their letters make a favorable first impression. To make the picture attractive, you must center the letter on the page, leaving equal margins on the sides and at the top and bottom; space the letter parts carefully; follow consistently a standard pattern of indention and punctuation; and make the letter absolutely free of strike-overs, erasures, and other marks which mar its appearance.

On page 499 four business letters have been reproduced in miniature. Each letter presents an attractive picture. Note that the letters follow slightly different styles, all of which represent standard practices: block style without indentions; semiblock style with regular indentions; semiblock style with deep indentions (beginning after the salutation); and the double-spaced style which is used only in a very short letter.

(3) Follow standard practice in continuing a letter on a second page.

A business letter should be as short as possible without being abrupt or confusing. However, if a letter must be continued on a second page, use a second sheet; never write on the reverse side of a

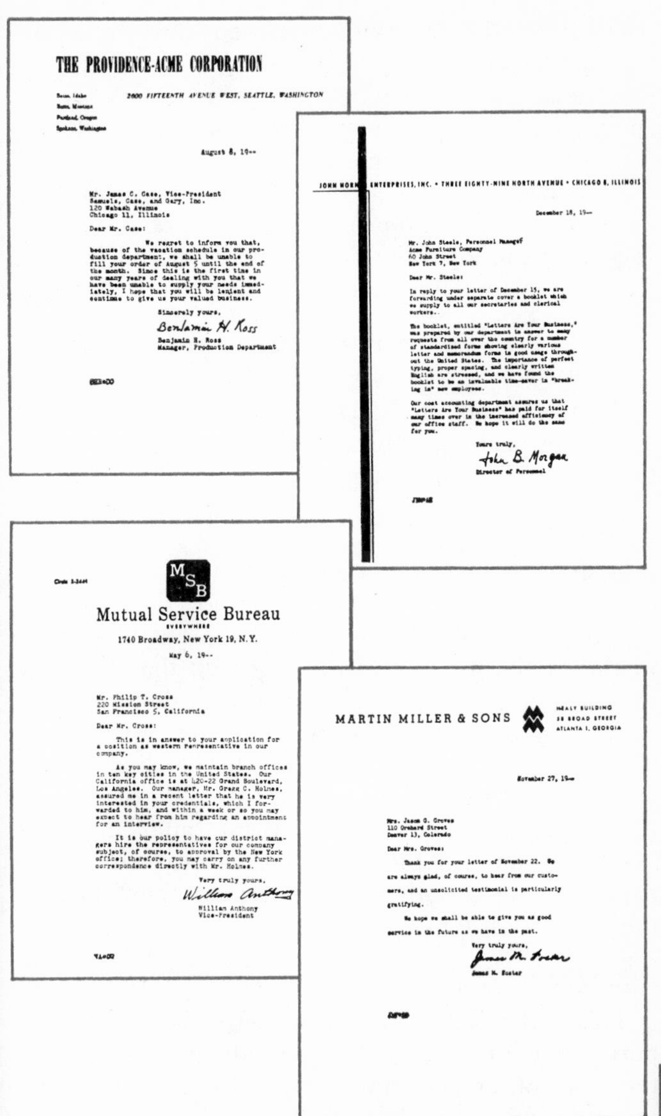

THE PROVIDENCE-ACME CORPORATION

Boise, Idaho
Butte, Montana
Portland, Oregon
Spokane, Washington

2600 FIFTEENTH AVENUE WEST, SEATTLE, WASHINGTON

August 8, 19--

Mr. James C. Case, Vice-President
Samuels, Case, and Gary, Inc.
120 Wabash Avenue
Chicago 11, Illinois

Dear Mr. Case:

We regret to inform you that, because of the vacation schedule in our production department, we shall be unable to fill your order of August 5 until the end of the month. Since this is the first time in our many years of dealing with you that we have been unable to supply your needs immediately, I hope that you will be lenient and continue to give us your valued business.

Sincerely yours,

Benjamin H. Ross
Manager, Production Department

JOHN NORM[...] ENTERPRISES, INC. • THREE EIGHTY-NINE NORTH AVENUE • CHICAGO 8, ILLINOIS

December 18, 19--

Mr. John Steele, Personnel Manager
Acme Furniture Company
60 John Street
New York 7, New York

Dear Mr. Steele:

In reply to your letter of December 15, we are forwarding under separate cover a booklet which we supply to all our secretaries and clerical workers.

The booklet, entitled "Letters Are Your Business," was prepared by our department in answer to many requests from all over the country for a number of standardized forms showing clearly various letter and memorandum forms in good usage throughout the United States. The importance of perfect typing, proper spacing, and clearly written English are stressed, and we have found the booklet to be an invaluable time-saver in "breaking in" new employees.

Our cost accounting department assures us that "Letters Are Your Business" has paid for itself many times over in the increased efficiency of our office staff. We hope it will do the same for you.

Yours truly,

John B. Morgan
Director of Personnel

MSB
Mutual Service Bureau
EVERYWHERE
1740 Broadway, New York 19, N.Y.

May 6, 19--

Mr. Philip T. Cross
220 Mission Street
San Francisco 5, California

Dear Mr. Cross:

This is in answer to your application for a position as western representative in our company.

As you may know, we maintain branch offices in ten key cities in the United States. Our California office is at 420-22 Grand Boulevard, Los Angeles. Our manager, Mr. Gregg C. Holmes, assured me in a recent letter that he is very interested in your credentials, which I forwarded to him, and within a week or so you may expect to hear from him regarding an appointment for an interview.

It is our policy to have our district managers hire the representatives for our company subject, of course, to approval by the New York office; therefore, you may carry on any further correspondence directly with Mr. Holmes.

Very truly yours,

William Anthony
Vice-President

MARTIN MILLER & SONS

HEALY BUILDING
38 BROAD STREET
ATLANTA 1, GEORGIA

November 27, 19--

Mrs. Jason G. Groves
110 Orchard Street
Denver 13, Colorado

Dear Mrs. Groves:

Thank you for your letter of November 22. We are always glad, of course, to hear from our customers, and an unsolicited testimonial is particularly gratifying.

We hope we shall be able to give you as good service in the future as we have in the past.

Very truly yours,

James M. Foster

Letter Pictures

page. If a letter is to run over, you must anticipate the fact and so arrange the material that at least three lines can be written on the second page. Never complete a letter on one page and put just the leave-taking and signature on the next.

The first line on the second page of a business letter on $8\frac{1}{2} \times 11$-inch stationery should be about two inches from the top. The page number should be centered about four lines above the first line of writing.

(4) Make the six parts of the letter conform to standard practice.

While you are studying the following descriptions of the six parts of a business letter, refer frequently to the model letter on page 501.

1. *The Heading*

Business firms use stationery bearing their letterhead, which makes it unnecessary for the writer to supply anything but the date in the heading. Note in the miniature models on page 499 that the date may be placed either at the right or in the center.

When you write a business letter without a letterhead, you must give a complete heading: street address on the first line; city and state on the second line with a comma between them (after the zone number); date on the third line with a comma between the day and the year. If you use abbreviations, use them consistently.

2. *The Inside Address*

This is the part of a business letter which is not a part of a friendly letter. In the inside address you give the name of the person or the firm (or both) to whom you are writing and the address with the usual comma between city and state. Business firms file copies of

Heading	188 Fernwood Terrace Stewart Manor, New York December 1, 19—
Inside address	Mr. James Cameron Nassau County National Bank 41 Front Street Rockville Centre, New York
Salutation	Dear Mr. Cameron:
Body	On November 28, in sending you the regular payment ($84.50) on my loan, No. 728, I sent by mistake a check for $48.00 made out to the Urban Servicing Company. I am enclosing with this letter my check for the regular payment, properly made out to your bank. Will you please return to me the check I sent by mistake.
Closing	Very truly yours,
Signature	Andrew K. Billings Andrew K. Billings
	AKB:DW

Model Business Letter

the letters they write. Since the copies are filed under the name of the person or firm to which they are written, it is necessary to have an inside address on each letter. Ordinarily the inside address is placed four typewriter spaces below the heading or date and flush with the left-hand margin. For examples, see the following discussion of the salutation.

3. *The Salutation*

The salutation, or greeting, is placed below the inside address (two spaces on the typewriter) and flush with the left-hand margin. It is always followed by a colon. The salutation varies with the nature of the inside address as follows:

a. If you are writing to a firm or a group, not to any specific individual, the proper salutation is *Gentlemen:* (*Mesdames:* for an exclusively female concern).

EXAMPLES

Soundcraft Corporation
10 East 52nd Street
New York 22, New York

Gentlemen:

Scholarship Board
Harvard Club of New York
33 West 44th Street
New York 18, New York

Gentlemen:

b. If you are writing to a specific person but know only his official position and not his name, the correct salutation is *Dear Sir:* (or *Dear Madam:*).

EXAMPLE

Personnel Manager
Airborne Instruments Laboratories, Inc.
160 Old Country Road
Mineola, New York

Dear Sir:

c. If you are writing to an individual and have used his name in the inside address, the proper salutation is *Dear Mr. ——:* or *My dear Mr. ——:* (The *My dear* form is considered somewhat more formal. Note that the *dear* is not capitalized.)

EXAMPLES

Mr. D. H. White, Manager
Eastern Oil Company
60 East 42nd Street
New York 17, New York

Dear Mr. White:

Mr. Scott Farnum, Director of Advertising
The Bigelow Company
74 Fourth Avenue
Grantley, Maine

My dear Mr. Farnum:

In an address always use a title with a person's name. Permissible abbreviations are *Mr.*, *Messrs.*, *Mrs.*, *Dr.*, *Hon.* Others should be spelled out: *Professor* Roger Keane, *Reverend* Thomas E. Haupt, etc.

d. High government officials may be addressed as follows:

THE PRESIDENT

The President
Washington, D.C.

Dear Mr. President:

SENATOR

The Honorable John W. Smith
Senate Office Building
Washington, D.C.

My dear Senator Smith:

REPRESENTATIVE

The Honorable John W. Smith
House Office Building
Washington, D.C.

My dear Mr. Smith:

GOVERNOR

The Honorable John W. Smith
Governor of New Jersey
Trenton, New Jersey

Dear Sir: (formal)

Dear Governor Smith: (informal)

4. *The Body*

A business letter should observe the five *C*'s of business correspondence: correctness, clearness, conciseness, completeness, and courteousness. A business letter obviously is a means toward achieving a particular result. Businessmen are busy men. There is little room for chat and discursiveness in business letters, but there is room for courtesy. Use simple language, clearly and directly phrased. The following trite phrasings, once in common use, are no longer considered good form: *Yours of the 5th inst. received and contents noted; beg to advise* (*remain, state, etc.*); *enclosed please find; please be advised that; thanking you in advance.* For discussion of the contents of particular kinds of letters, see the treatment of the order letter, the letter of inquiry, the adjustment letter, and the letter of application on pages 507 to 512.

The first line of the body of a business letter is placed two typewriter spaces below the salutation. It may be indented either the usual five spaces of a typed manuscript or as far as the length of the salutation (see the letter pictures on page 499). Subsequent paragraph indentions will be uniform with the first one.

5. *The Closing*

In a business letter the standard form for the closing, or leave-taking, is *Yours truly*, or *Very truly yours*. Less formal but frequently used is *Sincerely yours.* In writing to high government and church officials, you may use *Respectfully yours*, but avoid this in ordinary correspondence.

The closing is begun just to the right of the middle of the page and is followed by a comma. Note that only the first word is capitalized.

6. *The Signature*

The signature is written in ink immediately below the closing and flush with it. Directly below the signature the writer's name may be typewritten, a wise custom in the light of the illegibility of many signatures. This typewritten repetition of the writer's name may be accompanied by his official position.

EXAMPLE Very truly yours,
James MacPherson
James MacPherson
President

An unmarried woman may place (*Miss*) in parentheses before her signature so that her correspondent will address her properly in his reply. A married woman may write her full married name in parentheses beneath her signature.

EXAMPLES Very truly yours,
(*Miss*) *Virginia Shaw*

Very truly yours,
Elizabeth Blake
(Mrs. Henry G. Blake)

(5) Make the envelope conform to standard practice.

The correct form for the return address and the address on the envelope of a business letter is the same as that for the friendly letter (see page 490). The address on the envelope should be identical with the inside address.

(6) Fold the letter according to standard practice.

The folding of a letter is determined by the size of the envelope. If a letter written on standard $8\frac{1}{2} \times 11$-inch stationery is to be placed in a long envelope, the letter is folded twice: up from the bottom about a third of the way, then down from the top so that when unfolded it will be right side up. If it is to be placed in a small envelope, the letter should be folded up from the bottom to within a quarter of an inch of the top; then the right side is folded over a third of the way and the left side folded over upon that fold. Insert the letter in the envelope with the fold at the bottom of the envelope.

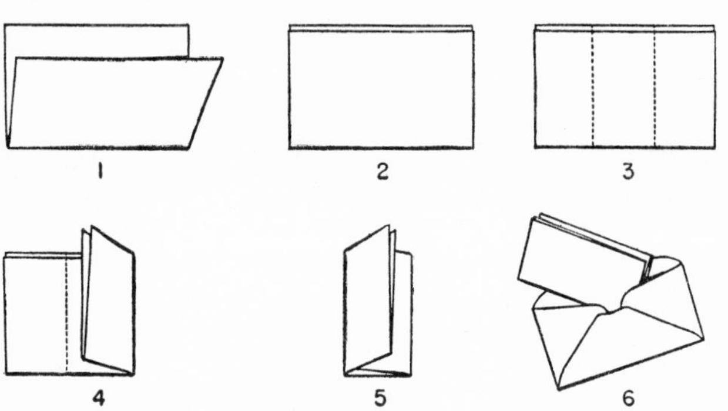

30c. Learn the requirements for various types of business letters.

A busy office will turn out in a single day a dozen different kinds of business letters, but the average person, in carrying on his private affairs, will have occasion to write only three or four types of letters. You will almost certainly have need at some time for the four types described on the following pages: the order letter, the letter of inquiry or request, the letter of adjustment or complaint, and the letter of application.

THE ORDER LETTER

The order letter is being outmoded by the prevalent use of printed order forms. However, there are occasions when it is necessary to write out an order in letter form. Study the model letter on the next page and the four requirements which follow it.

14 Oklahoma Avenue
Tulsa 6, Oklahoma
May 14, 19--

Guerber's Sports Equipment Company
85 Court Street
Marysville, Oklahoma

Gentlemen:

Will you please send me the following merchandise as advertised in the Marysville Journal for May 10.

2 doz. Easyflite golf balls @ $8.00	$16.00
1 pr. gabardine slacks, brown, size 32, length 31	8.75
2 white T-shirts, No. 86, size 36 @ $1.00	2.00
Total	$26.75

I am enclosing a money order for $27.00 to cover the order and a parcel post charge of $.25.

Very truly yours,
Ralph Gray
Ralph Gray

Model Order Letter

---

1. Set the list of ordered items off from the rest of the letter in a column arrangement.

2. Include all appropriate details as to quantity, catalogue number, style, size, and price. The symbol @ means *each* or *apiece:* 3 boxes @ $1.25 = $3.75. Sometimes it is wise to specify from what advertisement (magazine or paper and date) you have taken the information for your order. **30c**

3. Indicate how you are paying for the order: by check,

money order, C.O.D., or charge account. Include money for postage if you think it is expected.

4. If you wish the merchandise sent to an address different from the address in the heading, give the address in the letter.

A simple kind of order letter is that in which only one type of thing is ordered — theater tickets, a book, a fountain pen, etc. Such a letter is illustrated below.

345 Graham Road
Bellmore, New York
October 10, 19--

Box Office
Majestic Theater
245 West Forty-fourth Street
New York 18, New York

Gentlemen:

Please send me three tickets @ $2.40 for the matinee performance of Hamlet on Saturday, November 20. I am enclosing a check for $7.20 and a self-addressed, stamped envelope.

Very truly yours,

Catherine Moody

(Miss) Catherine Moody

THE LETTER OF INQUIRY OR REQUEST

Occasionally you may require information which can be obtained only by writing a letter. Writing for material to use in a research paper, for facts about travel in a certain locality, for a college catalogue, etc., are common situations of this kind. Be brief and direct. Make clear immediately what you wish; then stop.

118 Mountain Road
Kingston, New York
April 17, 19--

School of Agriculture
Cornell University
Ithaca, New York

Gentlemen:

Please send me your general catalogue and any additional literature you have on admission to the School of Agriculture and courses in dairy farming.

Very truly yours,

Walter Owen

Walter Owen

---

348 Converse Avenue
Maysville, Iowa
February 15, 19--

Bonar Plastics Corporation
1835 Washington Street
St. Louis 10, Missouri

Gentlemen:

For my Chemistry II class I am writing a research paper on the manufacture of plastics. I should appreciate very much your sending me any literature on this subject that you may have for free distribution.

Very truly yours.

Mary Robinson

Mary Robinson

Model Letters of Inquiry or Request

THE LETTER OF ADJUSTMENT OR COMPLAINT

When you write to a business firm to ask for correction of an error or to register a complaint of any kind, you will get better results if you restrain your annoyance and adopt a courteous tone.

14 Oklahoma Avenue
Tulsa 6, Oklahoma
May 24, 19--

Guerber's Sports Equipment Company
85 Court Street
Marysville, Oklahoma

Gentlemen:

On May 14 I sent you an order which included two white T-shirts, No. 86, size 36, @ $1.00. When the shipment arrived I found that you had neglected to send the shirts. I assume that this was merely an oversight in packing and will appreciate your sending me the shirts.

Very truly yours,
Ralph Gray
Ralph Gray

THE LETTER OF APPLICATION

Of all the letters discussed in this chapter, the letter of application is most important for you who are about to leave high school. Whether you wish a permanent job or temporary employment for the summer months, you are aware of the importance of making a favorable impression with your letter. Since the letter will undoubtedly be one of many received by your prospective employer, you must make sure that it is correct in every detail and sufficiently convincing to make the reader consider your application further.

It should, if possible, be typewritten.

There are certain clearly definable requirements for a good letter of application.

1. Begin with a statement of the position for which you are applying. Mention how you learned about it.
2. State all the facts an employer would certainly want to know: your age, education, experience.
3. Indicate, if you can do so naturally, that you are familiar with the requirements of the position and explain why you believe you can meet them.
4. Give references (usually three) with their addresses. If you have held other jobs, be sure to include among your references one of your former employers. Include also an adult who is acquainted with you and your family. Since you are still in school, a recommendation from a member of the faculty is appropriate. Before giving someone's name as a reference, ask his permission.
5. Request an interview at the employer's convenience.
6. Be especially careful with all the details of letter form, neatness, spelling, grammar, etc. You would not wish to lose a good position simply because you were too lazy to look up the spelling of a word or to copy your letter a third or fourth time to insure its being perfect.

Model Letter of Application

321 Fifth Street
Park Manor, Illinois
June 3, 19--

Benary Publishing Company
P. O. Box 172
Park Manor, Illinois

Gentlemen:

Please consider me an applicant for the secretarial position which you advertised in this morning's Herald.

I am eighteen years old and will graduate from Commercial High School this month. Since my sophomore year I have been taking business and commercial courses and have had the elementary and advanced courses in shorthand, typewriting, and bookkeeping, as well as courses in office practice, business mathematics, business law, English, social studies, and art. Being of Spanish ancestry, I am able to speak and write Spanish fluently.

Last summer I was employed as a part-time secretary by Mr. Allen Doyle in his real-estate office on Hilton Avenue, and during this school year I have worked two hours a day in the high school office. Both these positions have given me experience in office routine and in dealing with people.

The following have given me permission to use their names as references:

Mr. Allen Doyle, Edgemont Realty Company, 63 Hilton Avenue.
Mr. Allen Cartwright, office manager, Commercial High School.
Dr. James Anderson, principal of Commercial High School.

I shall be glad to come for a personal interview at your convenience. My telephone number is Parkhurst 3107.

Very truly yours,
Florence Gonzales
Florence Gonzales

BUSINESS LETTER EXERCISES

● EXERCISE 3. *The letter picture.* Following the models on pages 499 and 501, lay out on a piece of typewriting paper a perfectly arranged business letter, using neatly drawn lines for the body of the letter. Use your own address and the present date in the heading. Make up an inside address. Be sure the salutation is proper.

● EXERCISE 4. *The inside address and salutation.* The following inside addresses are mixed up. Rewrite them in correct block form. Beneath each write the proper salutation.

1. Postal zone 27, Fred Emerson, a professor at Columbia University, West 116th Street, New York City.
2. Miami University, Director of Admissions, Oxford, Ohio.
3. 49 East 33rd Street, Harper and Brothers, postal zone 16, New York City.
4. Representative from your district in the House of Representatives in Washington, D.C., Robert E. Thomas.
5. Personnel Director of the Bradley Manufacturing Company, Cass City, 82–84 South Avenue, Illinois, John T. Brooks.

● EXERCISE 5. *Order letters.*

1. Write a letter to the Board in Control of Intercollegiate Athletics, Yost Field House, Ann Arbor, Michigan, ordering two tickets for the Michigan–Minnesota game on November 7. The tickets cost $4.00 each.

2. Write to any firm you wish ordering at least three different articles advertised in a magazine or newspaper. Order more than one of some of the articles. Follow the model order letter on page 507.

● EXERCISE 6. *Request letter.* Write a letter to the Dean of Admissions of any college or university stating that you wish to apply for admission at a certain date and requesting an application blank and other necessary information.

● EXERCISE 7. *Adjustment letter.* Write a letter to a business firm asking why you have received a bill for an order for which you have already paid C.O.D. Give all important details, dates, etc.

● EXERCISE 8. *Letters of application.*

1. Using your local newspaper, select a help-wanted advertisement and answer it with a letter of application. Clip the advertisement to your letter when you hand it in.
2. Write to the manager of a summer camp, applying for a position as a counselor on the camp staff during the coming summer.
3. If you are going to work immediately upon graduation from high school, you probably have in mind the kind of position you intend to apply for. Write an imaginary letter of application for such a position.

PART SEVEN

SPEAKING AND LISTENING

CHAPTER 31

Public Speaking

LEARN TO SPEAK EASILY AND WELL IN PUBLIC

There is nothing difficult about learning to speak in public. The principles of public speaking are largely the same as those of social conversation. If you can converse acceptably, you can learn to speak before an audience, because public speaking is like conversation with a large instead of a small group of listeners. There is one other important difference: conversation is unprepared and hence informal and random; public speaking is prepared and hence more formal and purposeful.

Preparing the Speech

Sometimes the most troublesome phase of public speaking is finding something to talk about. If you are assigned a topic, consider yourself lucky. If the president of your club says to you, "At our next meeting we should like you to tell us about your camping trip," you can devote your time to organizing material and practicing delivery. But if he says, "We'd like you to speak to us at our next meeting on any subject you choose," you will very likely spend many hours deciding on an appropriate subject.

31a. In choosing a topic consider the occasion, the interests of your listeners, and your own interests and experience.

The occasion may suggest a topic. At a meeting held just before a national holiday, the significance of the coming holiday might be an appropriate subject; for example, "What should we be thankful for?" An annual meeting held to elect officers may be an appropriate occasion for tracing the history of the organization. Before you decide on a topic, find out the purpose of the meeting, the other speakers on the program, and the time allotted to your talk.

The interests of your listeners may suggest a topic. A subject that is appropriate for an audience of parents might not be suitable for an audience of teen-agers. Ask yourself, "What are my listeners interested in? What are their hobbies, problems, ambitions?" Talk about what concerns them.

Your own experiences may suggest a topic. If you have just completed a canoe trip, put together a jalopy, served as a nurse's assistant during the summer vacation, or done anything else different or unusual, you may wish to talk about your experience. If you do, you will find that words will come easily to you because of your familiarity with the subject and your enthusiasm. Your listeners will enjoy your talk more readily because you speak from personal knowledge.

● EXERCISE 1. Select a topic suitable for a talk on each of the following occasions. Explain orally the reasons for your choice.

School honor society meeting
Banquet tendered to a victorious school team
Commencement
Parent-teacher association meeting

Civic improvement association meeting
Chamber of Commerce meeting
School assembly
Community chest rally

31b. Set down your purpose in sentence form.

Have a definite purpose. To hit a target you must take careful aim. If you want your speech to be effective, you must have a purpose clearly in mind, and you must select and arrange the content of your talk to achieve that purpose. Speaking without an aim is like walking through a desert without a compass.

You must do more than talk *about* a topic. You must have a goal in view, a change you wish to bring about in the minds, attitudes, or actions of your listeners.

There are five recognized purposes of public speaking: to inform, convince, impress, entertain, and move to action. In speaking about any topic, the choice of subject matter will depend upon the speaker's objective. Thus the content of a talk on George Washington might vary as follows:

Purpose	*Content*
To inform	Relate the details of his life
To convince	Advocate following his advice on foreign alliances
To impress	Emphasize his valor, wisdom, integrity
To entertain	Narrate anecdotes of his life and times
To move to action	Urge contributions to a Washington memorial

As a beginning step, set down your purpose in sentence form and use it as a provisional title of your talk. Later you can substitute a shorter and more catchy title. The advantage of writing your title as a sentence is that it clarifies thinking, focuses attention on the aim, and guides in the selection of material. Typical sentence titles are:

Benjamin Franklin lived a fruitful and varied life. (*To inform*)
Capital punishment should be abolished. (*To convince*)
Have high ideals! (*To impress*)
I had my share of troubles the first time I went fishing. (*To entertain*)
Vote for my candidate for president of the Student Council! (*To move to action*)

31c. Gather materials from your own background, from interviews with others, and from printed sources, preferably in that order.

An inexperienced speaker tends to make the mistake of searching for articles and books bearing upon the topic he is to discuss before he explores other means of gathering material. The result is that his talk, when he delivers it, lacks originality and sounds like a rehash of others' thoughts and experiences. Reading has its rightful place in preparation—but it is not a first step.

The first source of material should be your own thoughts and experiences. What do *you* think about the topic? Why? Reflect, and then jot down your own opinions and experiences before going elsewhere for information. You will have the satisfaction of knowing that your treatment of the subject, whatever its shortcomings, is your own and not a warmed-over version of somebody else's ideas. What it may lack in substance is compensated for by freshness. It bears the stamp of your own personality.

Only after doing your own thinking should you discuss the topic with others. Formal interviews and conferences are not necessary. In conversations with friends and relatives you can steer the conversation around to the subject of your speech. In conversations with others about it, your thinking is sharpened, new ideas are acquired, and objections are proposed and answered.

The last source of material is the library.[1] By proceeding methodically here, you can save yourself time. To obtain a quick overview, first consult such general works of reference as an encyclopedia or an annual like the *World Almanac* or *Information Please Almanac*. Articles in reference works are usually brief and touch upon highlights only, but they provide a background against which other sources of information may be more readily understood.

The next step is to consult the card catalogue to find books on the subject. It is helpful to note the date of publication of the book and, in general, to examine recent publications before those written years ago.

The last step in your library research is to read recent magazine articles. *The Readers' Guide to Periodical Literature*, which lists magazine articles alphabetically by subjects and by authors, is an invaluable aid.

31d. Write notes on index cards.

Notes from your reading may be recorded on index cards. Such cards are convenient to handle, and they may be arranged in any order when the time comes to prepare an outline. Start each card with a subject heading and at the bottom give the source of the information recorded on it.

● EXERCISE 2. Select a topic for a five-minute talk to your class. Gather ideas for your talk. Use index cards to record your information. After you have

[1] For a complete treatment of reference materials see Chapters 20 and 23.

Extent of juvenile delinquency

A survey of 1,477 American cities by the FBI showed that 42.3 per cent of those arrested in 1955 for major crimes were under 18 years of age.

The New York Times Magazine
Sept. 2, 1956 Page 7

Model Note Card

collected all the information you need, submit to your teacher a list of your sources of information under the following headings:

1. Your own experience (*Tell what it is.*)
2. Interviews with others (*Who?*)
3. Reference books (*Name them. Give titles of articles and page numbers.*)
4. Other books (*List titles, authors, catalogue numbers, dates of publication.*)
5. Magazine articles (*List names of magazines, titles of articles, dates of publication.*)

31e. Mull over the information you have gathered.

Make the material your own by reflecting upon it. Your hearers will have more confidence in what you have to say if you are familiar with the subject.

31f. Outline your talk.

Engineers work from blueprints. So do architects, shipwrights, tool makers, and a thousand other creative craftsmen, including public speakers.

The blueprint or outline of a speech is the framework upon which a speech is constructed. It is drawn up after sufficient material has been gathered.[2]

● EXERCISE 3. Prepare a topical outline for the topic selected in Exercise 2. Observe the rules for form in making an outline, pages 382–84.

31g. Prepare a beginning which will arouse interest and lead into the subject.

In your opening remarks you should try to capture the attention of your audience and direct it to the subject you are going to discuss. Some effective ways of beginning a talk are:

By means of a striking statement

More people are killed in traffic accidents than in war.

By means of a question

How much weekly allowance ought a boy to expect?

By means of a narrative

After a crushing defeat Robert Bruce, the Scottish patriot, hid in a cave. His army had been crushed and his followers had left him. He had failed again—the third time! Despondent, he watched a spider spin a web. Again and again the web broke before it was completed, and each time the spider started afresh. That spider taught Bruce a lesson!

By reference to the occasion

Commencement brings back happy memories. Four years ago when we entered Louisville High School for the first time and sat in this auditorium, graduation seemed far off. Today, as we are about to be graduated, we look back on those four years and wonder where they have flown.

[2] For instructions in outlining see pages 381–86.

31h. Develop your ideas logically and persuasively.

By restatement

This is an important decision that faces us. What we decide now will affect the future of our club. We stand at a crossroads. We must consider every aspect because the decision is crucial.

By stating advantages and disadvantages

Let's hold a dance rather than a cake sale. A dance is more fun and less trouble to arrange. It will attract a greater number of young people. It will be more profitable.

By examples

Boontown High School held a successful dance last month. Townley High will hold one next week and Centerville High the week after. Ours is the only high school in the county that does not have a social affair every term.

By statistics

Of every four automobiles in the world, three are in the United States. In metropolitan Los Angeles, there are almost twice as many as in all South America. The car population of St. Louis is twice that of Japan. New York and Chicago have as many cars as France and Switzerland.

By reference to authorities

Dr. Donald H. Menzel, director of the Harvard Observatory, recently declared that interplanetary communication will be possible within the next ten years.

31i. Prepare a conclusion that will impress the central thought of your talk on your listeners.

The most common type of conclusion is a summary of the main ideas. Among the many ways of effectively ending a speech are an apt quotation, emotional appeal, or thought-provoking question.

● EXERCISE 4. From an anthology of speeches, read aloud the beginnings and conclusions of several talks. Discuss their effectiveness or ineffectiveness. Do the introductions arouse interest and lead into the subject? Do the conclusions drive home the main ideas?

● EXERCISE 5. Analyze a printed speech to discover the various means used by the speaker to develop his main thoughts. Summarize your findings orally.

Delivering the Speech

There are five methods of presenting a speech: impromptu speaking, extemporaneous speaking, memorized speaking, reading from manuscript, and a composite method.

An impromptu talk is organized and presented on the spur of the moment. It is delivered without preparation. A speaker relies on his general knowledge and experience to pull him through. Only experienced speakers should resort to this method.

An extemporaneous talk is carefully planned, but the choice of words is left until the moment of utterance. Usually an outline is constructed and memorized. The speaker, therefore, knows what he is going to say, but he makes no attempt to commit words to memory. This is the most flexible method of presenting a speech because words and content may be adapted to the reactions of the audience.

A memorized talk is written and learned word by word. This type of presentation is inadvisable because memorized talks usually sound artificial. Besides, it is almost impossible to memorize so thoroughly as to lose the fear of forgetting.

On rare, formal occasions, especially when exactness of expression is important, a speech may be written out and read from manuscript. A speech which is read lacks naturalness of expression. The presence of a manuscript hinders eye contact with the audience.

The composite method is a combination of two or more of the aforementioned methods. For example, a speaker may memorize his introduction and conclusion, read a quotation, and develop his main ideas extemporaneously.

Experienced speakers generally use the extemporaneous method. This method is also a good one for students to develop.

31j. Adopt a natural posture.

There are no hard and fast rules governing posture in speaking. In general, stand easily erect, feet a few inches apart and parallel, weight mainly on the ball of one foot, shoulders level, and arms at your sides except when gesturing. A speaker's posture changes as his purpose changes.

● EXERCISE 6. Before a full-length mirror, practice good standing posture for public speaking. Check your posture against the instructions given above. Move from one spot to another easily and without awkwardness.

Stand before the class as if you were speaking and invite constructive suggestions for improvement of your posture.

31k. Maintain eye contact with your listeners.

Look directly into the faces of your listeners. When you do this, your head will be up and your chin in—as they should be. Shift your attention from time to time so that each hearer feels you are talking directly to him.

311. Avoid excessive nervousness or stage fright.

Some nervousness is natural and desirable. Nearly everyone is a little tense before beginning to speak. Instead of being a liability, nervousness may be an asset. It is a sign that your body is keyed for maximum performance.

What must be guarded against is *excessive* nervousness or stage fright which prevents coherent thinking or smooth movement. Here are some practicable suggestions for preventing and overcoming stage fright.

1. *Know your subject thoroughly.* This is probably the best preventive. Begin to prepare well in advance of the scheduled date so that your thinking will have time to mature.

2. *Relax!* Try to feel at ease. Just before delivering the speech, breathe deeply and rhythmically several times. Yawning is also an aid to relaxing.

3. *Practice aloud.* Use different words each time you practice. Do not try to memorize. If you do not memorize, obviously you cannot forget! Have your outline at hand so that you become familiar with the sequence of ideas.

4. *Concentrate on your purpose.* Keep before your mind what you want your hearers to do, believe, or feel as a result of your talk. Forget yourself. Lose yourself in your subject.

5. *Move about.* Movement and gesture use up excess tension.

6. *Tell a humorous story.* Laughter will bring about relaxation.

7. *Welcome opportunities to speak in public.* Stage fright diminishes with experience in speaking. The most common cause of stage fright is lack of speaking practice. As you become accustomed to talking in public, your poise and confidence will increase.

31m. Use only natural gestures.

Gesturing is natural. Observe others conversing—they gesture to emphasize and clarify what they say. Observe yourself during a conversation. Unconsciously you also use gestures to stress your statements and make them clear.

Listeners like speakers who are active. A speaker who is as lifeless as a statue does not hold an audience's interest. Good speakers are animated.

Gestures should be appropriate. There are no set gestures to fit various ideas; different speakers use different gestures to express the same ideas. Common sense will dictate which gestures are appropriate for the ideas you wish to express.

Gestures should be graceful and spontaneous. They should be unforced, arising naturally out of the urge to communicate. They should be varied, changing as a speaker's ideas change.

Do not use gestures which are meaningless, awkward, flabby. Be careful not to gesticulate too much or to use one gesture repeatedly. Ordinarily it is inadvisable to gesture at the beginning or end of a speech.

Move occasionally when speaking. Move to show an important change of thought. When speaking to a small group, a shift of weight from one foot to another or an occasional movement from one spot to another will suffice. Before large audiences more obvious changes of position and more frequent movement are necessary for the sake of visibility.

● EXERCISE 7. Bring to class pictures of speakers in action which you have clipped from magazines or newspapers. Explain how the speaker's gestures seem to add to or detract from what he is saying.

● EXERCISE 8. Carefully watch and make notes upon a speaker's gestures during an assembly or a television program. Report orally on their effectiveness.

● EXERCISE 9. For each of the sentences listed below, do these three things: (a) express the idea by gestures only; (b) utter the sentence aloud without gesturing; (c) utter the sentence aloud and accompany it with a gesture.

1. Get out of here!
2. We must fight!
3. I appeal to you for justice.
4. We have nothing to hide.
5. Do as you are told.
6. The whole world envies our country.
7. Here he is.
8. Deep in the earth lies untold wealth.
9. Heaven will judge us.
10. Weigh both sides of the question.
11. Throw it aside.
12. Let's win this game!

31n. Speak in a conversational tempo.

Under ordinary circumstances speak at a conversational rate. In large auditoriums it may be necessary to speak somewhat more slowly than usual, but be careful not to be too slow. If your pace is too deliberate, your listeners' attention will lag.

Avoid "er" and "uh." These sounds serve no useful function and their repeated use is annoying.

31o. Enunciate clearly.

Vigorous lip and tongue action is essential for clear enunciation. Indistinct articulation results from a sluggish tongue and lazy lips.

● EXERCISE 10. Practice the following sound and word combinations before a mirror. Exaggerate your lip movements.

baw-bay-bee-boh-boo	bool-ah
maw-may-mee-moh-moo	raw beet
mee-maw	meat ball

● EXERCISE 11. Place the tip of the tongue on the gum ridge behind your upper teeth. Lightly and agilely practice:

t-t-t d-d-d t-t-t d-d-d
tah-tay-tee-taw-toh-too
dah-day-dee-daw-doh-doo
lah-lay-lee-law-loh-loo

● EXERCISE 12. Recite the following with energetic lip and tongue action, at first slowly, then with increasing speed.

The big bad boy bit the big black bear.
Rude food makes man brood.
Peter Piper picked a peck of pickled peppers.
Prunes and prisms, prunes and prisms.

SOME PROBLEMS IN ENUNCIATION

Omitting Sounds

Careless speakers omit essential sounds, either at the beginning of words, in the middle, or at the end.

● EXERCISE 13. Pronounce the following lists of words, giving especial attention to the enunciation problem indicated for each list.

Initial sounds

about	electric	exact
America	eleven	huge
because	eraser	remember

Medial sounds

accidentally	February	library
all right	finally	mystery
already	geography	poem
automobile	giant	poetry
champion	government	really
company	history	recognize
cruel	interesting	shouldn't
diamond	jewel	wonderful

Final sounds

child	East side	meant
gold	West side	nest
hand	abrupt	past
kind	chest	post
second	last	left

Difficult consonant combinations

cts: conflicts, facts, respects, restricts, tracts
dths: widths, breadths, hundredths
fts: lefts, shafts, shifts, tufts
lds: builds, fields, folds
pts: accepts, precepts, concepts
sks: asks, desks, disks, risks
sps: clasps, lisps, rasps, wasps
sts: adjusts, frosts, digests, insists, lists, mists, rests, tastes, tests

Adding Sounds

Adding sounds is a common fault. An example is *lawr* for *law*. Avoid this error when you speak.

● EXERCISE 14. Drill on the following words, being careful not to add any sounds.

athlete	elm	ticklish
burglar	idea	translate
chimney	grievous	twice
draw	lightning	umbrella

Substituting Sounds

The substitution of one sound for another is a frequent fault: *ciddy* for *city; dis* for *this; tree* for *three.*

● EXERCISE 15. Practice the following pairs of words, taking care to distinguish between them.

t–d		t–th	
beating	beading	boat	both
bitter	bidder	tree	three
matter	madder	true	through
metal	medal	taught	thought
latter	ladder	tinker	thinker
writing	riding	tin	thin

d–t͟h		w–wh	
bayed	bathe	Wales	whales
breed	breathe	watt	what
dare	there	weather	whether
day	they	wear	where
dose	those	wit	whit
read	wreathe	witch	which

Ng Confusions

In some words *ng* is pronounced **ng** [ŋ] [3] as in *sing* and *clinging*. In other words *ng* is pronounced **ngg** [ŋg] as in *finger* and *single*. Speakers sometimes confuse the pronunciation of *ng*, substituting **ngg** for **ng** or using **ng** when **ngg** is called for. If you know and practice the proper distinction between these sounds, you can avoid this common error.

1. *All words ending in* ng *are pronounced* **ng** [ŋ]. *If a suffix is added, the* ng *ending is still pronounced* **ng** [ŋ].

EXAMPLES	sing	singer
	cling	clinging
	long	longish

[3] International Phonetic Alphabet symbol. For a complete list of IPA symbols see the preface to Webster's New International Dictionary, Second Edition, or any textbook of phonetics.

EXCEPTIONS	**longer**	**longest** (*long-ger, long-gest*)
	stronger	**strongest**
	younger	**youngest**

● EXERCISE 16. Practice the following words aloud, taking care not to add a guttural click after *ng*.

bang, banging	gang, gangster	coming in
bring, bringing	fling, flinging	flinging up
hang, hanger	clang, clanging	going out
cling, clinger	long, longing	hanging on
ring, ringer	sing, singing	Long Island

2. *In all other cases* ng *is pronounced* **ngg** [ŋg].

EXAMPLES **anger, English, finger**

EXCEPTIONS **gingham, Bingham**

● EXERCISE 17. Practice the following words, taking care to add a guttural click after *ng*.

angler	hunger	mangle
angrily	jingle	mongrel
bangle	language	singly
bungle	languor	tangle
dangle	linger	tingle

● REVIEW EXERCISE A. Using the outline which you prepared in Exercise 3, deliver a five-minute speech to the class. At the conclusion of your talk your listeners will offer constructive suggestions covering content and delivery.

● REVIEW EXERCISE B. Deliver a seven-minute lecture to the class on a subject which you know thoroughly. You may accompany your talk with diagrams, pictures, or other visual aids. When you have finished, invite questions from the audience. Afterward the class will comment on your preparation, organization of material, introduction, development, conclusion, posture, eye contact, gestures, tempo, enunciation, and pronunciation.

CHAPTER 32

Listening

LEARN TO LISTEN INTELLIGENTLY

A great deal of knowledge and enjoyment comes through the ear. More than half your waking hours are passed in listening to your parents, friends, teachers, and to radio and television programs. In the twentieth century people are talked to and "talked at" more than ever before.

Since listening occupies such a large part of daily life, improvement of listening ability is important. It used to be assumed that everyone knew how to listen. Nowadays training in listening is recognized as necessary for everyone. Some do not know how to listen intelligently. Others do not listen as intelligently as they should. By practicing good listening habits, you can increase your ability to learn and enjoy.

Hearing and listening are not the same. Hearing is a passive activity. When you concentrate on your homework while a radio plays softly, you *hear* background music, but you are scarcely aware of what is being played. You are not really listening to it. Listening requires an active mind. The listener cooperates mentally with the speaker, gathering, sifting, and weighing the ideas that are spoken. Listening demands thinking.

● EXERCISE 1. Make a list of your listening activities for an entire day. Consider the various people to whom you listened, the places where you listened, and the kinds of talk listened to. The following list is only suggestive.

PERSONS	PLACES	KINDS OF TALK
teachers	school	instruction
parents	home	advice
clergyman	church	inspiration
storekeeper	store	information
friends	playground	encouragement

● EXERCISE 2. Explain why good listening habits are important to any of the following persons.

accountant	electrician	receptionist
actor	interpreter	reporter
architect	judge	salesman
carpenter	lawyer	secretary
chauffeur	mechanic	storekeeper
clerk	pilot	teacher
doctor	printer	waitress

Courtesy in Listening

Listeners and speakers influence one another. Together they compose a cycle of communication, each acting and reacting upon the other. Attentive listeners stimulate a speaker to do his best. Their interest helps him to be interesting. An inattentive audience, on the contrary, hinders a speaker. When listeners fidget, talk to one another, or look bored, a speaker's task, which is always difficult, is made doubly so. He cannot concentrate on his talk. His enthusiasm drops.

When you listen to a speaker, treat him as if he were a guest in your home. Give him your courteous attention.

32a. Observe good listening manners in informal situations.

Courtesy in listening requires you to observe the following etiquette when you are face-to-face with a speaker.

(1) **Listen to a speaker as you would like him to listen to you.** This is the Golden Rule of listening.

(2) **Use the speaker's name when addressing him.** "Mr. Jones, I hear that you coach a Little League baseball team."

(3) **Look at the speaker.** Give him your complete attention.

(4) **Keep your mind focused on what he says.** Do not let your attention wander.

(5) **If you disagree, express your point of view courteously.** Do not contradict flatly. "You make a strong case for football as a high school sport, but don't you agree that it is very dangerous, costly, and time-consuming?"

(6) **Listen without interrupting.** Wait quietly for your turn to speak. Your facial expression shows whether you are following the conversation or merely waiting for a chance to break in with your own comments. Relax!

32b. Observe good listening manners in formal situations.

Some of the preceding suggestions also apply in formal situations. Here are three additional hints on listening manners when you are a member of an audience.

(1) **Give your complete attention to the speaker.** Even if he is so far away that he cannot see you, do not read, study, doodle, fidget, look around the room, eat candy, chew gum, or chat with those seated near you. If you take notes, take them unobtrusively.

(2) **Applaud with your hands only.** Do not show your approval by whistling or shouting.

(3) Wait until the speaker is finished before leaving. If unusual circumstances require you to leave, slip out as quietly as you can.

● EXERCISE 3. Observe the listening manners of students in your classes. List examples of good and bad manners and explain orally how both speaker and listener were affected.

● EXERCISE 4. Assume that the Student Council has appointed you and several of your classmates as a committee to draw up a code of listening manners for assembly audiences. After drawing up a code with the other members of the committee, explain the reason for each item to the entire class.

● EXERCISE 5. In a three-minute talk explain how developing ability to listen can help you in high school, college, business, and social life.

Listening Faults

Untrained listeners commit a number of faults which affect their enjoyment and understanding.

32c. Avoid listening faults which hamper enjoyment and understanding.

Do not try to carry on a serious conversation while a radio, phonograph, or television set is playing. You cannot concentrate on two sources of vocal sound at the same time. The remedy to such a conflict is obvious: turn off the radio, phonograph, or television set until you complete your conversation.

Another listening fault is day-dreaming. Check the tendency to let your mind wander. When listening to a lecture, take notes. Note-taking helps correct the habit of mental wandering. Another way of correcting this habit is to question in your own mind the speaker's statements, especially expressions of opinion or assertions for which little or no proof is offered.

A third listening fault is the failure to see the point of an anecdote or illustration. Speakers often employ narratives, personal experiences, and humorous stories to drive home an idea. Unskilled listeners sometimes remember the story but miss the thought it illustrates. For example, Benjamin Franklin at the end of the Constitutional Convention referred to the carved design on the back of the presiding officer's chair. "I often wondered," he remarked, "whether that design represented a rising or a setting sun. Now I know it is a rising sun." What point was Franklin illustrating?

● EXERCISE 6. Only three listening faults have been listed above. With a little reflection others will come to your mind. Mention several, explain what they are, and suggest one or two means of overcoming each.

● EXERCISE 7. Show how an anecdote can be used to illustrate a serious idea. First, state in general terms the point you wish to make; then illustrate it by means of an anecdote. (Your school or local library has anthologies of anecdotes useful for illustrating various ideas.)

Listening in Class

In class you listen to learn. You listen to your teacher's instructions and to your classmates' answers, questions, and discussions. You profit by paying close attention. So do the other members of the class. When you listen attentively, you reduce the amount of time you need to spend in home study.

Those who speak in class should speak audibly and intelligibly so that everyone may hear and understand easily. Since speakers are affected by their listeners' attitudes, listeners owe them their alert attention. An inattentive listener is as much a barrier to learning as a poorly prepared speaker.

32d. Learn to follow the development of class discussion.

(1) Discern the difference between main and minor points.

(2) Weigh the pro's and con's of controversial issues.

(3) Ask questions when in doubt.

(4) Stay alert physically and mentally.

● EXERCISE 8. Make a survey of classroom listening habits in your school. Ask several teachers such questions as:

What are the effects of poor listening on pupils' achievement?

Do most pupils need to improve their listening ability? On what grounds do you base your answer?

What is the most common listening weakness?

How can pupils learn to be better listeners?

Ask several pupils the same questions. Report your findings to the class.

● EXERCISE 9. Listen carefully to a social studies or science lesson, or to any other lesson in which there is general class discussion. Prepare a report telling what main ideas were developed and what minor points were also developed. Explain how you were able to distinguish between main and minor matters. Were there any digressions? If so, were these digressions helpful or confusing to class and teacher?

Listening to Instructions and Directions

A great general once said, "Anything that can be misunderstood will be misunderstood." Sometimes instructions are not understood because they are not clear. Sometimes they are not understood because people do not listen sharply.

32e. Learn to listen intelligently to instructions and directions.

(1) Pay close attention to what is said.

(2) Ask questions about any point that is not clear to you.

(3) Repeat the instructions before carrying them out.

(4) Review the instructions as you carry out each step of the process.

● EXERCISE 10. Choose pairs of pupils to dramatize the proper way to listen to directions. One member of each pair gives directions for traveling to a point of interest some distance from the school. If necessary, the other person asks questions to clear up doubtful points and then repeats the directions to show that he understands.

● EXERCISE 11. Listen while your teacher reads aloud a set of instructions relating to any of the following or similar matters.

fire drills	air-raid drills
examination schedules	college applications
bus transportation	cafeteria regulations
assembly programs	study-hall rules

To show that you understand the instructions, repeat them aloud to the class.

● EXERCISE 12. Explain orally how to do any of the following. Use props when necessary. (This list is only suggestive. Choose other activities, if you wish.)

baking a cake	building a fire
putting on lipstick	erecting a tent
building a doghouse	tying a knot
pitching a baseball	applying a bandage
removing a tire	using a tool

After you have completed your explanation, call upon another pupil to perform in pantomime the activity you have just described or to repeat your directions step by step. This exercise is a test of your ability to explain clearly as well as a test of your classmates' ability to listen intelligently.

Listening with Discrimination

It goes without saying that you cannot remember everything you hear. Much of what is said is unimportant and can be ignored or forgotten. An intelligent listener knows how to discriminate; that is, he knows how to tell the difference between what is important and what is relatively unimportant.

32f. Learn to listen with discrimination.

(1) Learn to discover from the context the meanings of unfamiliar words.

The sentences surrounding an unfamiliar word often give you clues. Later, when you have an opportunity, you can look up in a dictionary the meanings of the words to be sure that your guesses were correct. For example, you can surmise the meaning of the italicized word in each of the following paragraphs from the rest of the paragraph.

Next week the Theater-of-the-Air will present a new drama entitled "Terror of the Night," written especially for television. It's a *macabre* play that will chill your spine and curdle your blood. The setting is an ancient, abandoned castle, the scene of ghostly dances. Don't miss it!

The speaker *mesmerized* his audience. He held his listeners spellbound with his eloquence. They listened as if in a hypnotic trance, quiet, obedient, unable to think for themselves.

Use Jones's Vanishing Cream to remove wrinkles! Watch those tell-tale *crow's-feet* disappear from around your eyes. Your skin will become as smooth as satin!

(2) Learn to distinguish between facts and opinions.

A fact is a statement of that which exists or has been done. It can be verified. "Water is composed of hydrogen and oxygen" and "Abraham Lincoln was the sixteenth president of the United States" are facts.

An opinion is a statement of what one believes or thinks about something. It is a viewpoint, a matter of taste or personal preference. "This country ought to take a leading part in international affairs" and "Eugene O'Neill was a better dramatist than John Galsworthy" are opinions.

When listening to evidence offered by a speaker, be careful to distinguish between his facts (which are objective) and his opinions (which are subjective). Different persons may hold different opinions based on the same facts.

● EXERCISE 13. Read aloud to the class a newspaper editorial, an excerpt from a speech, or a passage from a story which contains an unfamiliar word whose meaning can be discovered from the context. Call upon members of the class to explain the meaning of the word and to indicate the clues that made the meaning clear to them.

● EXERCISE 14. Select a word whose meaning you do not know, and look it up in a dictionary. Then use it orally in such a way that your classmates, if they listen carefully, can perceive its meaning from the context. The following list is suggestive:

abacus	liquidate
coiffure	martinet
flaunt	pedantic
florid	quixotic
haberdashery	scion
irascible	tycoon

● EXERCISE 15. Make a list of six facts. Compose six opinions based on these facts. Intersperse the twelve statements and read them aloud to your classmates to see whether they can tell the difference between a fact and an opinion.

● EXERCISE 16. Select a passage from a magazine article which contains facts and opinions. Read the passage aloud and call upon your classmates to point out the difference between the factual and the interpretive matter.

● EXERCISE 17. If you can obtain a tape recorder, record a portion of a news commentator's broadcast and play it to your class. Analyze the broadcast, distinguishing between facts and commentary.

(3) Learn to distinguish between main and subordinate ideas.[1]

A subordinate idea supports or clarifies a main idea. How can you tell the difference? There are four ways:

[1] See also the chapter on Co-ordination and Subordination, beginning on page 184.

1. *Pay particular attention to a speaker's opening remarks,* because speakers often announce in their introductions what their main points are going to be. For example:

You should go to college for three reasons, among others. First, to learn how to live wisely and happily. Secondly, to learn how to make a living. Thirdly, to learn how to carry on research for the benefit of mankind.

2. *Pay attention to ideas which are discussed at length.* A speaker usually spends more time on ideas which are important than on those which are unimportant. He repeats important ideas, usually in different ways, makes them clear by examples and anecdotes, and supports them by citing figures or quoting from authorities. Listen for restatements. Bear in mind that statistics and the testimony of experts constitute supporting evidence and are not usually main ideas in themselves.

3. *Pay attention to connecting words.* A speaker builds bridges between ideas in order to pass from one to another. When the ideas are of equal importance, he uses such helping words as *second*, *moreover*, *next*, and *finally*. When the next idea is a subordinate one, he uses such bridging words as *for example*, *for instance*, *because*, *since*, *although*, and *while*.

4. *Pay attention to the conclusion.* A speaker often repeats his main ideas just before he finishes. The conclusion of a talk, like the introduction, often lists the high lights that a speaker wants you to remember:

A college education, as we have seen, prepares a man for life, enables him to make a living, and trains him to engage in research which may benefit his fellow man.

(4) Learn to draw inferences from facts.

Thinking consists in forming conclusions based on information. An intelligent listener weighs evidence and draws inferences from it. Examine each of the following examples for the validity of the conclusion.[2]

Today is Friday the thirteenth. This morning I cut my cheek while shaving, my car broke down on my way to work, I lost my wallet, and I failed to get the raise I had expected. Thirteen is my unlucky number.

George Washington was a tall man. So were Thomas Jefferson, Andrew Jackson, and Abraham Lincoln. All great men are tall.

Seven of the regular Yankee players have batting averages of more than .300. No other team in the American League has so many players batting above that mark. Two Yankee pitchers have already won more than twenty games each. No other American League pitching staff has so good a record. The fielding percentages of all Yankee players are higher on the average than those of any other team. The Yankees are in first place because they have better pitching, fielding, and hitting than any other team.

Before going to bed last night, I put out the cat. This morning I found a dead field mouse on the terrace near the door of the house. There were tiny teeth marks on its body. The cat must have caught and killed it in her nocturnal prowlings.

(5) Learn to distinguish between ideas and illustrations of ideas.

Speakers often explain a principle by mentioning specific instances in which it applies. Careless listeners may recall the examples but miss the principle they illustrate. In the following excerpt, what general idea do the various instances exemplify?

[2] For additional work on drawing conclusions, see Chapter 26.

Nothing worth while is achieved without much time and effort. Webster spent thirty-six years on his dictionary. Bancroft required twenty-six years to write his *History of the United States.* Gibbon toiled for twenty years on his *Decline and Fall of the Roman Empire;* later he rewrote his autobiography nine times. Vergil devoted twelve years to writing the *Aeneid.* Field conceived the idea of a cable between Europe and America in 1854 but did not succeed in laying it until 1866, after six heart-breaking attempts which occupied twelve years of his life. Edison experimented more than 2,000 times before he found a suitable metal for electric lamp filaments.

(6) Learn to evaluate what you hear.

Mull over what a speaker has said. Ask yourself such questions as: Did he give a one-sided or a balanced presentation? Did he bolster his point of view with evidence? Are his facts accurate? Are his conclusions sound? What objections can be raised against his position? Do these objections weaken or nullify his arguments?

● EXERCISE 18. From an anthology of speeches or from a copy of the magazine *Vital Speeches*, select and read aloud to your classmates the opening of a speech which foretells the main points to be developed.

● EXERCISE 19. Read aloud the rest of the speech which you selected for Exercise 18 and call upon other students to show how the speaker:

1. Restates important ideas.
2. Illustrates an idea by means of an anecdote or example.
3. Indicates the relative unimportance of a subordinate idea.

● EXERCISE 20. Read aloud the conclusion of the speech used in Exercises 18 and 19, or that of any other speech, and show how the author repeats or summarizes the main ideas developed in his talk.

● EXERCISE 21. Compose two sets of facts similar to the examples given on page 544, but omit any conclusions. Read them aloud and let your listeners decide what inferences, if any, can be made from them.

● EXERCISE 22. Point out the central thought of the following talk. What illustrations does the speaker use to drive it home? Show how the conclusion repeats the main idea.

USE YOUR SPARE TIME [3]

Last month a man in Chicago refused a million dollars for an invention he had evolved *in his spare time.*

You are interested in this because it confronts you with the possibilities of *your* spare time. Did you ever stop to think that most of the world's great men have achieved their true lifework, not in the course of their needful occupations, but — *in their spare time?*

A tired-out rail splitter crouched over his tattered books by candlelight or by fire glow, at the day's end; preparing for his future, instead of snoring or skylarking like his co-laborers. Lincoln cut out his path to later immortality — *in his spare time.*

An underpaid and overworked telegraph clerk stole hours from sleep or from play, at night, trying to crystallize into realities certain fantastic dreams in which he had faith. Today the whole world is benefiting by what Edison did — *in his spare time.*

A down-at-heel instructor in an obscure college varied the drudgery he hated by spending his evenings and holidays in tinkering with a queer device of his, at which his

[3] From a speech by Bruce Barton published in article form in *The American Magazine.* Quoted in "Public Speaking as Listeners Like It," copyright 1935, Harper and Brothers. Reprinted by permission of the author and *American Magazine.*

fellow teachers laughed. But he invented the telephone — *in his spare time.*

Gentlemen, you, too, have spare time. The man who says: "I would do such and such a great thing, if only I had the time!" would do nothing if he had all the time on the calendar. There is always time — *spare time* — at the disposal of every human who has the energy to use it. USE IT!

● EXERCISE 23. Report on a radio or television talk on a controversial question. Did the speaker present both sides of the question fairly? What evidence did he offer to support his opinion? Were his facts accurate and his conclusions justified? What objections can you pose? In your judgment do these objections seriously weaken or destroy his case?

Note-Taking

32g. Learn how to take orderly notes.

There are several reasons for learning to take notes. First, taking notes on speeches helps you to concentrate. Your attention is less likely to wander. Second, you can more easily see the plan of the talk and the relationship of one point to another. Third, you have a record for further study and reflection. Finally, it is good training for college, where much of your instruction will be by means of lectures. You will have to know how to take notes if you are to succeed in your college studies.

There are two ways of taking notes. You should be familiar with both.

THE RUNNING SUMMARY

The most common method is a running summary. Here is a typical running summary of a talk delivered by a school principal before a meeting of a parent-teacher association. Notice the use of numbers to set off the main points and the use of abbreviations to save time.

"Danger signals of adolescents." 1. Difficult yrs. from 12–20. 2. Adolescent troubles preceded by danger signals. 3. No behavior characteristic is danger signal unless associated with fight or flight. 4. Flight means withdrawal from reality. 5. Fight means aggressive behavior. 6. Troublesome youth wears distinctive clothing, smokes, doesn't participate in family life, takes no part in sch. activ. or in wholesome recreation, fails in sch. 7. Good parents prevent trouble by keeping alert to danger sig. associated with flight or fight.

THE OUTLINE

Another method of taking notes is by outlining. This is a more difficult method, but it has the advantage of showing how a speaker's ideas are developed and related to one another. Compare the outline method with the running summary shown above.

DANGER SIGNALS OF ADOLESCENTS

I. Parents today have more difficult time than parents 50 yrs. ago.
   A. Yrs. 12–20 most troublesome.
   B. Adolescents display warning signals.

II. No behavior characteristic is warning signal unless associated with flight or fight.
   A. Flight means withdrawal from reality — daydreaming, shyness, etc.
   B. Fight means aggressive behavior — temper tantrums, disob., etc.

III. Five danger signals.
   A. Appearance — j. delinquents affect uniform garb.
   B. Smoking.
   C. Lack of participation in family life.

D. Lack of participation in wholesome recreation.
E. Failing sch. marks.

IV. Good parent prevents trouble. Makes correction unnec.

● EXERCISE 24. Listen to a radio or television speech or to a talk delivered at a school assembly and take notes in either running summary or outline form. Using your notes, give an oral digest of the speech. If other members of the class have listened to the same speech, compare notes.

● EXERCISE 25. As a result of your experience with Exercise 24, discuss the difficulties of note-taking. How can these difficulties be minimized or overcome?

● EXERCISE 26. Make a running summary or outline of an article which your teacher reads aloud. Compare your summary with those of your classmates.

● EXERCISE 27. Interview a college friend of yours with the purpose of finding out how he takes notes. Ask him, too, whether he found note-taking difficult when he first entered college and whether he can offer you any suggestions for improving your note-taking ability. Report your findings to the class.

Propaganda

The teachings spread by an organization or individual are called propaganda.[4]

Nowadays the word *propaganda* has unpleasant associations. It suggests wily and deceitful means of swaying people's minds.

But propaganda may be used for purposes of which we approve as well as for ones of which we disapprove.

[4] For a discussion of the steps in analyzing the logic of spoken and written matter, see Chapter 26, Clear Thinking, page 402.

A physician who tries to persuade an audience to eat sensibly is a propagandist. So is a parent who keeps telling his children that education is necessary for success in life and so, too, is a camp counselor who urges every boy to learn to swim. These people have no ax to grind. They are concerned about others' welfare. Their propaganda is beneficial.

An individual or group that tries to influence opinions or actions for selfish ends is engaging in propaganda which may be harmful. The professional propagandist is concerned with the effect of his efforts on you. He may not care whether or not that effect is beneficial to you.

32h. Learn to recognize and evaluate propaganda.

One test of propaganda is this: What is the motive behind it? If the motive is the advancement of the propagandist or the organization for which he works, the propaganda may be harmful. Examine it carefully for half-truths, distortions, and falsehoods. If the motive is your welfare or the good of society, and if the propagandist seeks no personal advantage, the propaganda may be harmless or even valuable. It is, however, still propaganda and not objective fact.

● EXERCISE 28. Report to the class examples of propaganda you have heard on radio or television, in the movies, in school, at home, or in the streets. Explain why you consider the propaganda harmful or beneficial.

PROPAGANDA DEVICES

The devices used by professional propagandists can be classified under two general headings: those associated with deliberate misuse of language, and those associated with faulty reasoning.

(1) Learn how propagandists deliberately misuse language with such devices as loaded words, name-calling, and slogans.

Words are powerful weapons. They can be used to persuade people to believe and act as propagandists want them to.

1. *Loaded words.* There are words which are loaded with emotion. You react favorably to some of them and unfavorably to others. *America*, *democracy*, *peace*, *science*, *loyalty*, *patriotism*, *home*, *liberty*, *progress* are examples of words which have positive appeal. Other words stir up unfavorable reactions. *Drunkard*, *poverty*, *slave*, *reactionary*, *imperialism* are examples of words that evoke negative responses.

High-powered propagandists use positively loaded words to evoke favorable reactions. They use them, for example, in the titles of subversive organizations:

League for Peace and Progress
Organization for a Progressive and Peaceful America
Society to Promote Liberty and Democracy

Advertisers make effective use of loaded words. A toothpaste advertisement promises to give you "The smile of beauty, the smile of health." A cereal advertises itself as "The breakfast of champions." A timepiece is called "The world's most honored watch."

Politicians use negatively loaded words to create opposition. "Don't be a reactionary! Vote against Proposition 5!" "Oppose these imperialist policies. Write to your senator today!"

Years ago eggs were classified as small, medium, and large. Advertisers changed the classification to medium, large, and extra-large. The result was an immediate upsurge in sales, a testimony to the power of loaded words!

2. *Name-calling.* This is a device by which a speaker attempts to defeat an opponent not by rational arguments but by calling him names or smearing his reputation. Mudslinging of this sort is not worthy of anyone. Do not repeat a smear and do not believe it until the person under attack has had a full opportunity to reply or until you have examined the evidence.

3. *Slogans.* Propagandists know the value of a slogan. It is simple, catchy, and easily remembered. An involved train of thought is hard to follow. A series of arguments is hard to remember. A slogan makes thinking unnecessary. It oversimplifies by reducing a chain of arguments to a few words.

Slogans play an important part in politics and advertising. When you hear a slogan, remember that it does not tell a complete story. It is a device to capture your attention and memory.

Here are some examples of effective slogans:

The life you save may be your own!
Ask the man who owns one!
Make the world safe for democracy.
The right is more precious than the peace.
Go west, young man!
Liberty, equality, and fraternity.

(2) Learn to recognize the propagandist's false reasoning, embodied in such devices as the testimonial, the unproved assertion, ascribing the wrong cause to an effect, begging the question, setting up a straw man, generalizing from insufficient evidence, and the band wagon.

Unless you are alert you may not perceive the illogical arguments used by propagandists to achieve their ends.

1. *The testimonial.* Sometimes statements by well-known personalities are used to persuade you to vote a certain way, buy a certain product, or adopt a certain belief. For example, a movie star endorses a cold cream; a famous baseball player says that such-and-such a razor is best; a society matron reports her satisfaction with a brand of cigarettes; a campaign orator announces that a popular singer is going to vote for his candidate.

Apply these questions to any testimonial:

a. *Is the speaker an authority in the field?* A renowned scientist, for example, should be heard with respect when he discusses scientific matters but with less confidence when he talks about music, art, or politics — subjects which are outside his area of competence.

b. *Is the speaker unbiased?* Is he paid for his testimonial or does he stand to gain in any other way by it? If so, there is a strong possibility of bias. At times it is difficult to discover bias. Knowing something about the speaker's background and reputation helps. Has he a reputation for accuracy and truthfulness, or has he frequently resorted to inaccuracies and exaggerations?

2. *The unproved assertion.* Repetition is not proof. Unless the restatement is accompanied by reasons, statistics, examples, or the statements of competent and unprejudiced authorities, it is no stronger than the original utterance.

The following declaration seems to prove a point. Actually it does not because there is no evidence offered.

My candidate is the best qualified of all. In character, experience, education, and intellectual ability he is superior to everyone who is running for this office. No one even remotely approaches his qualifications for the position. He stands head and shoulders above the other candidates. Everyone admits his superior merits. Therefore he deserves your vote.

3. *Ascribing the wrong cause to an effect.* Because one event follows another, the first is not necessarily the cause of the second. For example:

A speaker at a political gathering declared, "When our party was in power, there was no unemployment, wages were higher, and money was plentiful." He did not mention that the country was at war when his party was in office and that during wartime there is always a scarcity of manpower, an increase in wages, and an abundance of money because consumer goods are not available for purchase.

"I took some sulphur and molasses when spring began," a man remarked, "and I haven't had a cold since. Use sulphur and molasses to prevent colds." The absence of colds might have been owing to other causes.

A result can be credited to a specific cause only when all other possibilities have been ruled out of consideration. Do not jump to conclusions!

4. *Begging the question.* Sometimes a propagandist states his position as a truth that needs no proof. He fails to bring out arguments supporting his position, or he ignores the real issue. This type of fallacious reasoning is called begging the question.

At a school assembly a student speaker pointed out that all the student council presidents for the past four years were members of his party; for that reason, he implied, his party's candidates for office this year should be elected. He begged the question: What were the qualifications of his party's candidates and what were their viewpoints on the issues before the student body?

A debater argued that students should be permitted to smoke in school because they smoked outside of school. He ignored the real issue: Is smoking beneficial for teen-agers? If it is not, should the school permit it?

5. *The straw man.* A common device is to state an opponent's case incompletely and then knock it down as if it were a man made of straw.

A student argued that secret fraternities should be banned on the grounds that they were undemocratic, harmful to their members, questionable in their methods, and destructive of school spirit.

In rebuttal, a fraternity member said: "The only argument against secret fraternities is that not everyone may join." After this inadequate reconstruction of the opposing point of view, he proceeded to demolish it handily. He should, of course, have presented his opponent's case fairly and then attempted to refute the arguments point by point.

6. *Generalizing from insufficient evidence.* A conclusion should be based on adequate evidence. A few instances do not prove an argument unless they can be shown to be typical. Figures should represent a fair sampling of cases. Only quotations by reliable, qualified, and unbiased authorities should be used. If only a few logical reasons are presented, they should be strong and convincing.

A rabble-rouser on a street corner pointed out that several recent crimes were committed by members of the same race. "It goes to show," he shouted, "that all members of this race are alike." Obviously he should not form such a sweeping judgment on the acts of a few individuals.

7. *The band wagon.* Most people like to do what others are doing and believe as others believe. Propagandists know and capitalize on this human tendency.

"Everybody is joining our cause," they say. "Come along or you'll find yourself alone."

It requires will power and the ability to think for oneself to resist hopping on the band wagon. Do not be fooled into joining a movement simply because "others are doing it."

● EXERCISE 29. Out of your experience as a listener, give an example of five of the following propaganda devices and errors in thinking.

Loaded words	Ascribing the wrong cause to an effect
Name-calling	The straw man
Slogans	Generalizing from insufficient evidence
The testimonial	The band wagon
The unproved assertion	
Begging the question	

● EXERCISE 30. Copy a radio or television commercial which makes use of loaded words. Discuss their emotional overtones.

● EXERCISE 31. Report on a radio or television commercial which contains a testimonial by some well-known person. Is the person an authority on the subject he speaks about? Is he unbiased? Is he reliable?

● EXERCISE 32. Bring to class examples of slogans used in advertisements and in past or present political campaigns. Explain what makes a slogan an effective device for influencing thinking and action.

● EXERCISE 33. Ask your parents or friends whether they were ever deceived by propaganda. Find out the details and report the incident to your class. What propaganda devices were used in each case?

PART EIGHT

MECHANICS

CHAPTER 33

Capitalization

USE CAPITAL LETTERS ACCORDING TO STANDARD USAGE

Capital letters serve many purposes. They indicate the beginnings of sentences, an important aid to the reader; they distinguish names, titles, etc., from the rest of the sentence (*The Black River divides Port Huron*); they show respect (*the worship of God*). On the other hand, many uses of capital letters are merely conventions; i.e., they are usages customarily observed by educated people for no other reason than that they are customary. Readers expect capital letters to be used according to rules established by custom; in other words, according to *standard usage*. A writer should follow the conventional usage expected of him just as he follows the conventions of correct spelling, grammatical usage, and punctuation.

In the use of capital letters, as in all matters pertaining to language usage, variations and inconsistencies are common. In standard usage, for instance, the names of the seasons are not capitalized, but some newspapers do capitalize them. Newspapers also may adopt what they call the "down style" of capitalization in which words like *street*, *high school*, *club* are not capitalized as they are in standard usage when used with a particular name.

STANDARD USAGE	NEWSPAPER "DOWN STYLE"
Twenty-first Street	Twenty-first street
Bellmore High School	Bellmore high school
Hunting and Fishing Club	Hunting and Fishing club

The usage described in this book is standard ("up style") usage, which is followed in books and magazines. Review the rules and do the exercises so that you will be able to check accurately the capitalization in your own writing.

33a. Capitalize the pronoun *I* and the interjection O.

You will probably have little use for the interjection *O*, which is used only in such rare expressions as "O Happy Day, come soon!" The common interjection *oh* ("Oh, what a beautiful morning!") is capitalized only when it appears at the beginning of a sentence. It is always followed by a mark of punctuation, but *O* is never followed by punctuation.

EXAMPLES Help us, **O** mightiest of all!
He said he was sorry, **oh**, so sorry!

33b. Capitalize the first word in any sentence.

If failure to use a capital letter at the beginning of a sentence is one of your faults, you should review Chapter 5, "The Complete Sentence," because the error is almost invariably due to failure to recognize the end of one sentence and the beginning of the next

(1) Capitalize the first word of a formal statement following a colon.

EXAMPLE The following statement was released to the press: For reasons of national security, details of the defense program cannot be given to the general public at this time.

(2) Capitalize the first word of a resolution following the word *Resolved.*

EXAMPLE Resolved, That American aid to undeveloped countries should be increased.

(3) Capitalize the first word of a direct quotation.

EXAMPLE Mr. Jackson said, "Your sister is her own worst enemy."

Do not capitalize the first word of a quoted sentence fragment.

EXAMPLE I agree with Mr. Jackson's remark that my sister is "her own worst enemy."

(4) Capitalize the first word of a statement or question inserted in a sentence without quotation marks.

EXAMPLE Our problem is, How can we get somebody to help us?

33c. Capitalize proper nouns and proper adjectives.

A proper noun is the name of a particular person, place, thing, or idea. The opposite of a proper noun is a common noun, which is not capitalized.

PROPER NOUNS	COMMON NOUNS
James McCall	man
Canada	country
Mohawk River	river

▶ NOTE: Words which name a kind or a type (*spaniel, sloop, sedan*) are not capitalized. Names given to individuals within the type are proper nouns and are capitalized (Fido, *Blue Boy*, Buick).

A proper adjective is an adjective formed from a proper noun.

PROPER NOUNS	PROPER ADJECTIVES
England	English
Europe	European

Study the following classifications of proper nouns.

(1) Capitalize the names of persons.

Before writing names beginning with *Mc* or *Mac* (meaning "son of"), find out whether or not the person spells his name with two capitals. Custom varies: *McDonald*, *MacNutt*, *Macdonald*, *Macmillan*, *Macbeth*, etc. Names beginning with *O'* (meaning "of the family of") usually contain two capitals: *O'Reilly*, *O'Neill*.

The abbreviations *Sr.* and *Jr.* following a name are capitalized: *Henry Morgan, Sr.; Robert Lawton, Jr.*

(2) Capitalize geographical names.

CITIES, TOWNSHIPS, COUNTIES, STATES, COUNTRIES, CONTINENTS Garden City, Hempstead Township, Nassau County, New York, United States of America, North America

ISLANDS, PENINSULAS, STRAITS, BEACHES Sea Island, Iberian Peninsula, Strait of Gibraltar, Silver Beach

BODIES OF WATER Arrowhead Lake, Lake Superior, Red River, Atlantic Ocean, Baltic Sea, Cedar Pond, Peconic Bay

MOUNTAINS Rocky Mountains, Pikes Peak

STREETS Washington Avenue, Whitehall Boulevard, Dover Parkway, Pennsylvania Turnpike, Forty-second Street [In a hyphenated street number, the second word begins with a small letter.]

PARKS, FORESTS, CANYONS, DAMS Yosemite National Park, Belmont State Forest, Grand Canyon, Hoover Dam

RECOGNIZED SECTIONS OF THE COUNTRY OR WORLD the South, the Northwest, the Far East

(3) Do not capitalize *east, west, north,* and *south* when they indicate directions. Do capitalize them when they refer to recognized sections of the country.

33c

EXAMPLES Turn **e**ast at the next corner, and you will see the church on the **n**orth side of the street.
To understand America, visit the **Middle West**.
We were going **s**outh, and the car that hit us was going **e**ast.
We are going **S**outh for the winter.

The modern tendency is to write nouns and adjectives derived from *East*, *West*, *North*, and *South* without capital letters (a *southerner*, *southern* hospitality, *northern* cities, *middle-western* customs), but in the light of conflicting authorities, the capitalization of such words is also correct.

Adjectives specifying direction are not capitalized unless they are part of the name of a country: southern Ohio, eastern Russia, but West Germany, North Borneo.

(4) Do not capitalize a word used with a proper noun or adjective *unless* the word is part of a name, in which case it is a proper noun.

EXAMPLES the great **c**ity of Chicago, New York **C**ity; the beautiful **v**alley of the Hudson, the Hudson **V**alley; a Pacific **i**sland, Wake **I**sland
a popular Chinese **r**estaurant, Sing Lee's Chinese **R**estaurant; an Oregon **c**ollege, Oregon State **C**ollege

In spite of their origin, some nouns and adjectives derived from proper names are not capitalized: *mackintosh*, *macadam*, *morocco* leather, *china* dishes. Most words of this nature, however, may be written with or without capital letters: *roman* (*Roman*) *numerals*, *plaster of paris* (*Paris*), *venetian* (*Venetian*) *blinds*, *turkish* (*Turkish*) *bath*, *gothic* (*Gothic*) *style*, etc. When you are in doubt about the capitalization of words of this kind, refer to your dictionary.

● EXERCISE 1. Number on your paper from 1 to 25. In each of the following items you are to choose the correct one of two forms. After the proper number on your paper, write the letter of the correct form (*a* or *b*). In three of the items, both forms are correct; write both *a* and *b*.

1. a. the Amazon river
   b. the Amazon River
2. a. He said, "Wait for me."
   b. He said, "wait for me."
3. a. strait of Magellan
   b. Strait of Magellan
4. a. Oxford boulevard
   b. Oxford Boulevard
5. a. I heard him say he was "tired of being good."
   b. I heard him say he was "Tired of being good."
6. a. Norwegian settlers
   b. Norwegian Settlers
7. a. Aegean sea
   b. Aegean Sea
8. a. James Macdougall
   b. James MacDougall
9. a. Westchester County roads
   b. Westchester County Roads
10. a. north of the barn
    b. North of the barn
11. a. the Malay peninsula
    b. the Malay Peninsula
12. a. Twenty-Third Street
    b. Twenty-third Street
13. a. Grand Coulee Dam
    b. Grand Coulee dam
14. a. William Winter, Jr.
    b. William Winter, jr.
15. a. people of the Far East
    b. people of the far east
16. a. Southern fried chicken
    b. southern fried chicken
17. a. a French poodle
    b. a French Poodle
18. a. Clearwater Beach
    b. Clearwater beach
19. a. valley of the Ohio
    b. Valley of the Ohio
20. a. Grand Teton national Park
    b. Grand Teton National Park
21. a. Go south for three miles.
    b. Go South for three miles.
22. a. Jericho Turnpike
    b. Jericho turnpike
23. a. Western Pennsylvania
    b. western Pennsylvania
24. a. Timothy O'neill
    b. Timothy O'Neill
25. a. venetian blinds
    b. Venetian blinds

● EXERCISE 2. Copy the following, using capital letters wherever they are required; or prepare to write them from your teacher's dictation.

1. essex county
2. an african village
3. dallas, texas
4. latin america
5. two miles west
6. pioneering in the west
7. thirty-fourth street
8. great salt lake
9. glacier national park
10. the indian ocean
11. the catskill mountains
12. in the city of san francisco
13. a popular british composer
14. an english bulldog
15. mackinac island
16. a ford station wagon
17. ford truck
18. elmore county
19. the canadian wilderness
20. george o'connor, jr.

(5) Capitalize names of organizations, institutions, buildings, business firms, brand names of business products, ships, planes, trains, special events, historical events and periods, items on the calendar, government bodies, races, religions, and nationalities.

ORGANIZATIONS AND INSTITUTIONS Spanish Club, League of Women Voters, Princeton University, Arizona State College, Franklin High School, Plaza Theater, Roosevelt Hotel, English Department, Senior Class[1]

▶ NOTE: Do not capitalize such words as *hotel*, *theater*, *church*, *high school*, *college*, and *university* unless they are part of a proper name.

Onondaga **H**otel	a **h**otel in Syracuse
University of Michigan	a **u**niversity in Michigan
Emerson **H**igh **S**chool	a **h**igh **s**chool textbook
United States **P**ost **O**ffice	the local **p**ost **o**ffice

[1] Names of school classes may or may not be capitalized, but the modern tendency is to capitalize them; however, the words *senior*, *junior*, *sophomore*, *freshman* are not capitalized when used alone: *A freshman attended the meeting of the Senior Class.*

BUILDINGS, BUSINESS FIRMS, AND BRAND NAMES OF BUSINESS PRODUCTS Chrysler Building, Union Pacific Station, Pennsylvania Railroad, American Air Lines, Minnesota Mining and Manufacturing Company, Cheerios, Coca-Cola

▶ NOTE: The common noun which often follows a brand name is not capitalized except in advertising displays: *Tip-Top bread*, *Calumet baking powder*.

SHIPS, PLANES, TRAINS the *Constitution* (ship), the *Convair* (plane), the *Empire State Express* (train)

SPECIAL EVENTS National Open Golf Championships, World Series, American Legion Convention, Junior Prom

HISTORICAL EVENTS AND PERIODS Battle of the Coral Sea, Middle Ages, French Revolution, World War II

CALENDAR ITEMS Sunday, November, Christmas Eve, Labor Day, Book Week

▶ NOTE: Names of the seasons are not capitalized unless personified.

EXAMPLES a late spring
Spring in her green dress

GOVERNMENT BODIES Congress, House of Representatives, Securities and Exchange Commission, Treasury Department

▶ NOTE: The names of government bodies are capitalized when they are the exact names. Do not capitalize such general names as the following: *the state legislature*, the latest *department* meeting.

Do not capitalize the word *party* in *Democratic party*, *Republican party*.

RACES, RELIGIONS, NATIONALITIES Caucasian, Negro, Semitic, Roman Catholic, Baptist, Indian, Australian

(6) Do not capitalize the names of school subjects, except the languages. Course names followed by a number are usually capitalized.

EXAMPLES English, French, Spanish, Latin, German, Italian
algebra, art, chemistry, domestic science, modern European history
Algebra II, History III, Art 102

▶ NOTE: Schoolrooms and other nouns followed by a numeral or letter are usually capitalized: *Room 31*, *Parlor B*, *School District 18*, *Chapter 4.*

● EXERCISE 3. Copy the following, using capital letters wherever they are required; or prepare to write the list from your teacher's dictation.

1. cambridge university
2. the sophomore class
3. a neighborhood theater
4. hillsdale central high school
5. He is a sophomore.
6. a negro orchestra
7. a royal typewriter
8. summer vacation
9. the arcade theater
10. geometry
11. interstate commerce commission
12. biology II
13. the shafer building
14. memorial day
15. chemistry department
16. skippy peanut butter
17. republican party
18. national education association
19. sunset limited (train)
20. members of the department
21. the american revolution
22. the battle of bunker hill
23. the drake relays
24. fairview country club
25. a swedish restaurant

● EXERCISE 4. This exercise covers all capitalization rules presented to this point. Write in order in a list the words which should be capitalized in each sentence. When the capitalized words belong in one phrase, write them as a phrase: *Sunrise Highway*, *Jefferson Memorial Library.* Indicate in which sentence each word or word group appears.

EXAMPLE 1. As a child in montclair, new jersey, I used to play in anderson park.

1. Montclair, New Jersey
Anderson Park

1. Mr. glenn, our science teacher, took his sophomore biology classes to willow creek to collect specimens for the high school laboratories.
2. This winter we have been studying in social studies III the pioneers who settled in the west during the years following the civil war.
3. The university of wisconsin is situated on lake mendota in madison, the capital of the state.
4. Residents of five school districts in shannon county voted to build a new central high school and junior college as recommended by the state department of education.
5. In washington, d.c., during the annual spring trip of the senior class, those seniors who are members of the art club visited the national gallery of art.
6. The new massachusetts mutual building stands on the former site of the st. nicholas collegiate reformed church next to rockefeller center on the corner of fifth avenue and forty-eighth street.
7. Mr. frank mills, jr., is faculty adviser to the junior class and is personally acquainted with every junior in the high school.
8. One mile north of the village of turnerville, the lincoln highway crosses salt creek near the entrance to cameron state park.
9. The state theater and the park hotel on main street will be torn down to make room for the approach to the new marlborough bridge.
10. Harry mcdonald, who has a natural scotch accent, read some of robert burns's poems to our english class on monday afternoon.
11. Hamilton gardner, owner of the gardner baking company, makers of tasty crust bread and pastries, endowed the city's new hospital, which will be built in avon park and known as the gardner general hospital.

33d. Capitalize titles.

(1) Capitalize the title of a person if the title precedes the person's name. Capitalize a title used alone or

following a person's name only if it refers to a high government official or to someone to whom you wish to show special respect.

EXAMPLES Superintendent Williams, Dean Marsh, General Bradley, President Drake
Dr. Williams, superintendent of schools; Miss Marsh, dean of girls; John Drake, president of our class; but De Witt Clinton, Governor of New York; Charles Evans Hughes, Chief Justice [titles of high government officials]
the Senator, but the work of a senator; the General's orders, but the insigne of a general; the Chief Justice, the Secretary of Agriculture, the Duke of Windsor.

▶ NOTE: When used to refer to the head of a nation, the word *president* is always capitalized. Two capitals are required in *vice-president* when it refers to the Vice-President of a nation. The words *ex-* and *-elect* used with a title are not capitalized: *ex-President*, *Governor-elect*.

▶ NOTE: Capitalize words of family relationship when used with a person's name unless they are preceded by a possessive noun or pronoun: *Uncle Tom*, *Cousin Jim*, *my cousin Jim*. Do not capitalize words of family relationship when they are preceded by a possessive noun or pronoun; *your mother*, *Bill's sister*. Words of family relationship may be capitalized or not when used in place of a person's name.

EXAMPLES Ask Mother. [*Mother* is used in place of the woman's name.]
Ask mother.

(2) Capitalize the first word and all important words in the titles of books, magazines, newspapers, articles, historical documents, laws, and works of art: *A Tale of Two Cities*, *Saturday Review*, *New York Times*, Treaty of Paris, Sherman Antitrust Act, *The Calmady Children* (painting).

▶ NOTE: The words *a*, *an*, *the*, written before a title, are capitalized only when they are part of the title. Before the names of magazines and newspapers, they are not capitalized.

EXAMPLES ***The Last of the Mohicans, An Inland Voyage*** [*The* and *An* are part of the title.]
the *Principles of Sociology* [*The* is not part of the title.]
the *Saturday Evening Post*, the *Los Angeles Times*

(3) Capitalize words referring to the Deity, Christ, and Mary: God, Father, Saviour, His will, the Virgin.

▶ NOTE: Pronouns referring to God are usually capitalized, except the relative pronouns *who* and *whom*.

EXAMPLES **God revealed Himself to His followers.**
Pray to God, who helps the afflicted.

The word *god*, when used to refer to the pagan deities of the ancients, is not capitalized.

EXAMPLE **Achilles' mother asked the other gods to help her son.**

● EXERCISE 5. Number on your paper from 1 to 25. Copy after the proper number all items to which capitals must be added. Leave a blank space after the number of a correct item.

1. captain Blake
2. the congressman rose to speak
3. Mrs. Goldberg, the librarian
4. our class president
5. the governor of Alabama
6. the vice-president of the United States
7. Father Casey, an Army chaplain
8. ex-president Hoover
9. the leader of the guerrillas
10. a captain in the Army
11. the lord in his wisdom
12. aunt Louise
13. senator Feinberg
14. mayor Lane of Stamford
15. W. S. Thompson, assistant principal
16. the case of the missing mail (book)

17. the new republic (magazine)
18. the monroe doctrine
19. Mr. Lane, mayor of Stamford
20. your uncle
21. the Washington post (newspaper)
22. responsibilities of a senator
23. god whom we worship for his goodness
24. Ben Hogan, former national champion
25. the marshall plan

SUMMARY STYLE SHEET

Mexico *City*	a *city* in Mexico
Ocala *National Forest*	our *national forests*
Twenty-ninth *Street*	across the *street*
Houghton *Lake*	a shallow *lake*
the *South*	a mile *south* (*north*, *east*, *west*)
North America	*northern* Wisconsin
the Explorers' *Club*	a *club* for explorers
Ford Motor *Company*	an automobile *company*
Central *High School*	a new *high school*
Pomona *College*	four years in *college*
the American *Revolution*	a successful *revolution*
the Wrigley *Building*	a Chicago *building*
the *Fourth* of July	the *fifth* of July
the *Senior Ball*	a *ball* given by *seniors*
the *Freshman Class*	*freshman classes*
English, French, Latin	social studies, physics, art
History II	a course in world *history*
Winter's frosty breath	spring, summer, *winter*, fall
Principal Langley	Mr. Langley, the *principal*
the *President* (U.S.)	the *president* of our club
the *Senator*	a *senator's* duties
God made *His* will known.	tribal *gods* of the Indians
Don't tell *Mother* (or *mother*).	Don't tell my *mother*.
Uncle Bill	my *uncle*

Democratic *party*
Ivory *soap*
a Negro, a Presbyterian, a Swede
The Last of the Mohicans
the *Reader's Digest*

● EXERCISE 6. This exercise covers all capitalization rules in the chapter. Write in order in a list the words which should be capitalized in each sentence as you did in Exercise 4.

1. The republican club of edgemont county has established an office in the Roosevelt hotel.
2. In their english classes this term the juniors have read *giants in the earth*, a novel about the norwegian immigrants who settled in the dakotas.
3. According to professor Schwartz, Tennyson's *idylls of the king* was published in 1859, the same year that saw the publication of Darwin's *origin of species* and Fitzgerald's translation of the *rubáiyát of omar khayyám.*
4. The president went to national airport to bid farewell to the secretary of state who, with his secretary, was taking off for europe on an important mission.
5. Since he is not a high school graduate, Russell is taking courses at Springfield vocational school to prepare for a position with the Bowman engineering company, manufacturers of everlast electric motors.
6. After spending several winters in the northwest, my father sought a warm climate and moved to the south, finally entering the real estate business in madeira beach, florida, on the east side of the gulf of mexico.
7. To the glory of god, the early christian missionaries to north america succeeded in converting the indians from the worship of their pagan gods to the worship of him who loves rather than hates mankind.
8. Dr. Eugene Walker, jr., principal of the high school, explained why all sophomores are required to take history II and biology.
9. The treaty of versailles, which followed world war I, specified that germany should lose its colonies, the african colonies being made french and english mandates under the league of nations.

CHAPTER 34

Punctuation

USE PUNCTUATION FOR CLEARNESS AND ACCORDING TO STANDARD USAGE

Punctuation is used to make the meaning of a sentence clear to the reader. Some marks of punctuation are used to indicate in written English the pauses and stops which the voice makes in spoken English. They indicate not only where a pause should come but also the extent of the pause, the comma standing for a slight hesitation, the period for a longer one. Inflections in the voice are conveyed by the question mark and the exclamation point. Quotation marks and apostrophes serve to clarify writing. Although from the reader's point of view the apostrophe is the least essential mark of punctuation, apostrophes are used by careful writers according to very definite rules based upon custom. Just as you have learned to follow other conventions in grammatical usage and spelling, you should learn to follow the conventional uses of the apostrophe and other punctuation marks.

A complete statement of the correct uses of all punctuation marks is provided in this chapter together with exercises to help you fix these uses in your mind. Punctuating exercises is at best an artificial activity, however, and you must be very careful to carry over into your writing the punctuation principles you have learned. Since punctuation is so closely related to meaning, you probably should punctuate as you write, for while you are writing you continually use punctuation to group certain ideas together and to separate other ideas from each other. On the other hand, many writers prefer to concentrate first on getting their ideas onto paper; then they go back over what they have written and insert whatever punctuation is necessary to make the writing clear and conventionally correct. This latter process, known as proofreading, is a very important part of writing. Never consider a piece of writing finished unless you have proofread it carefully.

Using too much punctuation is just as bad as using too little. Do not overpunctuate. Use a mark of punctuation for only two reasons: (1) because meaning demands it, or (2) because conventional usage requires it. Otherwise omit punctuation.

End Marks

34a. A statement is followed by a period.

EXAMPLE **Summer vacation begins June 26.**

34b. An abbreviation is followed by a period.[1]

Ave.	Avenue
A.D.	*anno Domini* (Latin)
Dec.	December
Dr.	Doctor

34c. A question is followed by a question mark.

(1) Distinguish between a statement containing an indirect question and a sentence which asks a question directly.

[1] For fuller discussion of abbreviations see page 613.

34 a-c

EXAMPLES She wants to know what the assignment is. [statement containing an indirect question — followed by a period]

Do you know what the assignment is? [a direct question — followed by a question mark]

(2) Polite requests in question form (frequently used in business letters) may be followed by a period; a question mark would, of course, be perfectly correct.

EXAMPLES Will you please ship this order three weeks before Christmas.

Will you please ship this order three weeks before Christmas?

(3) A question mark should be placed inside quotation marks when the quotation is a question. Otherwise, it should be placed outside the quotation marks.

EXAMPLES John asked, "Have you heard from Joe?" [The quotation is a question.]

Did you say, "Meet me at eight o'clock"? [The quotation is not a question. The whole sentence, however, is a question.]

34d. An exclamation is followed by an exclamation point.

EXAMPLES What a beautiful dress!

How expensive!

For goodness' sake!

(1) Many exclamations begin either with "What a . . ." or "How . . ." as in the first two of the preceding examples. When you begin a sentence with these words, check your end mark carefully.

(2) An interjection at the beginning of a sentence is usually followed by a comma.

CUSTOMARY Ah, there you have me!
RARE Ah! There you have me!

(3) An exclamation point should be placed inside quotation marks when the quotation is an exclamation. Otherwise, it should be placed outside the quotation marks.

EXAMPLES "What a game that was!" exclaimed the coach.
How foolish of him to say in the fifth inning, "The game is won"!

● EXERCISE 1. Many periods and all exclamation and question marks have been omitted from the following passage. Copy in a column on your paper all words which you think should be followed by end marks. After each word write the end mark required. If a new sentence should begin after the end mark, write the first word of the sentence, giving it a capital letter. Before each word write the number of the line in which it appears.

EXAMPLE
1 "What an exciting picture" exclaimed my
2 companion as we left the theater wasn't it
3 too bad I couldn't agree with him the
4 picture had been . . .

1. picture!
2. theater. Wasn't
3. him? The

1 Janet Smith, wife of Herman T Smith, M D,
2 stopped her car behind an enormous truck "Whew"
3 she sighed. "What a lot of traffic" Presently the
4 cars at her right moved forward, but not the truck
5 ahead although in a hurry, she accepted the fact that
6 Sixth St at this hour was an overcrowded thorough-
7 fare, and she decided to be patient. The taxi driver

behind her, however, had a different idea he honked his horn the sound startled Mrs Smith, but what could she do anyone could see the truck was blocking her way. "How stupid some drivers are" she thought. The insistent honking continued, and Mrs Smith became annoyed when the truck moved on, she deliberately made a slow start and felt rewarded when the horn behind her broke into a deluge of noise.

When the light turned green at the next corner, she was about to press the accelerator when another horn, of deeper tone but just as unpleasant, broke out in the rear "All right All right" she exclaimed. "Hold your horses" When, after a number of similar incidents, she turned into her own drive, she was thoroughly sick of horns and ill-mannered drivers.

That evening, as Mrs Smith settled down to her favorite television program, her nerves were shattered again by a too familiar sound. "Good heavens" she exclaimed. "Will I never have any peace" Looking across the front lawn, she saw Hal Jordan's jalopy at the curb Hal was calling for Jimmy Smith. "Jimmy," she shouted, "come here at once" Jimmy stopped short in the second of his usual two leaps from stairway to door. "Jimmy, you tell that Hal Jordan he is never to honk that horn in front of this house again can't he walk up to the door and ask for you is he a cripple" Her words were drowned by Hal's obliging repetition of the two long and three short blasts Jimmy escaped, leaving his mother still talking but inaudible.

"Cut it out" she heard him yell "Do you love the sound of that horn"

When Dr Smith came in from a late call, his wife gave him an account of her experience with horn-blowers "I will propose to the Governor tomorrow morning," he said, "that auto horns be made inoperable when the car is not in motion wouldn't that be a good law" Mrs Smith stood in speechless admiration of her sensible husband.

The Comma

ITEMS IN A SERIES

34e. Use commas to separate items in a series.

EXAMPLES He was formerly on the staff of the embassies in Moscow, Berlin, Vienna, and Madrid.
We had a refreshing, exciting, entertaining experience.
There were toys for the children, tools for Father, and books for Mother.

▶ NOTE: Do not place a comma before the first item or after the last item in a series.

WRONG During the summer the workmen had installed, a new gymnasium floor, an improved heating system, and green chalkboards, in the high school building.

RIGHT During the summer the workmen had installed a new gymnasium floor, an improved heating system, and green chalkboards in the high school building.

(1) Publishers disagree about the use of a comma before the *and* joining the last two items in a series. Just as writers follow the practice preferred by their publishers, so you should follow the practice preferred by your teacher. There are some constructions in which the inclusion or omission of this comma affects the meaning of the sentence.

EXAMPLES American folk songs may be classified in the following categories: marching songs, work songs, ballads, old hymns, and spirituals. [five categories]
American folk songs may be classified in the following categories: marching songs, work songs, ballads, old hymns and spirituals. [four categories]

▶ NOTE: Words customarily used in pairs are set off as one item in a series: *bag and baggage*, *pen and ink*, *hat and coat*, *pork and beans*, *bread and butter*, etc.

EXAMPLE For lunch she served a fruit cup, macaroni and cheese, salad, ice cream and cake, and coffee.

(2) If all items in a series are joined by *and* or *or*, do not use commas.

EXAMPLE The weather man predicted rain or sleet or snow.

(3) Do not use a comma before the final adjective in a series if the adjective is thought of as part of the noun.

WRONG It was a cold, raw, dark, November day.

RIGHT It was a cold, raw, dark November day. [*November day* is considered as one word, one item. The adjectives modify *November day*, not *day*.]

RIGHT She is a pretty, charming, talented young woman. [*Young woman* is thought of as one word.]

▶ NOTE: If one of the words in a series modifies another word in the series, do not separate them by a comma.

EXAMPLE She wore a long, *bright blue* gown.

(4) Short main clauses in a series may be separated by commas.

EXAMPLE We worked, we played, we ate, and we gained weight.

● EXERCISE 2. The following sentences contain series requiring commas. Number on your paper from 1 to 10. Copy after the proper number the words in each sentence which should be followed by a comma, placing the comma after the word. Since the meaning of some sentences may be determined by the punctuation, you should be prepared to explain the punctuation you use.

1. Mr. James asked the waiter for coffee beans and ham and eggs.
2. States included in the Japanese beetle area are New York New Jersey Maryland and Delaware.
3. Everyone turned to watch the large pale yellow moon.
4. This policy covers medical expenses iron-lung rental hospitalization and transportation to a center of treatment.
5. The train pulled out and left me in a strange town without my luggage hat and coat and credentials.
6. The wagon train was approaching lonely wild Indian country.
7. The wind froze us the rain soaked us and the waves tossed us.
8. For their annual picnic this year the freshmen went to Belmont Park the sophomores to Long Beach the juniors and seniors to Cedar Lake.
9. He found that it was a friendly unsophisticated little town that he had chosen for his home.
10. She is pretty tall and blonde; her sister is small and dark and beautiful.

INTERRUPTERS

34f. Use commas to set off expressions which interrupt the sentence.

To set off an expression takes two commas unless the expression comes first or last in the sentence.

(1) Appositives with their modifiers are set off by commas.

An appositive is a word — with or without modifiers — that follows a noun or pronoun and identifies or explains it.

EXAMPLE A syndicated column by Bernard Silverman, the noted author, will appear in the *Times-News*, a local paper.

34f

When an appositive is so closely related to the word it modifies that it appears to be part of that word, no comma is necessary. An appositive of this kind is called a restrictive appositive. Usually it is one word.

EXAMPLES His cousin Arthur
The novel *Windswept*
Your friend Jean
William the Conqueror
The conjunction *and*

(2) Words used in direct address are set off by commas.

EXAMPLES I don't know, Alice, where your brother is.
Sam, please come here.
Your grades are disappointing, my boy.

(3) Parenthetical expressions are set off by commas.

The following expressions are commonly used parenthetically: *I believe* (*think*, *know*, *hope*, etc.), *I am sure*, *on the contrary*, *on the other hand*, *after all*, *by the way*, *incidentally*, *of course*, *in my opinion*, *for example*, *however*, *nevertheless*, *to tell the truth*.

EXAMPLES My father will, I am sure, let me have the car tonight.
The weight of the car, of course, determines the price of the license.

Knowledge of the above rule and of the expressions commonly used parenthetically is helpful in punctuating, but you should understand that the author's intention is the determining factor governing the punctuation. If he wishes the reader to pause, to regard an expression as parenthetical, he sets it off; if not, he leaves it unpunctuated. Sometimes, however, the placement of the expression in the sentence determines the punctuation. Study the following examples, noting the cases in which the comma is a matter of choice and the cases in which the placement of the expression governs the punctuation. All the examples given illustrate correct usage.

1. This is *indeed* a great piece of news.
   This is, *indeed*, a great piece of news.
   Indeed, this is a great piece of news. [comma required by placement]
2. We *therefore* agreed to sign the petition.
   We, *therefore*, agreed to sign the petition.
   We agreed, *therefore*, to sign the petition. [comma required by placement]
3. *I hope* this raise in salary will relieve your financial distress. [no comma because of placement]
   This raise in salary will, *I hope*, relieve your financial distress. [comma required by placement]

(4) Certain words when used at the beginning of a sentence or remark are followed by a comma. These words are *well, yes, no, why, oh*.

EXAMPLES Yes, you were elected.
Oh, I wouldn't be too sure about that.
Why, the entire argument is false!

(5) In dates and addresses every item after the first is *enclosed* by commas.

EXAMPLES Our sentimental idea was to hold a class reunion on June 18, 1966, at the old high school.
Address me at 222 Twin Oaks Road, Akron 3, Ohio, after the first of March.
Their son was born on Monday, May 1, 1949, in Baltimore, Maryland.

▶ NOTE: When only the month and day are given, no punctuation is necessary.

EXAMPLE It was on May 10 that we began work.

When the items are joined by a preposition, do not use commas.

EXAMPLE He lived at 331 Main Street in Passaic, New Jersey.

● EXERCISE 3. This exercise covers the 5 kinds of interrupters discussed on the preceding pages. Copy the sentences, inserting commas as needed.

1. The final act a general free-for-all had the first-night audience a dignified crowd holding their sides.
2. The wide circulation of the new magazine *Sports* has not been achieved of course without strong publicity.
3. Well if you cannot pass the test Helen you will get a low grade one that will disappoint your parents.
4. At 21 Dover Road Millville Tennessee we lived next door to the Andersons a family of ten.
5. On August 1 1956 the two offices of the firm were located at 500 Madison Avenue New York 22 and at 320 Mission Street San Francisco 5 California.
6. Yes to be frank the other team played better.
7. The poet Alice Duer Miller is perhaps best known for her poem *The White Cliffs* a moving narrative of a family in wartime.
8. The news on July 5 was filled with traffic accidents, which with its usual grim accuracy the National Safety Council had predicted.
9. Here as I see it is a question that will carry us a long way indeed.
10. Please forward our mail to 41 Fairview Boulevard Montvale Illinois until April 20; after that unless our plans change we shall be at home.

(6) A nonrestrictive clause is set off by commas.

A nonrestrictive clause is a subordinate clause which is not necessary to the meaning of the sentence but merely adds an idea to the sentence.

NONRESTRICTIVE **Joan Thomas, *who was offered scholarships to three colleges,* will go to Mt. Holyoke in September.**

The basic meaning of this sentence is *Joan Thomas will go to Mt. Holyoke in September*. The subordinate clause does not affect this basic meaning; it merely adds an idea to the sentence. It is a nonrestrictive clause because it does not restrict in any way the word it modifies — *Joan Thomas*. Clauses which modify proper nouns are nearly always nonrestrictive.

The opposite of a nonrestrictive clause is a restrictive clause.

RESTRICTIVE Joan Thomas is the only senior *who won scholarships to three colleges.*

Here the subordinate clause is necessary to the sentence, for without it the sentence would not say the same thing: *Joan Thomas is the only senior*. The subordinate clause restricts the meaning of *senior* — *senior who won scholarships to three colleges.*

Study the following examples of restrictive and nonrestrictive clauses until you understand the terms. Note the punctuation: *restrictive — no punctuation; nonrestrictive — set off by commas.*

RESTRICTIVE The city *which interests me most* is Hollywood.
NONRESTRICTIVE Bismarck, *which is the capital of North Dakota*, is in the south central part of the state.

RESTRICTIVE The man *who spoke to me* is my science teacher
NONRESTRICTIVE Mr. Orban, *who is my science teacher*, spoke to me.

Sometimes a clause may be interpreted as either restrictive or nonrestrictive. In such instances the writer must decide which interpretation he wishes the reader to give to the clause.

The boys took their problem to the librarian *who is an authority on reference books.* [interpreted as restrictive]

The boys took their problem to the librarian, *who is an authority on reference books.* [interpreted as nonrestrictive]

We may assume from the first sentence, which contains a restrictive clause, that there is more than one librarian. The boys chose the one who is an authority on reference books.

From the second sentence we may assume that there is only one librarian and that he is an authority on reference books.

My uncle who works at the Union Trust Company lives in New Jersey. [one of several uncles]

My uncle, who works at the Union Trust Company, lives in New Jersey. [only one uncle, no others]

● EXERCISE 4. Some of the sentences in this exercise contain restrictive clauses; others contain nonrestrictive clauses. Number on your paper from 1 to 20. If the italicized clause is restrictive, write *R* after the proper number; if it is nonrestrictive, write *Commas* to indicate that you would use commas in this sentence.

1. Friends *who do favors for you* may expect you to do favors for them.
2. The Welcoming Committee *who made us feel at home in a strange school* helped us through the first confusing days of the term.
3. Our new Buick *which Dad bought in Detroit* is a four-door model.
4. The Buick *which Mr. Burton drives* is like the one we saw on television.
5. She is wearing the sweater *that she received for Christmas.*
6. Her new sweater *which was a Christmas gift* is two sizes too large.
7. Men *who are timid* do not make good detectives.
8. Men *who are supposed to be the stronger sex* cannot stand pain so well as women.
9. American cities *which are outwardly very much alike* show distinctive characteristics on more intimate acquaintance.
10. Cities *which have abandoned streetcars for busses* are saving money.

11. The Soo Canal *which connects Lakes Superior and Huron* would be a prime bombing target in wartime.
12. I do not like girls *who apply make-up in public.*
13. These antiquated tariffs *which were necessary during the depression* are shutting off foreign markets from American manufacturers.
14. The people *who settled America* came here to escape tyranny.
15. The Hudson's Bay Company *which is the oldest trading firm in the world* was founded in 1670.
16. Sir Isaac Newton *who was an English physicist* is generally considered the father of modern science.
17. The book *that I have read for this report* is a novel about World War II.
18. On my return I found that the people *that I had expected to see* had moved away.
19. Mr. French *who does his own gardening* says he exhausts himself trying to keep up with his power lawnmower.
20. All the tickets *that had been sold* were recalled.

(7) A nonrestrictive participial phrase is set off by commas.

A participial phrase is a group of related words containing a participle (see page 36). Present participles end in *–ing;* past participles of regular verbs end in *–ed.*

Like a nonrestrictive clause, a nonrestrictive participial phrase is set off by commas because it is not necessary to the meaning of the sentence.

NONRESTRICTIVE My little brother, *playing in the street,* was struck by a car.

RESTRICTIVE A child *playing in the street* may be struck by a car.

NONRESTRICTIVE Mrs. Hampton, *frightened by the thunder,* locked herself in a closet.

RESTRICTIVE People *frightened by thunder* often try to hide.

NONRESTRICTIVE **The crowd broke up suddenly, *dispersing rapidly in all directions.***

RESTRICTIVE **I watched the crowd *dispersing rapidly in all directions.***

● EXERCISE 5. This exercise covers all 7 types of interrupters. Number on your paper from 1 to 20. After the proper number write all words in the sentence which should be followed by a comma. Write the comma after each word. Do not copy commas already in the sentence.

EXAMPLE 1. This old sloop which had been sailing for fifty years was still seaworthy.

1. **sloop, years,**

1. A plan which will clear up traffic snarls has been submitted to the Traffic Control Board which will consider it at Monday's meeting.
2. Mr. Forbes the new manager hired my friend Sally Winters a recent graduate of our commercial department.
3. Yes this is I believe a true account of my interview with Mr. Tucker the principal.
4. Before you start taking anything apart David I hope you will be sure that you can if necessary put it together again.
5. Astronomy which is a study of the heavens has always interested me more than geography which is a study of the earth.
6. The bus leaving at four o'clock will I am sure get you home by six.
7. Our house at 2125 Northern Boulevard Flushing New York was sold, and we moved to 433 West Thirty-fourth Street New York City.
8. The story *Markheim* which was written by Stevenson is on the other hand a psychological study of the thoughts of a murderer.
9. Mrs. McKay realizing that secrecy was important kept the story to herself not telling even her husband.

10. Everyone who intends to vote must register before March 1 at the Village Hall 220 Seventh Street.
11. You should understand my good friend that much as I should like to do so I cannot give money to every organization that thinks it needs help.
12. Passengers riding in the front of the wrecked bus were the ones who were most severely injured.
13. This school composed largely of boys and girls from farm homes must offer courses in agriculture the occupation which most of the boys will enter.
14. To tell the truth I never expected to see them again, but like bad pennies they returned the next day.
15. Ruth had moved from Harrisburg Pennsylvania to Tampa Florida on November 19 1955 and in March 1956 moved again to Columbus Ohio.
16. The Stevens's yacht which Mr. Stein and his men had not quite completed lay at anchor looking slick and shipshape.
17. Bob and Jim left alone in the house immediately raided the refrigerator which was full of tasty items for the party that Jim's mother was giving the next day.
18. Napoleon's brothers Joseph and Lucien tried to prevent him from selling Louisiana, but Richard Livingston the American ambassador and James Monroe Jefferson's special envoy succeeded in making the purchase.
19. Well after trying all morning to reach me the boys delivered the message, and I gave them a written reply one which in my opinion should have been satisfactory.
20. The letter which was addressed to Mrs. J. Thompson 18 Franklin Street Springfield went first to Springfield Massachusetts and then to Springfield Ohio.

MAIN CLAUSES

34g. Use a comma before *and, but, or, nor, for, yet* when they join main clauses unless the clauses are very short. 34g

EXAMPLES **Saturday's Council meeting was unusually productive, for no one raised any objections.**

The first two acts were slow moving, but the third act was full of action and suspense.

You go ahead and I'll follow. [main clauses too short to require punctuation]

When the conjunction joins two verbs, not two main clauses, a comma is not necessary.

EXAMPLES **I gave some good advice to Gerald and got some from him in return.** [The conjunction joins the verbs *gave* and *got*.]

I gave some good advice to Gerald, and he gave me some in return. [The conjunction joins two main clauses.]

▶ NOTE: You are allowed some freedom in the application of this rule. Many writers use the comma before these conjunctions — as they use the comma before *and* between the last two items in a series — only when necessary to keep the meaning clear.

NOT CLEAR **I grabbed the dog and the woodchuck limped away.**

CLEAR **I grabbed the dog, and the woodchuck limped away.**

NOT CLEAR **I didn't know whether or not to wait any longer for the postman had brought no word from you.**

CLEAR **I didn't know whether or not to wait any longer, for the postman had brought no word from you.**

As you can see from the preceding examples, a reader may easily be confused if the comma is omitted. This is especially true of the comma before the conjunction *for*, which should always be preceded by a comma when it means *because*.

For the sake of uniformity, however, you are to follow rule **34g** *in all instances in the exercises in this book.*

INTRODUCTORY CLAUSES AND PHRASES

34h. Use a comma after an introductory adverb clause, an introductory participial phrase, or a succession of introductory prepositional phrases.

Adverb Clause

EXAMPLE *While Mario put the costume on,* his accompanist played "Deep Purple."

▶ NOTE: An adverbial clause at the end of a sentence is not usually set off.

EXAMPLE His accompanist played "Deep Purple" *while Mario put the costume on.*

Participal Phrases

EXAMPLE *Watching the game from his elm-tree vantage point,* Elmer forgot to hold on.

▶ NOTE: Do not confuse a verbal noun ending in *–ing* and used as the subject of the sentence with an introductory participial phrase.

EXAMPLES *Washing and polishing the car* is fun. [verbal nouns as subject]
Washing and polishing the car, I developed some sore muscles. [participial phrase]

A Succession of Prepositional Phrases

EXAMPLE *At the edge of the deep woods near Lakeville in Cumberland County,* he built a small log cabin.

▶ NOTE: A single introductory prepositional phrase need not be followed by a comma unless it is parenthetical (*by the way*, *on the contrary*, etc.) or necessary to prevent confusion.

EXAMPLES By the way, I had a letter from Frances.
With the weak, competition is unpopular.
In the morning I am never wide awake.

34h

LETTER SALUTATIONS AND CLOSINGS

34i. Use a comma after the salutation of a friendly letter and after the closing of any letter.

EXAMPLES Dear Joe**,** Sincerely yours**,**

● EXERCISE 6. This exercise covers end marks and all comma uses. Copy the sentences, inserting punctuation and capitalization where necessary; or, if your teacher prefers, follow the directions for Exercise 5.

1. Trapped on a sand bar by the incoming tide the amateur clam diggers Pete and Don who could not swim had to be rescued.
2. In the first semester the following courses in homemaking will be offered: cooking sewing interior decoration baby care and feeding.
3. When a slight breeze blows the lake glistens and the huge white sails of the yachts all lean at the same angle.
4. John Carr Jr the only Eagle Scout in the troop organized the parade selected the flag-bearers hired the band and generally substituted for the scoutmaster.
5. In 1935 filming of the *Herald-Tribune* started and we now have on microfilm every issue from the *Tribune* of April 19 1841 up to last month.
6. When Chuck who was driving tried to show off his friend Lucille fearing an accident threatened never to ride with him again.
7. During band rehearsal on Friday Jimmy was sent downtown for the clarinet section needed new reeds.
8. When the general called Stackpole a major in the RAF and an official of the Kenya Colony government were standing at the table watching an experiment.
9. Some of the men were eating others were cleaning their guns and the sheriff was conferring with the troopers who had just arrived to assist in the hunt.
10. What a beautiful dress Margaret did you make it yourself or did you buy it

SUMMARY OF USES OF THE COMMA

34e. Use commas to separate items in a series.

34f. Use commas to set off expressions which interrupt the sentence.

(1) Appositives
(2) Words in direct address
(3) Parenthetical expressions
(4) The words **well, yes, no, why, oh** when used at the beginning of a sentence
(5) Items in dates and addresses
(6) Nonrestrictive clauses
(7) Nonrestrictive participial phrases

34g. Use a comma before **and, but, or, nor, for, yet** when they join main clauses unless the clauses are very short.

34h. Use a comma after an introductory adverb clause, an introductory participial phrase, or a succession of introductory prepositional phrases.

34i. Use a comma after the salutation of a friendly letter and after the closing of any letter.

The Semicolon

34j. Use a semicolon between main clauses not joined by *and, but, or, nor, for, yet.*

EXAMPLES Representatives of seventy-five nations attended the spring meeting of the General Assembly**;** they remained in session from April 5 to May 18.
Take with you only indispensable things**;** leave behind all heavy and bulky items.

A writer must have some basis for deciding whether to use two main clauses with a semicolon between them, or two sentences with a period (and capital letter). In most writing the division into sentences is preferable. A semicolon is used only when the ideas in the two clauses are so closely related that a period would make too distinct a break between them.

34k. Use a semicolon between main clauses joined by the words *for example, for instance, that is, besides, accordingly, moreover, nevertheless, furthermore, otherwise, therefore, however, consequently, also, thus, instead, hence, still.*

EXAMPLES Holiday traffic has always been a menace to safety**;** *for instance,* on one Fourth of July week end, four hundred persons were killed in traffic accidents.

Tension rose rapidly during yesterday's meeting**;** *nevertheless,* most of the Council members remained calm.

Matters involving Germany and Italy were discussed**;** *therefore* representatives from these countries were invited to attend the preliminary planning sessions.

When the connectives mentioned in this rule are placed at the beginning of a clause, the use of a comma after them is frequently a matter of taste. When they are clearly parenthetical (interrupters) they are followed by a comma. The words *for example*, *for instance*, and *that is* are always followed by a comma. The word *however* is almost always followed by a comma.

EXAMPLES The foreign situation was deteriorating rapidly; *that is*, governments could find no basis for agreement.

The foreign situation was deteriorating rapidly; *however*, all governments remained optimistic. [. . . all governments, *however*, remained optimistic.]

Most of the words listed in this rule, however, are rarely used at the beginning of a clause. They are usually placed later in the clause.

EXAMPLE Matters involving Germany and Italy were discussed; representatives from these countries were *therefore* invited to attend.

34l. Use a semicolon between main clauses if there are commas within the clauses; and between items in a series if the items contain commas.

EXAMPLES The Canby, a new theater on Bank Street, announced programs of Westerns, gangster pictures, and re-releases of blood-and-thunder movies; and the crowds, surprisingly enough, were enormous. [commas within the clauses]

The following business executives were elected to the Board of Education: John White, owner of White's Department Store; Allen Norton, vice-president of the Farmers State Bank; and Donald Corcoran, president of the American Cement Company. [commas within series items]

The Colon

34m. Use a colon to mean "note what follows."

As a mark of punctuation which "looks forward," the colon is commonly used in three constructions:

(1) Use a colon before a list of appositives or a list of any kind introduced formally by such words as *the following* or *as follows*.

EXAMPLES The car trunk was large enough for everything: rackets, golf clubs, fishing supplies, suitcases, a picnic basket, and heavy clothing. [before a list of appositives]

You will probably have to answer the following questions: How long have you been unemployed? Why did you leave your last position? What experience have you had? [before a list which is introduced formally]

▶ NOTE: When the listed items follow immediately after the verb, no punctuation is required.

EXAMPLE Foreign aid organizations sent food, clothing, medical supplies, toys, and books to Europe.

(2) Use a colon before a long and formal statement.

EXAMPLE Dr. Stoddard made the following observation: The time is coming when a general college education will be as common as a high school education is today . . . [Note that a formal statement like this need not be enclosed in quotation marks.]

(3) Use a colon between main clauses when the second clause explains or restates the idea in the first.

EXAMPLE These seat covers are the most durable kind: they are reinforced with double stitching and covered with a heavy plastic coating.

34n. Use a colon between numbers when you are writing the time, between volume and number or volume and page number of a magazine, and between chapter and verse of a passage in the Bible.

EXAMPLES 4:30 o'clock
Harper's 198:68–74
John 3:16

34o. Use a colon after the salutation of a business letter.

EXAMPLES Dear Mr. Green:
Gentlemen:

The Dash

34p. Use a dash to indicate an important break in thought.

EXAMPLES He might — and according to plans, should — have reinforced the Second Division.
The title — if, indeed, the poem had a title — has escaped me.

34q. Use a dash to mean *namely, in other words, that is,* and similar expressions which precede explanations.

EXAMPLE The referees had it in their power to prevent the fracas — they could have stopped the game at any time. [dash means *that is*]

In this use the colon and the dash are frequently interchangeable.

EXAMPLE The referees had it in their power to prevent the fracas: they could have stopped the game at any time.

Parentheses

34r. Use parentheses to enclose incidental explanatory matter which is added to a sentence but is not considered of major importance.

EXAMPLES Senator Saltonstall (R., Mass.) is chairman of the committee.
The recent election affected the stock market (see Diagram A) but only temporarily.

She pretended to be surprised (Mary is a good actress) so that no one would know she had been forewarned.

(1) For setting off incidental matter, commas, dashes, and parentheses are frequently interchangeable. Commas and dashes are more common than parentheses.

(2) Punctuation marks are used within parentheses when they belong with the parenthetical matter. Punctuation marks which belong with the main part of the sentence are placed after a closing parenthesis.

EXAMPLES Mr. Baker asked him (What a tactless question!) whether he had been fired.
If the petition is signed by Alyson (Does she spell her name that way?), others will probably sign it.

Underlining (Italics)

34s. Underline titles of books, works of art (pictures, musical compositions, statues, etc.), names of newspapers, magazines, ships, trains, and planes.

EXAMPLES The Ox-Bow Incident
the Blue Boy, Humoresque, The Thinker
the Louisville Courier-Journal, or the Louisville Courier-Journal
the Saturday Evening Post
the Mayflower, the Chief, the City of Houston

The use of quotation marks for titles is now generally limited to parts of publications; the titles of the publications themselves are underlined.

EXAMPLE Read Chapter 19, "The Great Experiment," in America's History by Todd and Curti.

▶ NOTE: When set in printer's type, underlined words are italicized.

The Ox-Bow Incident the *Saturday Evening Post*

The words *a*, *an*, *the*, written before a title, are underlined only when they are part of the title. Before the names of magazines and newspapers, they are not underlined within a composition.

EXAMPLE I took a few ideas from my history text, The World's History, and some others from the latest issue of the Atlantic.

34t. Underline foreign words, words referred to as words, and letters referred to as letters.

EXAMPLES I always have to look up the meaning of such Latin terms as carpe diem and caveat emptor.
The commonest English word is the; the most frequently used letters are e and t.

Brackets

In ordinary composition you will have practically no use for brackets. Commas, dashes, and parentheses are preferable as means of setting off parenthetical matter.

34u. Use brackets to enclose explanations within parentheses or in quoted material when the explanation is not part of the quotation.

EXAMPLES The following is a quotation from Mr. Gray's address of acceptance: "I am honored by it [the appointment], but I am also aware of the responsibilities which accompany it."
The senator criticized his own party ("We must reorganize it [the Republican party] before the election") and flayed the other parties.

● EXERCISE 7. This exercise covers commas, semicolons, colons, dashes, parentheses, italics, and brackets. Copy the sentences, inserting the proper punctuation.

1. The result of the election Grundy vs. Cole may indicate a popular change of attitude toward tariffs the candidate who favored protective tariffs was defeated.
2. Our sailing party there were eight of us went aboard the Sealark at 8 30 but we had to wait until 9 30 before the crew and wind and tide would permit us to sail.
3. After reading abbreviated versions of A Tale of Two Cities and Great Expectations many students they were the better readers of course read the complete novels.
4. Carrie went to the office to see Mr. Brown George Fred and I went to the superintendent of buildings and Betty went to the dean. We finally got what we wanted permission to hold an off-campus dance.
5. Mrs. Johnson my English teacher had me revise my composition three times first to correct the spelling second to revise some sentences third to remove all so's and and so's.
6. Any change in the loyalty of these subject peoples would never be known to the world for the people would not dare to express their opinions a few who tried are now dead and the government would quite understandably not admit its citizens were disloyal.
7. The smaller colleges on the other hand are in a difficult position their income has been cut their expenses have been increased.
8. There are good reasons why at this time candidates for teaching cannot be carefully selected for example there is a shortage of teachers and if standards are raised the shortage may become more acute a result everyone wishes to avoid.
9. An auto chair the kind that clamps over the back of the car seat will put the youngster up where he can see something something that is besides the tops of trees.

10. Professor Jones has condensed his directions into a mimeographed pamphlet Directions for Barbecuing Chicken that may be had on request to Department FC the New York Times 229 West Forty-third Street New York 18 New York.

Quotation Marks

34v. Use quotation marks to enclose a direct quotation — a person's exact words. Do not use quotation marks to enclose an indirect quotation — not a person's exact words.

DIRECT QUOTATION Mother said, "You may have the car until noon."

INDIRECT QUOTATION Mother said I could have the car until noon.

▶ NOTE: *Enclose* means to place quotation marks at both the beginning and the end of the quotation. Omission of quotation marks at the end of a quotation is a common error.

(1) A direct quotation begins with a capital letter.

EXAMPLE I heard her say, "Complete the lesson at home."

▶ EXCEPTION: If the quotation is only a fragment of a sentence, do not begin it with a capital letter.

EXAMPLE One critic called the book "an appalling waste of paper."

(2) When a quoted *sentence* is divided into two parts by such interrupting expressions as *he said, she replied, Jack added,* etc., the second part begins with a small letter unless some other rule requires a capital.

EXAMPLES "Go home," he pleaded, "before you cause more trouble."
"Have you," she asked, "been working this summer?"

34v

"Some safety devices must be installed," said the inspector; "for example, covers must be placed on all moving parts of the machines."

(3) If the second part of a broken quotation is a new sentence, it begins with a capital letter.

EXAMPLE "Drive carefully," he warned. "Speed is the cause of most accidents."

(4) A direct quotation is set off from the rest of the sentence by commas.

EXAMPLE She said, "We can reach them by telephone."

▶ NOTE: If the quotation is only a phrase, do not set it off by commas.

EXAMPLE Don't you believe in government "of the people, by the people, and for the people"?

(5) Other marks of punctuation when used with quotation marks are placed according to the following rules:

1. *Commas and periods are always placed inside the closing quotation marks.*

EXAMPLE "I know," he said, "that we can finish the job today."

2. *Semicolons and colons are always placed outside the closing quotation marks.*

EXAMPLES "Jim," my grandfather said, "you should stop being a burden on your family"; then he suggested that I leave school and get a job.
The following are what Mr. Sims describes as "highbrow reading": Homer, Shakespeare, the Bible, and Milton.

3. *Question marks and exclamation points are placed inside the closing quotation marks if they belong with the quotation; otherwise they are placed outside.*

EXAMPLES "Are the players ready?" asked the referee.
"How trying you are sometimes!" she exclaimed.
Were you surprised when he said, "Hop in"?
How disappointing it was to hear him say, "Your train has left"!

(6) A person's thoughts may be enclosed in quotation marks if they are expressed in the exact words in which he thinks them. If not expressed in the exact words (an indirect quotation) they should not be enclosed in quotation marks.

EXAMPLES Mary was astonished at her mother's stern refusal to let her go to the house party. "Surely," she thought, "Mother must realize that I am growing up. She can't really expect me to break a date with Pete." [exact words]

Mary was astonished at her mother's stern refusal to let her go to the house party. Surely her mother must realize that her daughter was growing up. She couldn't really expect her to break a date with Pete. [not exact words]

(7) When a quoted passage consists of more than one paragraph, place quotation marks at the beginning of each paragraph and at the end of the entire passage, not at the end of each paragraph.

▶ NOTE: Usually such a long quotation will be set off from the rest of the paper by indention and single spacing. In such a case, no quotation marks will be necessary.

(8) Use single quotation marks to enclose a quotation within a quotation.

EXAMPLE I remember her exact words, "For tomorrow read Frost's poem 'Mending Wall.' "

34w. When you write dialogue (two or more persons having a conversation), begin a new paragraph each time the speaker changes. **34w**

EXAMPLE "Hi, kids. Have you heard about Sandra and Bob?" Betty and I knew it was Sally Howe with some more gossip, and we also knew Sandra was on the other side of the row of lockers.

"Hi, Sally. How'd you like that French exam?" Betty was trying to change the subject fast.

"Oh, who cares about French?" she said. "Have you heard about Sandra and Bob?"

"Sally," I said in a feeble attempt to sidetrack her, "where did you get that cute pin? I've never seen one like it."

"Say, what goes on here?" Sally persisted. "I'm trying to tell you a story I heard about Sandra and that Bob Sharp and — oh, hello, Sandra. I didn't know you were here!"

"Serves you right, you little gossip!" Sandra approached menacingly. "Now what's that story?"

34x. Use quotation marks to enclose titles of chapters, articles, short poems, and other parts of books or magazines.

EXAMPLES Read Chapter 37, "Victorian Poetry."
I enjoyed Hollis Alpert's story "The Home of a Stranger" in the *New Yorker.*

▶ NOTE: Book titles and names of magazines are indicated by underlining (italics) (see page 596).

● EXERCISE 8. Copy the following sentences, inserting quotation marks and other required punctuation.

1. Do you think Miss Shapiro asked that you can be ready at four
2. Let's go Jean was all I heard you say.
3. What she asked have you done with the children
4. This is a mighty long job groaned Alice we should have started earlier.

5. He asked how old I was, and I replied I am old enough to know better.
6. Mr. Seegar said everyone knows the beginning of Alexander Pope's line which ends with the words where angels fear to tread.
7. I think that Shakespeare's phrase the primrose path appears in both Macbeth and Hamlet Mr. Stone replied.
8. Why John Morgan she exclaimed how dare you
9. Well they asked what about us are we what you mean by the lunatic fringe of the class
10. We'll be glad to help you Mrs. Riley I said the job won't take long if we all work at it.

The Apostrophe

34y. Use an apostrophe to form the possessive case of nouns and indefinite pronouns and to indicate the omission of letters in a contraction. Do not use an apostrophe to form the possessive case of personal pronouns.

APOSTROPHES TO FORM POSSESSIVES

(1) To form the possessive case of a singular noun, add an apostrophe and an *s*.

EXAMPLES Father's opinion
man's coat
Gus's hat

In words of more than one syllable which end in an *s*-sound, it is permissible to form the singular possessive by adding the apostrophe without the *s*. This is done to avoid too many *s*-sounds.

EXAMPLES Mr. Furness' car
the princess' wedding
Odysseus' travels

(2) To form the possessive case of a plural noun *not* ending in *s*, add an apostrophe and an *s*.

EXAMPLES women's fashions
children's games

(3) To form the possessive case of a plural noun ending in *s*, add the apostrophe only.

EXAMPLES boys' gymnasium
the Joneses' tennis court

▶ NOTE: Do not use the apostrophe to form the *plural* of a noun.

WRONG Bicycle's and truck's are not allowed on the parkway's.

RIGHT *Bicycles* and *trucks* are not allowed on the *parkways*.

PRONOUNS IN THE POSSESSIVE CASE

(4) The indefinite pronouns *one, everyone, everybody,* etc., form their possessive case in the same way as nouns.[2]

EXAMPLE Everyone's prediction was wrong.
He objected to everybody's getting a prize.

(5) Personal pronouns in the possessive case (*his, hers, its, ours, yours, theirs, whose*) do not require an apostrophe.

WRONG I thought the scarf was her's.
RIGHT I thought the scarf was *hers*.

WRONG You have seen baseball at it's best.
RIGHT You have seen baseball at *its* best.

WRONG Do you know who's book this is?
RIGHT Do you know *whose* book this is?

[2] Note the correct form of such words when used with *else:* everyone *else's;* somebody *else's*. Note that there is no apostrophe in *oneself*.

● EXERCISE 9. Copy the italicized words in the following list in two columns. Label the first column "singular possessive" and write the singular possessive form of each word in this column. Label the second column "plural possessive" and write the plural possessive form of each word in this column.

	Singular Possessive	Plural Possessive
EXAMPLE *citizen* privilege	**citizen's**	**citizens'**

1. *city* water supply
2. *girl* dresses
3. *friend* opinions
4. *deer* horns
5. *laborer* wages
6. *man* neckties
7. *dog* collar
8. *fox* tail
9. *student* books
10. *church* congregation

● EXERCISE 10. Number on your paper from 1 to 20. If the possessive case in each item in the list has been correctly formed, write a + after the proper number. If it has been incorrectly formed, write the correct form.

1. everyone's friend
2. bus' brakes
3. childrens' toys
4. this school's reputation
5. spectacles' rims
6. Is this your's?
7. Is it a girl's or a boy's school?
8. made it's way to port
9. tree's trunk
10. Victory is our's.
11. a street of worker's homes
12. in the Brown's yard
13. that nation's business
14. women's objections
15. broke it's back
16. travelers' passports
17. marines bravery
18. did its best
19. babie's bottles
20. the actors' parts

COMPOUNDS AND WORDS SHOWING JOINT POSSESSION

(6) In compound (hyphenated) words, names of business firms, and words showing joint possession, only the last word is possessive in form.

Compound Words

EXAMPLES **mother-in-law's visit**
commander-in-chief's order

Names of Business Firms

EXAMPLES Dun and Bradstreet's publications
Procter and Gamble's products

Joint Possession

EXAMPLES Dorothy and Ann's room
Jack and Tom's responsibility

(7) When two or more persons possess something individually, each of their names is possessive in form.

EXAMPLE Jack's and Tom's sweaters

SPECIAL USES

(8) The words *minute, hour, day, week, month, year,* etc., when used as possessive adjectives, require an apostrophe. Words indicating amount in cents or dollars, when used as possessive adjectives, require apostrophes.

EXAMPLES a minute's work, five minutes' work
a day's rest, three days' rest
one cent's worth, five cents' worth
one dollar's worth, five dollars' worth

● EXERCISE 11. In the following list the possessive relationship is expressed by means of a phrase. Change each so that the possessive case of the noun or pronoun will be used to express the same relationship. Write your answers.

EXAMPLE a vacation of two weeks a two weeks' vacation

1. gloves of David and Pat
2. the locker room of the boys
3. home of my brother-in-law
4. personality of a person
5. boat of Charles and Bob
6. opinion of the editor-in-chief
7. worth of three dollars
8. store of Barton and McLean
9. novels of Kenneth Roberts

10. top of it
11. accusations of the witnesses
12. a delay of a week
13. worth of ten cents
14. events of the day
15. wraps of the ladies
16. authority of the sergeant-at-arms
17. car of Bruce and Bill
18. a wait of ten minutes
19. rays of the moon
20. products of Johnson and Johnson

APOSTROPHES TO FORM CONTRACTIONS

(9) Use an apostrophe to indicate where letters have been omitted in a contraction. A contraction is a word made up of two words combined into one by omitting one or more letters.

EXAMPLES For **do not** the contraction is **don't.** [the letter *o* omitted]
For **it is** the contraction is **it's.** [the letter *i* omitted]
For **they are** the contraction is **they're.** [the letter *a* omitted]

▶ NOTE: The most common error in the use of the apostrophe in a contraction (except the failure to use it at all) comes from the confusion of *it's*, which means *it is*, with the possessive form *its* (*its* appearance), which has no apostrophe. Another common error, probably the result of carelessness, is the insertion of the apostrophe in the wrong place: *ca'nt* for *can't*, *does'nt* for *doesn't*, etc. Also note especially that *let's* in such an expression as "Let's go!" is a contraction of *let us* and requires an apostrophe for the omitted *u*.

34z. Use the apostrophe and *s* to form the plural of letters, numbers, and signs, and of words referred to as words.

EXAMPLES Mississippi is spelled with four *s*'s, four *i*'s, and two *p*'s.
Instead of a 3 and an 8 he had written two 3's.
How many +'s in this exercise?
Count the number of *and*'s in that paragraph.

● EXERCISE 12. Number on your paper from 1 to 25. Copy the following, inserting apostrophes where they are needed and changing the phrasal possessives to the possessive case. Some of the items are correct.

1. girls locker room
2. guns of a man-of-war
3. Its quite true, isnt it?
4. wind in its rigging
5. Lets find out whats up.
6. Ive found that cryings no use.
7. restaurant of Stengel and Thorpe
8. mens shoes
9. Whats its meaning?
10. a days fun
11. football of Fred and Herb
12. Whos in Jeans car?
13. this chains links
14. Im sure its early.
15. Theyll play if he lets them.
16. Her parents opinions are the same as hers.
17. womens handbags
18. Arent there two *r*s in *embarrass?*
19. boys magazine
20. Her numbers two *3*s and two *0*s.
21. publications of Bennett and Osborne
22. One works by oneself.
23. office of the boss
24. notebooks of Grace and Marie
25. Lets see whos here

● EXERCISE 13. Most of the necessary punctuation and capital letters have been omitted from the following passages. When a passage is assigned, copy it, making it as mechanically perfect as you can. The only changes you need to make in paragraphing are those required by dialogue. Some of the punctuation is incorrect, but in most instances you need only *add* punctuation and capitals. When you are in doubt as to a particular punctuation or capitalization problem, don't guess. Look up the rule.

1

In any discussion of the thrilling unbelievable deeds of Americas sports immortals the feats of Ty Cobb the georgia peach are sure to play a prominent part. In his twenty-three years in the major leagues Cobb scored more runs made more hits and stole more bases than any other player in history. His lifetime batting average the highest ever made was .367 he finished three seasons with an average better than .400 won the american league batting championship twelve times a feat never equaled and stole ninety-six bases in one season 1915 more than entire teams now steal. To increase his speed Cobb used to wear heavy shoes in training so that his playing shoes would feel light he was the first player to swing three bats while warming up pitchers who usually walk dangerous hitters didnt dare walk Cobb he was too dangerous on the bases, he played twenty-one years with the Detroit tigers taking time out in 1918 to join the chemical warfare division of the army. He was the first of baseballs heroes to be represented when in 1939 the baseball hall of fame was opened in Cooperstown New York

At 9 30 A M on columbus day which is not a school holiday in indiana a fire broke out in the chemistry laboratory of emerson high school the big new fireproof brick building on the north side of oxford boulevard. The third-period chemistry II class which is composed of seniors happened to be in the laboratory displaying a seniors presence of mind the students seized their chemistry notes their english texts and their french notebooks and shouting with glee hurled them into the flames. It was professor Montague I believe who at this exciting moment appeared in the doorway carrying one of the schools fire extinguishers. wow what a splendid conflagration he exclaimed whats cooking as he prepared to warm himself at the literary bonfire someone I am sure it was an accident knocked a bottle of sodium into a sink which was full of water. During the ensuing weeks the principals squad of detectives did its duty but didnt succeed in finding the pyromaniac who had caused all the excitement.

3

I was sitting in the front row of the bleachers Wednesday afternoon waiting for the start of the fifth inning of our game with plainfield high. These are Ann Wrights books Sue, she asked me to keep them while she went back to the high school for a minute but Ive got to go home. Will you watch them until she gets back This unexpected outburst from Jan Cunningham was accompanied by the arrival in my lap of a pile of literature science math and French textbooks a notebook and a pencil case I wondered why some girls carry so many books home. I dropped Anns library under the seat and turned back to the game. Someones voice bellowed in my ear knock the cover off it Pug, Pug you know is our best hitter. I forgot everything but the game at 8 30 that night Jan telephoned she wanted to know what Id done with Anns books. Anns books I asked vaguely oh yes I guess I left them there. where did you leave them Jan sounded desperate. Under the bleachers, Ann didnt come for them I said. Yes she did Jan explained, she looked for me and when she couldnt find me she thought Id taken the books home now she hasnt her books and its pouring outside.

I was sorry when I saw the books the next morning they had been swollen by the rain to twice their normal size, Jan said Ann and she were angry but it wasnt my fault was it.

CHAPTER 35

Manuscript Form

OBSERVE STANDARD PRACTICE IN PREPARING AND REVISING YOUR WRITTEN COMPOSITION

The Manuscript

Paper and ink. Write compositions on standard size (8 × 10½″) lined paper. Use black, blue, or blue-black ink. Follow the school policy concerning use of both sides of the paper.

If you typewrite, use standard size (8½ × 11″) white typewriting paper. Type double spaced and on only one side of the paper.

Labeling and numbering pages. Follow the school policy concerning the labeling and numbering of pages. Common practice is to write your name, the subject (English IV), and the date in that order, one below the other, in the upper right-hand corner of the first page. Number all pages, except the first, with Arabic numerals in the upper right-hand corner. It is a good plan to write your name beneath the page number on each sheet.

Margins. Leave a margin of at least one and a quarter inches at the left and one inch at the right side of the paper. The left-hand margin must be even; the right-hand margin may be slightly uneven. In typewritten manuscripts, place the first line of all pages after the first at least one inch below the top of the paper and leave a one-inch margin at the bottom of all pages.

The title. Place the title of the composition in the center of the first line of a ruled page, and skip a line between the title and the first paragraph. The title of a typewritten composition should be placed about two inches below the top of the page. Composition titles should not be underlined or placed in quotation marks, except in rare instances when the title is itself a quotation.

Indention. Indent the first line of every paragraph the same distance — about one inch in handwritten papers; five spaces in typewritten papers.

Long quoted passages may be made to stand out by indenting the entire passage. In typescript such passages are single-spaced.

Neatness. Do not mar the appearance of a composition by cross-outs, insertions between lines, and afterthought additions in the margins. If changes must be made in the final copy, make them neatly or rewrite the entire page. Strike-overs and messy erasures mar the neatness of typewritten work.

Revising the First Draft

All compositions should be written twice. The first draft of a composition is your own copy and need not conform to the manuscript standards noted above. Mark up this first draft with your revisions and corrections. When you are satisfied that you have made all necessary changes, write your final draft to be handed to your teacher.

Revision is an extremely important step in the composition process. You should look upon each theme, whether written for English or for any other class, as an attempt at perfection. Revision of a first draft should be done in three steps: (1) Evaluate the general organization of the whole composition. (2) Eliminate badly constructed sentences and poorly chosen words. (3) Check the mechanics.

Use the following check list each time you revise the first draft of a composition. With frequent use, the list will become so clearly fixed in your mind that you will follow it automatically.

REVISION CHECK LIST

Evaluate:
- Quality of material (effectiveness, relevance, etc.)
- General organization (sequence of ideas)
- Division into paragraphs (topic sentences)
- Transitions
- Variety of sentence structure

Eliminate:
- Errors in grammatical usage
- Sentence fragments and run-on sentences
- Awkward sentences
- Confusing sentences
- Wordy passages
- Clichés

Check:
- Spelling
- Punctuation (Don't forget the apostrophe!)
- Capital letters
- Hyphenated words at the ends of lines

ABBREVIATIONS

35a. In compositions do not use abbreviations except in certain special instances in which abbreviations are customary. 35a

WRONG One cold Mon. A.M. in Feb., as I was crossing a downtown st., a man rushed from a bldg. directly ahead of me and leaped into a car bearing a Cal. license.

RIGHT One cold Monday morning in February, as I was crossing a downtown street, a man rushed from a building directly ahead of me and leaped into a car bearing a California license.

(1) The following abbreviations are customary before a name: *Mr., Messrs., Mrs., Dr., Rev., St.* (Saint). The following are abbreviated after a name: *Jr., Sr.,* and the college degrees *A.B., Ph.D.,* etc. With the exception of the college degrees, these abbreviations are used only with a name.

WRONG We called a Dr. for the sr. member of the firm.

RIGHT We called a doctor for John Parsons, Sr.

(2) The following abbreviations are acceptable in all writing: A.D. (A.D. 485); B.C. (271 B.C.); A.M. (before noon); P.M. (after noon); *etc.* (and so forth); *i.e.* (that is); *e.g.* (for example).[1] Generally understood abbreviations for government agencies are acceptable: *FBI, TVA, SEC, NLRB.* Periods are not used with abbreviations of this kind for government agencies.

(3) Do not use the symbol & or + for *and*.

NUMBERS

35b. Do not begin a sentence with a numeral.

WRONG 8 students crowded into the car.

RIGHT **Eight** students crowded into the car.

35c. Numbers of more than two words should be written in numerals.

EXAMPLES 1,450,280; $125.75; 1935
two dollars; forty cents; thirty-three

[1] For other common abbreviations see page 483.

Be consistent in your use of words and numerals.

WRONG My brother makes forty dollars a week, but I make only $35.00.

RIGHT My brother makes forty dollars a week, but I make only **thirty-five.**

▶ NOTE: Rule 35c applies to ordinary writing. In mathematical, scientific, and statistical writing, most numbers are written as numerals.

Never spell out the year or page numbers following the word *page*.

35d. Hyphenate all compound numbers from twenty-one to ninety-nine and fractions used as adjectives.

EXAMPLES He spent **twenty-three** days in the hospital.
a **two-thirds** majority, but **two thirds** of the people

35e. Write out numbers like *second, twenty-fifth,* etc., instead of writing them as numerals with letter endings: 2nd, 25th, etc.

EXAMPLE I was standing **tenth** (not 10th) in the **third** (not 3rd) line.

The number of the day when given with the month is not used with the letter endings *st, nd, rd, th.* The name of a street, however, may be written with these endings.

EXAMPLES On June **25** we sail for Europe, and on August **21** we return.
133 West **34th** Street (also 34 Street or Thirty-fourth Street)

DIVIDING WORDS AT THE END OF A LINE

Division of words at the end of a line in order to maintain an even margin should be avoided but is sometimes necessary. A hyphen is used between parts of words divided in this way. Words should be divided between syllables, but accurate division of words into syllables is a technical matter. When you are in doubt, consult the dictionary. A few simple rules may be helpful in deciding where to place the hyphen.

35f. Divide a word at the end of a line between pronounceable parts only. One-syllable words should never be divided.

WRONG pray-ed [one-syllable word]
RIGHT prayed

WRONG demonstr-ate [parts not pronounceable]
RIGHT demon-strate

35g. A word having double consonants should be divided between the consonants.

EXAMPLES hap-py
com-mand

Words like *will-ing* and *err-ing* are exceptions. See rule 35j regarding prefixes and suffixes.

35h. Do not divide a word so that a single letter stands alone. If possible do not divide a word so that only two letters are carried over to the next line.

WRONG e-ventful, camer-a
RIGHT event-ful, cam-era

35i. Do not divide proper names or separate title, initials, or first name from a last name.

WRONG . . . . we were very much surprised to see Mr.
Campbell at the meeting . . . .

RIGHT .... we were very much surprised to see Mr. Campbell at the meeting ....

35j. Words having prefixes and suffixes should be divided between the prefix and the root of the word or between the root of the word and the suffix.

EXAMPLES pre-dict, usual-ly, atten-tion, will-ing

CORRECTION SYMBOLS

ms	error in manuscript form or neatness
cap	error in use of capital letters
p	error in punctuation
sp	error in spelling
frag	a sentence fragment
ss	error in sentence structure
k	awkward sentence
nc	not clear
ref	unclear reference of pronoun
gr	error in grammar
w	error in word choice
¶	Begin a new paragraph here.
t	error in tense
^	You have omitted something.

EXAMPLE OF SYMBOLS IN MARGIN OF A COMPOSITION

^ sp. Our games are lessons noble liveing. The
frag. playing field is in truth a school. Which
teaches the laws of honor. They ring through
p. every game, they are blazoned above every
playing field. They are among the oldest and
the most enduring things in the world. Under-
gr. p. laying every sport however often men may forget
it is the maxim "a fair field and no favor."

PASSAGE CORRECTED BY THE STUDENT

^ sp. Our games are lessons ^in noble ~~liveing~~ living. The

frag. playing field is in truth a school, ~~Which~~ which

teaches the laws of honor. They ring through

p. every game; they are blazoned above every

playing field. They are among the oldest and

the most enduring things in the world. Under-

gr. p. ~~laying~~ lying every sport, however often men may forget

it, is the maxim "a fair field and no favor."

CHAPTER 36

Spelling

LEARN TO SPELL CORRECTLY BY APPLYING SPELLING RULES AND AVOIDING COMMON SPELLING ERRORS

This chapter suggests a number of things you can do to improve your spelling:

1. Be careful.
2. Use the dictionary.
3. Keep a list of your own spelling errors.
4. Learn to spell words by syllables.
5. Learn a few helpful spelling rules.
6. Learn to distinguish between homonyms.
7. Learn lists of commonly misspelled words.

Spelling Habits

1. *Be careful.* Care in writing and in proofreading your compositions will eliminate errors in the spelling of simple words like *to, there, its,* which account for so many of the teacher's corrections on your themes.

2. *Use the dictionary.* Some students apparently think themselves allergic to the dictionary. They would rather take a chance on guessing than to expose themselves to the truth. But the only sure way to find out how to spell a word is to look it up.

3. *Keep a list of your own spelling errors.* We do not all misspell the same words. Although it is a difficult habit to establish, the habit of recording in your notebook the words you misspell in your compositions

will pay you a large return on the investment of a little time and patience.

4. *Learn to spell words by syllables.* This is the "divide and conquer" technique used with success by invading armies. It is equally effective in attacking a long and troublesome word. A long word divided into syllables becomes a number of short words. Short words are simpler to spell than long ones; hence you can simplify your spelling problem by acquiring the habit of dividing words into syllables and spelling them part by part.

Two common causes of spelling mistakes are the omission of a syllable and the addition of an extra syllable. A student who spells *probably* as though it were *probaly* has made the first kind of mistake. If he spells *lightning* as though it were *lightening*, he has made the second kind. Errors like these are errors in pronunciation which, in turn, are the result of not knowing the exact syllables in the word.

Dividing a word into its pronounceable parts (syllables) will help you to pronounce and to spell the word correctly.

● EXERCISE 1. Write each of the following words in syllables — place a hyphen between syllables. When you have completed the exercise and studied the words, take a test on them from dictation. Whether your divisions correspond exactly with the dictionary syllabication is not important, provided the words are divided into pronounceable parts and all letters are included and no letters are added.

1. modern
2. similar
3. library
4. surprise
5. privilege
6. perspiration
7. boundary
8. candidate
9. representative
10. entrance
11. lightning
12. accidentally

● EXERCISE 2. Follow directions for the preceding exercise.

1. athletics
2. disastrous
3. government
4. undoubtedly
5. equipment
6. temperament
7. recognize
8. business
9. sophomore
10. quiet
11. mischievous
12. curiosity

Spell by Rule

5. *Learn a few helpful spelling rules.* Although some spelling rules are hopelessly complicated, a few are simple enough and important enough to justify the effort required to master them. Study the following rules and apply them whenever possible in your writing.

IE AND *EI*

36a. Write *ie* when the sound is $\overline{\text{ee}}$, except after c.

EXAMPLES **believe, thief, fierce ceiling, receive, deceive**
EXCEPTIONS **seize, either, weird, leisure, neither, financier**

Write *ei* when the sound is not $\overline{\text{ee}}$, especially when the sound is ā.

EXAMPLES **freight, neighbor, weigh; height**
EXCEPTIONS **friend, mischief**

● EXERCISE 3. Write the following words, supplying the missing letters (*e* and *i*) in the correct order. Be able to explain how the rule applies to each.

1. for. . .gn
2. br. . .f
3. rel. . .ve
4. conc. . .ve
5. v. . .l
6. n. . .ce
7. c. . .ling
8. gr. . .f
9. p. . .ce
10. rec. . .ve
11. retr. . .ve
12. sl. . .gh
13. ach. . .ve
14. handkerch. . .f
15. perc. . .ve
16. th. . .f
17. s. . .ge
18. s. . .ze
19. bel. . .ve
20. w. . .rd
21. rec. . .pt
22. bel. . .f
23. f. . .nd
24. l. . .sure

PREFIXES AND SUFFIXES[1]

36b. When the prefixes *il–*, *in–*, *im–*, *un–*, *dis–*, *mis–*, *re–*, and *over–* are added to a word, the spelling of the word itself remains the same.

il + legal = **il**legal
in + elegant = **in**elegant
im + movable = **im**movable
un + necessary = **un**necessary
un + excused = **un**excused
dis + satisfied = **dis**satisfied
mis + understood = **mis**understood
mis + spell = **mis**spell
re + commend = **re**commend
over + run = **over**run
over + eat = **over**eat

36c. When the suffixes *–ness* and *–ly* are added to a word, the spelling of the word itself usually remains the same.

EXAMPLES mean + ness = mean**ness** final + ly = final**ly**

EXCEPTIONS Words ending in *y* change the *y* to *i* before a suffix: ready — read**ily**; heavy — heav**iness**; happy — happ**iness.**

● EXERCISE 4. Spell correctly the words indicated.

1. *rate* with the prefix *over*
2. *habitual* with the suffix *ly*
3. *agree* with the prefix *dis*
4. *green* with the suffix *ness*
5. *material* with the prefix *im*
6. *appoint* with the prefix *dis*
7. *apprehend* with the prefix *mis*
8. *practical* with the suffix *ly*
9. *abated* with the prefix *un*
10. *casual* with the suffix *ly*
11. *natural* with the prefix *un*
12. *stubborn* with the suffix *ness*
13. *legal* with the prefix *il*
14. *appropriate* with the prefix *in*

[1] A prefix is a letter or group of letters added to the *beginning* of a word to change its meaning. A suffix is a letter or group of letters added to the *end* of a word to change its meaning.

15. *appear* with the prefix *dis*
16. *movable* with the prefix *im*
17. *construct* with the prefix *re*
18. *animate* with the prefix *in*
19. *similar* with the prefix *dis*
20. *keen* with the suffix *ness*
21. *spell* with the prefix *mis*
22. *use* with the prefix *mis*
23. *avoidable* with the prefix *un*
24. *merry* with the suffix *ly*

36d. Drop the final e before a suffix beginning with a vowel.

EXAMPLES care + ing = car**ing** use + able = us**able**

EXCEPTIONS Keep the final *e* before *a* or *o* if necessary to retain the soft sound of *c* or *g* preceding the *e*: noti**ce**able, coura**ge**ous

36e. Keep the final e before a suffix beginning with a consonant.

EXAMPLES care + ful = care**ful** care + less = careless

EXCEPTIONS true + ly = tru**ly** argue + ment = argu**ment** acknowledge + ment = acknowledg**ment**

36f. Words of one syllable and words accented on the last syllable, when ending in a single consonant preceded by a single vowel, double the consonant before a suffix beginning with a vowel. When the last syllable is not accented, do not double the consonant.

EXAMPLES plan + ing = pla**nn**ing [one-syllable word]
forget′ + ing = forge**tt**ing [accent on last syllable]
occur′ + ed = occu**rr**ed [accent on last syllable]
prefer′ + ed = prefe**rr**ed [accent on last syllable]

36 b-f

prof′it + ed = profited [accent not on last syllable]
prefer + able = pref′erable [accent shifts; not on last syllable]

● EXERCISE 5. Write correctly the words formed as follows:

1. defer + ed
2. defer + ence
3. hope + ing
4. approve + al
5. benefit + ed
6. nine + ty
7. prepare + ing
8. counsel + or
9. write + ing
10. propel + ing
11. desire + able
12. control + ed
13. hope + less
14. move + ing
15. true + ly
16. run + ing
17. singe + ing
18. fame + ous
19. name + less
20. red + est

THE PLURAL OF NOUNS

36g. Observe the rules for spelling the plural of nouns.

(1) The regular way to form the plural of a noun is to add an *s*.

EXAMPLES chair, chairs book, books

(2) The plural of some nouns is formed by adding *es*.

The *e* is necessary to make the plural form pronounceable in the case of words ending in *s*, *sh*, *ch*, and *x*.

EXAMPLES dress, dresses bush, bushes
birch, birches box, boxes

(3) The plural of nouns ending in *y following a consonant* is formed by changing the *y* to *i* and adding *es*.

EXAMPLES fly, flies lady, ladies
enemy, enemies salary, salaries

(4) The plural of nouns ending in y *following a vowel* is formed in the usual way.

EXAMPLES monkey, monkeys donkey, donkeys

(5) The plural of most nouns ending in f or fe is formed by adding s. The plural of some nouns ending in f or fe is formed by changing the f to v and adding s or es.

EXAMPLES Add *s*: roof, roofs dwarf, dwarfs
chief, chiefs

Change *f* to *v* and add *s* or *es*:

knife, knives calf, calves
loaf, loaves wharf, wharves
leaf, leaves

(6) The plural of nouns ending in o *following a vowel* is formed by adding s. The plural of most nouns ending in o *following a consonant* is formed by adding es.

EXAMPLES *o* following a vowel:

rodeo, rodeos radio, radios

o following a consonant:

hero, heroes potato, potatoes
mosquito, mosquitoes

(7) The plural of most nouns ending in o and *referring to music* is formed by adding s.

EXAMPLES

piano, pianos soprano, sopranos solo, solos

(8) The plural of a few nouns is formed by irregular methods.

EXAMPLES

child, children tooth, teeth woman, women
mouse, mice ox, oxen goose, geese

(9) The plural of compound nouns (more than one word) is formed by making the *modified word* plural.

In the following examples, the phrases *in-law* and *of-war*, and the adjectives *martial*, *lieutenant*, and *by* are all modifiers. Note that it is the nouns modified by them which are made plural.

EXAMPLES mother-in-law, mothers-in-law
man-of-war, men-of-war
court martial, courts martial
lieutenant colonel, lieutenant colonels
passer-by, passers-by

(10) The plural of compound nouns ending in *–ful* is formed by adding *s* to the end of the word.

EXAMPLES cupful, cupfuls handful, handfuls

(11) The plural of foreign words is sometimes formed as in the foreign language.

EXAMPLES alumnus (man), alumni (men)
alumna (woman), alumnae (women)
datum, data
analysis, analyses
bacillus, bacilli
crisis, crises

(12) The plural of other foreign words may be formed either as in the foreign language or by adding s or es.

EXAMPLES index, indices or indexes
appendix, appendices or appendixes

(13) The plural of numbers and letters is formed by adding an apostrophe and s.

EXAMPLES There are ten 5's in this column.
There are two *s*'s in *necessary*.

(14) Some nouns are the same in the singular and plural.

EXAMPLES sheep, deer, trout, species, Chinese

● EXERCISE 6. Write the plural form of each of the following nouns. Be able to explain your spelling on the basis of the rules.

1. candy
2. sheep
3. piano
4. valley
5. alumnus
6. cameo
7. torch
8. chief
9. tomato
10. gas
11. fly
12. alto
13. brother-in-law
14. shelf
15. bench
16. major general
17. spoonful
18. hero
19. knife
20. goose

● EXERCISE 7. By referring to the rules on the preceding pages, explain the spelling of each of the following:

1. regretted
2. receive
3. illegible
4. coming (*e* dropped)
5. conferring
6. niece
7. contraltos
8. misstate
9. drunkenness
10. peaceable
11. ladies
12. conference
13. alumnae
14. leisure
15. occurred
16. writing (*e* dropped)
17. roofs
18. weigh
19. disappear
20. naturally

HYPHENATING

The surest way to find out whether or not a word is hyphenated is to look it up in the dictionary. The following somewhat oversimplified rules will, however, be useful in answering certain problems in the use of the hyphen.

36h. Hyphenate compound numbers from *twenty-one* to *ninety-nine*. Hyphenate fractions when used as adjectives before the words they modify.

EXAMPLES

thirty-three students
a **two-thirds** majority, but **two thirds** of the students

36i. Hyphenate a compound adjective.

EXAMPLES

a **second-story** room	a room in the **second story**
an **after-school** meeting	a meeting **after school**
dark-colored glasses	glasses of a **dark color**
door-to-door soliciting	soliciting from **door to door**
well-planned program	The program was **well planned.**

36j. When one of the modifying words is an adverb ending in *–ly*, omit the hyphen.

EXAMPLES *beautifully made* table
quietly prepared meal

36k. Use a hyphen with all prefixes before proper nouns and with the prefixes *ex–*, *self–*, *all–* and the termination *–elect* with any nouns.

EXAMPLES

un-American	ex-president
Pan-American	self-imposed
anti-Russian	all-star
pro-British	governor-elect
inter-Allied	

36l. Use a hyphen to prevent confusion or awkward spelling.

EXAMPLES

re-collect	prevents confusion with	recollect
re-form	prevents confusion with	reform
re-enlist	avoids the awkwardness of	reenlist
semi-invalid	avoids the awkwardness of	semiinvalid

Distinguish Between Homonyms

6. *Learn to distinguish between homonyms.* Homonyms present spelling problems because they sound alike but have different meanings and usually different spellings. You have probably had trouble distinguishing between *principle* and *principal*, *capital* and *capitol*, and other homonyms. Most of the paired words in the following lists are homonyms. Some are pairs that are frequently confused even though they are not pronounced exactly alike. Study the explanations and do the exercises.

already *previously*
I had *already* seen the movie twice.

all ready *all are ready*
Give the signal when you are *all ready*.

all right [This word really does not belong in this list, but it is included here because many persons think there is a word spelled *alright*, as though *all right* did have a homonym. There is no word *alright*. The correct spelling is always *all right*.]

altar *a table or stand in a church* or *a place for outdoor offerings*
The priest was standing beside the *altar*.

alter *to change*
If we are late, we will *alter* our plans.

altogether *entirely*
He doesn't *altogether* approve of me.

all together *everyone in the same place*
We were *all together* at Christmas.

born *given birth*
When were you *born?*

borne *carried*
He has *borne* his hardships bravely.

brake *device to stop a machine*
A defective *brake* caused the accident.

break *to fracture, shatter*
Try not to *break* any dishes.

capital *city;* also as an adjective, *punishable by death* or *of major importance*
Washington is the *capital* of this country.
Murder is a *capital* offense.
That is a *capital* idea.

capitol *building*
The *capitol* faces a park.

cloths *pieces of cloth*
Try the new cleaning *cloths.*

clothes *wearing apparel*
Her *clothes* are expensive.

● EXERCISE 8. Number on your paper from 1 to 20. Write after the proper number the correct one of the words given in parentheses in the sentences below.

1. The damage has (already, all ready) been done.
2. Father was (all together, altogether) too surprised to protest.
3. Events have (born, borne) out my predictions.
4. Pete is an (altar, alter) boy at St. Anne's Church.
5. If you (brake, break) a window, you will pay for it.
6. When you are (already, all ready) I will help you.

7. Belgrade is the (capital, capitol) of Yugoslavia.
8. If you will (altar, alter) the neckline, I will buy the dress.
9. My mother was (born, borne) in France.
10. Was his work (alright, all right)?
11. We use old sheets for cleaning (cloths, clothes).
12. We will (altar, alter) the building to suit tenants.
13. The dome on the (capital, capitol) is illuminated at night.
14. The club members have been (all together, altogether) only once.
15. Cars are (born, borne) across the river on a ferry.
16. Everyone was wearing his best (cloths, clothes).
17. How many states in this country have (capital, capitol) punishment?
18. I applied the (brakes, breaks) immediately.
19. Are you feeling (all right, alright)?
20. The family were (all together, altogether) on my birthday.

coarse *rough, crude*
He wore a suit of *coarse* cloth and used *coarse* language.

course *path of action; part of a meal; a series of studies*
He followed a straight *course.*
The golf *course* and the race *course* are outside of town.
Soup was the first *course.*
I am taking a *course* in cooking.

complement *something that completes* or *makes perfect*
The *complement* of 50° is 40°. [*completes* a 90° angle]
His part of the job *complements* mine. [Together they *complete* the job.]

compliment *a remark that says something good about a person; to say something good*
I am pleased by your *compliment.*
She *complimented* me on my cooking.

consul — *representative of a foreign country*
The American *consul* in Quito helped us during our visit.

council, councilor — *a group called together to accomplish a job;* a member of such a group is a *councilor*
The *council* met to welcome a new *councilor.*

counsel, counselor — *advice; the giving of advice;* one who gives advice is a *counselor.*
I accepted the wise *counsel* of my *counselor.*

des′ert — *a dry region*
We flew across the *desert.*

desert′ — *to leave*
He *deserted* his family.

dessert′ — *the final course of a meal*
The *dessert* was ice cream.

formally — *conventionally, properly, according to strict rules*
He spoke *formally* and with great dignity.

formerly — *in the past, previously*
I was *formerly* a member of that church.

its — [possessive]
The village is proud of *its* school.

it's — *it is*
It's a long way.

later — *more late*
We will arrive *later.*

latter — *the second of two*
When he gave me my choice of a football or a tennis racket, I chose the *latter.*

lead — [present tense] *to go first*
You *lead* and we will follow.

led — [past tense]
He *led* the army to victory.

lead — [pronounced lĕd] *a heavy metal;* also *graphit[e] in a pencil*
The industrial uses of *lead* are many.

● EXERCISE 9. Number on your paper from 1 to 20. Write after the proper number the correct one of the words given in parentheses in the sentences below.

1. Our (consul, counsel) in Rumania has returned to Washington.
2. I enjoyed the dinner but not the (dessert, desert).
3. Avoid (course, coarse) language.
4. Mr. Abrams was (formally, formerly) vice-president of the bank.
5. No (councilman, counselman) may serve more than three years on the council.
6. I do not enjoy parties conducted as (formally, formerly) as this one.
7. The walls of the room were papered but (its, it's) ceiling had been painted.
8. Some people are distrustful of (compliments, complements).
9. We are not sure which (course, coarse) to follow.
10. (Desert, Dessert) soil is fertile if irrigated.
11. Are you sure (its, it's) not too late?
12. I spent five summers working as a camp (councilor, counselor).
13. A golf (course, coarse) requires continual care.
14. I spoke to the mayor and the superintendent; the (later, latter) was more helpful.
15. I can't recall his ever giving me a (complement, compliment) on my writing.
16. All troops who (deserted, desserted) were finally caught.
17. The guidance (councilor, counselor) advised me to take the test.
18. During his senior year, Albert (lead, led) the team to a championship.
19. Have you finished your (course, coarse) in hygiene?
20. These supplies will (complement, compliment) those you already have.

loose *free, not close together*
The animals broke *loose.*
He stumbled in the *loose* sand.

lose [pronounced lo͞oz] *to suffer loss*
When did you *lose* your books?

miner *worker in a mine*
A *miner's* job is sometimes dangerous.

minor *under legal age; less important*
A *minor* cannot vote.
He raised only *minor* objections.

moral *good;* also *a lesson of conduct*
His good conduct showed him to be a *moral* person.
The class understood the *moral* of the story.

morale *mental condition, spirit*
The *morale* of the Army is high.

passed *verb*
He *passed* me at the finish line.

past *noun* or *adjective* or *preposition*
Some persons prefer to live in the *past* (n.) because *past* (adj.) events seem more interesting than present ones.
I went *past* (prep.) your house without realizing it.

peace *opposite of strife*
Everyone prefers *peace* to war.

piece *a part of something*
They ate every *piece* of cake.

personal *individual*
He gave his *personal* opinion.

personnel *a group of people employed in the same place*
The *personnel* of the company ranged in age from 16 to 64.

plain *not fancy;* also *a flat area of land;* also *clear*
She lives in a very *plain* home.
We crossed the *plains* in two days.
Our problem is *plain.*

plane *a flat surface;* also *a tool;* also *an airplane*
Plane geometry is a study of imaginary flat surfaces.
The carpenter used a *plane.*
A *plane* circled the airport.

principal *head of a school;* also *the main one of several things*
He went to the *principal's* office.
The *principal* cause of accidents is carelessness.

principle *a rule of conduct;* also *a main fact* or *law*
The judge accused the criminal of having no *principles.*
He understands the *principles* of mathematics.

quiet *still, silent*
A study hall should be *quiet.*

quite *completely, wholly;* also *to a great extent* or *degree*
I had *quite* forgotten his advice.
Bob is *quite* tall.

● EXERCISE 10. Number on your paper from 1 to 20. Write after the proper number the correct one of the words given in parentheses in the sentences below.

1. The judge regarded the crime as a (miner, minor) one.
2. A number of unexpected defeats destroyed the team's (moral, morale).
3. (Peace, Piece) had been maintained by the UN.
4. The meaning of his remark was perfectly (plain, plane).
5. These trucks are used for military (personnel, personal).
6. Word that the (principle, principal) wished to see me made me uncomfortable.
7. Do you understand the (principle, principal) of the gasoline motor?
8. If you don't wish to (lose, loose) the camera, keep it in the case.
9. The library was unusually (quite, quiet).
10. He had been a (minor, miner) in the Pennsylvania mines for many years.

11. The (principal, principle) characteristic of his poetry is its rhythm.
12. A (piece, peace) of the ship's mast was found.
13. Joe told me to (loose, lose) the dog from its leash.
14. A (personal, personnel) director is supposed to keep employees happy.
15. It was impossible to make the students be (quite, quiet).
16. When he (passed, past) me, I was going sixty miles an hour.
17. The (moral, morale) of the story was clear.
18. He went (passed, past) me like a flash.
19. You are a (miner, minor) as long as you are not of voting age.
20. He is a man who acts according to the highest (principles, principals).

stationary *in a fixed position*
The classroom desks are *stationary*.

stationery *writing paper*
I received three boxes of *stationery* at Christmas.

than [a conjunction]
I am stronger *than* she.

then adverb meaning *at that time*
Wear a green hat; *then* I'll recognize you.

there *a place;* [also used as an expletive (see page 24)]
We were *there* at two o'clock.
There were four of us.

their [possession]
The pupils bring *their* own lunches.

they're *they are*
They're going with us.

to [a preposition or part of the infinitive form of a verb]
Give the book *to* me, please.
We will have *to leave* early.

too adverb meaning *also* or *too much*
George is a sophomore, *too.*
It is *too* late to go now.

two *one + one*
We had only *two* dollars.

waist *your middle*
She wore a wide belt around her *waist.*

waste *unused material;* also *to squander*
Please empty the *waste*baskets.
Don't *waste* your time.

who's *who is, who has*
Who's coming?
Who's been here?

whose [possession]
Whose coat is this?

your [possession]
Is this *your* coat?

you're *you are*
You're a true friend.

● EXERCISE 11. Number on your paper from 1 to 20. Write after the proper number the correct one of the words given in parentheses in the sentences below.

1. The boys had neglected to lock (there, their) lockers.
2. I wanted to go to camp, (to, two, too).
3. Tie the rope around your (waist, waste).
4. The platform, we discovered when we tried to move it, was (stationary, stationery).
5. No one could remember (whose, who's) name had been drawn first.
6. This year's annual will be larger (than, then) last year's.
7. Where do you think (your, you're) going?
8. Some students regard the class as a (waist, waste) of time.
9. The work was (to, too) strenuous for me.

10. I used school (stationary, stationery) for my letters.
11. When (you're, your) homework has been finished, call me.
12. I do not know (whose, who's) going to solve the problem.
13. As soon as (their, they're) printed, we will ship the books.
14. Write your letters on business (stationary, stationery).
15. (Your, You're) lucky to have such a good job.
16. I cannot do any more (then, than) I have done.
17. Before we knew what the job was, (to, two, too) dollars an hour seemed to be good pay.
18. I'd like to know (who's, whose) responsible for this mess.
19. I was surprised at (you're, your) taking that attitude.
20. Chemistry has converted many (waste, waist) products into valuable commodities.

● REVIEW EXERCISE. Number on your paper from 1 to 40. After the proper number write the correct one of the words in parentheses in the sentences below.

1. Columbia is the (capital, capitol) of South Carolina.
2. Everything seemed to be (alright, all right).
3. Mr. Starkey (complemented, complimented) me on my English grade.
4. Have you discussed this problem with your (councilor, counselor)?
5. We were blown several miles from our (course, coarse).
6. The letters have (all ready, already) been mailed.
7. The amount of vegetation in the (dessert, desert) surprised us.
8. Mrs. Crane (formally, formerly) taught here.
9. Every nation must conserve (its, it's) resources.
10. My companion (lead, led) me down a dark passage.
11. We were (all ready, already) to start before dawn.
12. Try not to (lose, loose) your temper.
13. Success is the best (moral, morale) builder.
14. His (coarse, course) manners were not amusing.

15. We had been told not to ask for a second (piece, peace) of pie.
16. The new (altar, alter) is made of white marble.
17. I have read all of Steinbeck and Hemingway, and I prefer the (later, latter).
18. You must go to the (principal, principle) to get a working permit.
19. (Its, It's) time to think about getting a job.
20. There was (all together, altogether) no truth in the accusations.
21. Members of the (counsel, council) are elected annually.
22. A (capital, capitol) offense will cost you your life.
23. Everything is (all ready, already).
24. (Course, Coarse) wood absorbs more paint than fine-grained wood.
25. His work and mine are (complimentary, complementary).
26. Jack (past, passed) the ball to Joe.
27. When you are (all together, altogether) I'll take a group picture.
28. The mission was accomplished without loss of (personal, personnel).
29. The company embarked on the strongest advertising campaign in (its, it's) history.
30. What are the (principal, principle) products of Puerto Rico?
31. Some teachers prefer (stationary, stationery) seats in their classrooms.
32. There's a boy (whose, who's) going to succeed.
33. His performance was not outstanding, but it was (alright, all right).
34. Her (plain, plane) clothes did not detract from her beauty.
35. When we had cleaned our lockers, the (waist, waste) paper littered the floor.
36. The (principals, principles) of democracy have always been attacked.
37. Do you know (they're, their, there) new address?

38. Why didn't you follow your (counselor's, councilor's) instructions?
39. (Who's, Whose) pen is this?
40. Mrs. Smith gave us (complimentary, complementary) tickets.

Commonly Misspelled Words

7. *Learn lists of commonly misspelled words.* Frequent short spelling tests are an effective means of fixing correct spellings in your mind. On the following pages you will find a list of 300 commonly misspelled words. Taking no more than twenty at a time, have these words dictated to you. Study the ones you miss and record them in your list of spelling errors. When you have studied them (divided them into syllables and practiced writing each word several times), write them again from dictation. Spelling tests should be written, not oral.

THREE HUNDRED SPELLING WORDS [2]

accidentally
accommodate
accurate
acquaintance
across
aerial
aisle
all right
allotted
amateur

among
analysis
annihilate
anonymous

anxiety
apologize
appearance
appreciate
approaching
appropriate

approval
arctic
argument
arrangement
assassinate
association
athletics
atomic

attach
attack
attention
auxiliary
awful
awkward
bachelor
banana
bargain
basketball
battalion
beggar

beginning
believe

[2] The list does not include the homonyms listed on pages 629 to 637.

benefited
bicycle
biscuit
bookkeeper
breathe
bruise
bulletin
bureau

business
calendar
campaign
candidate
caricature
catastrophe
cellophane
cemetery
chaperon
classroom

college
colonel
colossal
column
coming
commission
committee
comparatively
competitive
completely

complexion
consensus
connoisseur
conscience
contemptible
convenience
copies
cordially

corps
correspondence

corroborate
courageous
courteous
criticism
criticize
customer
cylinder
defense
definitely
descendant

descent
description
desirable
despair
develop
dictionary
dining
diphtheria
disappear
disappoint

discipline
dissatisfied
doesn't
economical
ecstasy
efficient
eighth
eligible
embarrass
emphasize

endeavor
equipment
equipped

especially
etiquette
exaggerate
excellent
exercise
exhausted
existence

extension
extraordinary
familiar
fascinating
fatigue
February
feminine
fiery
finally
financial

foreign
forfeit
forty
fourth
fragile
genius
government
governor
grammar
grateful

guarantee
gymnasium
handkerchief
happened
harass
haven't
height
heroes
hoping
horizon

hospital
humorous
imitation
immediately
inasmuch (as)
inconvenience
indispensable
inevitable
influence
initial

inoculate
insofar (as)
interpreted
irrelevant
irresistible
kerosene
laboratory
leisure
license
lieutenant

lightning
loneliness
losing
luxurious
maneuver
marriage
masquerade
matinee
meant
medal

medicine
medieval
mentioned
microphone
minimum
mischievous

missile
misspelled
mortgage
movable

municipal
murmuring
naïve
necessary
nickel
ninety
ninth
negotiations
noticeable
nuisance

occasionally
occur
occurred
omitted
opinion
opportunity
optimistic
parallel
paralysis
parliament

particularly
pastime
penicillin
perhaps
permanent
perseverance
personally
perspiration
picnicking
planning

pleasant
pneumonia

possess
possibility
potato
practice
preceding
preference
prejudice
privilege

probably
procedure
prodigy
professor
pronunciation
propaganda
propeller
psychology
pursue
questionnaire

realize
receive
recognize
recommend
referred
rehearse
reign
relief
repetition
representative

restaurant
rhythm
satisfactorily
schedule
scissors
seize
semester
separate

sergeant
shining

siege
similar
sincerely
sophomore
souvenir
specimen
strategy
subtle
success
sufficient

supersede
suppress

surprised
syllable
sympathy
symphony
synonym
tariff
television
temperament

temperature
thoroughly
tomorrow
tournament
traffic
tragedy
transferred

twelfth
tyranny
undoubtedly

unforgettable
unmistakable
unnecessary
until
vacuum
vengeance
vicinity
villain
weird
writing

College Entrance and Other Examinations

At the present time, the percentage of young people wishing to attend college is greater than ever before. Deluged by applications for admission and for scholarship aid, colleges and other scholarship-granting agencies have been forced to become increasingly selective. If you are planning to go to college, you will probably encounter the selective process in the form of a test of your aptitude for college work and of your achievement as a high school student.

If a college is going to test you before it admits you, the chances are about eight in ten that it will test your verbal and mathematical aptitude and your skill in English composition. Verbal aptitude means your ability to deal with words, to understand them either alone or in combinations. Your skill in this area has a direct effect on your ability to do well in courses that require considerable reading and writing. Verbal aptitude is not developed in any particular courses you have had in school; on the contrary, you have been developing your verbal aptitude in all your reading, your listening, and your talking, since before you started to school. Composition, however, is taught in English class. When you are tested in composition, then, you are being tested on skills you have learned in class.

Since both verbal aptitude tests and English composition tests try to measure abilities you have rather than definite subject matter, there is not much that you can do in the way of specific preparation for them. You will not be tested on how well you know and can use any list of 500 or 1,000 specific words, or how glib you are in parroting ten rules of grammar.

What you can do in preparation, however, is to familiarize yourself with some of the standard ways of measuring verbal aptitude and compositional ability. The purpose of this chapter is to show you these methods. When any test you take makes use of them, you will, in a sense, be on familiar ground.

Always give careful attention to the test directions. Read them through at least twice. There may be a special way of marking your answer sheet; or there may be a slight variation from the directions you have followed in other tests. If you do not pick up these details, the chances are that you will not convey to the examiner the real knowledge that you have. In most modern tests, the means of communication between the student and the tester is the answer sheet. If you mark your answer sheet erroneously, there will be no proper communication.

Tests of Verbal Aptitude

Tests of verbal aptitude measure your knowledge of words. They test not only your understanding of single words, but also of words in context, of words in their relationship to other words, and of the meaning conveyed by whole passages of words. The commonest types of test exercises are synonyms, antonyms (opposites), word analogies, sentence completions, and reading comprehension exercises. Consideration of each individual type follows.

SYNONYMS AND ANTONYMS

In a synonym test you are asked to select out of four or five choices the word most similar in meaning to the word given to you. In an antonym test, you are asked to pick out the word most nearly opposite to the word given. The test directions read about as follows:

SYNONYMS: Each of the following questions consists of a word printed in capital letters followed by five words lettered A through E. Choose the lettered word which is most nearly *similar* in meaning to the word in capital letters.

ANTONYMS: Each of the following questions consists of a word printed in capital letters followed by five words lettered A through E. Choose the lettered word which is most nearly *opposite* in meaning to the word in capital letters.

You must be careful in reading these directions to make sure whether you are being asked to choose synonyms or antonyms, since some test questions will ask for one thing, an antonym for example, and will include a synonym as a wrong choice. Careful reading of directions will keep you straight. Following are three sample questions in which you are to find a synonym for each word given in capital letters:

i. ENERVATE: A. encourage B. enlarge C. bemoan D. weaken E. cut

ii. CATACLYSM: A. disaster B. catacomb C. cliff D. slope E. detriment

iii. ADUMBRATE: A. react B. darken C. resound D. visualize E. foreshadow

The answers here are i–D, ii–A, iii–E. Notice that in i a common misconception of the word's meaning is included among the choices. Many people are confused as to whether *enervate* means to take "nerve" away from a person or to put it in — hence *encourage* as a wrong choice. With ii and iii, the question forces you to a fairly accurate knowledge of the word in question. *Cataclysm* is something bad, but both *disaster* and *detriment* are bad. *Catacomb* may confuse because it has the same prefix as *cataclysm*. With iii, both *foreshadow* and *visualize* may suggest looking ahead; the particular kind of looking ahead must be clear to the test-taker.

● EXERCISE 1. Number on your paper from 1–5. Following the directions for antonyms on page 646, write your answers after the proper number on your paper.[1]

1. OBTUSE: A. popular B. compact C. brief D. light E. perceptive
2. QUIXOTIC: A. staid B. romantic C. polite D. plain E. slow
3. PALLIATE: A. deprecate B. color C. drop D. aggravate E. eradicate
4. EFFETE: A. wealthy B. raucous C. fresh D. masculine E. sad
5. ANTEDILUVIAN: A. sinewy B. abrupt C. agile D. modern E. forgetful

WORD ANALOGIES

The analogy, which is designed to measure your understanding of the relationships existing between words, is generally set up like this:

i. YAWN : ENNUI :: A. drink : hunger B. shout : triumph C. birds : prophecy D. miserliness : thrift E. equanimity : faith

[1] Answers for this and subsequent exercises are on page 675.

Directions for the analogy will read about as follows:

> Each of the following questions consists of two words which have a certain relationship to each other, followed by five pairs of related words. Choose the one pair of words which are related to each other in the same way as the original pair are related to each other.

In the sample question given, *yawn* and *ennui* have a certain relationship to each other. It can be verbalized as *a yawn is a sign of ennui* (or, since it is not yet clear whether *yawn* is to be considered a noun or a verb, *when you feel ennui, you often yawn*). Looking at the choices to find a similar relationship, you note that A will not do, since drinking indicates thirst, not hunger. B may be all right, since a shout is often a sign of triumph. In C, birds are not at all a sign of prophecy, though the Greeks and Romans often considered bird flights good or bad omens. Miserliness and thrift, in D, have a certain relationship, but it is not the *sign-of-something* relationship we are looking for; they are, to an extent, different degrees of a particular quality. And in E, a person who has faith may or may not have equanimity. In any case, it is a state of mind rather than a physical action indicating something else. B, then, is the only relationship that will work and is the best answer.

It will probably help you in doing analogies if you will verbalize each question. Something along the following lines is as good as anything: *Yawn is to ennui as shout is to triumph;* or, *a yawn is a sign of ennui; a shout is a sign of triumph.* Here is another sample to try:

ii. GIRTH : CIRCUMFERENCE :: A. weight : mass B. length : width C. height : altitude D. rectangle : circle E. color : stain

The first thing to do is to get the relationship expressed. *Girth* and *circumference* are in a limited way synonyms, although one is used most frequently with people or animals and the other with geometric figures; one is a short, earthy word and the other seems more abstract. Of course, C is the right answer, since *height* and *altitude* are in a way synonyms; in addition, *altitude* seems a little more abstract and more formal than *height*. *Weight* and *mass* make an attractive wrong choice, but they are not really synonyms, since *mass* conveys more the idea of magnitude than of heaviness. *Color* and *stain*, too, have something in common, but the best you can do there is to say that *stain* is a kind of color, usually a discoloration, different from the color that surrounds it. B and D seem designed only to catch the fancy of someone unacquainted with the meaning of one of the original pair.

● EXERCISE 2. Number on your paper from 1–5. Following the directions for analogies on page 648, write your answers after the proper number on your paper.

1. BRAVERY : LION :: A. shrewdness : mole B. wisdom : owl C. fox : stealth D. patience : elephant E. shark : fish
2. THINK : MEDITATE :: A. want : yearn B. study : scan C. paddle : swim D. mutter : talk E. hurry : run
3. RECTITUDE : CONDUCT :: A. wealth : society B. politics : government C. cowardice : fear D. manners : etiquette E. virtue : morals
4. CHEW : MASTICATE :: A. see : perceive B. eat : swallow C. walk : saunter D. go : peregrinate E. smile : scowl
5. VIRTUOSITY : MUSIC :: A. awkwardness : fall B. irony : sarcasm C. fluency : speech D. incisiveness : debate E. greed : voracity

WORDS IN CONTEXT

Moving on from the measurement of word relationships, the test of verbal aptitude may next examine the understanding of words in context. This is done sometimes by asking questions about words in long passages of writing, but more generally by a question that can be called the completion, or the sentence completion. The directions are something like this:

> Each of the following sentences has one or more blank spaces, each blank indicating that a word has been omitted. Beneath the sentence are five words, or pairs of words. Choose the one word, or pair of words, which, when inserted in the sentence, best fits in with the meaning of the sentence as a whole.

Here is an example of the sentence completion:

i. There are human beings so —— that they need drink or drugs to feel alive. A. perverse B. moribund C. unusual D. attenuated E. listless

The sense of the sentence is easy enough. Some human beings have a quality about them that makes them need drink or drugs. *Perverse* will not do, since perversity suggests a cantankerous frame of mind that is very alive, though not always pleasant. *Moribund* looks for a moment like a possibility, but a moribund person is a dying person and neither drink nor drugs will make such a person feel alive. *Unusual* doesn't explain satisfactorily why the people need something to feel alive. *Attenuated* seems to have nothing to do with the case and will probably attract only the students who don't know what it means and are guessing anyway. This leaves *listless*, which fits well. The sentence now makes complete sense, since *listless* describes a condition which can at least temporarily be relieved by artificial stimulation.

With a question as easy as this one, it will certainly not be necessary consciously to seek the answer so exhaustively. But each choice must be tried out, however quickly, to see what sense it makes; and the kind of trying out we have just gone through works as well as any. One more sample will probably suffice:

ii. The idea of giving —— credit for work done in —— school bothers many college teachers. A. upperclass . . . graduate B. legal . . . law C. full . . . marginal D. college . . . secondary E. academic . . . partial

Here we have an example of the sentence completion with two blanks. In completions of this kind you may find that the first blank, or the second, may be satisfactorily filled with more than one of the alternate choices offered. It is only when the two blanks are filled at the same time with the two words of the choice you are trying out that you can see whether you have found the right answer. Thus *upperclass*, *full*, *college*, and *academic* can all fit nicely into the sentence, and even *legal* could be forced in if necessary. Likewise, leaving the first blank empty, you could easily put *graduate*, *law*, and *secondary* into the second blank. But when the two blanks are filled at the same time, as they must be, A and B make little sense: graduate school work is certainly as good as upperclass work, though the demand for this kind of credit must be rare; and law school is certainly where legal credit, whatever it may be, is won. C fails because of *marginal school*. You can talk of marginal schools or colleges and be understood, but you do not speak of *marginal school*. Nor can you speak of *partial school* in E. D then is correct, as you can tell as soon as you try *college* and *secondary* in the blanks at the same time.

● EXERCISE 3. Number on your paper from 1–5. Following the directions for sentence completions on page 650, write your answers after the proper number on your paper.

1. The result, admittedly, was not to be so much a —— piece of research as an exploratory study. A. laborious B. rich C. finished D. real E. scholarly
2. Through efforts of many different agencies, there is now a widespread practice of —— of vitamins removed during the processing of food for human consumption. A. growth B. destruction C. concentration D. restoration E. exploitation
3. The master problem in the field of —— evolution is to describe, explain, and understand the life histories of the stars. A. stellar B. prehistoric C. authentic D. solar E. human
4. The Alexandrians labored under the difficulties that —— creative artists in an age when literature has passed one of its great periods. A. mold B. beset C. equate D. signalize E. inspire
5. Some students —— their colleges because they believe that only a certain group of institutions are within their reach ——. A. defend . . . scholastically B. reflect . . . socially C. corroborate . . . mentally D. describe . . . verbally E. choose . . . economically

READING COMPREHENSION

The aim of a test devoted to reading comprehension is to find out not only how well a student can understand what he has read, but also how well he can draw implications from his reading and make judgments about it. This might be called *total reading*. Reading comprehension exercises ask the student to get all he can out of what he reads.

The reading passages you will find in your tests

require no outside knowledge, aside from a knowledge of what words and sentences mean. The necessary information to answer all the questions asked is to be found in each reading passage itself.

Directions generally run something like this:

> The following test (or section) consists of passages of reading material, after each of which you will find a number of questions based on the passage itself. After reading each passage, answer the questions following it by choosing the *one* best answer for each question. Answer all questions on the basis of what is *stated* or *implied* in the passage.

Here is a sample passage followed by six questions:

> Being free from politico-educationist control, independent schools are free to experiment, to compete, to select their students and adapt their academic methods to the changing admissions requirements of our leading colleges. Attracting boys and teachers from many sections of the country, the boarding school offers an important counterpoise to the localism of the public school and provides essential training in the give and take of community living and community responsibility. A bad independent school, like a poorly run business, soon ceases to function; the good one provides, by virtue of small classes, teachers chosen for background in their fields and their understanding of boys, a twenty-four hour program of wholesome and purposeful work and recreation, an unparalleled opportunity to inculcate those intellectual, moral, spiritual, and social disciplines which make the effective citizen of the future. Several hundred such schools presently serve the country, and the records of their graduates need no embellishment.
>
> As a group these schools serve as the consistent strongholds of the basic disciplines of the English tongue, mathematics, history, and science — at the formative level. Leading public school advocates and

administrators are the first to proclaim the independent schools as the pace-setters for our great public school system, at present belabored by overcrowding, a shortage of competent teachers and classrooms, and the necessity of teaching down to the mediocre in response to growing public feeling that a secondary school diploma is a right for all, not a privilege for the competent. College admissions deans can document at request the demonstrated competence of independent school graduates to pursue advanced education.[2]

i. How does the independent school provide an "important counterpoise" to localism, according to the passage?

A. by paying no attention to local regulations
B. by enrolling students and securing teachers from many sections of the country
C. by adapting academic methods to the admission requirements of the country's colleges
D. by experimentation and competition
E. by a strong teaching program that forcibly broadens student outlook

ii. When the passage says "the records of their graduates need no embellishment," it means essentially that

A. the records are known to everyone
B. such records are uniformly good
C. the records are better than public school records
D. the records indicate a high degree of public service
E. such records speak for themselves

iii. Which of the following is *not* a present worry to public schools, according to the passage?

A. the availability of good students
B. the availability of good teachers
C. the availability of space
D. the necessity of holding down the rate of teaching
E. the necessity of graduating most students

[2] From "The Challenge to Independent Schools" by Harold H. Corbin, Jr., in *Lake Forest Academy: The First Hundred Years 1857–1957.*

iv. The passage implies that the real duty of the independent school is to

A. prepare students for college
B. provide a counterpoise to localism
C. provide leadership for the public schools
D. train effective citizens
E. serve as a stronghold of learning

v. In which of the following lines do you detect an exaggeration?

A. line 2 B. line 6 C. line 14 D. line 21
E. line 27

vi. As far as bias is concerned, how would you judge this passage?

A. It is strongly biased in favor of the independent school.
B. It is biased in favor of the independent school but attempts to be fair to public schools.
C. There seems to be no bias in the passage.
D. It is strongly biased in favor of public schools.
E. It is biased in favor of public schools but attempts to be fair to the independent school.

The questions you have just read are typical of the questions that are asked in reading comprehension exercises. Question i, for example, asks for the plain sense of the passage. The independent school, it is stated in lines 5–8, draws students and teachers from all parts of the country and thus provides an important counterpoise to localism. Hence B is the answer. You will note that some of the other choices, notably C and to some extent E, present advantages claimed by the passage for the independent school; but neither of these has any bearing on the question of localism. D is too general, and A states something that has no source in the passage and is undoubtedly not true.

Question ii, instead of asking you to find an answer in what you have read, checks to see whether you have understood a particular portion of the text. As in other questions, two or three of the choices are plausible, but only E provides the necessary paraphrase of the clause about embellishment.

Question iii again calls for the plain sense of the passage, but it does so negatively, by asking what the passage does not contain. The answer is clearly A. The passage nowhere states or implies that there are not good students in the public schools. It does, however, complain about the shortage of competent teachers and adequate classrooms and the necessity of "teaching down"; and it states that there is strong pressure to see that everyone gets a diploma, whether or not he is competent. The only thing to remember in dealing with this kind of question is to note carefully that the question is a negative one.

Question iv is an example of a question that goes somewhat beyond the passage and requires the student to draw an inference. There is nowhere in the passage an explicit statement of the essential aim of the independent, or of any, school. We know that the school does — or at least the passage says it does — do everything stated in all the choices. But in lines 11–18 the primary advantages of the independent school are summarized and it is asserted that all these advantages help inculcate the disciplines that make a good citizen. The passage implies then, and the question asks you to understand, that turning out a good citizen is really the primary aim of a school.

Questions v and vi require you to get outside the passage in another way, this time to judge it. All too frequently, students — and people in general — take literally anything they read. Questions of this sort suggest to the student that authors as well as students are fallible and that it is not a good idea to swallow anything without at least taking a careful look at it. Question v, to which the answer is C, is aimed at the "twenty-four hour program," which leaves little time for necessary sleep. And question vi requires him to stand off and judge the passage as a whole. There is no doubt that the author is a backer of the independent schools, though he does take time in the second paragraph to praise the public schools. The answer then is B.

● EXERCISE 4. Number on your paper from 1–5. After reading the following passage, answer the questions given at the end of it. Refer to the directions for reading comprehension on page 653.

This experiment, and the others that preceded it, settled once and for all the question of spontaneous generation of bacteria. Of course, many people repeated these experiments after Pasteur, and many failed; but it was a question of technique. Nowadays, it is commonplace to prepare a sterile solution that will remain bacteria-free indefinitely.

Researches that have been carried out since Pasteur's day have shown that bacteria are not nearly so simple as had been assumed up to that time. Although they are very small, they have a very delicate organization and very complicated chemical processes go on in them. They are just as complicated chemically as the individual cells that make up the bodies of higher plants and animals, and the idea of such complicated structures originating by chance in a medium containing nothing but organic chemicals is quite fantastic. As a recent writer has said: "Imagine a factory with smokestacks, machinery, railroad tracks, buildings, and so on springing into existence in a moment — following some natural event like a volcanic eruption. The same sort of event is assumed when one assumes that something as complex as a bacterial cell can originate in a pot of gravy." [3]

[3] From "The Origin of Life" by Norman H. Horowitz in *Engineering and Science*, November, 1956.

1. Spontaneous generation of bacteria means most probably the

   A. appearance of bacteria with no discernible cause
   B. automatic reproduction of bacteria by the splitting of the cells
   C. production of whole generations of bacteria in a single experiment
   D. idea that bacteria were very simple organisms
   E. production of bacteria by higher plants and animals

2. In this context, "it was a question of technique" means essentially that

   A. investigators tried these experiments to show how good their technique was
   B. since scientists knew the answer, they were interested only in how it could be arrived at
   C. investigators whose experimental technique was good would not fail
   D. many people found Pasteur's technique questionable
   E. investigators whose experimental technique was poor did most of the later experiments

3. The experiment mentioned at the beginning of the passage is probably an experiment to

   A. prepare a pot of gravy that produces bacteria
   B. show that bacteria are chemically complicated
   C. show that bacteria can be found in the higher plants and animals
   D. prepare a sterile solution that would remain bacteria-free
   E. demonstrate the spontaneous generation of bacteria

4. It is a popular assumption, the passage implies, that

   A. organic chemicals can generate bacteria
   B. complicated chemical processes go on in all matter
   C. bacteria have lives of their own
   D. bacteria cause decay in foods
   E. small things have a simple organization

5. A possible criticism of the comparison between the factory and the bacterial cell might be that
   A. the factory appears too suddenly
   B. there is no counterpart for the volcanic eruption
   C. factories do not have their own railroad tracks
   D. the factory is too big
   E. the factory is too complex

Composition Tests

The remainder of this chapter will be concerned with test exercises designed to measure your skill in the writing (and speaking) of English, a skill which has been developed chiefly in your work in school in a specific area. Many tests in this area are multiple-choice tests, like those we have already considered. Some allow room for individual reaction and require trained personnel to grade; and some, of course, allow the student freedom to respond as he will.

CORRECTNESS AND EFFECTIVENESS

Tests of English composition concentrate on three areas of a student's writing ability: correctness and effectiveness, organization, and taste and sensitivity. Correctness and effectiveness deals with the basic mechanics of writing: the spelling, the punctuation, the capitalization, the grammar and usage.

There are many different ways of testing this correctness and effectiveness of expression objectively. This chapter will show only two — spelling and a form of sentence correction.

Spelling

Spelling can be tested variously. Perhaps the most common form is the question consisting of five words, one of which may be misspelled. You pick out the wrong word if there is one; if there is not, you mark a 0 or a C on your answer sheet. The test questions usually hit the basic rules of spelling: *ie* or *ei*, double or single consonant, drop or keep a final *e* when adding a suffix, etc. You will occasionally find trick words from a favorite list, words like *plaguy*, *kimono*, *naphtha;* but generally the questions are straightforward. Here is a sample exercise in spelling.

● EXERCISE 5. Each of the following questions consists of five words, one of which may be misspelled. Choose the one word which is misspelled, and write its letter after the proper number on your paper. If all words in a group are spelled correctly, mark that question 0.

1. A. seize
   B. percieve
   C. salutary
   D. pronunciation
   E. righteous

2. A. catalogue
   B. laughter
   C. explannatory
   D. traveler
   E. ruse

3. A. peaceable
   B. edible
   C. salable
   D. syllable
   E. changable

4. A. picnicking
   B. dyeing
   C. prejudice
   D. foreigner
   E. desiccate

5. A. mischievious
   B. grandeur
   C. gorgeous
   D. athletic
   E. important

Sentence Correction

The other type of objective question covering correctness and effectiveness is a form of sentence correction. It asks you to look at a sentence which has four or five underlined places and pick out the one underlined place where there is an error. If there are no errors — and this is a possibility — you mark a special column of your answer sheet. This kind of question deals mainly with grammar and usage, although punctuation, capitalization, and spelling may be included too. One caution is necessary: these questions usually indicate the part of the sentence to be queried by underlining it; be sure to notice whether the underlining includes, or does not include, the punctuation. If a question wishes to test the use of a comma after the word *there*, for example, it will look like this: there,; if it wishes to test only the word, it will look like this: there,. Some examples follow.

● EXERCISE 6. Each of the following questions consists of a sentence with five portions underlined. One of these places may be incorrect, because of faulty punctuation, capitalization, grammar, or usage. Choose the one underlined part that is incorrect; or if there is no incorrect part, mark that question 0 on your paper.

1. The concept of face is an important element of the
A B
everyday philosophy of the mysterious East.
C D E

2. Eating, drinking, and to stay up late at night seemed
A B C
to be the only pleasures he could enjoy.
D E

3. His brother, who is five years older than himself, is more
A B C
inclined toward scholarly activity.
D E

4. *The Wings Of the Dove* is one of Henry James's more
A B C D E
difficult novels.

5. It always seems to be a case of us having to pick up the
A B C D
boys and take them home.
E

ORGANIZATION — THE SCRAMBLED PARAGRAPH

The second of the areas of composition in which a student is generally tested is organization. The most frequent exercise designed to measure organizational ability is the scrambled paragraph. This exercise takes a paragraph from any type of subject matter and presents the sentences to you in random order. Your job is to figure out the correct order, the order which will reform the sentences into a well-knit paragraph. This you do to some extent by studying the sequence of ideas presented; but primarily you have to concern yourself with the transitional words and phrases.

The directions and the questions for the scrambled paragraph are a little complicated, and may look a little frightening at first. Here is the way they go:

DIRECTIONS: The sentences below are in scrambled order. Read them and decide what would be the *best order* in which to put the sentences so as to form a well-organized paragraph. Each sentence has a place in the paragraph; there are no extra sentences.

In answering the questions, consider 0 to mean that nothing follows. Thus if you have arranged the sentences in the order CAB and are asked which sentence you put after B, your answer will be 0, i.e., *no sentence*. It will help you in answering the questions to jot down the correct order of the sentences in the margin; you will receive credit, however, *only* for answers marked on the answer sheet.

A sample paragraph is given on the next page.

A. If they came to college for the wrong reasons, they can be appealed to to work and succeed for the right reasons.

B. But of course it has to be done realistically.

C. People in college work should not look too sharply at the motives of entering students.

D. The least promising students must sometimes be discouraged from embarking on overambitious plans.

E. This lifting of sights for all students, even the least promising, is as important as any other function in a dean's office.

i. Which sentence did you put first?
ii. Which sentence did you put after A?
iii. Which sentence did you put after B?
iv. Which sentence did you put after C?
v. Which sentence did you put after D?
vi. Which sentence did you put after E?

The reason this looks so complex is that the testers are trying to give you credit for every correct relation you discern between sentences. It would be easier to ask you simply which sentence you put first, second, third, fourth, fifth. But suppose you picked the wrong sentence as the first one; then all your answers would be thrown off right down the line, even though you were perfectly well aware of the way the second, third, and fourth sentences should go together.

The sample paragraph is not a difficult one. Only two sentences, C and D, do not refer specifically to something that must have gone before. A refers to *they* twice, B uses *but* and *it*, and E talks of *this lifting of sights;* all these transition elements or links show you that these sentences must be in the body of the paragraph. D could begin a paragraph perfectly well, but not this paragraph, since none of the other sentences carries on the idea started in D. The choice for the first sentence then is C. Next you need a sentence that carries on the idea of students' motives — and A is clearly the only one that will do. Working on from there to see what must follow A, you find that B or E could do. But if it is to be B, you need next a reason why *it has to be done realistically*, and there is no reason given why your appeal to a student to work and succeed has to be realistic. So you move to E, deciding that *this lifting of sights* refers to the appeal mentioned — as it does. Once you have come this far, B and D fall quickly into place.

The correct order for the sentences, then, is CAEBD, and this you must determine before you answer the questions. *But note and keep firmly in your mind that you do not answer CAEBD on your answer sheet for questions i to v.* In the first place, there are six questions. And your answers for questions i to vi go CEDA0B, since you are indicating what sentence follows A, B, C, etc.

● EXERCISE 7. Number on your paper from 1–12. Following the directions on page 662, write the answers on your paper after the proper numbers.

1

A. There is an important difference between tests of ability and measures of interest and personality.

B. There is no question whether you have expressed correct interests.

C. In tests of ability, there are right, or at least best, answers.

D. In measures of interest and personality, however, the only right answers are the ones which correctly describe the person tested.

E. An interest in scientific activities, for example, is no more correct than an interest in literary activities.

1. Which sentence did you put first?
2. Which sentence did you put after A?
3. Which sentence did you put after B?
4. Which sentence did you put after C?
5. Which sentence did you put after D?
6. Which sentence did you put after E?

2

A. At first his affiliations were with the Whigs, but he found, as time went on, that the Whigs were less sympathetic with his views about ecclesiastical affairs than the Tories.

B. In the next four years he wrote a large number of political pamphlets, becoming perhaps the greatest political pamphleteer that England has ever known.

C. As a reward for his services, he anticipated that the Tories would provide him with some important post in the Church of England.

D. To Swift, this was a matter of vital importance, and about 1710 he transferred his allegiance to the Tory party.

E. During his visits to England in the early part of the century, Swift occasionally tried his hand at political pamphleteering.

7. Which sentence did you put first?
8. Which sentence did you put after A?
9. Which sentence did you put after B?
10. Which sentence did you put after C?
11. Which sentence did you put after D?
12. Which sentence did you put after E?

TASTE AND SENSITIVITY

The third area of English composition frequently, though somewhat less frequently, tested by objective tests is the area of taste and sensitivity. One kind of question measuring these qualities is very similar in form to the sentence completion. It presents a sentence with a blank in it and five choices for the filling of the blank. The difference between this and sentence completion, however, is that here more than one of the choices may be possible, as far as sense goes, but that only one of them makes the best sense, in that it corresponds to and completes the mood and the meaning of the sentence in question. The sentence often, though not necessarily, contains a figure of speech, and the choices are usually phrases or clauses rather than single words. Here is an example:

DIRECTIONS: In each of the sentences that follow there is a blank indicating that a part of the sentence has been omitted. Beneath each question are five words, phrases, or clauses which might be inserted in the blank space. Choose the best answer, considering the style and tone of the sentences and the meaning which the author intends to convey.

i. Some authors enclose digressions within digressions, like ——.

A. an endless chain
B. a play within a play
C. a pile of dishes
D. a tower of Babel
E. a nest of boxes

What you must do here, just as you did with the sentence completions, is to determine the intent of the author. But here you must worry about his artistic intent as well as about the sense of what he is saying. E is obviously the choice that makes clear the things-within-things effect the writer wants. C and D picture only a piling up; and the chain in A shows a series of equal links rather than a diminishing series of elements. If B were not clearly singular, the play within the play might be a possibility. But because we need more than one thing within a thing, this choice must be rejected. We settle, then — and it is an effective comparison — for the nest of boxes.

This sort of question is also to be found in passages of running prose. Here, however, the attempt of the tester is particularly to see whether you can sense the style of the author and realize what words fit well with it and what words would destroy the tone — and in some cases the meaning too. For this to be a fair test, the exercise will usually print a paragraph preceding the passage on which the questions are based so that you can get some feeling of the author's style before you are tested on it.

● EXERCISE 8. Number on your paper from 1–6 and follow the directions given on page 666. Note that a paragraph is given preceding questions 3–6 to give you an indication of the author's style.

1. People suppose that because the smallest circle ——, therefore the management of the world requires no more ability than the turning of a globe.

   A. still looks like a circle
   B. looks like a big circle if you magnify it
   C. has a circumference and a diameter
   D. is round too
   E. has as many degrees as the largest

2. A poet who follows Nature without using rhyme ——.

   A. falls on his face
   B. is doing a silly thing
   C. follows her on foot
   D. is making things rough for everybody
   E. is like a blindfolded man trying to see

Where Taurus lifts its head above the storm and presents nothing to the sight of the distant traveler but a prospect of nodding rocks, falling torrents, and all the variety of tremendous nature; on the bleak bosom of this frightful mountain, secluded from society, and detesting the ways of men, lived Asem the Man-hater.

Asem had spent his youth with men, had __3__

3. A. often been near them
   B. shared in their amusements
   C. ferreted out their inmost lives
   D. thrilled at their secrets
   E. nourished their young manhood

and had been taught to love his fellow creatures with the most ardent affection; but from the tenderness of his disposition he exhausted all his fortune in __4__

4. A. trying to remedy
   B. preventing
   C. stopping
   D. relieving
   E. sorrowing over

the wants of the distressed. The __5__

5. A. petitioner
   B. beggar
   C. lawyer
   D. suer
   E. man down at the heels

never sued in vain; the weary traveler never passed his door; he only __6__

6. A. quit
   B. cut out
   C. desisted from
   D. drew himself back from
   E. made a stop in

doing good when he had no longer the power of relieving.

Another exercise in taste and sensitivity presents a poem with a blank, gives you alternate lines, but asks you to judge each alternate line given. Thus, one of the lines is the proper one, one of the lines would be all right but for its meter, another but for its tone, and another has a meaning that does not fit. The directions and a sample follow:

DIRECTIONS: In each of the following passages of poetry there is a blank space indicating that a line has been omitted. Beneath each passage are four suggested lines which might be inserted in the blank space. One of the lines is appropriate, one of the lines is inappropriate in rhythm or meter, one of the lines is inappropriate in style or tone, and one of the lines is inappropriate in meaning. You are to determine the proper category for *each* line. On the answer sheet mark answer space —

A if the line is appropriate,
B if the line is inappropriate in *rhythm* or *meter*,
C if the line is inappropriate in *style* or *tone*,
D if the line is inappropriate in *meaning*.

I leaned upon a coppice gate
  When Frost was specter-gray,
And Winter's dregs made desolate
  The weakening eye of day.
The tangled bine-stems scored the sky
  Like strings from broken lyres,
And all mankind that haunted night

. . . .

i. Stayed snug and warm at fires.
ii. Huddled at fires.
iii. Had sought their household fires.
iv. Were with the cows in byres.

The key here is i–C, ii–B, iii–A, iv–D. The sense of i and ii fits in very well with the poem; but i exudes a false coziness with its *snug and warm* that is quite out of keeping with the poem; in addition, "warm at fires" is stylistically awkward. The two metric feet of ii make that line impossible for the iambic trimeter the poem needs. Of course, iii is the right line for this poem, and iv makes no sense.

● EXERCISE 9. Number on your paper from 1–8 and follow the directions given on page 669. Note that in the second poem the first line is a blank instead of the last.

Since I have felt the sense of death,
And death forever at my side —
Oh how the world has opened wide
Since I have felt the sense of death.
My hours are jewels that I spend,
. . . .

1. For I have seen the hours end.
2. For I have seen what men pretend.
3. Because I know they stop, my friend.
4. Because I have seen that my time can end.

. . . .
With liquor, love, or fights,
Lief should I rouse at morning
And lief lie down of nights.

5. If I had gathered treasure
6. If man were drunk always
7. Say, man were tipsy ever
8. Could man be drunk forever

The Interlinear Exercise

The interlinear exercise is a piece of prose into which some errors in grammar and usage and some infelicities and clumsy constructions have been introduced. These weak spots in the passage have not been marked in any way. The exercise is presented to the student with wide spaces between the lines and he is instructed to find and correct in his own words as many errors as he can. The grader notes the attempts at correction the student has made and marks them as to their acceptability, in accordance with the approved list of corrections he has to work with.

One point should be emphasized here, although it is covered in the test directions. There are only a certain number of errors that have been introduced into the text, and the testers are particularly interested in how the student goes about correcting them — if he finds them at all. You should look for these specific errors, or weaknesses, and make specific corrections of them rather than attempt to rewrite the whole passage. Rewriting takes up unnecessary time and frequently avoids the specific errors that you are supposed to find.

Here are the directions for the interlinear, and a sample showing how corrections are to be made:

DIRECTIONS: Reprinted below is a poorly written passage. You are to treat it as though it were the first draft of a composition of your own, and revise it so that it conforms with standard formal English. Wide spaces have been left between the lines so that you may write in the necessary improvements. Do not omit any ideas and do not add any ideas not now present. You may, however, change any word which you think is expressing an idea inexactly; and you may omit words, phrases, or sentences that are unnecessary.

You are not expected to rewrite the whole passage. Trying to do so will not only waste time but will also cause you to miss many of the specific errors you are expected to correct. Much of the passage is satisfactory as it stands. Leave such parts alone and concentrate on finding weak places that need changing.

In general, corrections should be made by crossing out the word, phrase, or mark of punctuation you wish to change and writing your own version above it. Any clear method of indicating changes is satisfactory, however. Simply make sure that what you intend is clear.

The captain advanced toward the column of Indians slowly waving the flag as he walked. One rider comes forth from the main body this was Cameahwait, chief of the Shoshones. Like Lewis was, he was a young man. In the center of the meadow of buttercups and Indian paintbrush, there was at last the meeting of the two. Down from the pony's bare back the secretary to the President of the United States was looked at by the savage.

The time would come when the American nation could be able to pour westward many regiments of blue-coated cavalry, and there would be long charades of covered wagons. Finally, puffing locomotives on steel tracks. But now the future of the great march to the Pacific hanged upon a man in tattered buckskin facing an Indian that was feathered on a paint pony.

Twelve errors appear in this short passage. They range from faulty sentence planning to misused words, and they include the dangling modifier, faulty parallelism, wrong tense, and misuse of preposition. The sample on the next page shows possible ways of correcting these. Let us take up the errors one by one and show alternative ways of correcting them. In this way, you will get an idea not only of the kind of thing the interlinear exercise generally contains, but also of the sort of correction that is expected.

The captain advanced toward the column of Indians slowly, waving the flag as he walked. One rider *came* ~~comes~~ forth from the main body. *T*his was Cameahwait, chief of the Shoshones. Like Lewis ~~was~~, he was a young man. In the center of the meadow of buttercups and Indian paintbrush, *the two* ~~there was~~ at last *met.* ~~the meeting of the two~~. ~~Down~~ *F*rom the pony's bare back, *the savage looked down at* the secretary to the President of the United States. ~~was looked at by the savage.~~

The time would come when the American nation could ~~be able to~~ pour westward many regiments of blue-coated cavalry, ~~and there would be~~ long *parades* ~~charades~~ of covered wagons, *and f*inally, puffing locomotives on steel tracks. But now the future of the great march to the Pacific *depended* ~~hanged~~ upon a man in tattered buckskin facing *a feathered* ~~an~~ Indian ~~that was feathered~~ on a paint pony.

Line 2: *Slowly* is misplaced. Now impossible to tell whether the advancing or the waving was slow. Place at beginning of sentence, or before or after *advanced.* Or leave where it is and separate with a comma from part of sentence it does not belong to.

Line 3: *Comes forth* is wrong tense. Change to *came forth.*

Line 3: Run-on sentence. *This was Cameahwait* . . . should be a new sentence.

Line 4: *Like* is a preposition, not a conjunction. Change to *Like Lewis,* or *As Lewis was.*

Line 6: *There was at last the meeting* is an awkward, flat, and unemphatic expression. Change to *In the center . . . the two at last met;* or at least, *the meeting at last took place.*

Line 7: *Down from the pony's . . .* is a dangling element — the Indian was on the pony's back. Change to *From* . . ., *the savage looked down at* or something similar.

Line 11: Tautology. Use either *could,* or *would,* or *would be able to,* not *could be able to.*

Line 11 ff.: Faulty parallelism. Sentence reads much better thus: . . . *pour westward many regiments* . . . , *long parades* . . . , *and finally puffing locomotives* . . . . Partial improvements here would receive partial credit.

Line 12: Wrong word. Should be *parades,* not *charades.*

Line 13: Sentence fragment. Tie the locomotives in with what precedes.

Line 15: *Hanged* not used in this sense. *Hung* is correct form, but *depended* is a better word here.

Line 16: Wordy and confusing. Change to *a feathered Indian.*

You will have noticed that the errors inserted into the exercise are chiefly those of correctness and effectiveness. This is always the case with the interlinear exercise. It cannot measure organization, and the nuances of taste and sensitivity tend to be overlooked as students search for the grosser errors; but it is an excellent measure for testing correctness and effectiveness of expression.

These, then, are the chief types of exercises that you will find in tests of verbal aptitude and of English composition. They are not the only exercises, to be sure; but if you run into different ones, the chances are that they will only be variations on those that appear here.

Treat these exercises as they should be treated. That is, familiarize yourself with what they are and the specific things they ask for. Understand the intricacies of the directions. But do not try to cram on exercises of this kind. Tests like these measure your general preparedness for further work rather than any special material you have worked over just before examination time. Continuing to read and to write is the best way of preparing for any test of verbal aptitude or of English composition.

Answers to Exercises

EXERCISE 1, page 647: 1–E; 2–A; 3–D; 4–C; 5–D.

EXERCISE 2, page 649: 1–B; 2–A; 3–E; 4–A; 5–C.

EXERCISE 3, page 652: 1–C; 2–D; 3–A; 4–B; 5–E.

EXERCISE 4, page 657: 1–A; 2–C; 3–D; 4–E; 5–B.

EXERCISE 5, page 660: 1–B; 2–C; 3–E; 4–0; 5–A.

EXERCISE 6, page 661: 1–0; 2–B; 3–C; 4–B; 5–C.

EXERCISE 7, page 664: 1–A; 2–C; 3–E; 4–D; 5–B; 6–0; 7–E; 8–D; 9–C; 10–0; 11–B; 12–A.

EXERCISE 8, page 667: 1–E; 2–C; 3–B; 4–D; 5–A; 6–C.

EXERCISE 9, page 670: 1–A; 2–D; 3–C; 4–B; 5–D; 6–B; 7–C; 8–A.

Index

KEY TO SUPPLEMENTARY DRILL

If additional drill is required, see Warriner and Blumenthal's ENGLISH WORKSHOP, **New Series**, Review Course. Each rule number in this text is keyed below to an appropriate lesson in the Workshop.

Text Rule No.	Workshop Lesson No.
1a	23
1b	23
1c	23
1d	24
1e	24
1f	26
1g	24
2c	25
2d	25
2e	25
2h	25
2i	25
2j	25
2k	25
3a	26
3b	26
3c	26
3d	26
3e-f	26
3g-h	26
3i-j	26
3k	26
4a	27
4b	28
4c	27-8
4d	28
4e	28
4f	27-8
4g	28
5a	33,35
5b	33,35
5c	34-5
6a	57-8
6b	61
7a	66
7b-c	66
7d	67
7e	67
7f	69-70
7g	71

Text Rule No.	Workshop Lesson No.
8a	76-80
8b	76
8c	81
8d	81
8e	81
12a	50
13a	47
13b	48
14a	51
14b-c	52
14d	52
24b-c	86
24d	87
24e	87
24f	86
24g	86
24h	88,91
25a-b	89
25c	89
25d	89
25e	94
25g	95
29a	92
29b	92
29c	93
29d	93
30b	96
30c	96
33c	1-3
34a-d	7
34e	7
34f	8,10
34g	11
34h	11
34j-l	16
34v-x	17
34y-z	18

CONTINUED FROM FRONT ENDPAPER